Lavery Library

EX LIBRIS
ST. JOHN FISHER COLLEGE

First published in the United States of America
1991 by RIZZOLI INTERNATIONAL PUBLICATIONS, INC.
300 Park Avenue South, New York, NY 10010

in association with Wexner Center for the Arts, The Ohio State University,
North High Street at Fifteenth Avenue, Columbus, OH 43210

Library of Congress Catalog Card Number
90-64092

ISBN 0-8478-1365-7

BREAKTHROUGHS

Avant-Garde Artists in Europe and America, 1950–1990

Wexner Center for the Arts

The Ohio State University

RIZZOLI
NEW YORK

C O N T E N T S

Foreword   vi

Robert Stearns, Director, Wexner Center for the Arts

Preface   viii

John Howell, Guest Editor

ART IN EUROPE AND AMERICA   **Art in Europe and America: The 1950s and 1960s**   3
THE 1950s AND 1960s
                                       Sarah Rogers-Lafferty, Curator of Exhibitions, Wexner Center for the Arts

                                       The Long and Short of It   13

                                       Dore Ashton

                                       Reconstruction: Art in Postwar Italy   23

                                       Giulio Carlo Argan

                                       Modern Nature   33

                                       Pierre Restany

                                       All the Newsprint That's Fit to Paint   49

                                       David Bourdon

                                       Stella and Hesse: Dispatches from the Sixties   59

                                       Brian O'Doherty

                                       Beyond "Big Serge": Dance in the Fifties and Sixties   69

                                       Lynn Garafola

                                       The Future of Music: The Fifties and Sixties in Retrospect   75

                                       Roy M. Close

                                       The Redemption of the City in Postwar Avant-Garde Film   81

                                       Paul Arthur

ART IN EUROPE AND AMERICA   **Art in Europe and America: The 1960s and 1970s**   91
THE 1960s AND 1970s
                                       Claudia Gould, Curator of Exhibitions, Wexner Center for the Arts

                                       Clean Slates   103

                                       Kenneth Baker

                                       EUROAMERICA: From Minimal Art to Arte Povera   113

                                       Germano Celant

                                       Intruders: Lynda Benglis and Adrian Piper   125

                                       Lucy R. Lippard

                                       "Give Up Painting" or the Politics of Art: A West German Abstract   133

                                       Walter Grasskamp

                                       Ways to Be   141

                                       Carter Ratcliff

                                       Bon Marché   151

                                       Allan Kaprow

                                       American Dance and Performance Art: The Sixties and Seventies   157

                                       Sally Banes

                                       Don't Look Back: Film and Video From Then to Now   165

                                       B. Ruby Rich

NEW WORKS FOR NEW SPACES
INTO THE NINETIES

New Works for New Spaces: Into the Nineties 177
Ann Bremner

Collecting Culture: Paradoxes and Curiosities 181
Patricia C. Phillips

Magdalena Abakanowicz 187

Gretchen Bender 189

Chris Burden 193

Malcolm Cochran 199

Fortuyn/O'Brien 205

Ann Hamilton 209

Tadashi Kawamata 215

Joseph Kosuth 221

Barbara Kruger 225

Sol LeWitt 231

Christian Marclay 233

MICA-TV 237

Gilberto Zorio 243

Trisha Brown 247

Spalding Gray 253

Bill T. Jones 259

Projects 265
William Horrigan, Curator of Media Arts, Wexner Center for the Arts

Notes for the Airwaves 266
Shu Lea Cheang

Casanova's Homecoming 270
Steve Fagin

Notes on Swoon 274
Tom Kalin

Character in Unconventional People 278
Leslie Thornton

Symptoms and Stories: The Narrative Cure 282
Julie Zando

Appendix: The Wexner Center's Inaugural Year 295

Acknowledgments 307

Index of Names 308

F O R E W O R D

This collection of writings, interviews, notes and illustrations casts a wide net over some
fundamental breakthroughs in recent art. While it stands alone as an anthology of
personal viewpoints, it also illustrates three related exhibitions and concurrent events
in dance, theater, music, film and the media arts presented by the Wexner Center for the
Arts at The Ohio State University during 1989–90, its inaugural year. These hundreds of
individual works provide a view of the mysteries and alchemy of what has been called
the avant-garde.

But what does avant-garde mean when it appears to have become the status quo?
What is a breakthrough in an era besieged by novelty-for-novelty's sake? The very
visibility of modern art and the market value collectors have placed on it beg these
questions. If art is acceptable and even valuable, can it be avant-garde? Do we expect it
to shock us with "the new" and then hate it when it does and berate it when it does not?
Can an object or idea, once at the cutting edge, retain a spark of inventive insolence
when it's seen in a historical context of any kind?

These questions touch on the seductive dilemma of the avant-garde, which can be
described most simply as a group devoted to the invention of new materials and techniques. Through its inventiveness, the avant-garde creates new ideas and often reshapes
its own forms and boundaries. Because of its inventiveness and willful disregard for conventions, the avant-garde typically has existed at the margins of society, unrecognized
and ill-rewarded for its contributions. The early call-to-arms of the French avant-garde was
epatéz les bourgeois, and in Europe artists had an informed urban populace to shock. By
contrast, the American vanguard confronted, for the most part, a serenely ignorant
society that, until recently, didn't take any notice at all. As American society finally has
taken notice, much new art has been consumed like so many shares of speculative stock.
It's an irony of contemporary capitalism that one generation's dross is spun into the next
generation's gold, pushing the true vanguard artist to search for new pastures.

Here we want to take notice for a different reason. With a historical mirror held up
by observers—curators and critics and artists themselves—it's quite possible to look at the
recent past and identify fundamental ideas and processes that made essential changes in
the artistic landscape. With a little perspective, we can try to see the edges that were and
are being cut. With that in hand, we can move ahead to nurture some next steps into the
future.

Throughout the four-plus decades surveyed in the Wexner Center's inaugural programs and hence in this volume, artists have groped for the future by investigating new
forms, materials and purposes for art. As they did so, they tended to perturb more than
they pleased and to raise more questions than they answered. Our survey begins in the
fifties, a time of summations and new beginnings when historical modernism was crystallized and ready for fresh interrogations in the visual, performing and media arts. Those
interrogations continued in the succeeding decades as once-new ideas were rejected,
revisited, discarded and rejuvenated according to their relevance for each succeeding
generation. The sixties, seventies and eighties witnessed the rise and recession and rise
again of movements such as Minimalism, Conceptual art and Arte Povera, the emergence
of new forms such as installation, performance, video and sound art, and the elevation
and demise of various countries, cities and even (as in the case of Manhattan's SoHo)
neighborhoods as creative centers. The essays gathered together here trace many ideas—
concepts of assemblage and of serial systems, interactions with popular culture and with
the natural environment, concerns for political issues and for formal essence—but one
theme, multidisciplinary investigations, seems particularly relevant both as a connecting
thread and as a determinant of the Wexner Center's own identity.

The cutting edge of art in the twentieth century has dissolved the boundaries between the disciplines of, say, painting and theater or sculpture and dance, or between art
and life itself. Pushing outward to new realms as well as sideways to other media, artists
have mingled dance with sculpture with music with painting with film with theater.
Armed with new technologies and new ideas, artists quite simply invented their ways

into the future, pushing in every direction, obliterating distinctions between media and joining various media in new ways. Through these artists' investigations the foundations for a new creative language were laid, but not laid to rest.

Both this anthology and the Wexner Center's program underscore this inevitably messy exploration, made all the more volatile in the context of the center's iconoclastic architecture. When, in 1982, The Ohio State University invited architects to propose designs for a new art center, it called for a showcase and a research center for the contemporary arts—not for a museum. Peter Eisenman and Richard Trott's solution offers an open-ended dilemma, a collection of unconventional spaces that requires taking risks. These spaces and their technical facilities force a reevaluation of what museums can do to act as centers of creative work and cultural exchange.

In planning the first exhibitions and programs for the center, the curators, program directors and I attempted to wrestle with the building's didactic philosophy and physical properties. This structure makes profound and disturbing demands through its own breaks with architectural conventions of form and function. Within its surroundings of reconstituted history (illustrated by its armory towers and grids, which refer to local mapping systems) and allusions to an unresolved future (suggested by the metaphor of its scaffold as "process"), we chose to offer a historical and conceptual backdrop for future programs. And so, for over a year we juxtaposed currency against history and history against currency: new works against their antecedents and vice versa.

This volume follows a format based on our trilogy of inaugural exhibitions—*Art in Europe and America: The 1950s and 1960s, Art in Europe and America: The 1960s and 1970s* and *New Works for New Spaces: Into the Nineties*. The first two exhibitions were historical selections, each including thirteen artists whose works have established and defied the standard interpretations of art history. For these exhibitions we selected works created at critical and transitional periods, often early in their artists' careers or during the headiest time of creative momentum. The exhibitions and related film/video series and performing arts presentations provided the core group of artists and works discussed in the first two parts of this book (though the essayists also augmented our selections by placing them in a larger context). Many of these works have become landmarks of contemporary art, but that is not the only reason they merit attention. We hope to reflect on the power and impact they had when they were first made and seen and on the influence their ideas continue to exert by attraction or repulsion.

New Works for New Spaces: Into the Nineties, the third show in the trilogy, was intended to confront just what the architects meant in calling their design a "center for the arts of the twenty-first century." Thirteen artists were invited to develop projects specifically for the exhibition and for the Wexner Center's building and environs—and they responded to this warehouse of systematic structures much as they might respond to the uneasy social environment in which they otherwise work. Their reactions were harmonious, argumentative, complementary or quizzical; their approaches, aggressive or subtle. The interviews in the corresponding section of the book chronicle the evolution of these thirteen specific works and so offer insights into their artists' working methods. Interviews with three performing artists and artists' pages by five media artists continue this section's emphasis on the creative processes behind "new works."

The building itself was, thus, a point of departure for our focus on invention in the art of the present, which is a product of the recent past. By examining these existing and newly created works, we have provided a springboard for the Wexner Center's future, as we will continue to present the work of artists who explore new territories, who continue the ideals of the avant-garde.

Robert Stearns

P R E F A C E

Considered as a whole, the choices of artists, artworks and critics included in this book, a volume with the sweeping title *Breakthroughs: Avant-Garde Artists in Europe and America, 1950–1990*, may seem somewhat arbitrary. In a sense, they are. The reader should think of the contents as representing selected figures in a landscape rather than a methodical map of an accepted territory.

Why? The truth is, we don't really believe in an all-slots-filled, balanced—that is, "objective"—version of the story of modern art anymore. While still granting history its integrity, we now have a more complex, less determinant idea of our objectivity. After more than a century of art that has self-consciously proclaimed itself avant-garde, that increasingly hard-to-define notion seems to have achieved at least one of its acknowledged goals: the blurring, if not the near-dissolution, of accepted boundaries, including those that would seem to limit the history of art to certain artists, certain influences, certain styles.

This volume represents a description of the avant-garde that explicitly observes the provisional nature of our understanding. A key criterion for commissioning the book's original essays was that of "witness," the notion of the critic as participant as well as evaluator. The choice of partisan historians ensured an inherent revisionism expressed in the disparate interests and divergent experiences of the several writers. The variety of voices and subjective brands of history resulted in multiple perspectives; it was felt that what was gained by such statements more than made up for the limitations of avoiding a more traditionally organized volume.

Another decision also ensured a dimension of difference: each critic-witness was to consider, either explicitly or implicitly, the context of the nineties in his or her necessarily abbreviated history; to impart a contemporary urgency, a sense of personal retrospective that would parallel the investigations of the artists themselves. The responses were as singular as the careers of their respective writers have been. The essayists writing for the first part of this book rethought the art of the fifties and sixties in ways linked only by their passionate involvement with the art and ideas of that time: from Brian O'Doherty's explicit references to the critic as a younger and, astonishingly, more conservative self to Giulio Carlo Argan's voice that still resonates, nearly half a century later, with the agony and the wonder of postwar European experience; from Dore Ashton's long view of the Romantic impulse's continued visibility in the twentieth century to David Bourdon's close-up look at one facet of Pop practice (the use of newspaper) and Pierre Restany's always personal yet always issue-fixated sense of art in its specifically European cultural context.

In the second section of essays, those covering art of the sixties and seventies, the general tone is less explicitly personal, more ideological, a patina that reflects the art of that period. Kenneth Baker examines Minimalism's closely argued premises and the alternatives that developed even within this movement's boundaries. Carter Ratcliff outlines the concentrated idiosyncrasy (sometimes known as pluralism) that makes each artist seem unrelated to anything but his or her own line of exploration. Lucy R. Lippard looks at individual visions in the context of larger social and political issues that provide a connecting background. Germano Celant explores the implications of Minimalism and one salient counter-argument to its prescriptions, Arte Povera, in the light of similarities and differences between European and American thinking and practice. Walter Grasskamp reports on the decisive work of German artists, perhaps the most significant European contribution to international art since the war.

Patricia Phillips sets the stage for the third section of this volume, *New Works for New Spaces*, by examining the Wexner Center's architecture and the concept of installation art. The focus then shifts from the notion of the critic-witness as essayist to that of the artist-curator interview. The dialogue between curator and artist, so often barely—if at all—visible in the work of art as finally exhibited, seemed an obvious analogue to the commissioned essays, reflecting as well an important stage in contemporary art making. Here, too, are found the individual voices and personal modes of thinking that characterize the preceding sections of critical essays.

The inclusion of essays and interviews on the performing and media arts confirms another fact of art practice in the second half of the twentieth century: that the cross-genre mixing of forms so prevalent in the avant-garde stems naturally from cultural developments that render strict categories relatively useless. The influence composer John Cage has had on the visual arts, for example, is crucial; to herd him and his peers into a separate if equal category makes no sense. Happily, in this volume, the performing and media arts are rightly seen in their appropriate contexts. The writers and interview participants in these areas exhibit individual voices and themes that underline the immediacy as well as the historical importance of dance, music, film and video from the fifties to date. Lynn Garafola follows the collaborative ideal in dance from Diaghilev to Merce Cunningham. Roy Close studies Cage's career and influence in close-up detail. Paul Arthur examines the significance of New York City as a metaphor for independent filmmakers. Allan Kaprow exposes the tangled web of practical circumstance and conceptual approach that blend behavior and theater into performance art. Sally Banes describes the connections between post-Cunningham choreographers and visual artists. B. Ruby Rich outlines the changing conditions of alternative film and the advent of video. This promiscuous polymorphism of categories is perhaps the most outstanding characteristic of what might be called avant-garde art today. From materials to concepts, it's clear that one major linkage between innovative artists from the fifties to the present is a genre-bending sense of wide-open possibilities.

Besides the multidisciplinary impulse, another identifiable trend might be a growing internationalism. In this era of global cross-pollination, such a reexamination of the intercultural links that began in full force after the Second World War is not only accurate history but a vital issue that bears on the ever-escalating multinational traffic that takes place today.

Despite its deliberate subjectivity, I'd like to think that this book, along with the art that inspired it, presents a relatively authoritative portrait of the historical decades under review and of the nineties, the period in which history proceeds even as the study of it is undertaken. I know, however, that history does not stand still for a formal portrait but continues to evolve even after its "facts" are registered; that other and radically different attitudes will emerge from a future rethinking of the same era, probably with different conclusions. *Breakthroughs* tells one kind of story and not another. More nearly at hand, this portrait is not complete until the act of seeing and reading by an audience takes place, an event that of course further alters the picture.

John Howell

ART IN EUROPE AND AMERICA

The 1950s and 1960s

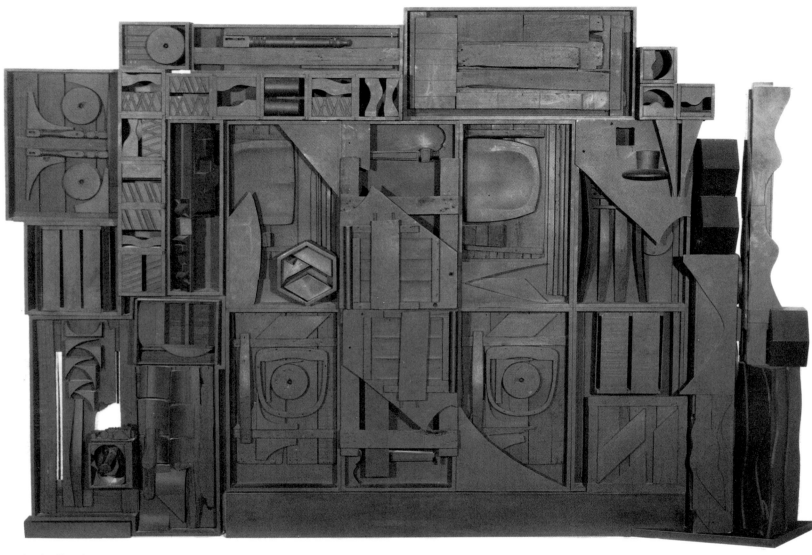

Louise Nevelson
Sky Cathedral: Night Wall 1963–70
painted wood
114" x 171"
Columbus Museum of Art, Ohio; gift of Eva Glimcher
and Derby Fund Purchase.
Photo: Todd Weier.

Art in Europe and America
The 1950s and 1960s

Artist refers to a person, willfully enmeshed in a dilemma of categories, who performs as if none of them existed.
Allan Kaprow

Rusted wheels, a scroll of latex, a bucket chained to a canvas, naugahyde and kapok, balloons filled with "artist's breath" and tins of "artist's shit." This is the stuff of art. These disparate objects form the material essence of art produced by individuals as diverse as Jean Tinguely, Eva Hesse, Robert Rauschenberg, Claes Oldenburg and Piero Manzoni. When they were created, the art world viewed these works as challenging and often shocking. Now they have acquired a patina of age and status—they're artifacts of a contemporary art that has already become historical. Yet their artists' innovations remain radical, even for jaded audiences a bit too comfortable with the unexpected.

Today Louise Nevelson's walls of black stacked boxes, among them *Sky Cathedral Presence* (1951–64), *Young Shadows* (1959–60) and *Sky Cathedral: Night Wall* (1963–70), are revered icons. Neither their assemblage methods nor their architectural scale strike viewers as unfamiliar or disquieting. But when Nevelson first showed her walls, they too thwarted expectations regarding sculpture and its presentation. Installed at New York City's Grand Central Moderns in 1958, her sculptures transformed the gallery—illuminated by only a few blue lights—into a stark, mysterious theater charged with intensely poetic, dreamlike associations. Nevelson wished to emphasize not the individual found and carved objects that filled the walls' nooks but the expressive quality of the totality as a place, as an environment—another once-radical concept now omnipresent in the formulations of installation art.

Over the past four decades, the form, content and context of art have undergone dramatic transformations and redefinitions as avant-garde vocabularies have passed into mainstream parlance. The impetus for change arose from the visions of artists who overtly or indirectly sought to dissolve previous aesthetic conventions and expectations and in the process established new ones. The institutionalization of expected discomfiture was one obvious and enduring legacy of avant-garde art from the fifties and sixties. Another was an open-ended, inclusive attitude toward art-making processes. Yet another was the absence of clearly defined boundaries: between the various components of the visual arts (painting, sculpture, graphics, photography) and between visual arts, performing arts, architecture and other disciplines. Situated in the "dilemma of categories" Kaprow describes, artists combined and moved between the two-dimensional and the three-dimensional, the visual and the aural, the static and the active, the isolated object and the total environment. Unexpected juxtapositions and multidisciplinary explorations became the norm.

The artistic breakthroughs of the fifties and sixties discussed in the following essays reveal the dynamic interactions of avant-garde artists whose activities and ideas often overlapped and developed simultaneously. As Dore Ashton reminds us in her essay, many of the ideas in international circulation during the fifties and sixties can be traced back to prewar developments, to earlier twentieth-century artists such as Marcel Duchamp, even to the eighteenth- and nineteenth-century wellspring of Romanticism. Nonetheless, the fifties and sixties witnessed the development and codification of a changing if not precisely new avant-garde. Our discussion begins in the fifties, when the collective spirit of modernism gave way to the individual pursuits heralded by the supremacy of individual gesture in Abstract Expressionism and when the seat of international artistic power shifted from European centers to New York City. The shadow cast by Abstract Expressionism would be particularly long, as its ideologies and forms became the standards against which much later experimentation would measure success: from the cool formalism of Minimalism in the sixties to the Neo-Expressionism of the early eighties. The avant-garde thus came to locate itself not only in a rush for what was novel and experimental but also in ongoing critical and aesthetic responses to previous experiments, previous breaks with convention.

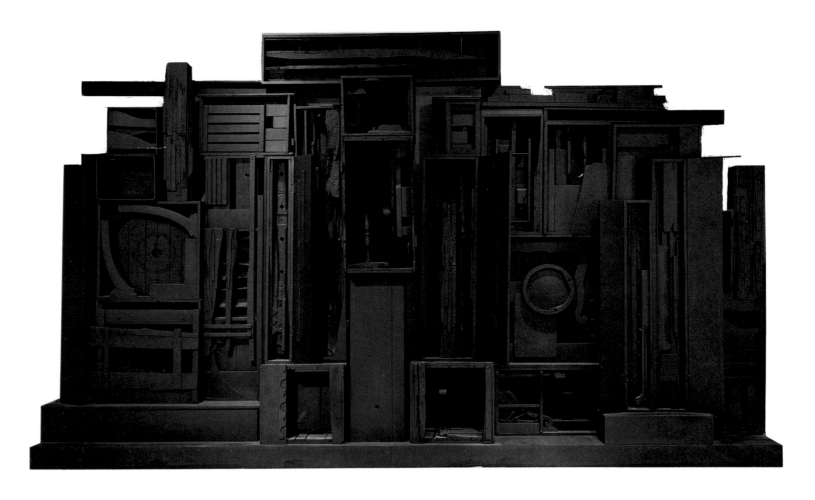

Louise Nevelson
Sky Cathedral Presence 1951–64
painted wood
117" x 174" x 29"
Walker Art Center, Minneapolis; gift of Judy and
Kenneth Dayton, 1969.

At once an end and a beginning, Abstract Expressionism summarized earlier twentieth-century abstraction and served as a point of departure for a new vision of art making based on the artist's action. In his seminal series of "Women," Willem de Kooning confounded figuration and abstraction, transforming his traditional subject of the female figure into a tense battleground of gesture, form and space—creating a new order amid the glaring chaos. The lush, energized handling of paint reveals his primary assertion that the subject of these works is less the figure than the space. De Kooning's work suggests the extraordinary and continuing impact of action painting: the issues he scrutinized set the stage for the further expansion and dissolution of traditional painting by younger artists including Jasper Johns, Robert Rauschenberg and Frank Stella.

The focus of international critical attention on the New York School in the fifties did not preclude equally inventive developments in Europe, and the inclusion of pivotal European artists and works in this volume contributes to the continuing reassessment of transatlantic artistic exchange. Ashton identifies common points of reference as well as distinctions between the American Abstract Expressionists and the European artists of the somewhat parallel tendency known as Art Informel. Pierre Restany compares the French Nouveaux Réalistes Yves Klein, Jean Tinguely and Niki de Saint Phalle with their American contemporaries Johns, Rauschenberg, Claes Oldenburg and Andy Warhol. Giulio Carlo Argan, on the other hand, considers developments in Italian art in the context of a specifically European imperative for postwar reconstruction.

Lucio Fontana, one of the artists Argan discusses, gave the notion of "breakthrough" physical as well as philosophical expression. Fontana created art that was not about making a mark on a canvas but about making a gesture in the realm of the world. The most infamous of his pursuits are the *Tagli* or slashes. In what many considered a violent gesture, Fontana literally cut with a knife into the surface of a carefully painted, monochrome canvas. His act was not a destructive one, however, but rather an affirmation and a symbolic entry into infinity. The most sublime of these gestures is perhaps the single slit on white ground, *Concetto spaziale, "Attesa"* (1960), in which all activities and decisions are compressed into one powerful, ultimate intrusion.

Piero Manzoni, a generation younger than Fontana, explored new artistic frontiers and presaged many later developments of Conceptual and performance art with an eclectic body of work as much about concept and process as about the object itself. His *Achromes*, constructed (not painted) of layered materials ranging from felt and cotton to stones and polystyrene, liberated the canvas from image, narrative, emotion and, perhaps most importantly, from the heroic presence of the artist. In some *Achromes* he used cobalt chloride, a light-activated substance that glows in the dark, to attain a dual

Louise Nevelson
Young Shadows 1959–60
painted wood
115" x 126" x 7 ¾"
Whitney Museum of American Art, New York;
purchase, with funds from the Friends of the Whitney
Museum and Charles Simon, 62.34.
Photo: Fredrik Marsh/Lynette Molnar.

identity determined not by the artist's controlled intervention but by the conditions in which the works are viewed. Manzoni's lines similarly subverted artistic tradition, reducing drawing to an event: he drew a line on a roll of white paper, then rolled it and placed it in a black container labeled with its date of execution and its length. With his infamous tins of *Merda d'artista* (Artist's shit, 1960) sold at the market price of gold, Manzoni sanctioned his excrement as not only artistic but valuable, turning the exalted myth of the artist's creativity into an ironic joke. With the balloons he packaged and sold as *Corpi d'aria* (Bodies of air, 1959–60) and those he inflated himself and titled *Fiato d'artista* (Artist's breath, 1960), he suggested that even air could be certified as art. Argan notes that Manzoni was one of the first postwar European artists to choose Duchamp as his artistic mentor, and the Italian artist shared not only Duchamp's taste for ironic and iconoclastic gestures but also his desire to meld art and life. In Manzoni's work this interest was perhaps most poetically expressed by *Socle du monde* (Base of the world, 1961), a magical pedestal for the entire world.

The French Nouveaux Réalistes posed equally radical challenges to established definitions of artist and art object, particularly in their investigations of theatrical and collabortive art-making techniques. Although his mature career spanned only a decade, Yves Klein produced an intensely flamboyant, controversial and influential body of work. In his *Anthropométries,* or imprints, Klein created paintings by directing models covered with blue pigment to leave bodily imprints on paper or canvas according to his instructions. Many of the imprints were made in front of an audience; others were completed in Klein's studio with extensive photo documentation reminiscent of Hans Namuth's photo essays of Jackson Pollock's working process. Klein insisted, however, that his work was the opposite of Pollock's action painting because of his detachment and function as conductor of the creations.

Jean Tinguely also crossed the boundary between art and action, turning movement itself into an artistic medium in his eccentric drawing machines and self-destructing environments. His kinetic reliefs of the mid-fifties, among his first explorations of movement in art, added a temporal dimension to the early modernist traditions of nonobjective painting. The *Balouba* series of the early sixties was inspired by the valiant independence struggle of the Balouba people in the Congo. At rest, these poignant sculptures appear to be odd collages of unrelated, found objects; once in motion, they become quivering dancers celebrating the Baloubas' heroic lives. This series is also among Tinguely's most serious exploration of color, influenced in part by his colleague and partner in life, Niki de Saint Phalle.

One of the few contemporary women artists to gain critical attention in the prefeminist early sixties, de Saint Phalle based much of her imagery on the female body and psyche, sources that would become central to feminist discussions of women's art and women artists in the seventies. Inspired by the pregnant figure of Clarice Rivers, wife of painter Larry Rivers, de Saint Phalle's *Nanas* embody the complexities of female existence. The name "Nana" reveals these paradoxes: the term refers to both the *femme fatale* of Emile Zola's novel and to a French expression for the role of the mother who holds the family together. The *Nanas*' small heads and large rounded bodies recall fertility goddesses in the tradition of the Venus of Willendorf. The artist described these forms as referring to societal clichés such as the emphasis on women's bodies over their minds but also transcending such definitions through the figures' exuberant, independent stature.

Collaborations and multidisciplinary investigations—rooted in the earlier cross-fertilizations of Dada—characterized both the European and the American avant-garde of the fifties and sixties and often linked European and American artists. De Saint Phalle and Tinguely collaborated not only with each other, as in *M.O.N.S.T.R.E.* (1964), but also with other visual artists and with artists working in other disciplines. Klein's *Anthropométries*, de Saint Phalle's "shooting paintings" and Tinguely's self-destructing assemblages, such as *Homage to New York* (1960), combined aspects of visual and performance art. Venturing further into the theatrical arena, Tinguely and de Saint Phalle worked with Rauschenberg, composer John Cage, dancer/choreographer Merce Cunningham and poet Kenneth Koch on *The Construction of Boston*, an experimental performance produced in New York in 1962.

Robert Rauschenberg's theatrical activities—the sets and costumes he designed for Cunningham's dance company and for other performers as well as the performances he presented himself—were very much about moving beyond accepted parameters and building a new artistic language. *Minutiae* (1955) shows Rauschenberg's masterful interplay of the everyday and the sublime—newspaper comics, delicate lace and blood red paint—in an exquisite stage-set construction that is an independent complement to, not merely a descriptive backdrop for, a dance of the same name performed by Cunningham with music by Cage. The form and content of Rauschenberg's artworks similarly sought to redirect traditional expectations by combining made and found, two- and three-dimensional objects. In *Memorandum of Bids* (1957), one of the "combines" included along with the legendary *Bed* in his first solo exhibition at the Leo Castelli

Piero Manzoni
Socle du monde 1961
iron
32 ¹³⁄₁₆" x 40" x 40"
Herning Kunstmuseum, Denmark.
Photo: Thomas Pedersen and Poul Pedersen.

Jean Tinguely
Balouba vert 1962
mixed media
54" x 20 ¹³⁄₁₆" x 16 ¹³⁄₁₆"
Louisiana Museum of Modern Art,
Humlebaek, Denmark.
Photo: Strüwing.

Lucio Fontana
Concetto spaziale, "Attesa" 1960
waterbase paint on canvas
46 ⅜" x 35 ⁷⁄₁₆"
Collection of Teresita Fontana.

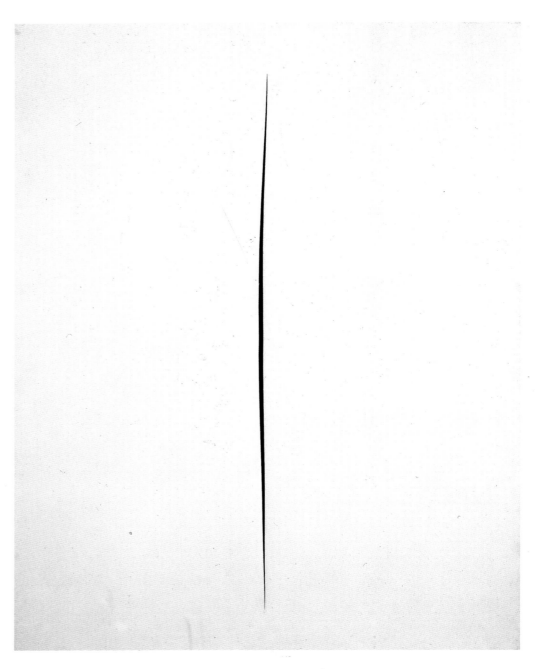

Gallery in 1958, he matched painterly brushwork with paper ephemera. In *Gift for Apollo* (1959) he chained a rough wooden construction to a common pail, with the title offered as an ironic reference to the Greek sun god's glorious chariot transporting the sun through the heavens.

Rauschenberg's art took many different directions; Jasper Johns' pursuits were intensely focused. Johns' early flags and targets were recognizable as signs that also functioned abstractly. Formally *White Target* (1957) is only a ring of concentric circles, but as a symbol its meaning is immediately clear. This dichotomy underscored the controversy Johns' work provoked and revealed his primary subject as the act of seeing. Similarly, his numbers were simultaneously functional and dysfunctional; printed over one another in *0 through 9* (1961), they create an image of numerical metamorphosis and exemplify the constant shift between depiction and presentation in his work.

There is a pervasive link between Americans such as Rauschenberg and Johns and Europeans such as Klein, Tinguely and de Saint Phalle in their common affinity for the everyday and the concrete (the source of the "realism" Restany found in Nouveau Réalisme), whether evidenced in commonplace imagery, cast-off objects or actual movement and action. This enthusiasm was continued by American Pop artists, but—as Restany and David Bourdon both point out—with subtle differences. Bourdon traces one example of the commonplace, the use of newsprint as subject and medium, through the fifties and sixties and so clarifies the roles Johns and Rauschenberg played as intercessors between the Abstract Expressionists and the Pop artists as well as the increasingly iconic, monumental and ironic tenor the everyday acquired in American Pop art. The voices of the Pop artists varied, as is apparent in Claes Oldenburg's affinity for the commonplace object and Andy Warhol's for the mass-media image. Their work, however, shares a similar function in its confounding of distinctions between "high" and "low" art, an issue with continuing resonance for contemporary artists.

Top
Andy Warhol
Daisy 1970
mixed media installation with photographs, pipes,
tanks, water
132" x 248" x 96"
Private collection; courtesy Ronald Feldman Fine Arts,
Inc., New York.
Photo: D. James Dee

Above
Claes Oldenburg
Giant Pool Balls 1967
sixteen fiberglass balls, each 24" diameter,
on wood rack
24" x 120" x 108"
Los Angeles County Museum of Art; anonymous gift
through the Contemporary Art Council, M.69.88.
Photo: copyright 1989, Museum Associates, Los
Angeles County Museum of Art.

Oldenburg's soft sculptures are often ironically lumpy versions of hard-edged techno-logical forms. Both the electrical outlet (*Three-Way Plug*, 1975) and the telephone (*Soft Pay-Phone*, 1963) were designed to facilitate communication in our technological world. Oldenburg rendered them ineffectual through exaggerated scale and illogical materials. He has pushed this concept to architectonic dimensions in the visionary monument drawings and public art projects that have occupied him during the past twenty years. *Giant Pool Balls* (1967) relates to a proposal for an "imaginary monument," *Moving Pool Balls in Central Park*, an idea realized ten years later in Münster, West Germany. The pool balls—twenty-four inches in diameter—play with the notion of play while also existing as quintessential minimalist volumes in space.

Warhol's life and work, his fascination with mass media and his stinging criticisms of it, became inextricably intertwined. His work, perhaps more than that of any other artist discussed here, has become so familiar, commercially successful and iconlike that it is difficult to understand and remember its avant-garde impact. But not all of Warhol's works are so predictable and familiar. *Daisy Fountain* (1970), for example, is not particu-larly well known, though it does embody several of the strongest characteristics of the artist's vision, characteristics shared by other innovative artists of the fifties and sixties: his involvement with new technologies, his directorial role in the art-making process and his desire to create theatrical effects as art. First exhibited at the United States Pavilion of Expo 1970 in Osaka, Japan, *Daisy Fountain* was commissioned by the Los Angeles County Museum of Art for its seminal *Art and Technology* exhibition, which brought together artists and scientists to create art, another manifestation of interdisciplinary and collabo-rative investigations. Warhol initially wanted to work with holograms; since another artist was already doing so, he selected instead another three-dimensional photographic process. His basic concept was a rain machine: a curtain of water positioned in front of photographs of plastic daisies. Although hampered from the beginning by technical difficulties, the project finally was completed with Warhol, as one witness remarked, "forcing everyone to act" and so orchestrating the collaborative process.

Warhol's later career provides an extreme example of the avant-garde's potential for eventual adoption by the mainstream, but the challenge of conveying the shock of initial innovations is common to the discussions of many artists represented in this section of *Breakthroughs*. Confronting this issue directly, Brian O'Doherty shares with us his own first reactions to Frank Stella and Eva Hesse's very different works and thus vividly recaptures a moment when their ideas were new and unexpected, whether irritating or intriguing.

When Stella moved to New York in 1958, he immediately became immersed in the aftermath of Abstract Expressionism. Johns' flag paintings presented themselves as signposts at this dramatic crossroads. Struck by Johns' notions of repetition and mono-chromatic color, Stella began his chilling and provocative "black" pictures: shocking, nonreferential images that were uncomfortable hybrids of hard-edged geometry and painterly gesture. After the "black" paintings, he began the "aluminum" series in which he introduced small notches in the exterior edges of the canvases. These helped to emphasize shape over the pictorial field, allowing the exterior shape to cause zigs and zags in the interior bands of paint. With these two series, Stella dismantled and subverted previous painting conventions, defining a new pictorial ideology that became a corner-stone for Minimalism in the sixties and seventies.

As the vocabulary of Minimalism grew rapidly alongside that of Pop art, the avant-garde began to operate in cohesive groups moving in opposition to one another as well as to their common forebears in Abstract Expressionism. Minimalism and Pop art quickly triggered their own creative reactions. Over a brief period of five years, Eva Hesse produced an extraordinary body of work that testified to the strength of expressive, process-oriented alternatives to the shared coolness of Minimalism and Pop art. Her visceral, hybrid objects poised between sculpture and painting are in many ways a counterpoint to Stella's painting and to the exactitude of Minimalist sculpture and materials. Her reliance upon synthetic materials, chance and hand-made construction gave her the freedom to create works that are compact in form but explosive in emotion. The repetitive and reductive quality of her works is minimalistic, but their tactility and frontality is highly expressive and painterly.

The opposing visions of Stella and Hesse together form one bridge between the artists and essays of *Art in Europe and America: The 1950s and 1960s* and those of *Art in Europe and America: The 1960s and 1970s*, the second part of this volume. The juxta-position of Stella and Hesse in O'Doherty's essay provides a springboard to the fuller discussion of contrasts between Minimalism and anti-formal alternatives to it—and of Conceptual objects and actions and Neo-Expressionist and other post–Minimalist work and ideologies—in the subsequent section of *Breakthroughs*.

The final three essays in this section—by Lynn Garafola, Roy M. Close and Paul Arthur—shift the focus of discussion from the visual arts to dance, music and film, respectively. Garafola traces attitudes toward movement, narrative, collaboration and decor in the work of George Balanchine, Maurice Béjart, Martha Graham and Merce Cunningham, choreographers who definitively reshaped the traditions of ballet and modern dance. Close places the innovations of John Cage, pervasive influences on all the arts, in context with those of other significant European and American composers, among them Pierre Boulez, Karlheinz Stockhausen and Morton Feldman. Arthur locates a New York "school" of American avant-garde film in an urban milieu that defined subjects, styles and modes of production. Suggesting the configurations of this period's avant-garde in other specific disciplines, these three essays also reveal precedent-shattering and precedent-setting developments that often paralleled those in the visual arts. For example, the interests in assemblage methods, found materials, popular-culture sources and multidisciplinary hybrids so prevalent in the visual arts also figured in avant-garde music, dance and film. Collectively, then, Garafola, Close and Arthur establish another connection between the first two parts of this book: the continued presence of concerns shared by artists working in different disciplines and the continued significance of inter- and cross-disciplinary investigations.

Sarah Rogers-Lafferty

The Long and Short of It

Dore Ashton

During the late forties and early fifties American Abstract Expressionists and their European colleagues of Art Informel redefined painting and established a legacy of individual freedom that continues to influence subsequent generations. In the following essay Dore Ashton ruminates on the attitudes that motivated these avant-garde artists at mid-century. That era, she argues, is to be measured not only against today's activities but also by its remaining traces—the art objects it produced. Ashton combines the historian's long view—a review of modern art from the nineteenth century to today in terms of modulations between classicism and romanticism—with the critic's sense of history as a constant reevaluation of evidence. Threading a line of argument between the past as objective and fixed and history as only relative, she arrives at the ineluctable fact of the art itself. Ashton brings to this assessment her own dual perspective as historian and critic. An on-scene witness during the halcyon days of Abstract Expressionism, she has worked as a critic for the New York Times, *has written several essential histories of art and presently teaches art history at the Cooper Union of Art and Architecture in New York.*

Willem de Kooning
Woman 1949–50
oil on canvas
64 ¼" x 46 ¼"
Weatherspoon Art Gallery, University of North Carolina at Greensboro; Lena Kernodle McDuffie Memorial Gift, 1954.
Photo: David Roselle.

Art history, a confection of the mind, is protean and always subject to alteration when it alteration finds. It cannot be bid to stop. If we try to fix the outlines of something that occurred after the Second World War, known in Europe as Art Informel (Informalism) and in the United States as the New York School (though almost no one in it was a born New Yorker), those outlines inevitably waver, expand and even dissolve. Certainly the configuration of artists who by convention are called action painters or Abstract Expressionists cannot be reduced to a stylistic category. Flamboyant, extravagant, hard-drinking, angry, tormented, introspective—adjectives so often used about artists of that period and that, to some degree, do qualify, hardly suffice to describe a historical movement, or even a moment. The only way to do that, more or less, is to take the long view. In the long view, the activity in the realm of the visual arts that erupted after the disaster of the Second World War can be seen as a chapter in the intellectual history of Romanticism, and who knows, even now, if that chapter is closed?

Romanticism itself has had a hard time finding a definition, but there are certain basic attitudes that emerge from it. Foremost is the belief that, as Vico put it in 1725, "the imagination is so much more robust in proportion as the reasoning is weak." Nearly a century later Keats would speak of "Negative Capability" and define it as "when man is capable of being in uncertainties, mysteries, doubts, without any irritable reaching after fact and reason." Soon after these early Romantics came many singular artists and poets who would celebrate what they called the Imagination, placing it above the powers of mere formal logic. They gathered up evidence that there was something that could speak to and from the senses that was superior to classic notions about the act of thinking. All through the nineteenth century, which culminated with the enshrinement of psychology as the discipline most capable of defining the arts, artists were energetically attacking positivistic views of the world. Intuition was raised to the power of a major faculty and artists began to see themselves as nonverbal contributors to knowledge. Once it was established that the arts were purveyors of a certain type of knowledge, the old quarrel between classicists and romantics had to be shifted to other grounds. The quarrel goes on, but in new, pseudoscientific lineaments. Many still doubt that the visual arts contribute to intellectual history. After the war, the French philosopher Maurice Merleau-Ponty warned his readers on many occasions never to "underestimate the painter's labor and study, that effort which is so like an effort of thought and which allows us to speak of a language of painting."

In fact, it was often in the language of painting that the most significant artistic attitudes in the postwar period were articulated. Ever since the early years of the century, painters had been beacons for creators in the other arts. During the years of the early Russian avant-garde, one of its major poets, Velimir Khlebnikov, repeatedly declared: "We must boldly follow the painters." Gertrude Stein in the same period pronounced her only influence to be Cézanne. Vanguard composers took up Cubism in France, and, during the Abstract Expressionist years, young American composers often said that they were influenced not by composers but by Jackson Pollock (in the case of Earle Brown) or Philip Guston (Morton Feldman). Something was going on in painting that inspired. It had the savor of freedom, that value most cherished and most poignantly explored by the Romantics.

Even a cursory glance at the diction of artists active after the Second World War shows the word "freedom" flitting through their pronouncements with greater or lesser philosophical precision. Theirs was a freedom that painters such as Pollock, Arshile Gorky, Willem de Kooning and Barnett Newman, to mention just a few, felt had been wrested from aesthetic despair. The quick march of artists to the tune of "isms" that had preceded them in the century had become intolerable as a prospect. No one could deal with the cacophony of often conflicting ideologies in the arts. They felt—as had each of the twentieth-century vanguard movements before them—that they had reached ground zero. As they struck out to demolish the conflicts of their past, they said, more or less, what the hell, we have nothing more to lose. This remarkable discovery proved to be

Top, Willem de Kooning, 1964.
Photo: © Hans Namuth, 1989.

astonishingly liberating. Harold Rosenberg caught the spirit in his celebrated definition of action painting:

> At a certain moment the canvas began to appear to one American painter after another as an arena in which to act—rather than as a space in which to reproduce, re-design, analyze or "express" an object, actual or imagined.[1]

Although Rosenberg referred only to his cohorts in the United States, he could easily have extended his assessment to the Europeans who, with equal intensity, sought to create a great convergence of feelings as they manipulated the physical matter of paint. While Rosenberg spoke of "action painters" and saw their behavior in terms of European existential philosophy, European commentators such as Jean Paulhan noted identical tendencies in postwar Europe but spoke of Zen Buddhism, stressing the nonrational character of Art Informel. The mood described by both critics was certainly inherited from the troubled years between the wars that had led artists to flee the strictures of classical logic, to establish what one American critic called an "intrasubjective" viewpoint and to extoll its corollary—the existence of individual freedom.

Many half-formed thoughts that had occurred to nineteenth-century precursors were completed in the period between the wars. Although the abstract artists in the wake of Constructivism and the artists in the wake of Expressionism saw themselves as antagonists (among them certain Surrealists), all were convinced that something pure, something unsullied by reason, could be fetched up from subliminal sources. Most artists were interested in the art of the so-called primitives because it seemed, as it had seemed to Vico, more authentic, closer to truth. Many spoke of an innocent eye, raising Baudelaire's curious notion of naïveté to a principle. While some artists dallied with Freudianism, others paid particular attention to the vernacular sources of art. Some equated individual freedom with political freedom. Others saw it in the creative act alone. All, regardless of their camp, had freedom on their minds. Such issues lingered and were reinterpreted after the Second World War. In Europe several forceful artists returned to earlier concerns, articulating them with a new expostulatory decisiveness. Jean Dubuffet defended painting as "a richer language than that of words," saying that it is "closer to the cry or

the dance." Like others before him in the century, he saw the primitive as somehow superior. In 1951 in the United States Dubuffet offered a lecture that the young American Claes Oldenburg relished, in which he blasted colleagues who thought that assembling shapes and colors pleasing to the eye was a worthy job. Painting, he said, was "an instrument of thought":

> ...painting, especially much better than words, allows one to express the various stages of thought, including the deeper levels, the underground stages of mental processes...Painting now can illuminate the world with wonderful discoveries, can endow man with new myths and new mystics, and reveal, in infinite number, unsuspected aspects of things...[2]

New myths and new mystiques were very much on the minds of many American artists who thought of themselves as departing from the classic, the Greek tradition, into some unknown territory in which all human passions, as Nietzsche had taught several of them, should be reflected. Sometime in the forties Barnett Newman had already remarked that "the artist today has more feeling and consequently more understanding for a Marquesas Island fetish than for the Greek figure." He and his friends Mark Rothko and Adolph Gottlieb would later address the issue of myth directly in their work and would renounce the banalities of painting in which, as Dubuffet had remarked, there were mere shapes and colors pleasing to the eye. The ingathering of all the emotional forces they

15

imagined required that they abandon the canons of earlier abstract artists. Rothko and Newman solemnly declared that there could be no good painting about nothing, and in 1945 Rothko wrote that "the abstract artist has given material existence to many unseen worlds and tempi. But I repudiate his denial of the anecdote just as I repudiate the denial of the material existence of the whole of reality."

There was concern with freeing the human image from the desuetude into which it had fallen on both sides of the Atlantic. It was thought at the very least that some semblance, some analogue of the long-worked motif of the human figure could be rescued from the depths of the psyche. Many artists after the war believed that elements of so-called reality were perfectly permissible and in some cases necessary. Jean Fautrier, who always hovered on the edge of explicitly articulating recognizable subject matter, stated categorically in 1957 that "the unreality of an absolute informal aesthetic gives us nothing—a gratuitous game. There is no form of art that can give emotion if it doesn't mix in a part of the real." In the United States it was Willem de Kooning who repeatedly asserted the right of an artist to work simultaneously with abstract and representational elements, to be utterly free in his choices. At a lecture at The Museum of Modern Art in 1951, well attended by members of the new art world that had so rapidly materialized after the war, de Kooning said "spiritually I am wherever my spirit allows me to be," adding:

> Some painters, including myself, do not care what chair they are sitting on. It does not even have to be a comfortable one. They are too nervous to find out where they ought to sit. They do not want to "sit in style." Rather, they have found that painting—to be painting at all, in fact—is a way of living today, a style of living, so to speak. That is where the form of it lies. It is exactly in its uselessness that it is free.[3]

At the time de Kooning was delivering this statement he was already preparing his exhibition of paintings on the theme of women—a coup of major significance that became a true *succès de scandale*. Gathering up his satiric and what he himself called his "vulgar" impulses, as well as his vast acquaintance with expressionist art of previous eras, de Kooning, with savage delight, shattered the hopes of the purists who had already begun to ensconce "Abstract Expressionism" in a formal context. De Kooning later

Robert Rauschenberg
Gift for Apollo 1959
freestanding combine
43 ¾" x 29 ½"
The Museum of Contemporary Art, Los Angeles;
The Panza Collection.
Photo: Squidds & Nunns.

Willem de Kooning
Woman 1965
oil on wood
80" x 36"
Hirshhorn Museum and Sculpture Garden, Smithsonian
Institution, Washington, D.C.; gift of Joseph H.
Hirshhorn, 1966.
Photo: Lee Stalsworth.

Willem de Kooning
Woman Accabonic 1966
oil on paper, mounted on canvas
79" x 35"
Whitney Museum of American Art, New York;
purchase, with funds from the artist and Mrs. Bernard
F. Gimbel, 67.75.
Photo: Sheldan C. Collins, New York.

Jasper Johns, 1964. Photo: © Ugo Mulas.

Jasper Johns
Subway 1965
sculpmetal over plaster and wood
7 ⅝" x 9 ⅞" x 3"
Collection of the artist.
© Jasper Johns/VAGA, New York, 1991.

reminisced about his move to the figure with his usual verbal agility:

> It's really absurd to make an image, like a human image, with paint, today, when you think about it...But then, all of a sudden, it was even more absurd not to do it...It did one thing for me: it eliminated composition, arrangement, relationships, light—all this silly talk about line, color and form—because that was the thing I wanted to get hold of.[4]

With similar declarations, many artists of the generation who are identified with the New York School established a moral climate in which the integrity of the artist rested on the principles of freedom and emotional honesty—a climate healthy for the revolt in the ranks of the next generation.

That revolt cannot be easily confined and historically defined. In the long view, the behavior of such figures as Robert Rauschenberg, Jasper Johns, Claes Oldenburg and Eva Hesse is quite consistent with the attitudes of the older generation. The sixties saw a riotous diversity released, but even those who challenged the fathers had been inspired by their adventurousness. In the way they spoke of their undertakings, these artists availed themselves of the diction of the earlier generation that had leaned so much on existentialist terminology. Hesse, for instance, wrote in the late sixties: "I have learned that anything is possible. I know that the vision or concept will come through total risk, freedom, discipline." Both Rauschenberg and Johns asserted their right to do anything—even to affix real objects to their canvases and, if they chose, to engage the other senses in their total effects. When Rauschenberg experimented with sounds, he could certainly be said to have extended the long romantic tradition of synaesthesia established so brilliantly in Baudelaire's famous poem "Correspondences." The old Wagnerian ideal of the total work of art haunted the twentieth century and was often realized in the activities of this generation, for this was the generation that moved away from the static work of visual art into that vaguely theatrical genre, the Happening. This was also the generation that announced its interest in the urban environment. First Rauschenberg and then Oldenburg emphasized the value of New York's street life and its detritus. They were interested in objects of the everyday world and mechanically reproduced imagery. In short, they desired to embrace the entire world of impressions and emotions—an ideal carried over from the previous generation. The prime impulse was to avoid what de Kooning had called silly talk about line, color and form.

Artists in Europe were in the same mood. The most radical were those who no longer saw painting in terms of an inviolable picture plane. Lucio Fontana, for instance, pried his viewers loose from their expectations by physically mutilating the picture plane. His slashed canvases with their intimation of real space illustrated the principles he had established in his *White Manifesto* in 1946, the opening salvo of which stated: "It is necessary to overturn and transform painting, sculpture and poetry." He and many others were working feverishly to overturn. From works on walls that incorporated bits of reality (Rauschenberg, for instance, with his famous bed) to the hybrid event called the Happening, which incorporated fragments from nearly all the arts, was a short step. In Europe, particularly among the members of that shifting world group called Fluxus launched in the early sixties, the arts overflowed their boundaries with alacrity. A German member of Fluxus, Wolf Vostell, observed: "What fascinated me were the symptoms and emanations of a constant metamorphosis in the environment and in which destruction in general, and in artistic expression, together with dissolution and juxtaposition, are the strongest elements." Jean Tinguely made it his mission to elevate process over product to the degree that even the destruction or dissolution process was inherent in his work. *Homage to New York*, his great performance at The Museum of Modern Art in 1960 in which he created a self-destroying machine that, to the consternation of officials, went up in flames, was another sharp signal to other artists that anything was possible.

Tinguely and his American counterparts had borrowed from their mentor, Marcel Duchamp, a smile of irony. To most commentators they seemed to be making a definitive break with what were then considered the rather ludicrous, earnest pieties of the Abstract Expressionists. Tinguely spoke of "much freedom and the *acte gratuit*" and announced that nonsense is "a dimension that irony can be built into." Rauschenberg declared that a pair of socks was no less suitable to make a painting with than wood, nails, turpentine, oil and fabric. The same year, 1959, Johns wrote: "Sometimes I see it and then paint it. Other times I paint it and then see it. Both are impure situations and I prefer neither." Impurity, the expressed ideal of de Kooning, goes all the way back to the early Romantics, and even irony, as personified by the life and work of Marcel Duchamp, was not invented by him. The preoccupation with objects, their personification or mystification, appeared long before among the Surrealists and was drawn from their

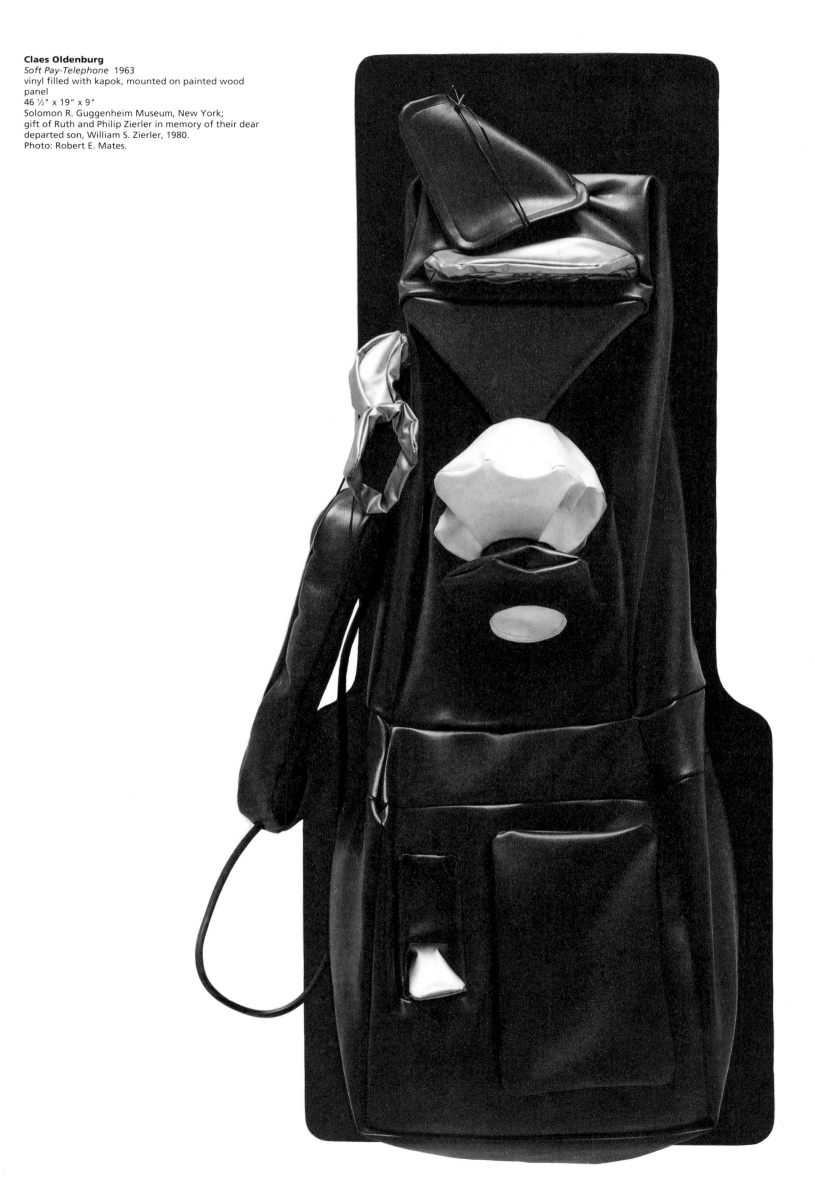

Claes Oldenburg
Soft Pay-Telephone 1963
vinyl filled with kapok, mounted on painted wood
panel
46 ½" x 19" x 9"
Solomon R. Guggenheim Museum, New York;
gift of Ruth and Philip Zierler in memory of their dear
departed son, William S. Zierler, 1980.
Photo: Robert E. Mates.

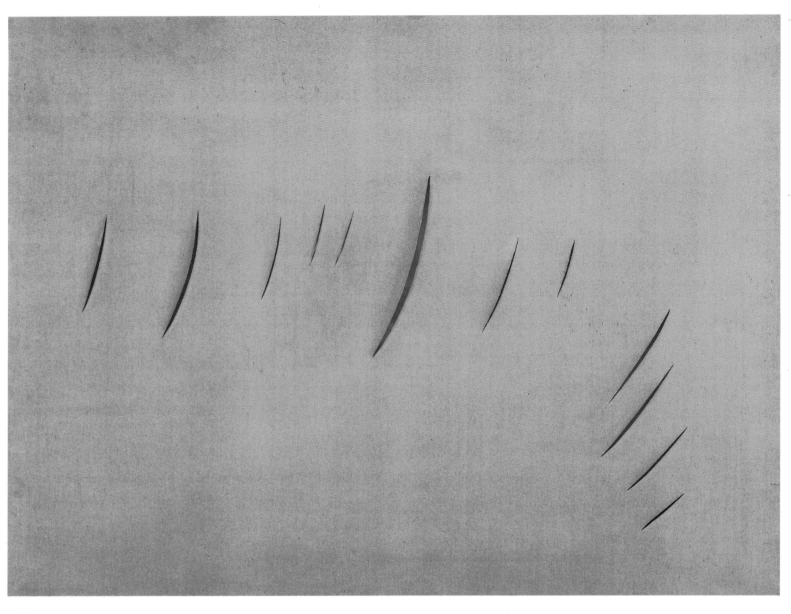

Lucio Fontana
Concetto spaziale, "Attese" 1959
aniline on canvas
40 ⅜" x 50"
Collection of Teresita Fontana.

meditation on the views of the eccentric Romantic pantheon.

Irony demands distancing. For the earlier and nonironic postwar artists, it had entailed a psychological withdrawal. They had distanced themselves from repellent aspects of modern life by scanning far horizons and ancient myths. From myth, with its dependence on metaphor, some had moved to the direct, sometimes ritualistic gesture. Subsequent artists seemed to recoil from this rarefied quest. They thrust themselves back into life with all its paradoxes and tried to smile. Their distancing took the form of a suspicion of metaphor and a refusal to take for granted the intellectual value of nondiscursive art. Johns firmly repudiated what he called "aesthetic hierarchy":

> The most conventional thing, the most ordinary thing—it seems to me
> that those things can be dealt with without having to judge them; they
> seem to me to exist, as clear facts, not involving aesthetic hierarchy.[5]

Echoing Johns, the young Frank Stella during the same period came forward with an uncompromising rejection of illusion, asserting his views by working with preconceived schemas on the surfaces of his paintings.

Although to many the new ironic stance that became highly visible during the sixties marked a significant break with the past, there is some question as to how much this break will appear definitive to future historians. Most of these artists continued to make paintings and sculptures. Most continued to display a certain confidence in nonverbal meaning implicit in works of visual art. In the long view, the artists who emerged on the stage during the sixties to deliver their various retorts to the fathers—those who altered conventions by expanding painting into sculpture and sculpture into environments—were still well within what Rosenberg had so deftly summarized as "the tradition of the new." That itself was, finally, a Romantic tradition.

But there is always the short view—the view from within our quotidian lives. From where we stand today, it seems that the seeds of our situation were sown during the sixties. Our situation might perhaps be characterized as anti-Romantic. There is a

verifiable loss of faith in the existence of immanent meanings. Tradition is seen as parody. The ideal of personal freedom is assumed by many artists today to be a mythical one since freedom as such, if it exists at all, is relative. An appetite for tendentious art has been whetted by the pervasive emphasis on information. Artists join everyone else as onlookers. They look, for instance, at what is often called "other" art, or the art of the others—it used to be called primitive art—with clinical eyes seeking not confirmation but information. They seek what Keats denied: facts and reason. There are few philosophical assumptions not grounded in quasi-scientific theories drawn from linguistics or the social sciences. It has become much more difficult for artists to assume that there is a language of painting which, with its immanent capacity to move, can add to the realm of knowledge. Perhaps loss of faith is the salient characteristic of this end of the century. Perhaps what distinctively separates the artists working now from those of the fifties and sixties is the inexorable relativism that prevails, a relativism that goes far beyond the Romantic relativism discussed by Baudelaire when, in *L'Art romantique*, he said:

> Absolute, eternal beauty does not exist, or rather, it is only an abstrac-
> tion skimmed from the general surface of different forms of beauty. The
> particular element in each form of beauty comes from the emotions and
> as we have our own particular emotions, we have our own form of
> beauty.

Since few are convinced today that there is much particularity in emotions, few could endorse Baudelaire's attitude. What has been called postmodernism includes in its project a downgrading of the individual with his particularities and oddly resurrects certain of the positivistic ideas that had so incensed the early Romantics. From the fin-de-siècle view, the ideals that inflamed the imaginations of the artists of the fifties and sixties seem little more than amusing. Revisionist art history has been at work. Yet, the works— those paintings, sculptures, combines, films of Happenings—remain with us. History may have found alteration, but its primary materials remain vital. □

Reconstruction
Art in Postwar Italy

Giulio Carlo Argan

Since the end of the Second World War, Italian artists have made notable and influential contributions to the development of vanguard art, yet their work has been less known to American audiences than that of their French and German peers. Contemporary Italian art has appeared in the United States most often as a phenomenon of discrete groups (Arte Povera, the three "C's" of Francesco Clemente, Enzo Cucchi and Sandro Chia) severed from history and context. In the following discussion of postwar Italian art, Giulio Carlo Argan views changes in aesthetic attitudes as inextricably linked to political events. This approach befits an observer who has witnessed nearly a century of abrupt upheavals in European culture. The dean of Italian art historians (and a noted scholar of baroque as well as modern art) and a former mayor of Rome, Argan is a model of the classic European art critic: mindful of tradition, attuned to contemporary culture and politically engaged. He examines the search for models to guide the "rebuilding" of postwar European culture and discusses in particular the work of Lucio Fontana and Piero Manzoni, artists who redirected the traditions of prewar abstraction through their investigations of new materials and art-making practices. Argan places Fontana and Manzoni's radical innovations into a specifically European cultural matrix of pan-national political, social and art history.

Giulio Carlo Argan's essay was translated from the Italian by Marguerite Shore.

After the Second World War, throughout a devastated Europe, people talked of nothing but reconstruction. It wasn't just houses, railroads and industries that had been destroyed; in the minds of victors and vanquished alike, all faith in the wisdom of governments and in the irrevocability of human rights had been lost as well. How did one go about rebuilding in such a crisis? Restore the status quo, thereby possibly re-creating the circumstances that had led to war? Or rebuild for a different and, perhaps, better world? But which world? The twentieth century had begun triumphantly, promising peace, well-being and brotherhood between peoples. It had then produced two tremendously destructive wars, tyrannical political regimes, racial persecutions and genocides, and condemnations of all nonconformist intellectual activity. And the war's end did not bring peace but a state of Cold War between forces that had been allied in the struggle against Nazism and Fascism. New weapons, which could destroy all mankind, created the threat of a new, infinitely more disastrous war.

The totalitarian regimes and the war had provoked a profound crisis in European intellectual life. Serious culture had not been compromised, but until the war it had not intervened in politics; at most, it had demonstrated a disgust for the cultural vulgarity of Fascism and Nazism. In Italy the most prominent cultural leader had been the liberal philosopher Benedetto Croce; he was opposed to Fascism, naturally, but also to the experimental tendencies of contemporary culture. He felt it wasn't his place to worry about social problems, economics, politics and the conditions of the working class.

European intellectuals were not to blame for the grim politics of Fascism and Nazism, but they could not deny partial responsibility. Few if any of them had acted to prevent the rise of these forces, yet Nazism and Fascism had violated all human rights and condemned all modern art and literature. The low point was reached with the German occupation of almost all Europe; not only political freedom and social dignity but the primary conditions of existence were abused. At that point intellectuals felt they had to take part in the liberation struggle; they fought as partisans alongside workers and peasants, becoming familiar with their problems, their culture, their politics. Now, after the war, one thing was clear: reconstruction had to be a collective enterprise, not one left to a ruling class responsible for the disasters that had occurred. Proposals for the future implied a critique of the past: in what manner had culture hastened or slowed down the involution of bourgeois culture? To what degree and within what limits had it promoted the revolutionary, or merely reformist, impulses that were seen in society as a whole? Repeatedly, avant-garde art movements had been connected to revolutionary notions; yet, after the First World War the avant-gardes were disbanded, except in Russia. There vanguard art had been directly involved in the development of a great socio-political revolution but was brutally suppressed once the revolution was realized.

The postwar reconsideration of the avant-gardes can be distinguished from the neo-Cubism of the same period, when Cubism was seen as a sort of interlanguage, outside any national tradition. In Italy, Emilio Vedova proposed the revival of the revolutionary impulse of Futurism, altering its meaning to turn it into a rebellious force against all forms of repression. Reconstruction had to form a new avant-garde. There were other difficulties: the culture that was sought was meant to be harmoniously, if not uniformly, European, but the Yalta Agreement had divided Europe into two areas with opposing ideological orientations. In terms of art, there was a clear split: on the one hand, figurative art intended to stimulate the proletarian struggles; on the other, a nonfigurative absolute, which aimed to separate artistic fact from any sensory emotion. Both tendencies claimed to be committed to the socio-political situation and leftist in orientation. Realism was presented as art for the revolution, abstractionism as intrinsically revolutionary art.

•

Prior to the Second World War, the polestar of Italian culture had been the idealism of Croce, but even before the war, art and criticism had attempted other paths: the Viennese school and pure visibility, the phenomenology of Husserl, the psychological theories of Freud and of Jung, the dialetical materialism of Marx. After the war, Jean-Paul Sartre was

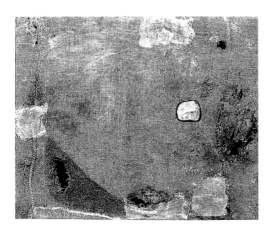

Alberto Burri
Sackcloth 1953 1953
burlap, sewn, patched and glued over canvas
33 ⅞" x 39 ⅜"
The Museum of Modern Art, New York;
Mr. and Mrs. David M. Solinger Fund.

the philosophical mind that guided European culture. He was interested in the problem of an art that was not assigned a precise political task but that acknowledged its intrinsic political nature. If art proceeded neither from a priori models of nature and history, nor from a preconceived aesthetic, it had value as pure phenomenal reality, as existential fact. Art necessarily had a relationship with the political situation of its own time, which was a condition of its existence, but just as it could not be identified with an ideology, so it was no longer seen as tied to the system of industrial production. Sartre's existential philosophy contradicted the thesis of the synthesis of the arts, a pivotal thesis of the first and second avant-gardes, of the Neo-Plasticism of de Stijl, of Russian Constructivism, of industrial design.

Since the German occupation, French painter Jean Fautrier had most explicitly reflected the existentialist concept of art. In his *Ôtages* (Hostages) he aimed neither to represent nor to express but to realize concretely, in anguished materials, the existential condition of the human being deprived of all personal liberty and dignity, who, from one moment to the next, might be deprived arbitrarily of his very existence. Jean Dubuffet's deformation of language was also linked, though less directly, to the "philosophy of crisis." And this "philosophy of crisis" corresponded to a total crisis in art, which, with its detachment from every aesthetic premise and from every historical precedent, from every preconstituted language, descended to grade zero and eventually began again with chance materials and the instinctive gesture of the artist. Throughout Europe artists had moved from figurative to nonfigurative work. In Italy, as early as 1947, a group of pure abstractionists (Piero Dorazio, Achille Perilli, Pietro Consagra, Giulio Turcato) had formed in Rome; another group, Origine, which included Alberto Burri, Giuseppe Capogrossi, Mario Ballacca and Ettore Colla, followed in 1950.

●

Even before the war, the avant-garde had proposed a synthesis of the arts, with the unanimous goal of an aesthetic education that would also be an education in liberty and a factor in bringing social-democratic reform to the social order. In France, with Le Corbusier, and in Germany, with Walter Gropius, rationalist architecture was presented as a wide-ranging project of reform, which covered everything from urban planning and building improvements to industrial design. In Weimar in 1919, Gropius established the Bauhaus, a school for all the arts acting in conjunction to establish a new, fully democratic social reality. He sought the most important artists of the time to teach there, and the faculty included Vasily Kandinsky, Paul Klee, Oskar Schlemmer, Josef Albers and László Moholy-Nagy. In 1925 the school moved to Dessau and then in 1930, shortly after Ludwig Miës van der Rohe became its director, to Berlin. Social-democratic in orientation and supportive of experimentation in the most modern tendencies of all fields of artistic research, the school was eliminated by the Nazi government in 1933.

With the support of advanced industrialists, currents in rationalist architecture and industrial design spread throughout Europe, including Italy, but there Fascism's repressive and backward impetus curtailed such developments. As with Nazism in Germany, art under Fascism had to be a function of the state, of the political regime in power, rather than of society. It could not produce buildings for habitation and work but had to focus on settings for mass political demonstrations. In Italy, the architects of the Fascist regime did more damage than the wartime bombardments. Rational architecture was practically excluded from large public projects. Due to its social, progressive commitment, it was considered incompatible with the reactionary state.

Once the war was over, it was logical that rational architecture, democratic and internationalist by nature, would be considered a guiding force in the program of reconstruction. Instead it was the object of severe criticism on the part of Bruno Zevi, a young architect who had studied in the United States and who, upon his return to Italy, had fought in the liberation forces. According to him, it was the American Frank Lloyd Wright rather than Le Corbusier or Gropius, who ought to be the model and guide for a European art that went beyond reconstruction to reestablish a European artistic culture. Wright was an established and celebrated architect whose work had been known in Europe since 1910, and his creative genius was well recognized. Why was he to be relaunched as an ideal guide for a reconstruction that was meant to be more than mere restoration? Like the European rationalists, Wright favored a democratic, internationalist architecture: according to his ideas, however, democracy meant not only equal civil rights but also the free and positive relationship of each individual to his own vital environment, and internationalism was not the unification of styles but the total independence of each tradition. Wright's "organic" architecture was more modern than European rational architecture because it didn't come out of a preconceived notion of space, of society, of architectural form; it was limited to the material that the artist took from nature and shaped with the inventive force of his own gesture. In fact, his architectural

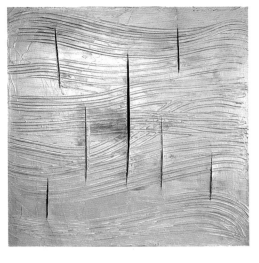

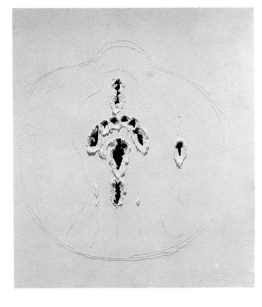

Lucio Fontana
Concetto spaziale, "Venice Moon" 1961
oil on canvas
60" x 60"
Collection of Teresita Fontana.
Photo: Paolo Vandrasch.

Lucio Fontana
Concetto spaziale 1968
oil on canvas
40" x 32 ⅛"
Fondazione Lucio Fontana, Milan.
Photo: Paolo Vandrasch.

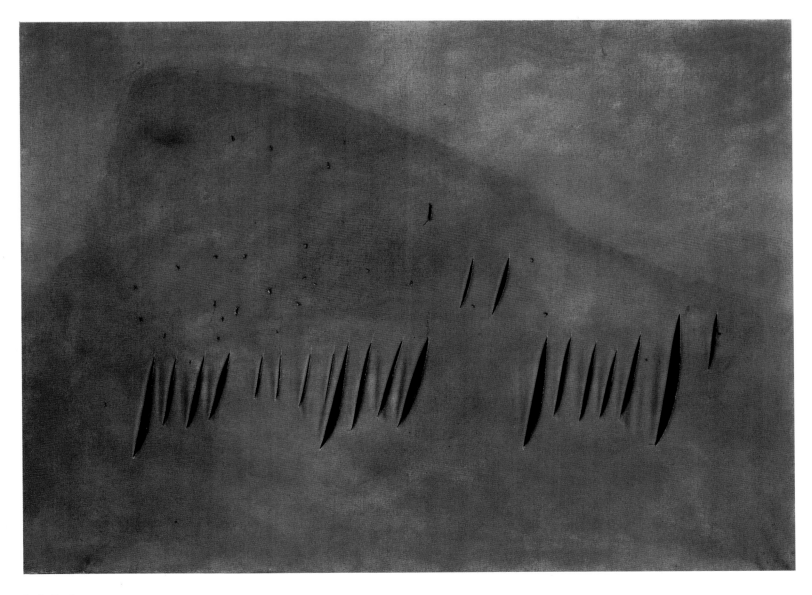

Lucio Fontana
Concetto spaziale, "Attese" 1959
aniline on canvas
38 ¾" x 52"
Fondazione Lucio Fontana, Milan.
Photo: Paolo Vandrasch.

Lucio Fontana, Milan, 1964. Photo: © Ugo Mulas.

plasticity was more advanced than the European avant-garde because it was freed from the compulsion to define itself in antithesis to an impoverished tradition. In order to be a force for reconstruction, which was anything but completed, art couldn't be involved in revivals, nor could it set itself up in opposition to the past. It had to have its own dynamic, to have a more intense, manifest, conscious existence.

At the beginning of the fifties, Alberto Burri showed his first *Sacchi* (Burlap) pieces. Without direct analogy to Wright's architecture, these works also had an intensified, expressive potential in their materials. Avoiding any symbolic intention, the artist presented his paint-splattered fragments of sackcloth directly, even flagrantly, which strengthened the relationship between material and image. Yet, with some reason, critics found those early works by Burri to be the expression of an inner creativity, and the more *povera*—worn-out and consumed—the real material, the more taut and secure that creativity.

●

The phenomenon that was most salient, but also terminal and conclusive, for postwar European art was, in Milan, the close affinity and, at the same time, the extreme contradiction between an older artist, Lucio Fontana, and his young student, Piero Manzoni. Fontana had begun work as a sculptor in the thirties and forties, in conjunction with a group of early abstractionists in Milan. His predilection for the most daring modernity and for decoration led him to be interested in architecture and industrial design and brought him into contact with Marcello Nizzoli, the renowned designer for Olivetti. (In 1939 Nizzoli's typewriter was shown at The Museum of Modern Art in New York.) During the war, Fontana lived in Argentina; in 1946 he launched a radical avant-garde movement with his *Manifesto blanco* (White manifesto), which was followed, in 1951, after his return to Italy, with the *Manifesto tecnico dello Spazialismo* (Technical manifesto of Spatialism).

The new avant-garde had a relationship with the sciences rather than with a revolutionary ideology, for Fontana believed that it was scientific research and technology, not political ideology, that had changed the face of the world. From the thirteenth century on, Western art had been a representation of space; now it was a continual invention of space—not of an absolute and geometric space but of individual spatial situations, which were also temporal since there was no longer an a priori distinction between space and time. These situations were determined by movement, which was the unifying factor, and their goal was a substantial identity rather than a synthesis of the arts. Fontana wrote, "Man is vacant of pictorial and sculptural forms…The tranquil life has disappeared…The aesthetics of organic movement is replacing the empty aesthetics of fixed forms." His ideas about nature were not very different from those of Wright: he too saw nature as a dynamic, mutable, intensely vital relationship of matter and movement rather than a formal, preconstituted model, a totality of laws. And man was not an object with respect to a subject; he too was nature and participated in its existential rhythm. The specific function of art was to recover the primary values of both nature and existence. "We postulate an art free of all artifice…we refute the aesthetic falsities invented by speculative art." This was to be an art free of every "adaptation to natural forms, a function of all man's energies, in creation and in interpretation. Existence is integrally manifest with the fullness of its vitality."

In Fontana's work, theory and practice are not separate. The *Concetti spaziali* (Spatial concepts) are at the same time concepts and figures of a space that doesn't exist save as phenomenon and becomes phenomenon through a creative act of will. Yet there is a preliminary operative stage; a compact and uniform color is applied in equal coats to the taut canvas, a purely manual, craftsmanlike labor, like painting a door. The repetition of the gesture, the compactness of the surface and its coloration provoke the artist to an abrupt reversal of behavior: projecting fragments, perforating and later sharply cutting the surface. Space emerged with the rupture of a boundary, with the reestablishment of a continuity between "this side" and "that side" of a surface. And it was space as absolute, pure entity, which couldn't contain anything and which had an existence of its own; space was a state of being and not a condition of being. And the being led to time as act, as phenomenon, as consciousness.

At a time when people tended to identify the value of art with the meaning of the artist's gesture, Fontana's gesture in the large cuts in the colored surface was distinguished by its instantaneousness, its resoluteness, its precision. Fontana had worked as a decorator and designer and had no prejudices against the scientific technology of industry; he didn't rule out the possibility of a relationship, and often, in his research into the environmental development of space, he took advantage of the most sophisticated lighting apparatuses. The gesture of projecting fragments or of rending the canvas with a cutting blade had the force and resoluteness of the movement of a machine, but these

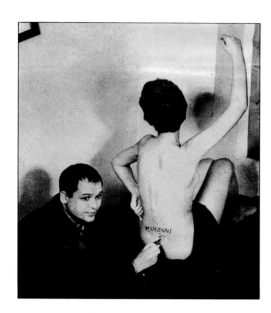

Above and right, Piero Manzoni, 1961. Photos courtesy of Galleria BLU, Milan.

were unique and unrepeatable acts of will, the effect of which was also an object, an unrepeatable one: the canvas. Thus it was an object that was the opposite of the serial, exclusively quantitative production of industry. At this point the artist could compete with the velocity, the precision, the infallibility of the machine; with a gesture, he freed himself from that inferiority complex with respect to mechanical means, which Günter Anders called "technological shame," and which constituted one of the causes of modern man's alienation.

Fontana's goal was another modernity, an absolute reality that gave both time and space the sole dimension of the absolute present. Yet in fact he was the last "pure" artist, asserting the absolute value of art as quality and of the creative gesture of art, which technical invention could not replace. At the time he was, with reason, considered the most advanced of modern Italian artists, the leader of a new, open-minded avant-garde. In reality, he was the defender of the concept of art as creation and even as beauty. But at the same time, he demonstrated the limits to which those concepts had to be reduced in order to coexist with the new value concepts introduced by industrial culture.

It was Fontana's most talented student, Piero Manzoni, who understood the internal contradiction that was concealed beneath the luminous clarity of the master's art. Manzoni died in 1963, not yet thirty years old. He came to art after studying philosophy, and in terms of painting, his point of departure was the geometric purism of Mondrian and de Stijl. Manzoni was friendly with Enrico Castellani, who had studied architecture in Belgium, and the common objective for the two artists was the overcoming of Italian abstractionism, of which Fontana represented the most advanced, almost insurmountable, frontier.

In 1957 Manzoni made his first *Achromes*, working directly on the surface of the canvas or gesso support without using paint. In 1959 Castellani and he established the magazine and then the gallery *Azimuth* with the goal of coordinating European research that went beyond abstractionism. They were connected to Yves Klein and the French Nouveaux Réalistes. Their wide-ranging research didn't stop with pictorial representation; it addressed numerous problems: the canvas as object, traditional techniques and procedures, prejudicial aesthetics about the essence and statutes of art, the market.

At this point, it was inevitable to summon up the historical example of Dada, which, with its fundamental nihilism, had not entered into the revision or revival of the avant-gardes and their view toward a cultural reconstruction of Europe. In Italy, Manzoni was the first to see that Duchamp was one of the most important protagonists of the century, the first artist for whom there was no work of art that wasn't also an idea about the essence and historical condition of art. Clearly there was a relationship, and not just a dialectical one, between the paintings Manzoni made out of wrinkled canvas, sponges and rolls and his overtly scandalous and sacrilegious "performances": nude models, their skin signed to guarantee their natural beauty; balloons blown up with "artist's breath" and small tins of "artist's shit," ironic comments on the myth of art as a product of the artist's interior; tubes containing kilometers of lines designed to mock the idea of space. He courted scandal and he got it, and those whom he scandalized, in good or bad faith, ended up seeming ridiculous: members of parliament who called for the intervention of the state, magistrates who threatened to take legal action to punish the offense to art's ideal nature held sacred by the bourgeois public. In fact, Manzoni's appeal to Duchamp

Piero Manzoni
Achrome 1960
polystyrene soaked in cobalt chloride
25" x 19 ¼"
Private collection; courtesy Sperone Westwater,
New York.
Photo: Phillips/Schwab.

Piero Manzoni
Achrome 1960
polystyrene soaked in cobalt chloride
13 ¾" x 10 ¼"
Private collection; courtesy Sperone Westwater,
New York.
Photo: Phillips/Schwab.

and to Dada was the the negative conclusion of the long debate concerning the raison d'être and the function of art as a component of a European culture.

Manzoni's Dadaist gestures didn't constitute a terminal period of self-negation of his own work. They were contemporary to the period of his committed search for a different and superior absolute value for art, beyond all aesthetic theories, all traditional idealism or realism, all criticism in literary terms, all divulged opinion, and beyond market publicity. Art was undergoing a serious crisis, not because of incompatibility with industrial techniques but because of the failure of the commonly accepted concept of art's cultural justification. In short, the crisis was an internal one. There were similar motivations behind Nouveau Réalisme in France, with artists such as Klein and Niki de Saint Phalle, supported by the critic Pierre Restany.

●

Manzoni implied a negative judgment of so-called programed art, which was developing throughout Europe in the fifties, and which, in Italy, culminated in an exhibition organized in 1960 by Olivetti in Milan. Programed art could trace a direct descent from the Bauhaus and, more specifically, from the experimentalism and teachings of Moholy-Nagy. The theoretical assumptions of the movement, which also spread to South America, were based on the reduction of aesthetics to the psychology of perception and to the study of self-generated visual images. Committed to scientific methods of research, for which the making of art was a tool of experimentation and demonstration with educational ends, practitioners of programed art considered the artist's personality irrelevant and favored instead organized group research. They rejected ties to the art market and cultivated an

Piero Manzoni
Laine de Verre 1961
fiberglass and felt on board
15 ¼" x 17 ¼" x 1 ⅜"
Albright-Knox Art Gallery, Buffalo;
The Martha Jackson Collection at the
Albright-Knox Art Gallery, 1974.

Top
Piero Manzoni
Corpo d'aria, No. 11 1959–60
wood box containing a balloon and a metallic base
4 ¹³⁄₁₆" x 19 ³⁄₁₆" x 4 ¹³⁄₁₆" (closed)
Courtesy Galleria BLU, Milan.

Below Left
Piero Manzoni
Merda d'artista 1961
Nos. 003, 006, 010
1 ⅞" (height) x 2 ⅝" (diameter)
Courtesy Galleria BLU, Milan.

Below Center
Piero Manzoni
Linea di lunghezza infinita 1960
wood cylinder
5 ¹⁵⁄₁₆" (height) x 1 ¹⁵⁄₁₆" (diameter)
Courtesy Galleria BLU, Milan.

Below Right
Piero Manzoni
Linea m. 6 1959
ink on paper
10 ¼" (height) x 2 ⅜" (diameter)
Courtesy Galleria BLU, Milan.

exclusive relationship with schools, and without developing specific applications to industrial design they advocated adherence to industrial means of production and distribution of images. The ultimate goal of programed art was the correction of the negative, alienating effects of mass visual communication within the environment.

Beyond these extreme positions, the problem of art as a component of the value system of a European culture no longer existed; the very concept of a central European culture no longer made sense. Precisely at the end of the fifties, American Pop art—ruling out all historical issues and questions as to art's conception, techniques and goals—radically changed the possibilities of art's affinities and accessibility. □

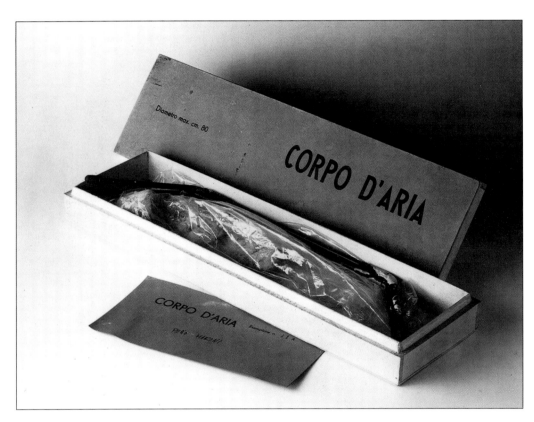

Piero Manzoni
Linea lunga, 7200 meters 1960
zinc and paper
26 ⅜" x 38 ⅜"
Herning Kunstmuseum, Denmark.
Photo: Thomas Pedersen and Poul Pedersen.

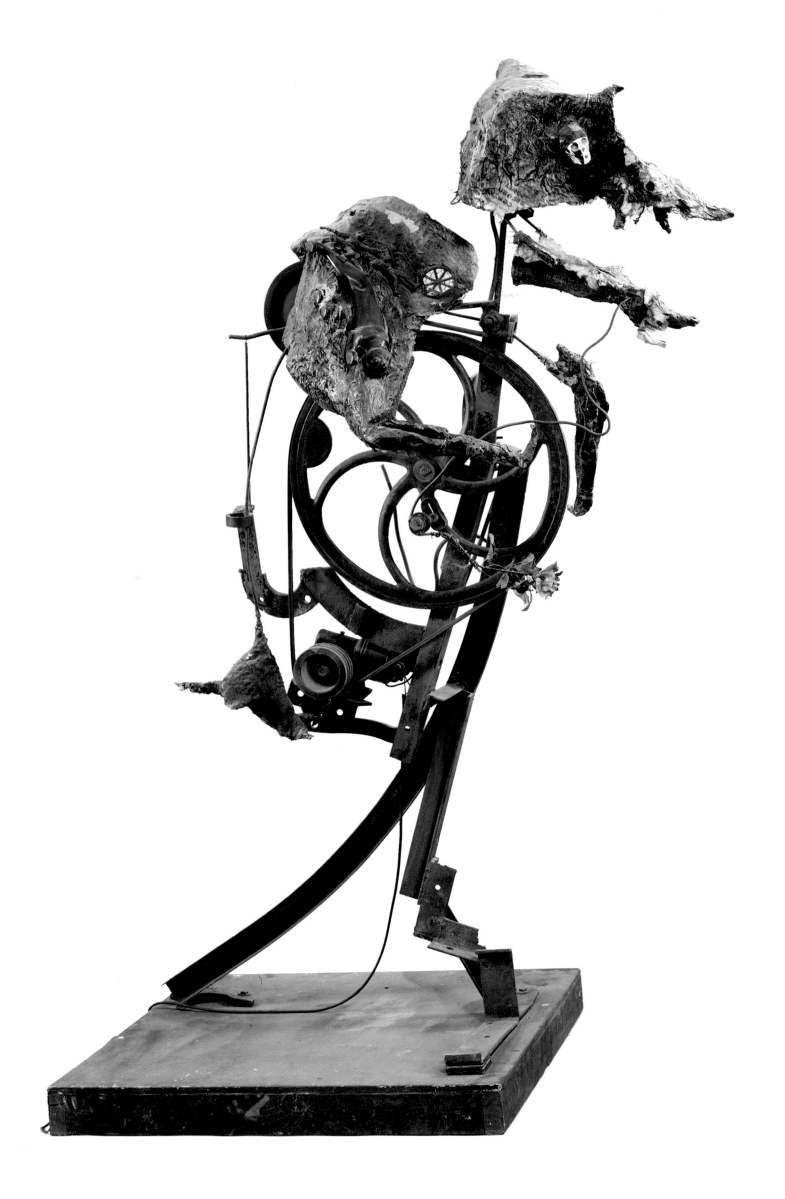

Modern Nature

Pierre Restany

One of the most intriguing connections between avant-garde European and American artists in the fifties and sixties was the fascination with the "real"— everyday objects, commonplace images, literal movement and action—shared by the French Nouveaux Réalistes and the American Pop artists. In the following essay, Pierre Restany chronicles the development of Nouveau Réalisme, a movement he helped to launch, assessing its affinities with Pop art as well as distinctions between the two movements. While noting and naming the several philosophical congruences and divergences among artists and curators of the period, Restany also displays his sheer relish at the give and take of ideas in a moment of new beginnings.

Restany's text is an adaptation of his essay "Chelsea 1960," which was originally written for the catalogue of the exhibition Paris–New York *at the Centre Georges Pompidou in Paris in 1977. Published here for the first time in English, Restany's comments track the intertwined careers of French and American artists—and the author—through impressionistic memories of exhibitions and encounters in New York and Paris. As one of the few French critics to embrace postwar developments in American art, Restany forged early and important links between artists on both sides of the Atlantic through the exhibitions he organized and his prolific writings.*

Pierre Restany's essay was translated from the French by Joachim Neugroschel.

The first half of the sixties was one of those peak periods in art. For fifteen years, the bitter commercial rivalry between Parisian and New York art dealers had led to the almost complete break of relations between the American Abstract Expressionists and their opposite numbers in European Art Informel (Informalism) and Tachism. The imperatives of the market, translated into terms of cultural imperialism and chauvinism, interfered with the free spread of artistic information. And this was true of an entire generation—the generation of 1945. Beginning in 1960, the tables were turned. A new generation of artists was more interested in examining their similarities than in cultivating their minor differences. What did these later artists have in common? Their awareness of the exhaustion of the Abstract Expressionist style and the discovery of a modern sense of nature—industrial and urban.

The basic artistic utterance of doubt and angst following the Second World War was the rejection of the world through the rejection of injustice. The painterly gesture of individual revolt and the rejection of the outer world produced an art of nonfigurative escape. The artists of 1960 no longer shared this postwar mood; they wanted to participate in the reality of the contemporary world rather than flee into imaginary spaces. And, in both Paris and New York, this reality was the world of the factory, of the serial object, of publicity and mass media, the world of consumerism and big cities.

This common situation fitted in with different cultural perspectives. The first industrial revolution had turned America into a nation. When the sense of modern industrial nature reentered the logic of American ideas in 1960, it emerged as a reflection of the maturity of an industrial culture, as a national folklore. In Europe, the new cityscape was forcefully imposed by two successive world wars. Modern nature appeared as a sensitive discovery, a philosophical rupture, the reflection of a youth rediscovered at the price of heavy sacrifices. Among the American artists of 1960, we note an aesthetic concern, a sense of continuity, esteem and respect—beyond stylistic divergences—for their elders, who had made New York a capital of contemporary art. Among the Europeans, the basis for realistic appropriation was far more extremist from the very start: they had no special regard for the uncharismatic personalities of the previous generation.

On the other hand, European and American artists shared an emotional bias that made encounters and exchanges possible: a generous but lucid technological humanism that blended both fascination and derision, imagination and conscious control. In his *Architecture de l'air* (1959), Yves Klein dreamed of returning to a state of nature in a technological Eden. In 1966, Robert Rauschenberg and Billy Klüver founded E.A.T. (Experiments in Art & Technology), an association of artists and engineers whose goal was the systematic study of all the possibilities of language offered by contemporary technology.

The rational optimism that marked the technological humanism of the early sixties was the common denominator of numerous and highly diverse approaches that made up the prehistory of Pop art and conditioned its international expansion. This common denominator defined both a field of activities and a border. Certain New York exhibitions of works by Jean Tinguely, Arman, Martial Raysse, Alain Jacquet and Christo were historic benchmarks in American artistic life during that era, just as the European activities of Rauschenberg, Jasper Johns, Allan Kaprow, Claes Oldenburg and Andy Warhol left an enduring imprint on European culture.

•

In the Paris of the late forties and fifties, when abstract art was all the rage and the geometric-versus-lyrical battle was at its height, it looked as if the debate on art were taking place within nonfiguration. Abstraction was either "cold" or "hot" and the rational construction opposed the instinctive gesture. No one yet noticed the artists for whom the surrounding world and its forms constituted the basis of an autonomous expression. Scattered and quasi-clandestine experiments were conducted by several people who eventually asserted themselves, creating the nucleus of the group that became known as Nouveaux Réalistes. In 1949, Raymond Hains and Jacques de la Villeglé selected and ripped their first torn posters off the walls. Tinguely, relocating from Basel

Two views of Yves Klein at *L' Anthropométries de l'époque bleue,* 9 March 1960. Photos: © Harry Shunk.

Opposite
Yves Klein
Anthropometry: Princess Hélena 1960
oil on wood
78" x 50 ½"
The Museum of Modern Art, New York;
gift of Mr. and Mrs. Arthur Wiesenberger.

Previous page, Yves Klein, 1960.
Photo: © Harry Shunk.

Below
Yves Klein
ANT 85 1960
blue pigment on paper, mounted on linen
61 ½" x 138 ¾"
Private collection.
Photo: Bill Mc Lemore.

to Paris in 1953, delved into the motion and animation of found objects. In 1946 in Nice, Klein had been inspired with his theory of universal permeation with pure color and had produced his first efforts in monochrome pastels, but it was not until 1955, following his definitive return to France after endless travels in Europe and a long sojourn in Japan, that he had his first show in Paris.

By the late fifties, when the New York art world was discovering Rauschenberg's combine paintings and Johns' flags, Richard Stankiewicz's assemblage sculptures and the first Happenings of Kaprow, Oldenburg and Jim Dine, the Parisian art world was having parallel experiences. In 1957 Hains and Villeglé organized their retrospective anthology of torn posters; in 1958 Klein mounted his famous exhibition *Le Vide* (The void), and the Klein/Tinguely encounter, illustrated by the exhibit *Vitesse pure et stabilité monochrome* (Pure speed and monochrome stability), marked a new pivotal point in the oeuvre of the Basel sculptor.

Tinguely executed his *Homage to New York* in March 1960 in the courtyard of The Museum of Modern Art in New York. Klein staged his painting-performance *L'Anthropométries de l'époque bleue* at the Galerie Internationale d'Art Contemporain in Paris, also in March, while Arman made his first accumulations of objects in Nice and put on his exhibition *Plein* (Full)—the antithesis of Klein's *Le Vide*—in Paris that October. Nineteen-sixty was also the first year of Daniel Spoerri's trap paintings and Niki de Saint Phalle's shooting paintings and of new directions from Raysse (ready-made assemblages), Christo (cans and packages) and Gérard Deschamps (patchworks). Mimmo Rotella had previously been working in isolation in Rome, showing his first posters at La Salita in 1953 and 1954 (while Rauschenberg presented collage paintings at Galleria dell'Obelisco); now Rotella came into contact with his Parisian colleagues Hains and Villeglé, who had been joined in 1957 by the ultra-letterist poet François Dufrêne.

In this maelstrom, the Parisian avant-garde was finding its leading spirits and its vision. Its underground days were over. A specific event sanctioned this fait accompli. On 26 October 1960, at the home of Yves Klein, I founded the group of Nouveaux Réalistes, in the presence of Arman, Dufrêne, Hains, Klein, Raysse, Spoerri, Tinguely and Villeglé. (César and Rotella, although they had been invited, were absent, but they participated in further activities of the group, which eventually also took in Niki de Saint Phalle, Christo and Deschamps.) During and immediately after the three years of their collective action (1960–63), the Nouveaux Réalistes were the artisans of the New York/Paris cross-cultural encounter.

The few avant-garde galleries of that era were the crucible of this encounter. The pioneers, Colette Allendy and Iris Clert, were joined by Jean Larcade and Daniel Cordier. From 1961 until its closing in 1966, Galerie J functioned as a hub for the Nouveaux Réalistes and then as an ongoing experimental laboratory. The extreme scarcity of havens for the experimental milieu of Paris in the late fifties may seem surprising today. But it was understandable, given the pressure of the surrounding conformism, the direct result of the exorbitant power wielded by the major, mainstream private galleries of the time. They had managed to attain this control because of the dearth of initiative in museums and public institutions, which had primarily promotional aims. The conditions were

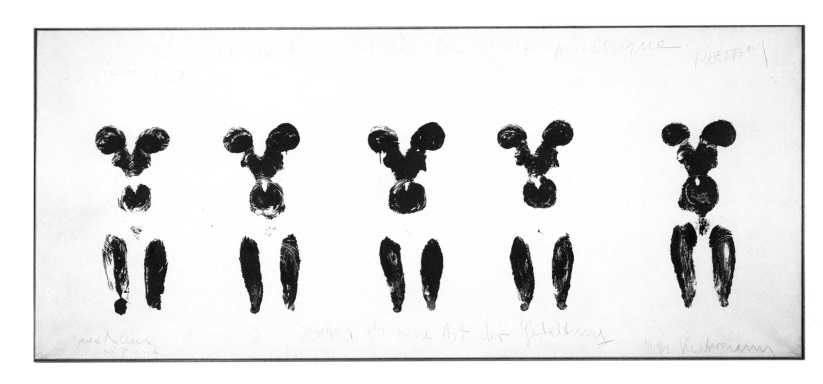

Niki de Saint Phalle, 25 February 1961.
Photo: © Harry Shunk.

Niki de Saint Phalle during her first "shooting,"
Paris, 15 February 1961. Photo: © Harry Shunk.

especially precarious for young artists who could not sell their work. Nor was the situation of marginal American artists any more enviable during the triumphant era of Abstract Expressionism, even though the American system of education, which in those days was far more flexible than the French system, allowed them to benefit from teaching jobs or stints as artists-in-residence at colleges and universities.

•

In January 1960, Jean Tinguely sailed to New York on the *Queen Elizabeth*. The Staempfli Gallery was going to show his classic geometric mobile reliefs and also four *Métamatics*, the drawing and abstract painting machines that had already been exhibited with increasing success: first by Iris Clert in July of 1959, then at the Institute of Contemporary Art in London and finally at the Biennale of the Young in Paris. The renown of Tinguely's *Métamatics* had already spread beyond the confines of Europe. The historical Dadaists who lived in Paris—Jean Arp, Tristan Tzara, Man Ray—saw his show at Iris Clert. Marcel Duchamp, who was visiting the capital as he did almost every summer, did not miss the opportunity to come and "create" ready-made abstract art. Upon returning to New York, Duchamp spoke about the *Métamatics* to the members of his entourage.

The Staempfli exhibition sparked a reserved interest. Emily Genauer of *The New York Herald Tribune* summed up the overall impression: "Machine-made abstraction is clever, but is it art?" Tinguely didn't care, he was too enthralled with New York. He saw Rauschenberg again, he familiarized himself with the works of John Chamberlain, Bruce Conner and Stankiewicz. Tinguely sent raving letters to all his European friends: they [the American Neo-Dada artists of pre-Pop] are doing BIG Things, that's right, big things, it's fabulous!

This discovery of American "bigness," conceived both as an exact proportion of space and as a potential rhythm of energy, was an experience common to all the young European artists who "took the trip" in the early sixties. But Tinguely was the first to translate it into reality. A trip to Philadelphia with Duchamp to see the extensive Arensberg Collection confirmed his notion that in America "you have to see big." Yves Klein's spiritual influence was abetted by Stankiewicz's formal influence: the idea of making a large-scale self-destructing machine in *Homage to New York* was taking shape.

Everything accelerated. Tinguely met Billy Klüver, a Swedish engineer at Bell Telephone Company, who had already worked with Johns and Rauschenberg. He got together with painter and filmmaker Robert Breer, who also was interested in movement in art and whom he had already known well in Paris. Klüver and Breer, who were very excited about the idea of *Homage to New York*, personally helped to bring it about. Marcel Duchamp spoke about it to his friend William Copley, the billionaire painter, who informed Sam Hunter, who then talked to Peter Selz, curator of painting and sculpture exhibitions at The Museum of Modern Art. Selz visited the Paris Biennale, where he found André Malraux gazing at *Métamatic no. 15.* The Museum of Modern Art functioned as the mecca of modern art. Its prestige was incontestable throughout the world, even among the retrograde chauvinists of the School of Paris. So, when MoMA offered Tinguely the chance to present his self-destructing machine in the museum's sculpture garden, he jumped at the chance.

Thus began an adventure that was to culminate on 17 March 1960, when *Homage to New York* was set on fire in the sculpture garden of the Modern. Tinguely's gigantic monument was a crazy quilt of scrap iron incorporating diverse objects: bicycle wheels, wagon wheels, radio sets, an addressograph, two *Métamatics* and a piano. This temporary architecture, crowned by a weather balloon and a cloud of foul-smelling smoke, was slated for thirty minutes of animation and then doomed to destruction by remote control. *Homage to New York* was an overwhelming success. Here was America in the throes of its apocalyptic cult of the machine at the very moment that Rauschenberg, Johns, Stankiewicz and Chamberlain, in the metropolis of New York, were becoming the center of the Neo-Dadaist trend.

By the time Tinguely returned to Paris only a few days later, he was a changed man. He had discovered his means and methods. He lived on the momentum of his appropriation of scrap iron until the spring of 1963, when he gradually began to move away from the found object and work towards forms that were more and more finished, constructed and uniformly covered with the black paint so dear to Alexander Calder. For three years, Tinguely engaged in intense activity, multiplying his machines, exhibitions, events. He played a decisive role in founding the group of Nouveaux Réalistes in October 1960, especially through his preliminary discussions with Klein, Hains and myself. For Tinguely, this was a period of major commitment to collective action, of incessant commuting between Paris and New York, and the start of his life with Niki de Saint Phalle, "the shooting painter."

Of a French and American background, Niki de Saint Phalle was born in Neuilly, near Paris, and brought up in New York. She was deeply involved in Anglo-American literary circles, thanks to her first husband, the writer Harry Matthews, who was very close to the poets Frank O'Hara and John Ashbery (the latter then earned his living as art critic for the Paris *Herald Tribune*). De Saint Phalle, along with Tinguely, contributed a great deal to tightening the bonds between Parisian and New York artists. Her shooting paintings were target reliefs encompassing pouchs of pigment, at which viewers were invited to fire a revolver or a rifle. Struck by the bullet, the pouches burst and the pigment spurted out, impregnating the plaster with a colored dripping worthy of Pollock at his best. In June 1961, her first show, *Feu à volonté* (Fire at will), at Galerie J—which was transformed into a rifle range—made de Saint Phalle an overnight sensation, four years before the appearance of the *Nanas*, her best known works, in 1965.

The years 1958–60 in New York seethed with all kinds of evolutionary ferment. While Abstract Expressionism remained the official mainstream movement, a whole series of opposing and experimental phenomena kept seeing the light of day at an increasingly rapid pace. First of all, there was a formal evolution: Abstract Expressionism began to approach everyday figuration (Alfred Leslie, Larry Rivers). This figuration willingly utilized an extrapainterly addenda that constituted assemblages (Rauschenberg's combine paintings). The object acquired an expressive autonomy (in his racks and medicine chests, George Brecht took over Joseph Cornell's boxes). The references to Duchamp's readymades and Kurt Schwitters' Merzbau and Merztheater were brought up to date and

Jean Tinguely
Fragment from *Homage to New York* 1960
painted metal, wood and cloth
80 ¼" x 29 ⅝" x 87 ⅞"
The Museum of Modern Art, New York;
gift of the artist.

Niki de Saint Phalle
Nana c. 1965
mixed media
50" x 36" x 31"
Albright-Knox Art Gallery, Buffalo;
gift of Seymour H. Knox, 1978.

applied in terms of free experimentation. As of 1959, Allan Kaprow defined the "artforms" of the environment and the Happening and put them into practice in *18 Happenings in 6 Parts*. He was immediately followed by Jim Dine and Claes Oldenburg (the environments *Street* and *House*).

The most active center was the Reuben Gallery, which followed in the footsteps of the Hansa co-op gallery, gathering Lucas Samaras, George Brecht, Red Grooms, Jim Dine, Rosalyn Drexler, Robert Whitman and others: these artists specialized in junk art, drawing directly on industrial folklore and passing quite naturally from garbage to Happenings. In fact, the gallery devoted its entire 1960–61 season to the new form of expression.

A certain number of personalities emerged from this cultural simmering to occupy a special place: Johns, Rauschenberg and Stankiewicz, because of the quality of their work, its precise cultural references, their past, their contacts with Europe, particularly Paris, and their promotional underpinning. Johns and Rauschenberg showed with Leo Castelli. Castelli, his associate Ivan Karp and Richard Bellamy of the Green Gallery were the first to foresee an overall evolution of the situation. Stankiewicz, who had been loyal to the Hansa cooperative, exhibited his sculptures of assembled objects at the Stable Gallery (which also originally showed Warhol and Robert Indiana). Kaprow instantly took the lead as theorist and practitioner of Happenings, thanks to the rigor of his thinking and the breadth of his vision. He fascinated the poet and critic Alain Jouffroy and his friend Jean-Jacques Lebel, who introduced Europe to Happenings, a discovery that also inspired Wolf Vostell of Germany and Ben of France.

Behind the reference points of the nascent Happenings, we see the personality of John Cage. Knowing, as we do, that Cage taught at Black Mountain College, that, in 1952, he performed his "concerted action" there—a fusion of painting, dance, film, projections, recording, radio, poetry, piano, lecture ("with the audience in the middle")— we can say that he staged the first Happening *ante litteram*. Cage's friendship with Rauschenberg began during that period. Rauschenberg took part in the "concerted

Niki de Saint Phalle
Black Venus 1967
painted polyester
110" x 35" x 24"
Whitney Museum of American Art, New York; gift of
the Howard and Jean Lipman Foundation, Inc., 68.73.

action," as did Merce Cunningham. And when Cunningham founded his dance company, Cage became its musical director and Rauschenberg its artistic director. During 1958–59, Kaprow took Cage's courses at the New School for Social Research, New York (together with George Brecht, Al Hansen and Dick Higgins). Cage's influence, virtually that of a Dada guru, dominated the pre-Pop era of the years 1955–60, in which he acted as a catalyst for the synthesis.

●

The great New York event of 1961 was the exhibition *The Art of Assemblage*, curated by William C. Seitz, which was shown at The Museum of Modern Art in October and November. This was an ambitious undertaking: in the open perspective of the Cubist tradition of collage and Dada's subversive shattering of languages, the goal was to survey the modern sense of nature, the "assemblist" vision derived from the industrial urban folklore of our "collage environment": neons, advertising, auto graveyards, public discharges, mass production, etc.

Seitz had a clear inkling of the launching of this new adventure of the object. During his preliminary field trip to Europe, he had spent a long time in Paris. There, in May 1961, he had seen the exhibition *40° au-dessus de dada* (Forty degrees above Dada) which I had curated at Galerie J. We had a long talk, and I showed him the works of the Nouveaux Réalistes. Together, we commented on *The Second Manifesto of New Realism*, which I had published for the exhibition. We realized that our minds ran along the same lines, and I believe Seitz's exhibition partly reflected the conclusions we had reached at our

Jean Tinguely, Niki de Saint Phalle and Robert Rauschenberg during *The Construction of Boston*, New York, 1962. Photo: © Hans Namuth.

meeting. His exhibition juxtaposed the Nouveaux Réalistes and their European cousins, such as the Italian Enrico Baj and the Englishman John Latham, with a vast sampling of the new generation of American artists: Rauschenberg, George Brecht, Ed Kienholz, Bruce Conner, Robert Moskowitz, Marisol, Robert Watts, Lucas Samaras, et al.

The Art of Assemblage had a twofold consequence. In Paris it sanctified a rapprochement with the New York artists, which had been prefigured by a show that I had curated in June 1961 with Jean Larcade at the Galerie Rive Gauche. Titled *Le Nouveau Réalisme à Paris et à New York*, this show included Klein, Arman, Johns, Rauschenberg, Stankiewicz, Tinguely, Hains, de Saint Phalle, Chamberlain, Lee Bontecou, Chryssa and César. "What we are discovering in both Europe and the United States," I wrote in my introduction, "is a new sense of our contemporary industrial, mechanical and urban nature." The confrontation was based on chronology and exact themes: a Klein fire painting and a Johns wax, a composition of auto body fragments (Chamberlain) and a crushed car (César), a relief in letters (Chryssa) and a shredded poster (Hains), a Stankiewicz and a Tinguely. In New York Seitz's exhibition gathered together diverse elements of the assemblist movement, giving it a large-scale coherence while emphasizing the expressive possibilities of the object and the flexibility of the new modes of language. A new expression, with multiple forms and dimensions, emerged on the horizon of modernity.

The pure assemblist trend, embodied by George Brecht, Ray Johnson (the forebear of mail art) and Dan Flavin (who, having not yet discovered neon, was crushing tin cans on painted surfaces), seemed too thoroughly integrated in everyday life and action to be immediately salvageable in the art market. Meanwhile, a more aestheticizing line was emerging: James Rosenquist, abandoning an Expressionism in half-tints, discovered the billboard style and the contrasts of shock images. Warhol, who was about to launch the industrial process of phototransfer into art history, had not yet assumed the paternity of this seminal action, which consisted of translating comic-strip characters into the gestural style of Action Painting. Roy Lichtenstein retrieved comic strips. George Segal molded his plaster casts like a physician. As for Oldenburg, after terminating his phase of cardboard cut-outs, assemblages of scrap wood and laminated paper (*Ray Gun*), he entered the period of *Store* (environments of painted plaster objects regarded as organic elements of the environment of his storefront studio at 107 East 2nd Street). His polemic with Kaprow about the definition of the Happening strengthened him in his fragmented vision of the world. Kaprow's conception was resolutely assemblist; Oldenburg's was organically analytical, the immediate data of his perception of a fragment of daily life. Oldenburg's evolution was exemplary. He symbolized what became the Pop method: the exaltation of a slice of daily life by appropriating an established socio-cultural technique. When Lichtenstein "invented" his comic-strip style, Warhol his phototransfers and Rosenquist and Tom Wesselmann their billboards, and when Segal placed his silhouettes of urban postures in their functional context, a whole American vision of the world crystallized in the mold of a language—the visual revolution was translated into reality.

In April 1961 Leo Castelli asked Yves Klein to exhibit his blue monochromes in his gallery. Reissuing Klein's blue period works after a four-year hiatus was a long shot in the effervescent New York of Neo-Dada, assemblages and Happenings. Klein knew it was risky, but, yielding to the temptation of America, he tried his luck. First he took the precaution of explaining himself to the New York audience in a programmatic speech reviewing the major developmental phases of his approach, which he had thoroughly analyzed and described in 1960 in *Le Vrai devient réalité* (Truth becomes reality), his text for *Zéro no 3*. He set about rewriting the manifesto at the Chelsea Hotel in collaboration with Neil Levine and John Archambault. This inspired and illuminating piece titled *Manifesto of the Chelsea Hotel* was published in the catalogues of many posthumous Klein exhibitions (he died of a heart attack in Paris on 6 June 1962).

Klein's talk had no effect on the public—either in New York or in Los Angeles, where the show was mounted at the Dwan Gallery one month later. When he presented his blue monochromes at Castelli in April 1961, there was a striking gap between the content of his show and the cosmic diversity of his current preoccupations. The tone did not come off, especially after Klein tried to define himself in relation to Action Painting, at the precise moment when that portion of his audience that would have been most favorable to him had completely broken away from the properly gestural and painterly aspect of the problem. As Oldenburg subsequently told me, "Klein arrived either too early or too late." (Actually, it was only as of 1967–68, with the appearance of earth works and the gradual conceptualization of Minimal art, that the most intellectual faction of specialized American opinion opened up to Klein's message and reconsidered all its implications.)

In the spring of 1962 I received an important visitor in Paris: Sidney Janis, the leading dealer of Abstract Expressionism. He promptly got to the point: the international situation brilliantly sketched by Seitz in *The Art of Assemblage* merited a sharper and more precise illustration. Given Janis' contacts with the Galerie Rive Gauche, our conversation led me to assume that the confrontation would take place on the historical and thematic level on which I had situated *Le Nouveau Réalisme à Paris et à New York* the previous year. We agreed on a selection of Parisian artists and on the use of the term "New Realists" as an overall title.

The exhibition *The New Realists* opened on 31 October 1962. It instantly dawned on me that this exhibition spelled a farewell to Schwitters, a farewell to Duchamp, a farewell to the problem of objective appropriation! Here was a great style of realistic representation. The logical interlocutors (Rauschenberg, Johns, Stankiewicz, Chamberlain) of the Parisian Nouveaux Réalistes had been replaced by the most accomplished practitioners of the new aesthetic-analytical line: Oldenburg, Dine, Segal, Indiana, Lichtenstein, Warhol, Rosenquist. I was generally struck by the mastery of techniques demonstrated by the American artists, especially by Oldenburg's quality; Segal's *Bus Driver* and Indiana's *Black Diamond American Dream* also made a lasting impact on me, as did Warhol, who was absorbed less in his phototransfers than in his amateur films, which he had just started shooting with a secondhand camera.

Arman, Christo, Hains, Klein, Raysse, Rotella, Spoerri and Tinguely made up an extremely compact and coherent panorama of Nouveau Réalisme and its problems of object appropriation. Their works blatantly contrasted with the spirit of figurative representation in the American selections, making them look like venerable ancestors. From the European side, they were surrounded by the Swedes Oyvind Fahlström and Per

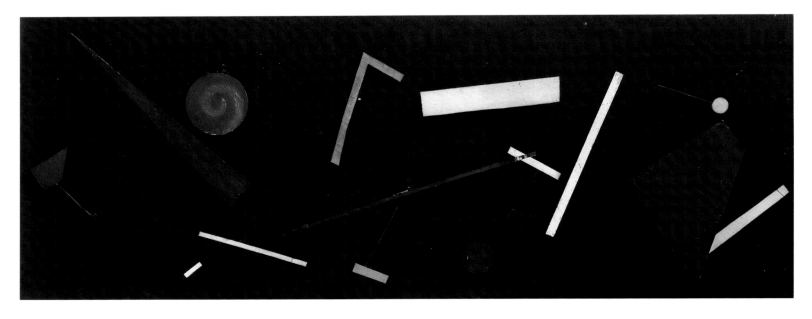

Jean Tinguely
Relief métamécanique 1956
mixed media
18 ¹³⁄₁₆" x 49 ³⁄₁₆" x 6 ¹³⁄₁₆"
Louisiana Museum of Modern Art,
Humlebaek, Denmark.

Olof Ultvedt, the Italians Enrico Baj, Gianfranco Baruchello and Mario Schifano, and the Englishmen Peter Blake, John Latham and Peter Phillips. This composite appendage, while not lacking quality, was justified chiefly by the desire to underscore the diversity of the European selections.

The general reaction of the press was confused and at times, frenzied. Reviewers were shocked by the term "New Realists." This country, which, since colonial days, has cast the same dazzled and bewildered eyes at its reality as the first settlers once did, expects a "realist" style to be noble, not popular and, as Max Kozloff put it, "new vulgarian." The journalists fell back on the term "Pop," a label borrowed from England, where Lawrence Alloway had used it "at a certain moment between winter 1954–55 and 1957" to designate the investigations of popular culture conducted at the London Institute of Contemporary Art by a small group of independent artists (including Richard Hamilton and Reyner Banham): "pop" for "popular." A second wave of young British painters developed around this thinking nucleus, forming a motley nebula (from the brilliant superdraftsman David Hockney and the porno-poet Allen Jones to the assemblist-wizard Joe Tilson).

The critics had understood, and that explained their surliness. Since the old lion Sidney Janis had joined the Castelli gang, it would take only a few months, perhaps less, and only a few collectors—and everyone would be picturing Lichtenstein in front of a comic strip, Warhol in front of a tin can or a photo of a movie star, Rosenquist in front of a billboard, and Oldenburg in front of a store window on the Lower East Side. The game was won: Pop art, Pop music, Pop songs—a veritable phenomenon of civilization. The forecasts came true at lightning speed.

Jasper Johns
0 Through 9 1961
oil and charcoal on canvas
54 ⅛" x 41 ⅜"
Hirshhorn Museum and Sculpture Garden,
Smithsonian Institution, Washington, D.C.;
gift of Joseph H. Hirshhorn, 1966.
Photo: John Tennant.

Two installation views of *The New Realists* exhibition
presented by the Sidney Janis Gallery, New York, 1962.
Photos: Eric Pollitzer, courtesy of Sidney Janis Gallery,
New York.

Tinguely lived in his American mode for several years. He went back to New York with Niki de Saint Phalle in 1962, and both took part in a Cage-style Happening, *The Construction of Boston*, which was scripted by poet Kenneth Koch and organized by Rauschenberg and Merce Cunningham. On the same trip, Tinguely presented his *Study for an End of the World Number 2* in the Nevada Desert; its self-destruction was telecast by NBC. In December 1964, when Iolas in Paris put on *Méta*, a fourteen-piece retrospective of Tinguely's oeuvre since 1954, James Johnson Sweeney, with the financial support of Jean and Dominique de Menil, purchased the entire show for Houston's Museum of Fine Arts. Nevertheless, when talking to the sculptor after each trip abroad, one sensed a growing surfeit in regard to the American milieu. Tinguely was far more alive to the industrialization of culture than to the phenomenon of institutionalization. As of 1963–64, Tinguely began to experience the end of the machine age. His works grew more and more "anachronistic." They tried to escape the sway of everyday time, ignoring the new times of the second industrial revolution. They returned, with all the elegance of kinetic constructivism, to the Cubist sculpture from which they had issued.

Tinguely's internal evolution led him to fall back on Europe, or rather on references to the European sensibility. Europe feted the triumphant return of one of its prodigal sons, his native Switzerland sparing no pains to wipe out its long years of total indifference. Tinguely's oeuvre definitely entered the history of modern sculpture. Niki de Saint Phalle followed Tinguely. The European apotheosis of their collaboration came with their sets for *Éloge de la folie* (In praise of folly) at the Ballets Roland Petit (1966, with Raysse) and with the sculptural installations *Hon* (She, with P.O. Ultvedt, Stockholm, 1966) and *Paradis* (Paradise, French pavilion at Montreal, 1967).

●

For us Europeans, America is still waiting to be discovered. At every moment of our existence, it lurks continuously in the subconscious of our memory, as the temptation of energy or the outburst of willpower. It is this illusory access that causes so many misunderstandings and spectacular reversals in the way European artists appreciate the American reality. You can't take New York like an aspirin.

Discovering America isn't enough; you have to grasp it and play the game. Europe is a continent divided into nations that are so many egotistical and particularistic gardens. Europe is the continent of qualms; they proliferate here like hares in wheat. America is a unified continent. It doesn't know what to do with qualms. You love it or you leave it. Accepting it doesn't mean you can't help it evolve, but that's a whole other story—an American story.

The Nouveaux Réalistes gave in to the American temptation. In 1960, they were probably the only Europeans capable of starting a basic dialogue with the young American artists of their generation. The dialogue took place. The subjective lessons drawn by the participants remained their personal business. A Rauschenberg probably did not grow any more European, nor a Tinguely any more American. But the objective lessons gained from the experience were positive. America was demystified for the European artists of 1960. It became an unconditionally open milieu. One cannot ask America for more than it can give, and America itself is very demanding. □

Robert Rauschenberg
Memorandum of Bids 1957
combine painting
59" x 44 ½"
Sonnabend Collection, New York.

All the Newsprint That's Fit to Paint

David Bourdon

With its appropriations of imagery, materials and techniques from popular culture, Pop art has exerted a continuing influence on avant-garde art, raising still-debated questions about the fundamental nature and function of art in contemporary times. In the following essay, David Bourdon—author of Warhol (1989) and a critic who helped present Pop art during its heyday to general audiences as a writer and editor at the Village Voice, Life and Vogue—focuses on a formal device, the use of newspaper as content and medium, that connects Pop art to antecedents in the vanguard movements of Cubism, Surrealism and Abstract Expressionism. By looking at the diverse motives behind various artists' use of a common element, Bourdon examines a familiar subject from an unexpected point of view. He intimates that the radical choice of a mass-media product as a major component of art making has had a far-reaching impact on thinking about art and cultural criticism. Ironically, the newspaper, that most disposable and ephemeral of modern mass media, continues to make news.

Extra! Extra! Read all about it! "POP GOES THE EASEL!" When Pop art invaded the art world in the early sixties, it triggered an enormous amount of press coverage. The news was less apocalyptic, of course, than the incidents that commandeered many front-page headlines: world crises such as Soviet missiles in Cuba, an American U-2 shot down in the Soviet Union, the construction of the Berlin Wall and the death of Marilyn Monroe. But beyond the front-page headlines, the news in the art section impressed many readers as equally dire. Here, the big story was the near-total eclipse of Abstract Expressionism by Pop art, an event as welcome in the minds of some people as Attila and his troops running wild on Manhattan's 57th Street. Pop art was feared because it turned "civilized" values upside down; the artists who made it were viewed not only as uncreative but as blatantly imitative of the most vulgar, lowbrow forms of art—comic strips, commercial packaging designs and advertising illustrations. Seldom has a new art movement been so copiously chronicled in newsprint.

Pop art would scarcely exist without newsprint, which in many cases provided the painters with their subjects and their content. As artists turned to the mass media for inspiration, they discovered that no visual medium was more accessible and cheaper than the daily newspaper. It offered them a wealth of pictorial sources—headlines, news photographs, display ads and comic strips—that they could reprocess in their paintings. Newspapers—as well as magazines, posters and other varieties of printed paper—were an abundant source for "found" or ready-made images. Some artists cut up and collaged actual newspapers to incorporate in their pictures, treating them as free art materials. News clippings were both embodiments of and metaphors for the real world, injecting a degree of immediacy and topicality. Their presence called into question the traditional hierarchies of subject, which favored "big" themes like history painting over "little" genres like still-life painting.

Pop-oriented artists seemed to gravitate toward the subject of newspapers because they are so readable and understandable, contrasting sharply with the abstruse nature of serious abstraction. Newspapers also signify the ephemeral, throwaway character of popular culture, another contrast with the Abstract Expressionists, who sought to imbue their art with a timeless, even spiritual quality. A meaningful aesthetic dialogue was virtually impossible between Abstract Expressionists and Pop artists; it might have been easier to imagine a conversation between Fra Angelico and Popeye.

Newspaper imagery—and in some cases actual newsprint—turns up in the work of artists as diverse as Andy Warhol, Roy Lichtenstein, Robert Rauschenberg, Jasper Johns and Willem de Kooning. They are anything but isolated cases, because newspapers, both real and simulated, have a lengthy history in art. Picasso and Braque and their fellow Cubists frequently collaged newspaper clippings in their pictures. Their Italian counterparts, the Futurists—Umberto Boccioni, Carlo Carrà and Mario Sironi, among others—also incorporated actual newspaper clippings to provide contrasting textures and colors to their compositions. Although the Cubists and Futurists employed other types of printed paper as well, their use of newspaper was particularly shocking, a thumbed nose at art history and conventional good taste. But the shock was justified by wit—expressed not only in the surprising juxtapositions of disparate forms but also in visual and verbal puns. Such puns enliven Juan Gris' *Man in Café* (1914), for instance, a picture of a seated figure who is shown reading *Le Matin*, constituted in part by actual news clippings, including a story headlined "*On ne truquera plus les oeuvres d'art*" ("one will no longer fake works of art").

Among Americans, Man Ray utilized a theater page from a November 1916 copy of the *New York Sun* to serve as the background in *Theatr* [sic](1916), a collage to which he added elements of drawing and bits of pasted paper; the page of newsprint includes display ads for D. W. Griffith's *Intolerance* and Broadway productions starring theatrical luminaries such as Ruth Chatterton, John Drew and David Warfield. For a Paris ballet production in 1923, Gerald Murphy devised a spectacular backdrop that monumentalized the eye-catching look of the bold headlines ("UNKNOWN BANKER BUYS ATLANTIC") on the front page of a hypothetical American newspaper. A couple of years later, Arthur Dove scissored the art page of a newspaper into the shape of a man and combined the cutting with printed illustrations of consumer goods to produce a collage that he sardonically titled *The Critic* (1925); he showed what he thought of such scribblers by putting his paper man on skates and outfitting him with a vacuum cleaner.

Although the Cubists pioneered the use of actual newspaper clippings in their collages, other artists had used newsprint imagery at an even earlier date, for example, in the trompe l'oeil images created by nineteenth-century American still-life painters such as William M. Harnett and John Frederick Peto. In their zeal to show off their skills as master illusionists, they produced many pictures in which newspaper clippings and a great many other varieties of printed paper—such as postage stamps, admission tickets, dollar bills and calling cards—are presented against a flat background. They owed much of their fool-the-eye success to the fact that they selected "preflattened" subjects that virtually eliminate any illusion of three-dimensional depth, thereby resulting in compositions in which the depicted images are totally congruent with the picture plane. Peto and Picasso epitomized very different art worlds, but they shared an impulse to make newsprint an attention-getting device, provoking viewers to do a double take.

Newspapers were given a new lease on aesthetic life when they began to play a vital, highly visible role in the art of Robert Rauschenberg and Jasper Johns, two of the most resourceful innovators in the generation of artists who emerged in the fifties. Both adopted the fluid, painterly brushwork of the Abstract Expressionists who preceded them and combined it with commonplace, ready-made imagery, which prophesied Pop art. These two artists—the main links between two opposed schools of art—frequently incorporated cut-up newsprint as components in their collages and occasionally made a complete sheet of newspaper function as the primary image in a work of art.

Rauschenberg collaged newspaper sheets in some of his Black Paintings, a series of monochrome, minimalist pictures he made in 1951–52. One of his purposes in gluing the paper onto canvas before painting the entire surface with a thin layer of paint was to introduce a contrasting texture. A typical work consists of two vertically abutting panels, with portions of two sheets of newspaper covering most of the lower panel and continuing onto the lower edge of the upper panel. The pages are positioned sideways, as if to discourage their legibility, but viewers can easily make out and read columns of classified ads, as well as display ads for the A & P supermarkets and O. K. Cash Stores, a sports story headlined "Cubs Outlook—Lose Fewer Contests than Last Season" and a crossword puzzle.

As Rauschenberg's paintings evolved, he continued to make prominent use of printed matter. Comic strips became a staple ingredient in his art from 1953 to the end of the decade. He included several panels from Terry and the Pirates in *Yoicks* (1953), superimposing the comic strips on a patterned fabric ground that he painted with red and yellow horizontal stripes. Over the years Rauschenberg would demonstrate an unquenchable zeal for printed ephemera, ranging from newspaper ads and magazine illustrations to calendar pages, election fliers, wanted-by-the-F.B.I. posters and, in *Memorandum of Bids* (1957), a recycled "contract ledger" form.

By the mid-fifties, Rauschenberg was scandalizing the art world with his provocative "combine paintings"—artworks in which he juxtaposed passages of painterly brushwork with a multiplicity of collaged papers and cloths (comic strips, news photographs, doilies and ties) as well as three-dimensional "found" objects (stuffed birds, electric fans, a chair or an automobile tire). Though obviously indebted to past masters of collage, such as Picasso and Kurt Schwitters, Rauschenberg's "combine paintings" greatly amplified the scale and format of the medium as well as its repertory of "found" materials. The resulting compositions appear to be more improvised than planned, half "made" and half "found," providing a kaleidoscope of diverse visual information that suggests a blitz of "high" and "low" cultural images. He collaged comic strips and reproductions of European works of art in *Charlene* (1954); newsprint in *Red Interior* (1954); paint-splattered comic strips, including Popeye, in *Satellite* (1955); and a page of color comics, a reproduction of Botticelli's *Primavera*, sports photographs and a row of a paint manufacturer's color chips in *Rebus* (1955). He even worked comic strips into the freestanding stage-construction he designed for Merce Cunningham's dance *Minutiae* (1954). As composer John Cage noted in writing about Rauschenberg's art: "There is no more subject in a *combine* than there is in a page from a newspaper. Each thing that is there is a subject. It is a situation involving multiplicity."

Rauschenberg's readiness to welcome vulgar "found" images into his art was antithetical to the ideals of many Abstract Expressionists, with the singular exception of Willem de Kooning, who also contributed, if inadvertently, to the use of newsprint in painting. De Kooning, intrigued by the sometimes romantic and poignant banality of

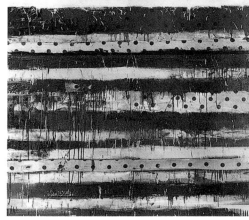

Robert Rauschenberg
Yoicks 1953
oil, fabric and paper on canvas
96" x 72"
Whitney Museum of American Art, gift of the artist, 72.210.

Opposite, Robert Rauschenberg, New York, 1964.
Photo: © Ugo Mulas.

Robert Rauschenberg
Minutiae 1954 (replica)
freestanding construction: oil, fabric, paper, metal,
plastic, wood with mirror on string
84 ¾" x 81" x 30 ½"
Cunningham Dance Foundation Inc., New York.
© Robert Rauschenberg/VAGA, New York, 1991.
Photo: Lynette Molnar.

advertising and commercial art, produced several works that were particularly relevant to the Pop artists who followed. Among these works was a noted oil-on-paper study (1950) for one of his celebrated "Women": taken by a color photograph of a young woman in a magazine ad, he collaged her smile—all bright red lipstick and sparkling white teeth—in place of his painted figure's mouth. Four years later, he brushed into being a blond Venus with large eyes and lustrous lips, titling the work *Marilyn Monroe*, which surely demonstrated his interest in this goddess of pop culture.

Offset newsprint images appear in de Kooning's abstractions from 1948 to 1956. They are primarily there because he sometimes pressed a flat sheet of newspaper onto the wet surface of a large painting in order to slow the drying of the pigment or to cover up a section of the work in progress while he concentrated on an adjacent area. When he later peeled away the pages, he found offset, reversed impressions of the newspaper in the paint, and he occasionally chose to let those pale traces of news photographs and classified and display ads remain.

A ghostly bathing beauty peers through a scrim of pigment in *Attic* (1949). Along the top edge of *Gotham News* (1955–56), scrutinizers will find a small display announcement (upside down) advertising Cary Grant and Grace Kelly in *To Catch a Thief*. *Easter Monday* (1956) has newsprint images along most of the right side and all along the lower edge, including photographs of people in the news and a display ad for refrigerators. *Easter Monday* also features a listing for the Broadway musical *Pajama Game* and a display ad for a movie starring Richard Burton as Alexander the Great.

Like the news clippings in the work of Rauschenberg and the Cubists, de Kooning's offset newspaper images implicitly invite viewers not only to look at his paintings but also to read them. The newsprint contributes an additional dimension of significance to the otherwise abstract paintings by injecting a topical element, documenting a specific time and place and offering clues to the cultural context in which the pictures were made. Not the least intriguing aspect of these pictures is de Kooning's extraordinary finesse at simulating the appearance of collage without violating the texture of his paint surface. He had discovered, perhaps accidentally, a way to incorporate newsprint imagery without having to glue pieces of paper to his canvases.

The happy marriage of printed illustrations and pigment achieved by de Kooning apparently offered little appeal to Rauschenberg, who continued to shun uniform, homogeneous surfaces as he affixed a wide assortment of textured materials and three-dimensional objects to his combine paintings. In the late fifties, however, he developed an ingenious form of "transfer drawings" that enabled him to transmit the look of mechanically printed photographs onto paper. He selected illustrations from newspapers and magazines (frequently from *Time*, *Life* and *Sports Illustrated*), moistened them with a solvent (turpentine or cigarette-lighter fluid) and placed the damp side against his drawing paper. He then rubbed the reverse side of the illustration with the tip of a pencil or an empty ball-point pen, thereby transferring it onto the paper. The technique enabled him to "collage" printed pictures from many different sources, yet produce a unified surface. The resulting images retain the appearance of printed photographs but also resemble hand-made drawings insofar as they reveal the direction and pressure of individual pencil strokes.

Like Rauschenberg, Jasper Johns incorporated newsprint in a great many of his works of the fifties, often completely covering his canvases with fragments of glued paper, then painting over the collaged ground in encaustic. He, too, combined the painterly brushwork of Abstract Expressionism with commonplace imagery—in his case, familiar symbols and emblems, such as targets, American flags and sequences of letters and numerals. As his layered brush strokes are irregularly deployed, certain areas of the encaustic remain thin and translucent, enabling viewers to read the underlying news-print. In *Flag Above White with Collage* (1955), scrutinizers can make out such phrases as, "If there is tragedy in this story," "she is small freckled and shy" and "Hey Kids! Books for Boys."

When later asked about the iconographic significance of his collage materials, Johns replied that, while his use of newsprint was deliberate, "whatever printing shows" generally has "no significance" for him. In choosing particular pieces of newsprint, he sometimes looked for different kinds of color or particular sizes of type. *Green Target* (1955), another encaustic-on-newsprint picture, has a symmetrical composition that consists of four concentric rings around a disk. Up close, viewers can peer at the underlying newsprint collage and find department store display ads and a news photograph captioned "Woman Hurt as Autos Crash." Legible newspaper clippings also appear below the paint surface in *Device Circle* (1959), *Out the Window* (1959) and *Painting With Two Balls* (1960).

Johns' art historical importance—and his special relevance for Pop artists—is based to a large extent upon his successful reconciliation of commonplace representational imagery with the aesthetic theory that modern painting should shun spatial illusionism and orient itself to the literal flatness of the picture plane. By choosing to paint "preflattened" subjects, such as targets and flags, he avoided the illusion of three-dimensional depth; by limiting his palette in such works as *White Target* (1957), he rejected even the suggestions of recession and projection that color contrasts might provide.

Few everyday objects are flatter than an unfolded, double-page sheet of a newspaper, so Johns took such a sheet, affixed it somewhat above center on a slightly larger canvas, brushed the entire surface with gray encaustic and titled the resulting work *Newspaper* (1957). Once again, the newsprint is intermittently visible, offering scattered glimpses of words and images: "Khrushchev portrait reveals," "Quest for knowledge" and advertising illustrations of automobiles. The identity of the newspaper appears deliberately concealed, perhaps so that it will be seen as a generic object rather than as a specific publication. The contrast between the newsprint in Johns' pictures and that in Rauschenberg's *Black Painting* is striking: the latter work is a comparatively dynamic composition that directs our attention toward overall shapes, while *Newspaper* draws us to its densely articulated, if enigmatic, paint surface.

Real newsprint virtually disappeared from Johns' work after 1962, the year in which he painted *4 the News*. In this puzzling picture, consisting mainly of four vertically tiered, gray panels, he wedged an entire folded newspaper into a slot that he created between the top two panels. The newspaper, a metaphor for worldly reality, is ambiguously positioned, as if emerging from the picture plane or plunging through it. The painting evidently refers to Peto's trompe l'oeil representations of newsprint, because Johns stenciled block letters and numbers along the bottom edge: "4 THE NEWS PETO JOHNS

62." Images of newspapers would recur later in Johns' art, but not in collage form.

By the time Johns painted *4 the News*, Roy Lichtenstein and Andy Warhol had already pioneered an alternative approach to newspaper imagery, meticulously simulating the appearance of printed illustrations in large, hand-painted pictures, mainly derived from comic strips, advertising art and packaging design. Johns' and Rauschenberg's use of commonplace imagery had helped prepare the way for Warhol and Lichtenstein, who seemed no less literal but far more brazen because they aggrandized their ready-made subjects. (Both artists used opaque projectors to enlarge their clippings, tracing the outlines of their "found" compositions onto canvas.) They based their paintings on commonplace items, displaying a preference for banal and ephemeral subjects with connotations of "low" culture. This was particularly ironic in Warhol's case, because he had been a successful commercial artist, producing an enormous amount of magazine and newspaper illustrations throughout the fifties. About 1960, newspapers and magazines, previously the setting for his typically whimsical commercial art, became the subject of his serious, paintings.

During 1960–61, Warhol painted a series of works based on the four-color comic strips that appeared in Sunday newspaper supplements. He focused on the most famous superstars of that domain, renowned figures such as Dick Tracy, Superman, Popeye and

the Little King. By contrast, Lichtenstein's comic-strip characters were generic types; his square-jawed heroes in military uniforms and his beautiful young women with tears in their eyes looked familiar, but they didn't seem to originate in any known war, romance or science-fiction strips.

Warhol and Lichtenstein based several of their early, black-and-white Pop pictures on commercial illustrations of consumer products in display ads, transforming printed ephemera into provocative paintings. Lichtenstein derived his *Girl with Ball* (1961) from a one-column newspaper ad for a resort hotel in the Pocono Mountains. In search of "a tawdry type of commercialism," he claimed to find "a great source of inspiration" in the yellow pages of the telephone directory. Warhol painted stark images of a telephone, a typewriter, a well-stocked refrigerator, a water heater, a storm door and *TV $199* (complete with the General Electric logo and the price prominently overlapping the console). Lichtenstein's pictures are neatly rendered with sleek black contour lines, while Warhol's earlier works are painterly in a fairly conventional way, featuring the smeared edges and runny paint that were almost mandatory in the work of second-generation Abstract Expressionists.

Through coincidence, both artists also painted diptychs with before-and-after motifs. Lichtenstein depicted a woven piece of cloth before and after repair in *Like New* (1962). Warhol's *Before and After III* (1962) presents two side-by-side views of a woman's profile before and after cosmetic surgery on her nose. He derived the image from a New York plastic surgeon's display ad in the *National Enquirer*. In transposing small, rather graceless illustrations onto large canvases, Lichtenstein and Warhol created startling pictures in which deadpan irony and a campy sense of humor seemed locked in a chilling embrace.

Of all the Pop artists, Warhol was the most infatuated with tabloids. He doted on them because of their lively combination of scandals, celebrity photographs and gossip columns. Tabloid headlines epitomized for him the pervasiveness and instant fame that the mass media could generate. Between November 1961 and June 1962, Warhol hand-painted three pictures, each six feet high and all blowups of actual pages from New York tabloids. The first of them, *A Boy for Meg* (1961), portrays the front page of the 3 November *New York Post*. The headline refers to Great Britain's Princess Margaret, whose photographic portrait is rendered as a schematic black-and-white picture. The artist's hand-painted simulation of a smaller portrait of Frank Sinatra at the top of the page is similarly unconvincing as a newspaper photograph. Although Warhol had based many of his drawings over the years on printed photographs, these portraits are his first—and not very convincing—attempt to make a painting look like a photograph.

Warhol's second newspaper painting presents the spread-out back and front pages of the 29 March *Daily News*, headlined "Eddie Fisher Breaks Down/In Hospital Here: Liz in Rome." (The pop singer was suffering because his wife, Elizabeth Taylor, was filming *Cleopatra*, and her costar, Richard Burton, was playing his role as Marc Antony to the

Jasper Johns
White Target 1957
wax and oil on canvas
30" x 30"
Whitney Museum of American Art, New York;
purchase, 71.211.
Photo: Robert E. Mates, New Jersey.

Roy Lichtenstein
Girl with Ball 1961
oil and synthetic polymer paint on canvas
60 ¼" x 36 ¼"
The Museum of Modern Art, New York; gift of Philip Johnson.

hilt.) In Warhol's third newspaper painting, *129 Die* (1962), he introduced the subject of accidental and violent death, which soon became a central theme in his art. The picture derived from the 4 June *New York Mirror* reporting the crash of an Air France Boeing 707 in Paris. *129 Die* may have been Warhol's last attempt to make a hand-painted copy of a photograph.

One reason that Warhol's newspaper paintings don't altogether succeed is that he lacked the patience to simulate the dot patterns of printed news photographs. He therefore eliminated the entire middle range of gray tones and translated the pictures into flat areas of solid black and white. Lichtenstein was more consistently successful in emulating the look of mechanically printed illustrations. Using a stencil with a grid of small holes in it, he imitated the Benday process, a technique (invented by American printer Benjamin Day) for translating shaded or tinted areas into a system of dots for reproduction by line engraving. Lichtenstein's dots, though produced manually, functioned as a metaphor for mechanical reproduction.

Toward the middle of 1962, Warhol discovered he could order photographic silkscreens made from almost any newspaper or magazine illustration, as well as conventional black-and-white photographic prints. (Silkscreening is a photomechanical stencil process utilizing a fabric screen that has been chemically treated so that certain areas are impervious to pigment, while other areas let the pigment pass through. The process is similar to photoengraving, translating the picture into a series of halftone dots.) Within a short period of time, he was screening photographic blowups of grisly car accidents and glamorous likenesses of Marilyn Monroe, Elvis Presley and Elizabeth Taylor on hand-painted grounds. With silkscreens now expediting his production, Warhol could really plunder the popular press for suitable images and print them up in grids on canvas.

As Warhol had lifted some of his ideas from Rauschenberg and Johns, it was perhaps only fitting that they, in turn, adopted his silkscreen technique. By the end of 1962, Rauschenberg was using quantities of silkscreens to transfer news photographs and art reproductions to canvas. The technique enabled him to print a photograph in any size and as many times as he wanted, without ever having to worry about how to make it adhere to the canvas or blend in texturally with adjacent areas of paint. Prior to his discovery of silkscreens, he had to use printed photographs in the actual size in which he found them, and if he wanted to use them more than once, he had to find another copy of the same magazine or newspaper. From now on, the picture sources would no longer determine the scale in which he could use them. Rauschenberg created a spectacular series of silkscreened paintings during the next couple of years, including the thirty-two-foot-wide *Barge* (1963), with its arresting kaleidoscope of photographic images. His subjects during this period included sports players in action, technological hardware, urban street scenes, traffic signs and Old Master paintings.

Rauschenberg continued to use silkscreens to transmit newsprint into his art throughout the seventies and into the eighties. In *Currents* (1970), a six-by-fifty-four-foot silkscreen drawing on paper, he amassed a melange of newspaper images, including front pages from the *New York Times*, the *San Francisco Examiner*, the *Minneapolis Tribune*, the *Wall Street Journal* and the *Los Angeles Herald Examiner*. Many of the headlines are distressing—"ARABS BOAST: WE BOMBED JET," "KILL ARMY WIFE, 2 IN LSD RITE" and "PANTHER BRAWL ROCKS COURT"—and, for once, Rauschenberg appears somewhat overwhelmed by his material, getting mired in reportage. In his beautiful *Hoarfrost* series (1974–75), however, he again elicited an unsuspected lyricism from newsprint. Many of these unstretched paintings consist primarily of texturally diverse fabrics, ranging from gauze to silk. As with his earlier "transfer drawings," Rauschenberg found the means to translate his "found" images, including many pages of newsprint: he sprayed a fine mist of solvent over the papers and then sent them through a press, imprinting ghostly images and typography upon the fabric. His unswerving infatuation with newsprint frequently gives his works a topical edge.

Johns, by contrast, only turned to silkscreens on rare occasions, most notably when he wanted to create the illusion of a long line of newspaper pages in *According to What* (1964), his large-scale, multipanel homage to Marcel Duchamp. Although the newspaper pages in this work imitate the look of collage, they are actually silkscreened, the image being repeated several times in a diagonal row that acts as a connecting link between a few of the panels. The significance of the newsprint in relation to the other imagery remains enigmatic.

Except for Rauschenberg, most of the Pop-oriented artists ceased to pluck their images out of the daily news after the sixties. Warhol briefly returned to the subject of newspaper front pages in 1981, when he produced a few silkscreened canvases, such as *Fate Presto*, which reproduced a front page from the Neapolitan newspaper *Il Mattino* chronicling a recent Vesuvian disaster. By that time, his ardor for other people's publica-

Andy Warhol
A Boy for Meg 1962
paint on canvas
72" x 52"
National Gallery of Art, Washington D.C.; gift of Mr.
and Mrs. Burton Tremaine.

tions had cooled as he was publishing his own monthly magazine *Interview*, founded in
1969. Fragments of consumer advertising turned up in some of his last paintings and
drawings, where motorcycles, price tags and the Dove soap and General Electric logos are
combined with Leonardo's *Last Supper*.

It is possible, but not very likely, that Pop art could have come into being without the
ubiquitous presence of newsprint. By appropriating images and works from newspapers,
magazines, billboards and street signs, artists introduced a new and invigorating topicality in their paintings, arresting the passing ephemera of daily life and causing viewers to
look again—both at the artworks and at the environmental and cultural contexts in
which they were made. Pop art coaxed people to reexamine the far-reaching ramifications of Cubist collage and to marvel once again at the extent to which bits of newsprint
can excite our imagination. While altering our perspectives on past art, the Pop sensibility
also influenced many younger artists, processors of words and images as diverse as Ashley
Bickerton, Jenny Holzer and Barbara Kruger. Most of yesterday's newspapers are historic,
throwaway artifacts. But those that were recycled into provocative works of art remain
astonishingly fresh. □

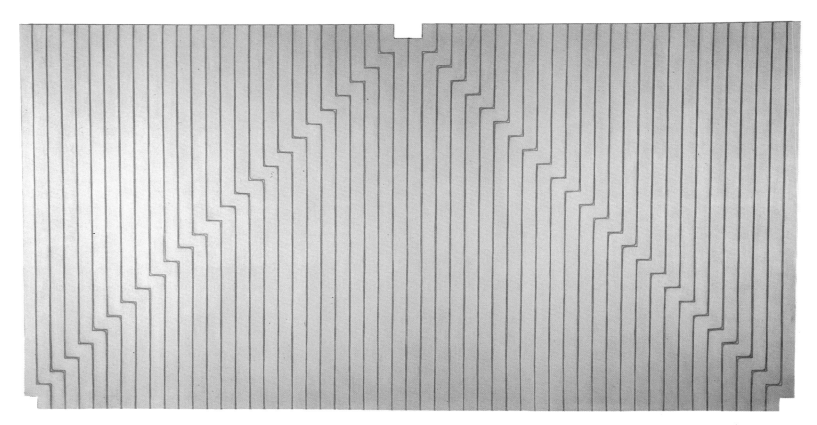

Frank Stella
Union Pacific 1960
aluminum paint on canvas
77 ¼" x 148 ½"
Nathan Emory Coffin Collection of the Des Moines Art
Center; Coffin Fine Arts Trust Fund, 1976.

Frank Stella
Untitled 1959
cardboard and enamel paint on wood
33" x 61 ¼"
Wexner Center for the Arts, The Ohio State University,
Columbus; purchased in part with funds from The
National Endowment for the Arts.

Stella and Hesse

Dispatches from the Sixties

Brian O'Doherty

From our perspective, it's difficult to understand the shock engendered by Frank Stella's paintings in the early sixties and Eva Hesse's sculptures a few years later. Then Stella's works announced the avant-garde's startling repudiation of Abstract Expressionism and Hesse's marked an equally unexpected rejection of Minimalism. Now Stella is practically an icon, favored with multiple retrospectives at The Museum of Modern Art, and Hesse's oeuvre has become one of the most important influences on current art practice. In the following essay, Brian O'Doherty examines the changed cultural context in which these artists' works have come to appear authoritative and notes the numerous overlays of ideological criticism that have distanced us from the experience of their radicalism. O'Doherty's solution to the dilemma posed by hindsight is to muse upon the perceptions of an earlier self first confronting stunningly unconventional objects. By recovering such a persona he enables us to experience again something like that original, unfamiliar confrontation.

The self of whom O'Doherty writes was both critic—for the New York Times *in the early sixties—and artist. His well-known history of and commentary on the modern gallery space* Inside the White Cube *appeared as a series of essays in* Artforum *in 1976 and subsequently in book form. He continues to exhibit his own art (as Patrick Ireland) while also serving as the director of the Media Arts program for the National Endowment for the Arts.*

A short time can feel like ages. When you think of postwar art you sometimes feel you've lived from the Jurassic Period (Abstract Expressionism) to the age of mammals (Neo-Expressionism) and beyond. Embedded in that past are fossils of your former self, each crushed in its perceptual stratum. Think of the art you saw in the making, its positive or negative fate, its retrieval on grounds irrelevant to its inception, the unloading of new content upon it, its reinterpretation according to formalist inquisitions, ideological diagnoses, Marxist accusations, quantifications of desire, denial, repression, power; think of the uses and abuses to which it was and is put, supporting contrary positions, dispossessed absolutes, covert moralities, personal kinks, fantasies of history, illusions of gender, all the while accommodating the past to the hysterical present. As readings extend to the context of context, you feel you are standing at the edge of a pool where the ripples at your feet have forgotten the dropped stone. After all that, how do a few works from the early sixties by Frank Stella and Eva Hesse look to me?

The artworks in question, both Stella's and Hesse's, were originally highly original. If there is anything sadder than a failed artwork, it is a very successful one. Now, museum-broken, early works by these two artists lie under layers of other art, which replaced them in hostile takeovers, and submit themselves to radically changed modes of critical inquiry. The aesthetics by which they were first rationalized tend to be period aesthetics. The premises of these apologias are both justified and discredited by these artworks' survival. How much, we may ask, do the ideas of the artist, as inventor and subsequent witness, survive when he or she is dispossessed by the technology of inquiry, a process confused by commerce. It gets down to how we assign meaning to objects and how that meaning is socialized. This involves value.

But why bring down the house on a few works by Stella and Hesse? After all, examinations such as this generally confine themselves to ratifying the status quo. It is not allowable to propose a reversal of the work's value. Despite revisionist fashions, art history, once it certifies its icons and once that certification is reinforced by commerce, is virtually irreversible. Yet our own internal revisions continue through life, as we warm and cool towards the art that, like some indispensable luggage, accompanies our journey. It happens that these two artists and these particular works are implicated in my own history in different ways. Both provoked and astonished me back then, and both assert themselves restlessly on those occasions when I rehearse my past.

There is a profound difference in my perception of each artist. For Hesse (d. 1972) is gone and Stella (b. 1936) is a living institution. Hesse's work is final, she can no longer alter it. What Stella does now can inflect the way his early work is seen. When I look back, I see two vigorous ghosts: the "early Stella," young, hungry and aggressive; and the very young Hesse, buoyant, street-smart, vulnerable and a lot of fun. A third ghost completes a triangle, but that will wait.

Few moments in postwar art history announced themselves with such radical authority as Hesse's eccentric sculpture and Stella's "black" paintings. They declared their originality uncompromisingly. How original is originality? How is it noticed, rewarded, rejected? What assumptions prepare its brief? It is always defined against something, and when it lacks this launching pad, it is not originality but irrelevance or madness. Sometimes relevance arrives a long time later (as with El Greco and Vermeer). Often a master's last work remains in limbo, because, as Blake might say, its authors are in the future. Being too far ahead is as bad as being too far behind. Originality is always perceived within a carefully evolved set of conditions, refers to these conditions for its authority and, in our culture, is deeply connected with perceptual and psychological fatigue. Originality, by this definition, may not be so much original as inevitable. What is certain is that originality and its substitutes are much prized.

Keats has reported to us in a lush sonnet his experience "On First Looking into Chapman's Homer." He doesn't report on the second time. But, when looking at art that has become familiar, do we remember the first time? And seeing it again—and again— are we accompanied by that primary spectator? How much of seeing is remembering?

Repetition tends to blind us, and the work, which once so excited us, becomes part of the signage as we drive the postmod thruway. But for me, seeing early Stella is remembering. From the distant past, a skinnier figure stares at these Stellas and is discomforted and ultimately annoyed.

This first spectator's experience is so vivid that he still rushes up to give evidence every time I now see an early Stella. Who is he, this earlier O'Doherty? Someone conducting his education in public through the pages of the *New York Times*, hired by what we would now call a neoconservative, John Canaday (whose passion was for Jacques Louis David and whose resistance to new art was, I believe, in part the response of an out-of-towner with the instincts of a satirist to New York's closed circles). The somewhat Candide-like newcomer was unprepared for the blasts of hostility directed towards him as he entered a battlefield in the uniform of the *New York Times*. Canaday, whose mildly dandyish appearance belied the fierceness of his columns, had wanted "balance" in the *Times'* coverage. His blanket condemnation of Abstract Expressionism had drawn upon him, in a notorious letter, the opprobrium of New York's intellectual community. That letter probably ended Canaday's career as a serious critic of contemporary art. He became, however, a folk hero to some, especially to visually illiterate literary figures whom the wordless image frequently insults. C. P. Snow, rubicund and wearing an all-purpose smile, appeared between desks at the *Times* eager to meet the man who had slain the dragon of Abstract Expressionism; I directed him to St. George's glassy cell.

The first impression that critical ingénue (myself, alas) received when first he laid eyes on Stella's work was of mean aggressiveness. The granular surfaces sandpapered the retina; the slight waver of the hand-painted lines seemed a kind of etiolated joke on the painterly stroke; the flat surface denied access as if the canvas were backed with steel plate; the relentless repetition punched away with a monotony that seemed almost sadistic; even the slight "bleed" around the paint into the duck managed to offend, as if an accident had been delivered on order. The evidence did not offer sufficient cause to the first looker as to why he should feel so disturbed, itself a further irritation. What was presented should have been mild enough: all-over painting, generated concentrically from the center. The center, compressed by these repetitions, which were curiously a-geometric, should have popped, but it remained inert. The whole picture thrust itself forward in one aggressive blow. The distant critic, who had never seen anything like it, found in it negative force, denial, rage. Why was the painting mad at him? And why was he mad at the painting?

Whose rage was this anyway? And at what? In a formalist world, which then obtained, the rage could be at closed options. As late modernism became obsessed with history—speculating on history was the OTB of the sixties—art cornered itself in an esoteric endgame. Surely this aggressive bet laid on the modernist gaming board was too extreme. After the brushstroke, the line; after emotional posturing, the laid-back cynic; after the metaphor, the brutal fact. Was this not a kind of dialectical farce? Or a spectacular formal tizzy? This was too easy. The Gordian knot should be unraveled, not cut.

But what provoked this anger? How could these innocuous formalities outstrip their own rutting of the visual field? The result of these perceptions, resolved immediately over an ancient typewriter as Brooks Atkinson smoked his pipe at the next desk, was a ripe sample of negative criticism that Stella, to his honor, never resented to its perpetrator. Reading that review now is still a complex experience for me, its author. How does one take as a text a former self? Without disowning it, but being responsible for what it has done? Does one kneel like Barbarossa in the snow? Or rationalize an accommodation with the overwhelming historical judgment? Or build a more sophisticated case to confirm that early opinion and fling it against the juggernaut of consensus? All that would be too easy, and in America difficulty is, after all, morality's mask. On rereading, the text betrays more than the writer was then aware of. For returning one's proxy to that past, I'm aware of something marginally felt then—a sense of unchallenged powers ordering the future according to their specifications. What that remote critic was feeling, imperfectly, without much comprehension, was the institutionalization of the avant-garde. In the crazy atmosphere of the sixties, history had become manipulable. Historical patterns had become as legible as the newspaper, their teleologies transparent as glass.

And from the wings, a new combo debuted in the rocking sixties: the art historical avant-garde. The co-option of art by commerce was accompanied by the co-option of art history by the avant-garde. And this had—has—a profound monetary effect, for in the sixties, the financial stakes were, for the first time in modern art in America, high. This liaison—between art history, the avant-garde and commerce—was to become a powerful establishment in which the academic partner was a brilliant if manipulated collaborator. Contemporary art became material for postgraduate study. Institutionalizing the new through the Ph.D. thesis was a radical change in academic practice. The pioneering

Frank Stella, New York, 1964. Photo: © Ugo Mulas.

example of William Seitz' brilliant thesis on Abstract Expressionism was followed by a flood as the university opened its doors to the present.

In addition, the reviewer, an empiricist, found himself in a lonely position between the hostility from without and the assumptions from within, where his reception of new art often made him a minority of one. For the *Times* then—unlike its present judicious and open posture—saw itself as a stern guardian of culture. He discovered that in taking the job he had succeeded a devoted apologist for Abstract Expressionism whom Canaday had dismissed as inimical to his own prejudices. A difficult and eventually untenable atmosphere. Yet the job was exhilarating in that you saw new art hot from the studio and had to deal with it in a few hours. The politics of the art community were ignored by the reviewer, for which lack of observance the community exacted its price for several subsequent years.

But given all that, why did the work offend him? He was not alone. William Rubin, in his meticulous, indeed inspired, reading of Stella's art, refers to angers and violations felt by others. It seems absurd, but the very grain of the canvas, not to speak of the grain of the personality, rubbed him the wrong way. The aggression came at you like a tiger. At the same time, paradoxically, there was a depressive sense of a void. What decorum of perception was transgressed here? Was the work shouting out the formal equivalents of obscenities? What finally persuaded him was a new kind of heartlessness. The paintings fucked you and wouldn't give an inch of emotion in the process. They must be violently emotional to have produced this response, but that emotion seemed masked or de-sublimated in a kind of indifference. Complex issues here, involving contradiction, logic, paradox, irony, anger, arrogance.

What remains of all this in the light of Stella's subsequent regal triumph? We are told that it's not whether you win or lose but how you play the game that counts. The critical equivalent is not whether you were right or wrong (the distant critic was spectacularly wrong) but how you got there, and was it, in Matthew Arnold's word, "interesting"? Every genuinely new work has gathered as part of its provenance an initial negative response that eventually becomes part of its credentials. The first witnesses bear witness to their assumptions, prejudices, social and political values and historical obtuseness. Their responses become part of the history of unenlightenment. Art history in the modernist era continually set up these straw men to be blown away with the gale of historical inevitability. Yet the objections of the first negative observers often contain an astute insight. The response is correct, we may say, but the response to the response is often faulty. For instance, with Manet's first works, the negative dispatches frequently mentioned his coldness. Modernism has taken this emotional chill and seen it as setting us on the road to pure painting, the autonomy of the picture and the fetishes of modernism which are now hiding their faces in disgrace.

Is there some blurred set of principles here? That what is new about new art is recognized by both its positive and negative recipients. That new art's power resides in what is most despised by the negative audience. That the conflict comes from the interpretation of that quality by two radically opposing mind-sets. That these two climates of opinion are part of the artist's subject matter and, like any subject matter, can be manipulated. And that the opportunity for such manipulation depends on the inter-section of several vectors, which create a favorable opportunity for intervention: a preeminent mode of art past its prime, but still dominating the thinking of a second generation; a new generation which has passed through this dominant mode as a student/artist and so knows the enemy first-hand; the expectation of a dialectical re-sponse in the audience; a response dialectically correct but unanticipated in its particulars; a context of advanced gallery and critic(s) that together articulate the indispensable justifying "ideas"; and an establishment straight man, in which position I temporarily found myself. I was not charmed with my part in this scenario.

Looking at some of these paintings now, their uncompromising insistence on their own agenda still makes me uncomfortable. A quarter century of ritual sanctification has elevated each "black" painting like a host in the transubstantiations of commerce. Their extraordinary originality has been confirmed and numbed by the brushing of tens of thousands of glances. The "black" paintings received their justifying apologies in a formalist climate, but they have survived that and the slow deposition of other content upon them. What is their content now? Their dystopian titles, as explicated by Brenda Richardson in her excellent catalogue, were carefully analyzed so as not to distort the paintings' formalist meanings. But those titles were entirely synchronous with the aggression and virtual cynicism of the paintings.

What is the relation of a title to a work? Exactly the same relation as a person's name to a person. It starts off as a label and ends up thoroughly implicated in that person's being. Paintings, like people, get to look like their names. The "black" paintings' basic paradox is that they carry an emotional wallop through means that appear to have preempted emotion. This was, of course, formalism's dilemma: to establish a connection between what was seen and what was felt meant casting lines of opinion across an abyss. Inevitably, the postmature formalism of the sixties was replaced in the eighties by socio-political ideologies reading texts. Now, perhaps, Stella's early titles—and the cavalier brilliance of his titles is unending—can be seen as ironic *bon mots* about the paintings and their interpreters.

In those early works, Stella's elimination of passion, false rhetoric and the obliging demon of metaphor was itself a passion, a kind of familiar American positivism. Each work fits exactly around its idea and so, locked in a reciprocal grasp, forces every issue. The paintings achieve, through brilliant cancellations, the impact of the Abstract Expressionist art they displaced. Through sheer force of will, they generate an "expressionism" new in its conceptual intimidation, signaling (along with Donald Judd's and probably Dan Flavin's work) a sudden and profound change in the artistic climate. Things (and objects) would never be the same again.

How could I have seen all this negatively and have flung at it such names as the Master of Ennui and the Oblomov of boredom? Quite easily, I will submit. What I missed was the complexity of feeling: that such negative force was itself a force, indeed a kind of criticism of its own premises that sought to widen then-current issues far beyond the visual into the conceptual; that in its impatience and apparent arrogance, it had confounded metaphorical excess with an irreducible fact. These paintings are now, for better or worse, some of the best produced in this appalling century.

●

Installation view of Frank Stella's solo exhibition at the Leo Castelli Gallery, New York, 1964. Photo: Rudolph Burckhardt, courtesy of Leo Castelli Gallery.

This looks ridiculous. Outrageous, spunky, crazy. A huge bandaged frame, wound and bound with such force that the tearing of the gaffer's tape (is it gaffer's tape?) is in my ears. And looping up out of the top of that frame, a bar of curved steel (iron?) throws a hard curve down near my feet (step back), then flashes into the lower part of the wound (wounded?) frame. This thing's on the wall and off the wall (joke?) and leaves me hanging because the mind wants to run like a squirrel for a familiar tree. What does she see when she looks at it? She's over there (cluttered studio), looking off-hand. She's not talking. Her intensity raises the temperature. Very female. But this work hasn't got a gender. Assured, daring, gutsy. Not afraid. Not thinking of the gallery as the inevitable foster home. The gallery will have to deal with it. That loop of iron is aborted out of a missing picture. But the space within the frame isn't pictorial. If it isn't, then that "frame" isn't a frame. It's not framing anything. I've nothing to connect it with. Now I know what Eva's been doing since those early black drawings (like abstract fists) I called "gnomic" and she said she didn't see how that applied at all. I meant compressed and pithy. You can roll your eye through this big hoop. Walk over to the other side and roll your eye back. What to say to her? It's like nothing I've ever seen.

That was in 1965, when I first saw *Hang-Up*. I'd met Eva Hesse when Mel Bochner brought her to a party at Nancy and Bob Smithson's. Or was it Sol LeWitt who brought her? Everyone liked her; she was always a concentrated presence with those sloe-eyes and bundled-up air. I remember brown sweaters and a ready smile. By that definition made earlier, she may have been the most original artist I ever met. Her work seemed a kind of grand folly, because there was nothing to connect it to. Lucy Lippard, her friend and inspired champion, had no such problem. She included Eva in a show in 1966 called *Eccentric Abstraction*. Lucy, equally intense and vivid in her own perceptions, was at the center of this group which included obsessives like Eva and Sol devoted to repetition and

Eva Hesse
Hang-up 1965/66
acrylic on cloth over wood and steel
72" x 84" x 78"
Art Institute of Chicago; gift of Arthur Keating and
Mr. and Mrs. Edward Morris by exchange, 1988.130.

Eva Hesse. Photo courtesy of Robert Miller Gallery.

insistence. Lucy has clarified the historical moment when Eva's work appeared, its role in the famous Castelli warehouse show of 1969, and shown its relationships to the work of her friends, particularly LeWitt, who supported her work generously. Indeed, Eva and Sol, of all the group, were the most pleased when I introduced them to Morton Feldman, whom they had long admired. I think Feldman's ideas of structure found sympathies with Sol, while his notions of indeterminacy within that structure were relished by Eva.

Eva, whose life was lived with what you might call the second Minimal generation (after Judd, Stella and Flavin), was included in the Whitney's *Anti-Illusion: Procedures/ Materials* (1969) exhibition (one of the Whitney's best ever, right on the money, or rather on the mark, since there was no money in process). This was the severest criticism of formalism to date, and it showed how widespread that criticism was. New work seems to arrive in a kind of sloppy simultaneity, which leads to pop meditations on the zeitgeist, which is always stumbling around in the vicinity of the avant-garde. Eva's work was right there at the beginning, but its beginning was such that it has never quite come into focus in the imperial (male?) fashion of breakthrough and conquest. It was done intensely and modestly, with a wary sense of the dangers of preeminence (after a splash in *Artforum* she said "I hope I'm not on everyone's shitlist"). It is the farcical practice of such notes as this to contrast A and B, how A is not B, though B illustrates aspects of A, etc. But since I've been asked to deal with Stella and Hesse, I cannot but note the superb confidence of Stella, the sense of someone who knew exactly what he was doing back then: focused, intense, prodigious. With him, you knew where you were, but you didn't want to be there. With Hesse, you didn't know where you were (or at least I didn't), but you did want to be there. No matter what's on it, a canvas is always a canvas, and painting, however bizarre, is always painting. Eva's sculpture (which didn't look like sculpture, though in the sixties we knew that game too) looked as if a delirium had ravaged the orders of Minimal/Serial thinking.

It felt expressionist, but it offered no biography. Its masticated forms sought disorder in the templates of order, and she fused these opposites into Siamese twins often connected by strings. How opposites are experienced may deliver them from the narrow corridor in which they ricochet back and forth. The great mature works all announced their dialectical foils frankly: order as advanced by Minimal/Serialism, the idea of beauty, and formalism. (She said to me once: "I hope your work doesn't become too pure.") She wanted to surprise herself with the ugly and the absurd, categories she repeatedly used in her thinking and writing. The weight of such words as arbitrary, crazy, absurd, outrageous, risky force up their rejected siblings: orderly, sane, safe, quiet, logical, beautiful, predictable, appropriate—the rational language of classicism. Her categories searched beyond the orthodox social contract through which we keep chaos at bay; they pushed into a kind of darkness that, like her final artworks, frequently had no edge or border. There was a sense of the work having had a rough passage through some difficult terrain, which remained foreign rather than mysterious. Perhaps that was how it got that unusual quality of generalized feeling without an identifiable emotion, a sense of something kept just out of focus but provoking only a limited curiosity as to its nature—which kept you fixed on the materials and means. She explored and worried these materials until they often appeared half-digested by a process of rumination. Her mental life and the body of her work were unusually fused. Yet this was not the classic expressionist practice, the redemptive self passing through its own dark mirror. But we may ask, what self was in operation? What mind? What body?

The anthropomorphic posture of much of the work is undeniable; it hangs (*Contingent*, 1969), leans (*Accretion*, 1968), slumps from wall to floor (*Area*, 1968), settles and spreads out (*Augment*, 1968), always aware of gravity's gentle tug (some of her other colleagues conceived of gravity as dead weight, inertia, a pulverizer of space). The distribution pieces often look as if a mind were thinking and verbalizing. *Repetition 19, First Version* (1967) repeats the concept "container" but articulates it differently each time through morphological nudges. The bocketty containers are set in a kind of anti-grid, which keeps the space "fluctuating, unfixed—what Hesse once called 'wild space'" (Lucy Lippard). The extended belt of *Sans II* (1968) is like a long sentence in which the emphasis—and thus the meaning—changes as each unit argues against its uniformity but not against its position. In that argument, each unit repeats itself until, like a word stunned with redundancy, it becomes available for another kind of meaninglessness.

If the substance of her pieces—often tarry, dark, semi-transparent—is the work's organic body, the reciprocal whirlpools, sheaths and ripples of air induced by the forms may be its "mind." Against the even constant of gravity, a uniform "ground," space swerves and flows around the forms with the speed and antic certainty of thought. But the body is not anthropomorphic as in frank expressionism, it is somehow alien. In the early days, the question of gender confused me, for some of that work is both male and

Eva Hesse
Repetition 19, First Version 1967
painted newspaper over wire screening
each approximately 10" high x 8" diameter (irregular).
The Museum of Modern Art, New York; gift of Mr.
and Mrs. Murray Charash.

female—or neither. She suggested a swap of one of my ogham sculptures for one of her "wursts," with the string hanging out of it, but its ambiguous associations—penis/ tampon—so confused me that I deprived myself of a work I would now cherish. Several of the later works can be reinstalled differently each time according to their intrinsic justification, just as Feldman's indeterminate compositions can be replayed differently each time while maintaining their signature motif. Meaning is prevented from accumulating in psychological pools, distancing the work from easy assimilation.

As a rule the work proceeds from order to varieties of apparent chaos. From the outside, the boxes of the Accession series present teeming registers of perforated steel. Inside, fingers of plastic tubing project in a spiky, chaotic rug. The downward glance is wounded by their agitation. The rational and somewhat inert outside encloses a mad turbulence, a quota of "wild" space. Pointing every which way, the ciliation deepens into a twilight vibrating with energy born of obsession. As the box's body (its material substance) is conjugated by its mind ("thinking" space), it becomes eerily brainlike. From the outside, perfect order; then, as one's glance slips across the rim, its dialectical twin. Inside and outside, two categories that Minimalism, in its disinfection of anthropomorphism, sought to make homologous, were here reinterpreted—one might say reinfected—while keeping a wary eye on the Minimal proscription. As when I saw *Hang-Up*, there was, again, nothing else like this.

•

Stella's early work presented a very cool surface seething with contradictions and acidic ironies. Hesse's work seemed to have a deep emotional bias, but the more you pursue it, the more elusive it becomes. The two artists' paths cross at a point where they might, I think, recognize each other's destination. The work of each artist wears a mask, and the mask is a classic one of late modernism, schooled in formalism, set on its destruction, obsessed with originality, intent on transforming the heroic rhetoric of its immediate predecessors into everyday discourse. If their work is now a sign of those times, it was a time for such signs. And what do they signify?

The feelings that these artists negotiate through their formal and antiformal strategies were new back then. The works made me feel strange and different, as if another mind was forcing me to think its thoughts; the experience wasn't in the least comfortable. But nothing is more perishable than the new or the illusion of newness. Even the recognition of the new is an old feeling now. It has become a category, which is a preface to meaning. But what I felt back then was access to a new mode of feeling, as if new forms could discover and invent new emotions. Or did they merely reinvent ways of feeling old emotions? Or was the emotion merely that of recognizing the new? Do modes of feeling, like modes of perception, change? How much of that feeling was period feeling? Do the works provoke it still? How do they resist assimilation, if they do? How can one recondition them for the present (particularly Hesse's; her too brief career takes on a miraculous cast in memory)? I first saw each artist's work from very different vantage points: the Stellas from an establishment bastion; the Hesses from within a group of like-minded friends, of which she was one. By coincidence, this essay has given me the opportunity to look back, like Keats with Chapman, at the work of the two artists who left me with probably the most forceful impression of originality I've had. ☐

Eva Hesse
Area 1968
latex on wire mesh and metal wire
240" x 36"
Wexner Center for the Arts, The Ohio State University,
Columbus; purchased in part with designated funds
from Helen Hesse Charash, 1977.001.
Photo: Lynette Molnar.

Beyond "Big Serge"
Dance in the Fifties and Sixties

Lynn Garafola

The relationship of avant-garde dance to the visual arts in the fifties is an oblique and knotty one. Lynn Garafola, a dance historian who has written extensively on impresario Serge Diaghilev, finds that choreographers at mid-century, whether working in modern dance or ballet, in America or Europe, were looking back within the field of dance to deal with that modernist pioneer's legacy, making only sidelong glances at other genres. Garafola examines the innovations of four choreographers—George Balanchine and Maurice Béjart in ballet and Martha Graham and Merce Cunningham in modern dance—as they tackled basic issues of movement, narrative, collaboration and the relationship of dance and design and, in the process, broke free from Diaghilev's pervasive influence.

To some extent, the dance artists' searches paralleled those of contemporary visual artists also taking the measure of once-potent prewar traditions and influences. How to "make it new" after so much early twentieth-century "newness" was the question of the day for choreographers and visual artists alike. As Garafola notes, the beginnings of some answers for dance eventually turned into points of contact between ballet and modern dance and between vanguard choreographers and visual artists. She traces the beginnings of a ballet–modern dance connection that is one of the most striking features of today's international dance scene and a nascent cross-pollination between art and dance that would flower in the mid-sixties.

Carolyn Brown and Viola Farber in Merce Cunningham's *Summerspace* (1958), decor and costumes by Robert Rauschenberg. Photo: Richard Rutledge, courtesy of Cunningham Dance Foundation Inc., New York.

"Big Serge," as his dancers liked to call Diaghilev, never did things by halves. Even his shadow was colossal, and today, more than sixty years after his death, it continues to hover over the art world. In the last decade, his fame has actually grown, thanks to a spate of exhibitions and headline-making auctions that have rekindled interest in his fabled Ballets Russes. Purveyors of celebrity collaborations also have discovered his legacy. At the Brooklyn Academy of Music's Next Wave Festival, his name is routinely trotted out, his enterprise ("the best-known venture in artistic collaboration the world has ever known," as one Next Wave program essay put it) invoked as a kind of Good Housekeeping Seal. Yet few of his ideas remain in circulation. Nowhere is this more striking than in the field of design, revolutionized by choreographers of the postwar decades. With the choreography of George Balanchine, Martha Graham, Merce Cunningham and Maurice Béjart in the fifties and sixties, dance finally put Diaghilev behind it.

Between 1909 and 1929, Diaghilev redesigned the stage for ballet. He did this by using easel painters—first, Russians allied with the World of Art; then, Westerners associated with nearly every movement after Cubism. He did it by making a virtue of collaboration and by turning the stage into a public gallery—marrying modernist art to ballet chic. Diaghilev's heirs took the letter rather than the spirit of his work to heart. They made decors a necessity, but not painters of the highest caliber; made a fetish of collaboration, but forgot about the avant-garde. Ballet of the thirties and forties reduced Big Serge's approach to an unimaginative formula.

This was even true of the choreographer who first challenged Diaghilev's "method." Russian-born and trained, George Balanchine joined the Ballets Russes in 1924. He knew a good deal about music, but almost nothing about painting. "Oh, *really*?" he replied when told that the sets and costumes of *Le Chant du Rossignol*, his first ballet for Diaghilev, were by Matisse: Balanchine had never heard of him. Numerous artists, more than at any other time, worked for Diaghilev in those years. Most of them did no more than a single production, and this, typically, was a one-man "cocktail" mixed by Diaghilev. Choreography took a back seat to design. *Les Matelots* had a dozen backdrops; Balanchine's *La Pastorale*, a "mazurka" of practicables that left hardly any room for dancing. Even *Apollo*, which Balanchine regarded as a turning point in his development, was loaded with wigs, tutus, props, a staircase to the empyrean, backdrops with flowers, flying cherubs and chariots.

In the thirties and forties, Balanchine was content to leave the artistic direction of his enterprises to others. Both Boris Kochno, in Europe, and Lincoln Kirstein, in the United States, adopted Diaghilev as a mentor, and though they added to his roster of painters, neither abandoned his decorative approach. Both dressed Balanchine up—in settings by Christian Bérard, Pavel Tchelitchev, Mstislav Dobujinsky, Kurt Seligmann, Dorothea Tanning, Eugene Berman, designers who brought a whiff of something like Surrealism to the choreography. This, however, was developing along other lines. In 1941, with *Concerto Barocco* and *Ballet Imperial*, Balanchine created his first fully plotless works. The late forties and fifties witnessed many more, and with them, the appearance of a new design aesthetic.

In 1945, when *Concerto Barocco* entered the repertory of the Ballet Russe de Monte Carlo, Berman refused permission to use his scenery, claiming its technical execution was unsatisfactory. So the ballet was performed in practice clothes against a plain cyclorama. Three years later, the artist changed his mind, and Balanchine, remounting the work for the New York City Ballet, reinstated the painted decor and Berman's synthetic rubber costumes. But audiences preferred their *Barocco* bare, as did Balanchine, and in 1951, he "undressed" the ballet, substituting for tutus the classroom-style tunics we know today. *Barocco* was not an isolated phenomenon, but an expression of the design credo that now became a trademark of his mature choreographic style. That same year, he discarded what remained of Kurt Seligmann's "cerements, bandages, tubes, wraps and tourniquets," as Kirstein picturesquely described the artist's costumes for *The Four Temperaments*. Since 1946, the year of the ballet's premiere, Balanchine—scissors in hand—had been snipping away at them. Now, at a single stroke, he eliminated them entirely, replacing them with simple leotards. This was not the first time dancers had worn leotards in a ballet; Diaghilev's 1928 *Ode* held that distinction. But it was the first time they wore them as a company uniform and the first time that uniform became identified with the postwar landscape of anxiety.

Beginning with *The Four Temperaments*, leotards became the dress code for works that bared the anguish of sex and the ambiguity of sexual identity. Like *The Four Temperaments*, *Agon* (1957) and *Episodes* (1959) were plotless; their chance encounters, mechanical pleasures, calculated seductions and abrupt departures embedded in images that stood classical tradition on its head. In *Agon*, the danseur supported the ballerina from the floor, while in *Episodes*, she emanated from his body like a physical synecdoche, a faceless design of arms and legs. The abstraction of Balanchine's choreography stripped its "drama" to essentials, just as the leotard transformed the dancer into an image of generalized humanity. Shorn of particularity, existing in a timeless present, Balanchine's "leotard" ballets distilled the experience of modernity into a mythic moment.

Although few choreographers went as far as Balanchine in purging their work of narrative, myth was a common inspiration in the forties and fifties. Martha Graham's best works of the period often took their narrative structures from ancient myths reinterpreted after Jung and reconceived along the antirealistic lines of Japanese theater. Like the "leotard" ballets, her inventions all turned on sex. But where Balanchine, a romantic manqué, exposed the tragedy of incomprehension between the sexes, Graham, a liberated Puritan, agonized over female sexual expression and guilt. Myth gave this obsession respectability; in *Night Journey* it wasn't Graham onstage working out the problems of middle age, but Jocasta meditating on the archetypal dilemmas of the human condition. Isamu Noguchi, who designed most of Graham's works between 1944 and 1967, brilliantly underscored that intent. His settings were both minimal and suggestive, a landscape of sexual symbols—shafts, coils, platforms, columns with protruding mounds and cylinders—that universalized her themes by locating them within a design of timeless formality. Today, Noguchi's designs seem infinitely fresher than the phallocentric dramas they were called upon to illustrate.

Balanchine and Graham threw over the Diaghilev legacy by uniting the functions of choreographer and artistic director. In a far more radical act, Balanchine usurped the role of the designer and made his creation superfluous. One suspects he enjoyed the swipe at Diaghilev; it made up for the clutter in ballets like *Apollo*, which Balanchine now also stripped down. At the same time, it must have gratified the modernist to find his choreography—at long last—identified with the American avant-garde.

Merce Cunningham's scenic innovations threw over the Diaghilev legacy too. Balanchine had gotten over the hurdle of collaboration by eliminating the designer. Cunningham kept the designer, but eliminated collaboration. The costumes for his earliest dances were mostly souped-up leotards, of his own or dancer Remy Charlip's invention, and the stage was usually left bare. But almost as soon as the Merce Cunningham Dance Company was formed in 1953, visual artists made their appearance. Robert Rauschenberg's first work for Cunningham was *Minutiae* the following year, and over the next decade he created sets and costumes for almost two dozen pieces. By 1970, Jasper Johns, Frank Stella, Andy Warhol and Robert Morris had also worked for the company, and Marcel Duchamp had let Cunningham adapt *The Large Glass* (1915–23) for *Walkaround Time* (1968). Unlike Balanchine, who "dressed" non-leotard ballets in styles no more adventurous than postsurrealism, Cunningham broke with the Surrealist tradition entirely, choosing his designers from New York's art world of the fifties. For the first time since Diaghilev's discovery of the avant-garde in World War I, dance had embraced contemporary art, and for the first time, the contemporary had nothing to do with international modernism.

Cunningham, however, tossed out far more than Diaghilev's modernism. Collaboration also went, both as a theoretical idea and a practical method. For most of his career as a producer, Diaghilev had followed in Wagner's footsteps, creating works that aspired to a fusion of their component arts. At the Imperial Theaters in pre-Revolutionary Russia, a half-dozen scene painters and costumers might work on a production. Diaghilev, by contrast, usually employed a single designer; he sat him down with the composer and the choreographer and asked for his input. It was hard to know sometimes who came up with an idea, and egos were often ruffled by program credits. Egos were also bruised by Diaghilev's "meddling"; he made Picasso redo the designs for *Pulcinella* (which so infuriated the artist he tore up his drawings for the costumes) and scrapped or at least modified all of Juan Gris' original ideas for *Les Tentations de la bergère*. Nor did collaboration always result in unity. Too many cooks, it turned out in *Firebird* and *Romeo and Juliet*, could spoil the broth.

George Balanchine's *Episodes* (1959) in a 1963 production by the New York City Ballet. Photo: Fred Fehl.

Martha Graham as Jocasta, Robert Cohan as Tiresias, and Bertram Ross as Oedipus in Graham's *Night Journey* (1944). Photo courtesy of the Martha Graham Center of Contemporary Dance.

Cunningham, by contrast, did everything he could to eliminate power from the artistic process. In his democratic polity, designer, composer and choreographer worked independently, free of the constraints imposed by either a unifying idea or a dominant personality. "What we have done," he has said, referring to his decades-long association with composer John Cage, "is to bring together three separate elements in time and space, the music, the dance and the decor, allowing each one to remain independent. The three arts don't come from a single idea which the dance demonstrates, the music supports and the decor illustrates, but rather they are three separate elements each central to itself." Cunningham's "non-collaborative collaborations," as they have been called, thus set a premium on individuality. Cunningham wasn't interested in making a whole that "gelled." Except for a time structure—so many parts, so many minutes in each part—agreed upon in advance, music and dance went their own ways, "meeting" for the first time onstage. It was in performance, too, that Cunningham first encountered the set, and this, too, heightened the possibility of surprise, as did the improvisational elements built into many works. "It is an anarchic process of working," Cunningham once said. "Each person and the work he does is independent, and he acts with the others, not competitively, but complementarily."

It wasn't only power that Cunningham removed from Diaghilev's collaborative recipe. In a work like *Story*, where Rauschenberg recreated the set for each performance from whatever "junk" he could lay his hands on, Cunningham did away with the idea that design was a commodity. Although Diaghilev kept most of what he commissioned, he had a sharp eye for the art market and, after the First World War, demanded that painters "brush" their own sets, adding to their value as collectibles. (When bankruptcy loomed in the late twenties, he chopped up Picasso's curtain for *Le Tricorne* and sold it at a high price to a German collector.) But junk? Fresh green boughs from Prospect Park? A nightgown from a thrift shop? Ironing shirts or painting a picture onstage (as Rauschenberg sometimes did in *Story*)? Rauschenberg or no, not much here was salable, either because the sets weren't permanent or the materials hadn't any value. If Diaghilev brought dance into the art market, Cunningham did everything possible to keep the two separate.

Like Rauschenberg, Cunningham opened his work to the vernacular and the ordinary. Yet for all the walking, all the improvised tasks and indeterminate structures, he remained committed to movement that was specialized and, to most of the general public at least, close to impenetrable. However much he turned his attention outward on the world, his art belonged to an avant-garde elite, the painters and composers who saw the company through its first, lean decade. If Cunningham lowered the barriers between art and life, he never broke with the idea of dance as high art.

The choreographer who destroyed this last Diaghilev shibboleth was Maurice Béjart. French-born and ballet-trained, he came on the scene in the fifties, not a propitious time in Europe for a choreographer interested in experimentation. Ballet was riding high, and so was the past—in repertory no less than personnel. In England, Petipa's *Sleeping Beauty* played hundreds of performances; a half-dozen Diaghilev ballets were revived, and Frederick Ashton, after toying with abstraction, switched to making story ballets. In Paris, Serge Lifar, Diaghilev's last leading man, returned to his post as head of the Paris Opéra Ballet (he had been dismissed at the end of the Second World War for collaborating with the Germans) and fell back on recipes and associates inherited from the twenties. Even the Ballets des Champs-Elysées, a bright spot on the French postwar horizon, could escape neither the influence nor the alumni of "Big Serge." As for modern dance, outside Germany there was almost none to speak of in all Europe.

So Béjart studied ballet, first in Marseilles, where he grew up, then in Paris and London. He joined Mona Inglesby's International Ballet and became a leading man on its tours of the European backwater. In London, where he saw the New York City Ballet, he fell in love with the exuberant teen rituals of Jerome Robbins, discovering in *Interplay* and *Fancy Free* a "linguistic" freedom he had believed it possible to achieve only in literature. Another revelation was Martha Graham, whose company he saw in 1954. Here was an art of ongoing discovery, a theater that plumbed the psyche and bore witness in the utterance of archetype. Here also was a technique that owed nothing to ballet, yet worked the body expressively. Béjart filed this all away, along with the other influences that marked his passage through the fifties—existentialism, *musique concrète*, Kabuki, Noh, jazz, the "new novel," the theatrical ideas of Pirandello and Artaud.

He made his way without patrons or plum commissions or champions from the narrow circle of balletomanes. He liked to shock, imagining, for instance, an Annunciation where Gabriel gave Mary the news by telephone. He formed a small company, the Ballet de l'Etoile, and two years later, in 1955, created his first ballet to *musique concrète, La Symphonie pour un homme seul*. It was a critical success, although the general public stayed away, and a turning point in his career. He now repudiated nineteenth-century music and all his previous choreography; got rid of tutus, traditional narrative and romance. With Joyce, Proust and Hindu philosophy under his belt, he made ready his assault on high culture.

More than any other work, the 1959 *Le Sacre du printemps* revealed the new Béjart. The ballet was a sacred cow, the lost masterpiece of the legendary Nijinsky and Diaghilev's greatest *scandale*. The original, set in prehistoric Russia, depicted a fertility rite that ended with the sacrifice of a maiden. Béjart's version dispensed with the Slavic trimmings. It took place in the here and now and put the accent on youth; it made *Sacre* a rumbling, heavy-petting fest. With *Sacre* and the ballets that followed, Béjart said "yes" to the sexual revolution and packaged that "yes" as pop mysticism, psychology and politics.

Sacre established Béjart in the vanguard of European dance. In 1960, he renamed his company the Ballet of the XXth Century and set up shop at Brussels' Théâtre de la Monnaie. The security gave him freedom; in his new ballets and the total theater pieces that increasingly commanded his attention, he revealed the full extent of his iconoclasm. With its giant automatons and interpolated passages of electronic music, his *Tales of Hoffmann* was a shocker, as was his version of *The Merry Widow*, where he juxtaposed the events of the operetta with the atrocities of the First World War. "Masterpieces," he was fond of saying, "were made to be violated." And, so in *Baudelaire*, the poet's name echoed as "Bob Dylan," and in *Nijinsky, Clown of God*, exhortations to "save the planet" and "abandon your factories" mingled with quotations from various Diaghilev ballets. None of these devices was unique to Béjart. What set his work apart, above all from experiments in the United States, was the sheer scale of his productions, which grew ever more massive as the decade advanced. Not only did he routinely create for the opera house, but beginning in 1961, when he mounted *Les Quatre Fils Aymon* at the Cirque Royal in Brussels, he sought out nontraditional playing spaces geared to the masses he increasingly regarded as his true audience.

In New York, the choreographers associated with the Judson group also took to the streets in the sixties. But unlike Béjart, none had the means and few had the interest in taking their work to the "people." With his *Ninth Symphony*, to Beethoven's music, and his *Messe pour le temps présent*, with texts from Buddha, Nietzsche and the Songs of Songs, Béjart pulled the "people" in. He filled sports arenas, circus halls, city squares and Roman amphitheaters. The audiences were predominantly young, and many had never seen a ballet before. Béjart wowed them with a spectacle worthy of Cecil B. De Mille— hundreds of performers ranged in circles of cosmic union, whirling in Dionysian rapture, walking upward into light in an act of collective self-deification. No matter that the choreography was banal, that the dancing lacked finesse, that the ideas behind the concept were simplistic. The whole was modern and new; it stood opposed to the past and, from the jeans the dancers wore to their multiracial identities, spoke directly to the experience of the audience. Peaceniks, Buddhists, Maoists, third worldists, long hairs who thought that making love was better than making war and who, in the spring of 1968, staged a cultural revolution in Paris—Béjart belonged to them all, and they packed his performances as if they were rock concerts, love-ins organized under the sign of Aquarius. At the Avignon Festival that summer, *Messe* played to 60,000 people.

To the cultivated elite, it was all bread and circuses or Pop art with pretensions. This in fact was the source of Béjart's subversiveness; his work questioned—with evident success—the identity of ballet as high art. Such an identity was another of Diaghilev's legacies, for it was his enterprise that gave artistic and social legitimacy to ballet after its long decline in the second half of the nineteenth century. Béjart challenged not only that legitimacy but the social privilege on which it implicitly rested. His kids were both the disenchanted and the disenfranchised; culturally, they stood outside the opera house and all it represented in European society. In *Nijinsky, Clown of God*, Béjart summed up that tradition with a twelve-foot puppet of Diaghilev—paunchy, powerful, a high-society ringmaster posing as Jehovah. Big Serge wouldn't have liked it. But he would have gotten the message. Dance had put his legacy behind it. □

The Ballet of the XXth Century in Maurice Béjart's
Le Sacre du printemps (1959). Photo courtesy of ICM
Artists, New York.

The Future of Music
The Fifties and Sixties in Retrospect

Roy M. Close

As a musician, composer and philosophical eminence grise to the performing and visual arts as well as to music, John Cage has irrevocably influenced the arts in the second half of the twentieth century. Even today, he appears to be the dominant figure in twentieth-century music. In his iconoclastic strategies, Cage invented and put to use new vocabularies of sound involving noise and silence and new composition methods based on chance and technological innovations. In the following essay, music, dance and theater critic Roy M. Close describes the context in which Cage made his precedent-shattering gestures. Close outlines the differences and similarities between Cage and European composers such as Pierre Boulez—and so between American and European attitudes toward the renewal of music in the postwar period—and concludes that Cage and his contemporaries' legacy is "artistic freedom unprecedented in the history of music." How today's composers address the questions Cage raised in the fifties and sixties, Close notes, will affect the course of music in the nineties.

On 29 August 1952, at a recital in Woodstock, New York, pianist David Tudor gave the first performance of John Cage's *4'33"*, the first musical composition consisting entirely of silence. Timing each of its three movements with a stopwatch, Tudor sat motionless at the keyboard for the specified length of time. His only actions were symbolic: at the beginning of each movement, he lowered the keyboard cover; at the end, he raised it. Maverick Concert Hall, on the village outskirts, stands in a forest clearing and is open to the woods at one end. During the first movement, attentive listeners heard a breeze rustling the leaves of the nearby trees; during the second, a few drops of rain on the roof; and during the finale, it having dawned on them that not a note was to be played, the voices of disgruntled concertgoers—some of whom, Cage remarked twenty-five years later, "may be said to still be walking out."[1]

Many of the Woodstockians greeted *4'33"* as a tasteless practical joke and were sorely vexed at having been made the butt of it. The Dada streak in Cage's humor cannot be denied, but *4'33"* was much more than a tweaking of audience expectations: it embodied many of the principles of Cage's credo in the early fifties, an astonishingly fruitful period during which he permanently altered the course of experimental music in America.

By treating ambient sounds as music, Cage effectively redefined the art form, expanding its boundaries to encompass sounds unintended by the composer—including noise. By writing a piece without notes, he demonstrated that silence is as valid as sound in a work of music. By using chance operations to determine the length of the piece, he gave up a measure of control over it; in later works, his renunciation would be more complete. By springing it on an unsuspecting audience in the context of a traditional piano recital, he reaffirmed a commitment to music as theater that would reach its zenith with the sound-and-light spectacle *HPSCHD* (1969). Even the score of *4'33"* was innovative, for Cage's novel notation represented the passage of time as progress across a succession of virtually blank pages—the only marks were vertical lines indicating beginnings and ends of movements—at the precise tempo of eight seconds per inch.

●

Cage was not alone in embracing new values. During the decade that followed World War II, composers on both sides of the Atlantic sought to reinvent classical music, as it were, by contriving new methods of organizing sound. Their common objective, diversely pursued, was to create the music of the future.

The most important of the new methods was serialism. In Europe—building on the foundation laid by Arnold Schönberg, Anton Webern and Olivier Messiaen—Pierre Boulez and Karlheinz Stockhausen emerged as serial composers par excellence, leaders of a circle that included Henri Pousseur, Bruno Maderna, Luigi Nono and Luciano Berio, among others. Milton Babbitt, working independently in this country, likewise extended Schönberg's dodecaphonic technique to other parameters of sound. The differences among them were significant, as later events would show; but in the early fifties they all shared a common interest in discarding the past and starting over.

Boulez studied with Olivier Messiaen, from whom he acquired a taste for rhythmic complexity, but it was the twelve-tone works of Schönberg's disciple Anton Webern that fired his imagination. Their purity of form led him to envision a new musical language wherein not only pitch but all the salient characteristics of sound—rhythm, amplitude, attack and timbre—would be organized according to the same basic principle: that of the tone row. A tone row is a twelve-note theme consisting of the twelve semitones that make up one octave. The pitches may be arranged in any sequence, but each may be used only once; in addition, their order may not be altered for the duration of a work, though innumerable transformations and variations derived from it may be introduced.

Early in his career, Boulez employed total serialism the way a safecracker uses dynamite—as the best available tool for demolishing the musical detritus of the past—and composed intense, turbulent works such as the *Second Piano Sonata* (1948) and *Structures I* (1951–52). It was never his intention, however, to abandon artistic control

A page from the score of John Cage's *Music of Changes*. © 1961 Henmar Press Inc.; used by permission of C. F. Peters Corporation.

over the composition process; his purpose was to strike a balance between intellectual rigor and creative freedom. This he did most eloquently with *Le Marteau sans maitre* (1954), a landmark work that owes as much to Debussy as to Webern. Its serial techniques are vast and varied; its largely *mezzo* instrumentation—contralto, alto flute, viola, guitar and percussion—has spawned many imitators.

Like Boulez, Stockhausen was influenced by Messiaen, whose pointillistic *Mode de valeurs* he encountered in 1951 at the new music institute in Darmstadt, West Germany. For *Kreuzspiel*, completed later that year, he devised a system for manipulating each note individually, in effect creating a unique new musical universe that operated according to its own laws without recourse to even rudimentary thematic units. Unlike Boulez, Stockhausen was an early convert to the studio; at the Cologne radio station he produced *Studie I* (1953), the first composition made of sine tones. Largely because of his influence, Cologne became a hotbed of electronic music.

Babbitt, meanwhile, approached serialism with a mathematical passion. As the first to analyze the relationship of twelve-tone music and set theory, he introduced such terms as "combinatoriality" and "source set" into the lexicon of contemporary music. Babbitt's goal—not shared by Boulez, Stockhausen and the other European serialists—was to develop a consistent method for adapting Schönberg's twelve-tone row to all the other parameters of music: hence the size of the ensemble in his *Composition for Twelve Instruments* (1948). In 1957 he introduced "time points," a system for relating rhythmic intervals to those of pitch. The increasing complexity of Babbitt's music militated against accurate performances, however, and by 1960 he had retreated to the Columbia-Princeton Electronic Music Center, whose RCA Synthesizer could realize his compositions with unerring precision.

•

Perhaps the Woodstock audience shouldn't have been surprised by *4'33"*, for by 1952, the year of his fortieth birthday, Cage was a prominent member of the American avant-garde—so prominent, indeed, that the printed program of the recital, which included works by five other composers, listed Cage's name above that of Tudor, the pianist. That he espoused an unorthodox artistic viewpoint, in other words, was widely known. But in 1952 Cage enjoyed the respect of the musical establishment, which knew him as a composer of percussion music and inventor of the prepared piano, for which he had written more than a dozen works, chief among them the sublime *Sonatas and Interludes* (1948).

Cage met Boulez in 1949 and became his first American champion; among other good turns, he arranged for Tudor to give the U.S. premiere of Boulez's *Second Piano Sonata* in December 1950. Although there were points of agreement between them, Boulez and Cage soon parted company over the latter's use of chance to determine the content of his compositions. Despite Cage's insistence "that nothing was lost when everything was given away,"[2] his use of chance created a gulf that set him apart from his peers, many of whom believed that to abandon control over one's material was artistically irresponsible. Their disdain ran deep: in the late sixties, when Cage was soliciting music manuscripts for a book on contemporary notation, Otto Luening submitted a sheet of composing paper covered with a meaningless scrawl and titled *Rorschach Symphonic Sonata*. (Cage got the last laugh: he published it.) As for Boulez, he summed up his position when he remarked, "I love John's mind, but I don't like what it thinks."[3]

Cage's decision to use chance was prompted in part by his studies of oriental philosophy, which led him to conclude that music should resemble nature in the way it operates—that is, randomly. The only way of bringing this about, he concluded, was to eliminate the distorting influence of his own taste. In *Sixteen Dances* (1950) and the *Concerto for Prepared Piano and Chamber Orchestra* (1951), he used charts resembling magic squares; beginning with *Music of Changes* (1951–52), a forty-one-minute opus for solo piano, he has relied primarily on the coin-tossing procedures of the *I Ching*, the ancient Chinese Book of Changes.

Cage subsequently devised other means of freeing his music from his influence and pushing it steadily toward "indeterminacy," a term he used to describe music sufficiently unstructured to admit events unimagined by the composer. In *Imaginary Landscape No. 4* (1952), he guaranteed a high degree of unpredictability by employing as instruments twelve variously tuned portable radios. In *Music for Piano 21–52* (1955), the placement of notes was dictated by imperfections in the paper on which it was composed; in *Atlas Eclipticalis* (1961), by the locations of stars on celestial maps. The flamboyantly theatrical *Concert for Piano and Orchestra* (1957–58), the pièce de résistance of Cage's celebrated twenty-five-year retrospective concert, employed a great variety of graphic notation, the interpretation of which was left up to each musician. Increasingly, Cage declined to specify instrumentation or performance time, even for extant pieces; when *4'33"* was

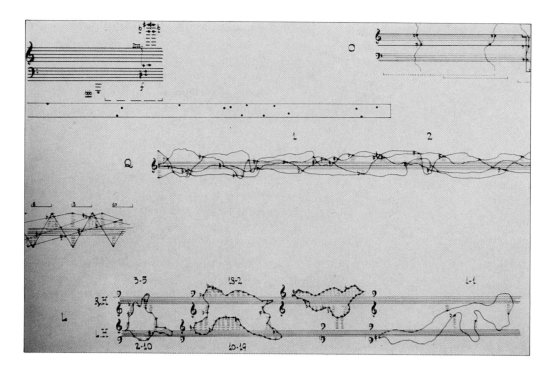

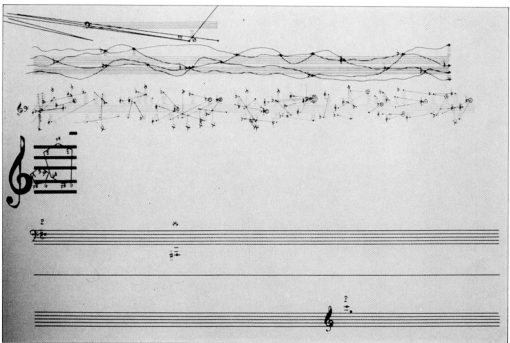

published in 1960, he wrote: "the work may be performed by an[y] instrumentalist or combination of instrumentalists and last any length of time."[4]

In the early fifties, Cage's circle included three composers of note, Earle Brown, Morton Feldman and Christian Wolff, who influenced and were influenced by him. In works such as *December 1952*, Brown abandoned traditional notation in favor of graphic scores that left many variables open to the discretion of the performers. Feldman, whose influences also included the Abstract Expressionist painters Jackson Pollock and Willem de Kooning, did likewise. In his *Projections* and *Intersections* series of the early fifties, he specified only the range—upper, middle or lower—to be played by each instrument during a given passage, leaving the fine-tuning to the players. Wolff, an early Minimalist, drastically reduced the repertoire of pitches and durations in some of his pieces.

By the sixties, as Babbitt was quick to point out, total serialism was largely a relic of the past; in Europe, especially, it had been superseded by other means of organizing sound—including chance operations. It is one of the ironies of the era that Boulez, who had broken off relations with Cage over the latter's use of chance, not only embraced chance in his *Third Piano Sonata* (1957) but coined the term "aleatory" music—after *alea*, the Latin word for chance—that has come to identify the genre as a whole. Three decades later, the notion that serialism was a creative cul-de-sac enjoys wide currency; yet it cannot be denied that serialism in one form or another engaged some of the most brilliant musical minds of the mid-twentieth century, that it produced a small legacy of masterpieces and that its influence is still widely felt.

If the fifties had been characterized by a common objective, the sixties were notable for diversity. Electronic music reached its zenith; so did music as theater; Minimalism was born; collage, a technique borrowed from the visual arts, found favor; composers such as Britain's Peter Maxwell Davies and Harrison Birtwistle wrote music that synthesized medieval and modern influences.

Electronic music had been around since the invention of the Theremin (1924) and Ondes martenot (1928), the first instruments to employ radio-frequency oscillators. Cage's *Imaginary Landscape No. 1* (1939) incorporated two variable-speed turntables and five phonograph records of the type then used by studios to test frequencies. Phonographs and discs were likewise used by Pierre Schaeffer, who founded Europe's first electronic music studio in Paris and there created the first examples of *musique concrète*—music consisting of sounds drawn from the real world and altered by electronic manipulation. Paris has been an important center for electronic music ever since, a status enhanced by the establishment in 1969 of the Institut de Recherche et Coordination Acoustique/ Musique (IRCAM), of which Boulez has been director since 1977. As previously noted, Paris had a European rival in Cologne, where Stockhausen held sway; unlike the practitioners of *musique concrète*, the Cologne composers were interested in generating new, purely electronic sounds. In the United States, electronic music flourished mainly in New York, home of the Columbia-Princeton Electronic Music Center, where Babbitt produced all his electronic works. There were pockets of electronic activity elsewhere, however, notably at the University of Illinois, home of the Illiac computer on which Cage and Lejaren Hiller collaborated on *HPSCHD*.

Although recorded electronic music did not demonstrate broad commercial appeal at the time, live electronic music was taken up by many composers, some of whom formed ensembles to perform it. The most prominent of these groups were Musica Elettronica Viva, founded by Frederic Rzewski and others, and the Sonic Arts Union, founded by David Behrman, Gordon Mumma, Alvin Lucier and Robert Ashley. Chief among the technological advances that enabled such groups to function was the Moog synthesizer, invented by Robert Moog in 1964, which made it possible to manipulate sounds as they occurred. Now a staple of rock bands everywhere, the synthesizer is one of the few components of sixties' experimental music to have been assimilated into popular culture.

A page from the score of Morton Feldman's *Intersection for Orchestra #1.* © 1962 C. F. Peters Corporation; used by permission.

Experimental music and theater have had a colorful history throughout the twentieth century. The premiere of Stravinsky's *The Rite of Spring* in 1913 provoked a riot in the auditorium; a year later the Futurist composer Luigi Russolo touched off another by giving a concert of noises produced by mechanical instruments of his own construction. Among the avant-gardists of the fifties and sixties, there were several composers of opera—Luigi Nono, Luciano Berio, Hans Werner Henze and Bernd Zimmermann—and one, Cage, who composed regularly for the dance.

Cage's dance compositions, oddly enough, are among his least theatrical, for he has long treated music and dance as mutually independent entities; the many works he

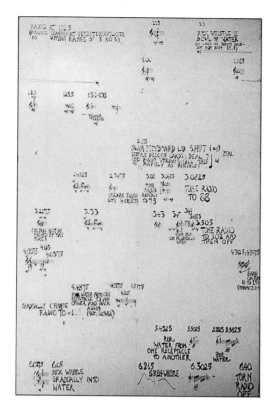

The score of John Cage's *Water Music*, separate sheets designed to be mounted as a poster.
© 1960 Henmar Press Inc.; used by permission of C. F. Peters Corporation.

composed for the Merce Cunningham Dance Company related to Cunningham's choreography only by virtue of their being performed simultaneously. His theatrical aptitude surfaced in other works, such as *Water Music* (1952), a celebrated early example, the props for which include a radio, whistles, pails of water and a deck of cards. Other noteworthy Cageian contributions to music theater include *Musicircus* (1967), consisting of dozens of independent performances occurring simultaneously in the same place, and *HPSCHD* (1969), a spectacular tour de force involving seven harpsichords, computer-generated music, slide projections and colorful lighting. The latter's scale was so grand that its premiere was held in a basketball arena.

At Black Mountain College in 1952, Cage organized a multimedia event—its components included live and recorded music, dance, poetry and painting—that inspired the Happenings of the sixties and, indirectly, today's performance art. Happenings could be elaborate or quite simple. George Brecht's *Motor Vehicle Sundown* (1960), for instance, required its performers to drive to a prearranged spot at dusk and perform various activities, such as blowing horns, turning lights on or off and opening or closing doors. LaMonte Young's *Piano Piece for Terry Riley #1* (1960), by contrast, directed the performer to push a piano against a wall and keep pushing; the piece was over "when you are too exhausted to push any longer."[5]

Several of Young's early works explored the ramifications of holding a single note for a long time, and these compositions were to have a lasting impact on the music world. Among the first members of the Theatre of Eternal Music, an ensemble formed by Young in 1962 to perform his pieces, was Terry Riley, whose *In C* (1964) launched the Minimal music movement of the seventies and eighties. Indirectly, then, Philip Glass, Steve Reich and John Adams are Cage's heirs.

It is hard to say whether the avant-garde music of the fifties and sixties will ever attract a large following. Whatever their differences as compositional methods, serialism and chance have met with equally chilly receptions from mainstream audiences. Younger composers, eager to please their listeners, have embraced tradition as enthusiastically as Cage and his peers rejected it. Yet they are the greatest beneficiaries of the Cageian revolution, for no doors are closed to them: the legacy of the fifties and sixties is artistic freedom unprecedented in the history of music. □

John Cage and Merce Cunningham.
Photo: © Fred W. McDarrah.

The Redemption of the City in Postwar Avant-Garde Film

Paul Arthur

The city has been a principal subject in art since the birth of modernism in the late nineteeth century. Film theoretician Paul Arthur describes the "shared inventory of aesthetic concerns, image motifs and social practices" that linked avant-garde filmmakers of the fifties and sixties with New York "schools" of visual arts and poetry and contrasts these filmmakers' images of New York with earlier experiments in urban documentary. Postwar New York was the major cauldron in which new ideas in all the arts were being brewed during the fifties and sixties, so it seemed to be the natural home for those who wished to pose avant-garde cinematic alternatives to mainstream movies. It was also conveniently far from Hollywood, and independent filmmaker-auteurs used its literal distance—as well as its general aura of progressive culture—to stake out a claim for a film art far removed from West Coast conventions, whether in aesthetics or conditions of production. The example of the filmmakers—including Jonas Mekas and Ken Jacobs—and films Arthur discusses persists as a seductive model, one that has led, and continues to lead, to notable cinematic achievements "outside the system."

Above, Joseph Cornell's *Nymphlight* (1957). Photo courtesy of Anthology Film Archives.

Opposite, Joseph Cornell's *GniR RednoW* (1955–56). Photo courtesy of Anthology Film Archives.

Multitude, solitude: identical terms, and interchangeable by the active and fertile poet. The man who is unable to people his solitude is equally unable to be alone in a bustling crowd.
> Charles Baudelaire
> "Crowds"

Ever since that moment in 1895 when the Lumière brothers recorded, among their *fair divers*, workers leaving a factory, the demolition of a brick wall fronting a Parisian intersection and a woodcutter plying his trade on a busy avenue, cinema and the modern city have been locked in an unequal, yet mutually enhancing, embrace. To a greater degree than still photography a half-century before, cinema *required* the presence of an urban matrix at all stages in its ever-thickening economy, from the manufacture of equipment to image production to the marketing and consumption of product. The city presented itself as a material resource and as a site, a repository of "ready-made" iconography, themes, characters and abstract configurations perfectly commensurate with film's mechanical bases and cultural heritage. Just as the capitals and magnets of modern culture—Paris, New York, Berlin, Moscow—shaped cinematic aspirations in their own image, cinema reciprocated by supplying to a mass audience convictions about urban existence embedded in a throng of literary and pictorial representations and social theory texts. An unprecedented instrument of discovery, film in its projection of the city was caught from the outset in a dialectic of uncharted visual forms and received wisdom.

The observation that the postwar American avant-garde has promoted, and in turn been sustained by, a distinct discourse of the urban, a concatenation of traditional motifs and a challenging of historical conditions by which those motifs gained acceptance, is at once self-evident and insufficient. In the forty-five-year history of the movement, the city has not constituted simply one *topos* in a general program of subjective inscription and modernist formal invention. Rather, a polyvalent concept of urban-ness can be said to underwrite the entire trajectory of independent film as part of a shadow armature whose other wing is the Hollywood industry. In an important sense, this work is *about* the city: a reification of its power and complexity, a transient sign of its personal nourishment and communal possibility. Even at the avant-garde's most determinedly pastoral—in films by Stan Brakhage, Bruce Baillie or Carolee Schneemann—the urban imprint in and of the filmic apparatus tempers visions of Romantic isolation in nature. And here the pressures exerted by, in Leo Marx's phrase, "the machine in the garden," are more pronounced than those of the locomotive rumbling in back of Thoreau's pond.[1]

The figuring of urban space and social relations is rarely a matter of direct reflection; it encompasses any number of textual levels and procedures. The city can be realized as a descriptively concrete surface of shapes and movements, a specific place caught at a given moment in history. But it is as frequently a byproduct of assertive or formulaic editing patterns, a residue of narrative evacuation, a rhetoric anchored in American anti-urban political philosophy or that same "sad city of the imagination" rehearsed in countless allegorical depictions since the Industrial Revolution. Celebrations of speed, density and heterogeneity (Joseph Cornell's *GniR RednoW*) are coextensive with figments of an eschatological ground-zero (Peter Emanuel Goldman's *Pestilent City*). As might be expected given the movement's bohemian origins and cultural positioning, what is absent is any semblance of overt class analysis or coherent social critique. For the avant-garde, irrespective of tone or mode of address, the city is by definition fragmentary, a collection of marginalized spaces and alienated perspectives.

Nonetheless, if these films have consistently refused the burdens of the synoptic, the explanatory, in reference to their urban situation, the city has hardly been consigned to "illegibility"[2] as a visual signifier. Expressive personal itineraries build skeins of association among otherwise diffuse details of the environment—the "poetic" mandate of the early avant-garde. In the Structural mode of the sixties and seventies, in which poetic linkage as well as narrative incident were suppressed in favor of foregrounded analogies

Peter Emanuel Goldman, 1965.
Photo: © Fred W. McDarrah.

between spatial articulation and the mechanisms of cinema, nonexpressive grids recast bare interiors and street scenes as mirrors for a cinematic ontology. The diarist, like the *flâneur*, merges self with society in the spontaneous rush of commonplace incident and glance; the practitioners of punk and deconstructive narrative mine conventions accumulated by mass culture around urban violence and sexuality. For various segments of the American avant-garde, the city is a master text to be read both with and against the material constraints of noncommercial production. And processes of reading tend to oscillate between two traditional tropes: the city as machine and the city as organism.[3]

Like *film noir* (that other great postwar visual manifestation of urban America), the avant-garde assimilates in haphazard fashion principles of social ecology posited in the reformist theories of the Chicago School and popularized by an entire generation of fictional and journalistic writing.[4] Attuned to Robert Park's well-known assertion that the city is a "state of mind," a body of organized attitudes and beliefs inhering in a set of customs, the avant-garde forges as it documents through the act of filming (supplemented by editing, publicizing, screening, etc.) a community of loosely bound, at times conflictual, interests. Although more abstract than a geographic neighborhood, avant-garde film binds its subjects and objects in a struggle against the encroachment of formalized controls, the administered "facelessness" of the postindustrial city. Due in part to the indexical nature of the medium, and because the economic stakes in this enterprise are so slight, there is practically no ground for the distant observer, the stance of touristic neutrality. Avant-garde filmmakers become, willy-nilly, urban activists—albeit in a profoundly conservative register—shoring up the ruins of *gemeinschaft*, of clan values

Christmas 1961: Eugene Archer, Adolfas Mekas, Sheldon Rochlin, Jonas Mekas, Emile de Antonio, from Jonas Mekas' film diaries. Photo courtesy of Anthology Film Archives.

Right, Jonas Mekas. Photo courtesy of Walker Art Center.

and face-to-face contact, in the very heart of decentered affiliation, a condition Carl Schorske calls "permanent transience."[5]

If the avant-garde's composite mapping of the look and ambient energies of the city must be granted a sociological dimension beyond the subcultural documentation of groups such as the Beats and punks,[6] its field of exploration is largely reducible to a single site, New York. A cursory glance at institutional canons convened around avant-garde film—the collection of Anthology Film Archives, the Whitney Museum's Biennial programs, the holdings of The Museum of Modern Art—reveals the vast majority of artists working in and around American society's embodiment of the "other": New York, defined in the popular imagination as the emblem of "difference, diversity and conflict."[7] San Francisco and Los Angeles constitute a second echelon with another half-dozen cities, including Chicago, Denver and Akron, gaining sporadic representation in the work of individual filmmakers.

There are manifold historical as well as cultural implications to the primacy of New York, but whatever else it may signify, the overlapping of film with the development of postwar "Schools" of New York poetry and painting points to a shared inventory of aesthetic concerns, image motifs and social practices. This complex relationship is one of the principal subtexts of Jonas Mekas' signal diary films. Until the mid-sixties this confluence helped frame the meeting ground of high modernism and a precarious urbanism.[8] Since that period, differences both among proliferating styles in independent film and between film and adjacent "avant-garde" arenas have become increasingly marked. Yet while New York as a figure for imaginative reconstitution has flared and abated in other arts, it has remained a more-or-less constant issue at the cinematic margins.

This last point raises the specter of documentary as a genre. In what ways can the American avant-garde be construed as a branch of documentary practice whose primary, though not exclusive, focus is the visual patterning of New York? The abiding aesthetic precedent of the European avant-garde of the twenties—its interest in dream and subjectivity, image distortion and the metaphoric properties of montage—has been elaborated with conviction and great gusto by P. Adams Sitney in his book *Visionary Film*.[9] Unacknowledged in Sitney's widely accepted account are myriad connections with the "city symphony" documentaries of the twenties and early thirties, a group of films interlaced both formally and culturally with the more abstractive tendencies of Fernand Léger, Jean Cocteau, et. al. Not only do the poetic urban essays of Walter Ruttman, Joris Ivens, Alberto Cavalcanti and Dziga Vertov reflexively align the energies of the modern city with the material bases of cinema, they foreshadow the double axis of image organization codified by the postwar movement into separate, highly visible and competing styles: spontaneous diarylike recording of objects, places or urban "pathways"; and rationalized schema for the dissection (in shooting, editing, and/or postproduction) of quotidian urban locations.

Prototypically, the city symphony's disjunct collection of non-narrativized detail is secured within the rigid physical parameters of a single space and, frequently, ordered by natural laws of the diurnal cycle. Like much of the later avant-garde, the city symphonies

Alfred Leslie. Photo: © Fred W. McDarrah.

Sally Gross, Alice Neel and Mooney Pebbles in Jack Kerouac, Robert Frank and Alfred Leslie's *Pull My Daisy* (1959). Photo courtesy of Walker Art Center.

Helen Levitt, Janice Loeb and James Agee's *In the Street* (1952). Photo courtesy of The Museum of Modern Art Film Stills Archive.

Michael Snow's *Wavelength* (1966–67). Photo courtesy of The Museum of Modern Art Film Stills Archive.

evolve structures that are dependent neither upon fictionalized characters and incidents nor upon purely abstract linkages between shapes and movements. Moreover, while not uncritical of the social realities they trumpet through formal innovation, neither do they engage in the left-liberal didacticism of Depression-era British and American documentaries such as Ralph Steiner and Willard Van Dyke's *The City* (1939). And although the moment of the city symphony in Europe was rapidly eclipsed by political exigencies and the solidification of national film industries, its American counterpart limns a thin but unbroken arc of urban celebration from Charles Sheeler and Paul Strand's *Manhatta* (1921) and Jay Leyda's *A Bronx Morning* (1931) to the postwar merging of avant-garde and documentary impulses in Helen Levitt, Janice Loeb and James Agee's *In the Street* (1952), Frank Stauffacher's *Sausalito* (1947) and *Notes on the Port of St. Francis* (1952), Francis Thompson's *N.Y., N.Y.* (1957), Shirley Clarke's *Bridges-Go-Round* (1958) and *Skyscraper* (1959) and the entire roster of Rudy Burckhardt's New York sketches, among others. In any adequate assessment of the postwar avant-garde, it is incumbent that such "city films," and the socio-aesthetic concerns they articulate, be superimposed over the experimental tradition said to flow from Jack Kerouac, Robert Frank and Alfred Leslie's *Pull My Daisy* (1959) and the early work of Stan Brakhage, Kenneth Anger, Marie Menken, Jack Smith and Ken Jacobs.

Jacobs in particular frequently has presented himself as a participant-observer in subcultural rituals constituted in equal measure by chance upheavals and the constraints of sociological demarcation. His attitudes are exemplified in this production note to *The Winter Footage* (1964/84):

> We lived alongside the Manhattan side of the Brooklyn Bridge, a ghost town nights and weekends. A big walker and looker, I became familiar with many objects comprising our neighborhood and invited them to the cine-dance I threw. Framing drew them together and split them in ways they could never understand but together we achieved some animation.[10]

Aside from whatever sustenance the avant-garde drew from the long chain of urban representation in film, there are demonstrable social and economic factors that condition the movement's obsessive, disparate treatment of the American cityscape—and these in

Ken Jacobs, 1979. Photo courtesy of Walker Art Center.

part help to distinguish the terrain of the avant-garde from that of documentary. One factor might be called the conflation of workplace, home and social environment, a predicament in direct opposition to the general profile of modern urban development. Quite simply, a substantial block of the most generative films confine themselves to a timely observation of their makers' immediate surroundings. Deflected versions of the depiction of the artist's studio, they do not sally forth into nature or other uncharted regions but hunker down in lofts, gaze from apartment windows or navigate the streets below waiting for (or actively engendering) a camera "event." This ingrown scrutiny, of which Warhol's Factory is the hyperbolic instance, shapes conditions of possibility for a spectrum that includes Jacobs, the Kuchar brothers, Ernie Gehr, Hollis Frampton, Andrew Noren and Michael Snow.

What inevitably passes in front of the lens, regardless of how it is spontaneously or retroactively arranged, bears the marks of an urban matrix. Without sinking into triviality, Manny Farber's gnomic comment that *Wavelength* (1966–67) is "a straightforward document of a room in which a dozen businesses have lived and gone bankrupt"[11] applies, with slight variations, to literally dozens of films. The detritus of Snow's loft and the clogged commercial street seen through its windows are scarcely neutral or contingent. They are not subdued into a purely conceptual logic by camera movement or by transformations in film stock and color. Rather, they actively mediate the creation of meaning, sparking all manner of correspondences with the work of the cinematic machinery and the consciousness behind it.

Something similar can be claimed for the settings of Gehr's minimalist urban ethnography, his intensified weighing and repatterning of familiar components of street movement studied from a window.[12] If in Gehr's work—and at times that of Jacobs, Noren, Barry Gerson and David Rimmer—the gaze of the observer retreats into long-held armchair contemplation, the charge of immediate, integral correspondence between the dailiness of the camera's vantage and the repetitive activities passing before it identifies the product of urban perceptual dynamics as a sort of crypto-cottage industry (not wholly removed from the ranks of disenfranchised, lower-class women dubbed "professional" street watchers).

The case is only slightly different for makers who mingle the filming of their own domiciles with recorded wanderings in the neighborhood or the city at large. Jonas Mekas reports from his earliest experiences: "If one has a camera and wants to master it, then one begins to film in the street or in the apartment."[13] In Mekas' diaries, as in some

Ken Jacobs' *Little Stabs at Happiness* (1959–63). Photo courtesy of the filmmaker.

of Frampton's predesigned encounters with the city, public spaces are returned to a private realm through an excess of expressive—or systemic—marks. Like the Situationist *dérive*, but without its pervasive boredom and alienation, the restaging of street life calls forth what Michel de Certeau refers to as "perambulatory optics," the formalizing of pedestrian movement as a counterweight to the panoptic power of vertical icons.[14]

A second factor reinforcing the avant-garde's conflation of social with personal patterning is the disjunction of sound and image or the absence of sound altogether. The increased costs of sound recording, mixing and printing, along with the relative inaccessibility of synchronous sound units, predispose filmmakers away from the fullness of a realist urban representation. Language is curtailed; no one speaks from or *for* the streets—not even, since the mid-sixties, the ubiquitous jazz scores which primed the eye and the emotions with rhythmic equivalencies for social interaction. Walter Benjamin, tracking Baudelaire, remarked that contact in the modern city favors the eye over the ear.[15] In these films, expected aural signs of the city's complexity, its impenetrability and depersonalization, are withheld or temporally displaced or replaced by nonmimetic elements.[16] Although in certain periods the disconnection of sight and sound has bolstered the avant-garde's cult of the autonomous image, it has paradoxically worked to sharpen sociological subtexts through the defamiliarizing of everyday events. What emerges is a visual field constantly oscillating between historical specificity and a "theoretical" appropriation of urban spatial distribution moored in concepts of a marginalized self. In this way, architectures as well as passersby maintain the bearing of a particular

Jonas Mekas' *Reminiscences of a Journey to Lithuania* (1971–72). Photo courtesy of Anthology Film Archives.

moment and social denotation as they participate in a reflexive operation of formal leveling.

Although it is risky to generalize about such internally diverse and culturally mismatched areas of artistic production, American avant-garde film is notably distinct in its urban address from, say, the contemporary novel or postwar painting and sculpture. They may all in one fashion or another "inhabit" the same milieu, drawing form or content from the decaying physical core of industrial capital (Tama Janowitz as well as Franz Kline). They may express the problematic nature of the urban subject through strategies of decentering and fragmentation or, alternatively, through upholding the discredited rubric of a unique self-as-style.[17] And in accord with their respective materials, the place of language and the linearity it affords can be rendered as insufficient or debased or merely solipsistic. Yet nothing in literature or the objecthood of art at once resists its own commodification—commercial, institutional or both—and maintains a direct spatial *orientation* in the city as does avant-garde film. In the collapse of mode of production, community dynamics and aesthetic axiom, this movement has constituted an imaginary history of urban life, a decidedly unofficial account whose thrust has been equally one of deciphering and renewal. □

Ken Jacobs' *Star Spangled To Death* (1957–69). Photo courtesy of the filmmaker.

ART IN EUROPE AND AMERICA

The 1960s and 1970s

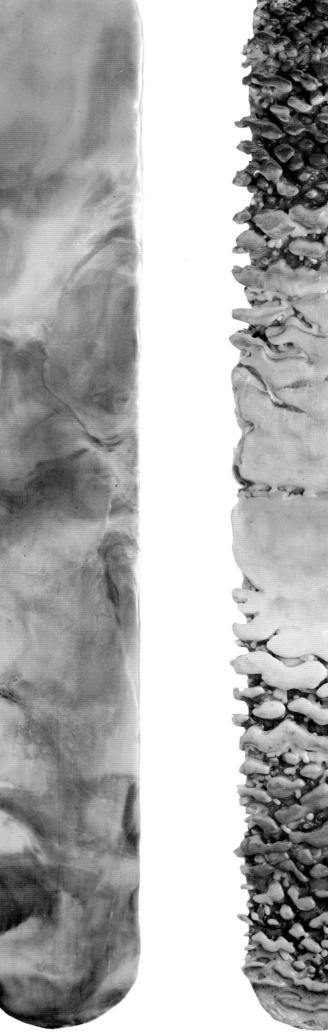

Lynda Benglis
Untitled 1968
encaustic-damar resin on masonite
36" x 4 ½"
Collection of Nancy and George Rosenfeld.
Photo: Fredrik Marsh.

Lynda Benglis
Plum 1971
purified pigmented beeswax and damar resin
on masonite and wood
35" x 5 ⅛" x 2 ¾"
Collection of Mr. and Mrs. Harry W. Anderson.
Photo: Fredrik Marsh.

Art in Europe and America
The 1960s and 1970s

*Obscenity is a moral concept in the verbal arsenal of the Establishment,
which abuses the term by applying it, not to the expressions of its own
morality, but to those of another. Obscene is not the picture of a naked
woman who exposes her pubic hair, but that of a fully-clad general who
exposes his medals rewarded in the war of aggression; obscene is not
the ritual of Hippies, but the declaration of a high dignitary of the
church that war is necessary for peace. Linguistic therapy, that is, the
effort to free words (and thereby concepts) from the all but total
distortion of their meanings by the Establishment, demands the transfer
of moral standards (and their validation) from the Establishment to the
revolt against it. Similarly, the sociological and political vocabulary must
be radically reshaped: it must be stripped of its false neutrality; it must
be methodically and provocatively "moralized" in terms of the Refusal.*
Herbert Marcuse
An Essay on Liberation

Marcuse's statement is clearly of its moment, 1968, but his thoughts transcend the
intervening years to reflect issues current in the last decade of the twentieth century. In
selecting this passage to introduce my comments on avant-garde art in the sixties and
seventies, I want to highlight such parallels, as well as the pervasive spirit of liberation
and anarchy Marcuse addresses. This spirit critically shaped the sixties and seventies and
so was crucial to many of the artists discussed in this second part of *Breakthroughs*.

The immediate postwar period was a time of reconstruction, of knitting life back
together, of trying to find—or manufacture—security. The fifties brought the tensions of
the Cold War to Europe and America and, as a defense against remembered and anticipated upheavals, political and social conservatism that emphasized family structures and
the home. Those conservative values were challenged in the sixties, and the resulting
polarizations shaped the seventies. Civil rights, women's rights and anti–Vietnam War
movements in the United States and the insurrections of 1968 in both Eastern and
Western Europe denounced established power structures, proposed radical alternatives
and sometimes encountered violent reactions. These eruptions served as catalysts,
opening the way for change. Economic and social systems based on inequality and racism
were questioned; the elements of the family and the role of women came under discussion. The use of drugs to "expand" the mind, as well as the acceptance of contraception,
proposed freedom as a physical and biological necessity, part of a new fabric in society.
As Marcuse's comments suggest, the effort to free ideas from rejected "Establishment"
values became a moral imperative. Liberation was the order of the day.

In the arts as in the social arena, impulses toward liberation often took the form of
challenges to perceived establishments. During the fifties and early sixties, artists on both
sides of the Atlantic challenged the relatively unified hegemony of American Abstract
Expressionism and European Art Informel (or Informalism). Their explorations led, on one
hand, to Pop art and Nouveau Réalisme and, on the other, to the Color Field painting
championed by Clement Greenberg and to Minimalism. In the later sixties and seventies,
the impersonal logic of Minimalism and the cool formality Greenberg prized became
particular targets for artists who again rejected an artistic establishment in favor of an
eclectic variety of individual expressions—the pluralism characteristic of the seventies.

The most pervasive establishment convention in the arts existed implicitly in the
"frames" of painting and the self-contained closure of sculptural objects. If artists in the
fifties created chaos inside the frame with a desire to destroy order (as in the works of
Willem de Kooning, Lucio Fontana or Piero Manzoni), artists in the sixties and seventies
took that chaos outside the frame and, in some cases, brought it into the streets. Lynda
Benglis, Joseph Beuys, Jannis Kounellis and Robert Smithson broke through the conventional frames of painting and sculptural objects. Performance art, which denied the
limitations of frames in its multidisciplinary expansiveness, flourished as an independent

art genre. Allan Kaprow staged his Happening *Bon Marché* in a Parisian department store; Adrian Piper took the actions of her persona performances onto subways and street corners. Painting, at least on wall-mounted canvases, took a back seat—albeit temporarily—to the sprawling contours of earthworks and installations, the "dematerializations" of Conceptual art and the living energy of performance art. In one of the essays accompanying this section of *Breakthroughs*, Walter Grasskamp notes that the self-given command to "give up painting" had special urgency for a number of youthful German artists in the sixties—a notable irony given the role of German art in painting's resurgence at the end of the seventies.

Avant-garde artists of the sixties and seventies seemed to delight in confronting icons, and they did not limit their attention to those held sacred by the art world. Particularly in the late sixties and seventies, many European and American artists took part in the larger struggles for liberation and empowerment Marcuse's statement reflects, and attitudes in the arts were affected by these struggles as well. Joseph Beuys made political activism an intrinsic part of his artistic persona, as Grasskamp notes, reintroducing political commentary in German art and serving as a model for both European and American artists. Women artists and artists of color found increased exhibition possibilities and critical exposure in the climate created by the feminist and civil rights movements. Sculptors Lynda Benglis and Louise Bourgeois, for example, received recognition in the light of interests in women's art, though their significance is scarcely limited to their identity as "women artists." Visual artists incorporated political agendas and specifically feminist, gay and lesbian and multicultural viewpoints into their works. Similar concerns motivated many performing and media artists, as both Sally Banes and B. Ruby Rich point out in their essays.

The Happenings presented by Kaprow and other artists and the interdisciplinary events of the international Fluxus group—both providing the groundwork for the development of performance art—typified the restless energy of the sixties and the imperative need to free artistic ideas and practices from their conventional frames. The Fluxus artists, like the earlier Dadaists, sought to confront what they saw as the vacuity of formalist aesthetics and to resurrect the potential for effecting social or political change through art. The interests of Fluxus are represented in this section through the work of Nam June Paik and Joseph Beuys. Both artists participated in the Fluxus events of the sixties and drew on these experiences to develop their own intermedia modes of expression.

Paik's multifaceted interests in music, performance, video and visual art led him to combine a range of new media. He showed his first television sculptures in a 1963 exhibition at the Galerie Parnass, a center of Fluxus activity, in Wuppertal, West Germany. Two years later in New York, he learned to use a portable video camera, then newly available, to shoot his own videotapes. The unstable images of television crept into stable homes during the fifties and sixties, and Paik played with this irony, attracted by the dualities of the safe and the unsafe, the static and the transitory, that television offered him. In *Magnet TV* (1965), the TV screen stands in for a canvas, replacing television's narrative and representational images with abstract patterns controlled by manipulating a magnet positioned on top of the set. In *TV Buddha* (1974) a wooden statue of the Buddha sits in front of a space-age television set that reflects its image, mirroring itself in a contemplative stare. Here Paik addressed the contrasts between an ancient culture and a modern one, a culture steeped in tradition and one obsessed with speed, movement and transformation.

Joseph Beuys presented himself as a visionary shaman with a personal, almost messianic, mission to work for utopian, humanistic goals. In his performances, installations and objects, he often combined mechanical or industrial materials with organic substances—fat, felt, wax—suggesting the need for a corrective balance in a world becoming too dehumanizing. *Scala Napoletana* (1986), Beuys' last major work, provides another kind of comment on the tenuousness of human existence. This work consists of a very delicate ladder—a type used for picking oranges—held upright by wires anchored to a lead ball on each side. The title refers to the Italian city of Naples, whose steep, narrow staircases were placed in jeopardy by a major earthquake in the early eighties. Beuys suggests parallels between the city's vulnerable position and the sculpture's precarious and transitory balance. At the same time, the work is an unmistakable reminder of the virile male within this fragile female city; Beuys' image suggests both a compassionate homage and a violation.

Jannis Kounellis, an artist associated with Italian Arte Povera, also creates metaphoric installations of unexpected objects, using symbols that represent his Greek and Roman heritage and combining social and aesthetic references. Elements of fire and music have been central to his work since the fifties. In *Untitled* (1980), he attached propane gas torches to seven musical instruments: cello, mandolin, flute, trumpet, drum, violin and trombone. Kounellis explored the connections between music and communication and the familiar associations of each instrument. A flute is phallic in shape yet "feminine" in its lightness of tone; a cello is "feminine" in shape but "masculine" in its voice. Music, as one of the arts, is associated with creativity; fire suggests the transformation of reality and the breakdown of rigidity. Kounellis' untitled installation, like many of his works, embodies ideals of personal anarchy and revolution akin to those referred to by Marcuse.

Sensitivity to political and social fragmentation forms a bond between Kounellis and the American sculptor Robert Smithson. In both artists' works transformation is opposed by inertia, entropy by order. The late sixties saw their paths crossing: each artist combined steel structures (the rational material of Minimalism) with coal and earth (the elemental materials of process art and Arte Povera). Kounellis eventually abandoned the use of these rational elements, but Smithson continued such contrasts in his "nonsites," interior installations of rocks, gravel, dirt and, often, mirrors. In one such "nonsite," *Gravel Mirror with Cracks and Dust* (1968), the reflective property of the mirrors jolts the disorder of gravel into perfect symmetry. Order and disorder, the rational and the irrational, collide. Excavated by Smithson from the foundation of an abandoned hospital in New Jersey, the gravel evokes awareness of time's passage through its references to past usage.

Lynda Benglis' poured pieces recall Smithson's *Asphalt Rundown* (1969), in which he poured a load of asphalt down an eroded hillside in Italy, or his *Partially Buried Wood-shed* (1970), in which he heaped earth over a former tool shed on the Kent State University campus. Though Benglis worked with synthetic and Smithson with natural materials, both produced metaphorical volcanos erupting uncontrollably, unframed and unconstrained. The sensuality and colorful exuberance of Benglis' works reveled in the gestural instincts of Abstract Expressionism, rejecting the rigidity of Minimalist sculpture. While the Minimalists economized and reduced, Benglis and Smithson accumulated and dispersed. In the poured pieces, Benglis proposed an alternative to the cold facture of Minimalism with the hot aesthetics of flowing lava.

Many of Benglis' works, such as her wax paintings, have an intense tactile appeal in materials and forms that viewers feel compelled to fondle. Others recall the organic and tactile forms of the Surrealists Jean Arp and Joan Miró. But while the Surrealists sought to explore the unconscious, Benglis investigates the consciousness of being a female artist in the male-dominated art world. As Donald Judd was controlling and compressing power inside the body with his rigidity, Benglis was doing the opposite—letting her power out as an artistic and personal statement of liberation.

Louise Bourgeois directs the idea of personal liberation specifically toward the body. This preoccupation is evident in her sculptures' sensuous forms—suggestive of fingers, phalluses and breasts—and materials: bronze, plaster, marble, rubber, wood and plastic. Her sculptures reveal a direct and often shocking investigation of the body as an un-known erotic territory. *Janus in Leather Jacket* (1968–71) addresses issues of anxiety and pleasure, entrapment and independence, in a bronze, double-phallus form, which refers by its title to the two-headed god of classical mythology, and hangs from the ceiling as if it were a slab of meat in meat locker. Again Bourgeois' work looks to Arp and Miró, this time in a more direct correlation to the Surrealists' study of the unconscious.

Paik, Beuys, Kounellis, Smithson, Benglis and Bourgeois all offer clear rebuttals to Minimalist art's insistence on impersonal, unified order. Tensions between Minimalism and alternative tendencies more concerned with disorderly process or personal expression form a strong connecting thread in the essays in this second part of *Breakthroughs*. Germano Celant reflects on this contrast in terms of disparate European and American approaches to art making. Kenneth Baker, Carter Ratcliff and Lucy Lippard find contradic-tions to the formalist precepts of Minimalism in the directions taken by American artists such as Smithson, Benglis or Bourgeois, whether chosen as a form of opposition (as might be said of Smithson or Benglis) or developed independently in a continuation of earlier lines of inquiry (as might be said of Bourgeois). Baker and Ratcliff also note that even the artists often discussed under the general umbrella of Minimalism did not form a mono-lithic totality.

During the sixties Agnes Martin's work was often interpreted through analogies with Minimalism, but her paintings also have affinities to those of the Abstract Expressionists. Her grids naturally denote order, but her pencil, ink or brush opens subtle textural differences within the framework of regularity. The canvas and the pencil produce infinite grids, as lines create infinite space in both directions. Her work's elusive visuals open it into areas of the spiritual. Martin's work is positioned between order and chaos and so can be linked both to earlier traditions of expressionism and to Minimalism.

Donald Judd's sculpture is the antithesis of this hybrid, the most concrete example discussed here of Minimal forms and ideas. Each of Judd's works contains a totality of

Nam June Paik
Magnet TV 1965
black and white, 17-inch television set with magnet
28 ⅜" x 19 ¼" x 24 ½"
Whitney Museum of American Art, New York;
purchase, with funds from Dieter Rosenkranz,
86.60a-b.
Photos: Robert E. Mates.

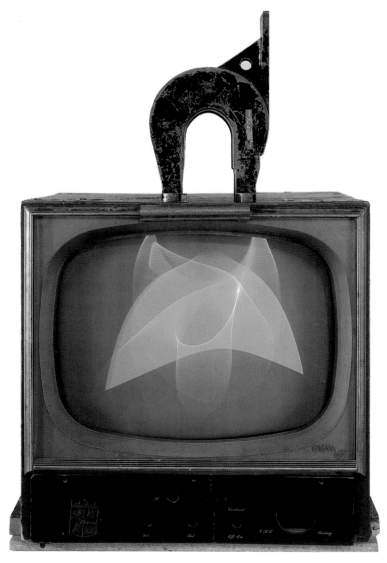

color, surface and volume controlled by a completely balanced and unified system. This unity can be attributed to his industrial materials and the hands-off process with which he works. By contrast, Martin's hands-on approach distances her work from pure Minimalism. In Judd's *Untitled* (1965), a horizontal "progression" fabricated in lacquer paint on aluminum, hues of cadmium red and purple reveal this artist's affection for color and materials even in the midst of Minimal reductions. *Untitled* (1966), a single boxlike volume, again shows the artist's concern for sensuality joined with his concurrent passion for the ordered and systematic. This self-contained unit of amber plexiglass and stainless steel invites viewers to an internal dialogue as they are faced with their own shimmering reflection within the void.

A concern with process, which links Americans such as Smithson or Benglis with Europeans such as Beuys or Kounellis, offered one possible response to the impersonal tenor of Minimal art. By contrast, Conceptual artists such as John Baldessari built on this tendency. Avoiding any sensuality of materials, Baldessari employs any variety of media—photography, text, film, video, books, drawings, paintings and any combination of the above—that allows him to concentrate on information. His work is situated between the banal and the profound, between the language of Los Angeles and Hollywood and the language of Duchamp and Wittgenstein. In his deadpan text paintings from the late sixties, Baldessari sends messages about the structure of representation and of art, posing humorous questions and answers about ideas of subject matter, space and how to examine a picture, as if he were giving grade-school art history lessons.

More traditional approaches to painting experienced a significant revival in the late seventies and early eighties. In the United States, this trend was nourished by concurrent developments in Europe and by reactions against the depersonalized and rational aesthetics of Minimalism and Conceptual art. Susan Rothenberg's embrace of one favored motif—the horse—recalls Jasper Johns' iconic usage of common images as a ground for formal explorations of media and techniques. Rothenberg's horses are not drawn from real life; they are impressions that look as if they were painted in a dream state. In this way, they are personal and emotional icons, addressing the sensations, more than the objective properties, of color and form.

Sigmar Polke's paintings reflect the changing language of art more clearly than do Rothenberg's stable and formalist paintings. Polke's appropriations of familiar images to canvas aligns him with the American Pop artists and the postwar boom of consumer products and the media. His interest in popular images and cultural icons leaves him open to all representational modes and styles. Squeezed, as were the Dadaists in the early part of this century, between high and low art, kitsch and irony, Polke pokes fun at Minimalism, Conceptualism and abstraction, producing canvases that employ those very concepts. His signature technique—a choreographic application of paint on such appro-priated materials as photographs, wallpaper and printed fabrics—allows him to employ an endless variety of materials and styles. Although his work may appear scattered, random and without order, he is a prime example of a postmodern artist whose investi-gations are rooted in the reorganization of established conventions in painting.

Despite renewed interests in painting, other image-making approaches remained strong in the late seventies and early eighties and often drew on the same postmodern eclecticism of sources and techniques: narration, appropriation and compilation. For a number of artists, issues of identity related to gender, race and sexual orientation became paramount. The British team of Gilbert and George, who began collaborating in 1968, shifted the focus of their work during the seventies from performance tableaux as "living sculptures" to large-scale photocollages that often address homosexuality. In these compositions, Gilbert and George are still frequent subjects, acting as dandy, voyeur, anonymous bystander or active participant. Often gridlike in format, the composite images confront the vanity and the banality, the beauty and the bad taste that exist simultaneously in contemporary life. *Lick* (1977), from the *Dirty Words* series, shows its title as a graffiti inscription on the top half of a twelve-panel grid. The composition's central, black-and-white sections depict life on the street and behind barbed wire in a very forthright manner. Clad in dandy fashion, Gilbert and George stand at the sides, as if they were two red bookends framing the composition, looking out and across at each other.

As Gilbert and George raise the question of identity in a generic and open way, Adrian Piper raises the question of her own individual identity: as visual artist, performer, writer, professor; and as a female from a racially mixed background. Piper's performances and artworks always define herself, as well as the community in which she lives. Her projects can be consciously offensive or moving, but they are almost always unsettling. The multimedia environment *Four Intruders Plus Alarm System*s (1980) demonstrates Piper's approach to social commentary and the freewheeling use of varied stimuli she developed in her performances. In this installation, Piper places four light-boxed images of black men into a small, roomlike space where funk music blares. At four listening stations, visitors to this installation listen to tape-recorded monologues of racist comments. Piper reveals and critiques the racist attitudes of contemporary society and, by exposing these attitudes, forces viewers to confront their own prejudices as a first step toward overcoming them. In her refusal to accept limitations—whether imposed by the conventions of art or by a racist society—Piper exemplifies the demand for liberation that characterized art in the sixties and seventies.

Claudia Gould

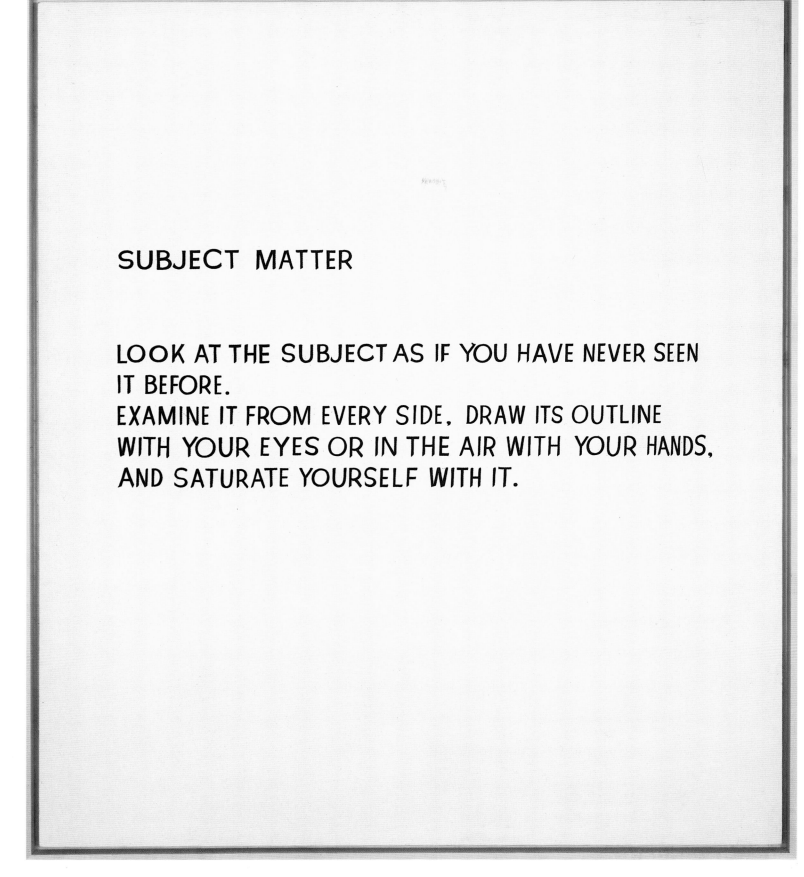

John Baldessari
Subject Matter 1967
acrylic on canvas
67 ¾" x 56 ½"
Courtesy Sonnabend Gallery, New York.
Photo: Fred Scruton, New York.

Louise Bourgeois
Janus in Leather Jacket 1968
bronze
12" x 22" x 6 ½"
Courtesy Robert Miller Gallery, New York.
Photo: Fredrik Marsh.

Joseph Beuys
Scala Napoletana 1985
wooden ladder and two spheres of lead
176" x 10"; diameter of spheres, 20"
Estate of Joseph Beuys; courtesy of Lucio Amelio,
Naples, Italy.
Photo: Fredrik Marsh.

Louise Bourgeois
Rondeau for L 1963
bronze
ll" x ll" x l0 ½"
Courtesy Robert Miller Gallery, New York.
Photo: Peter Bellamy.

Clean Slates

Kenneth Baker

In the following essay Kenneth Baker highlights a central dilemma facing artists in the early sixties: what to do after the boundary-battering example of Jackson Pollock's painting? How could an American avant-garde redefine itself in the gap between European tradition and Pollock's negative retort to it? One answer was to turn away from nakedly expressive painting completely, as Donald Judd did with his industrially fabricated, geometrically controlled objects. Another possibility was to delve into the intensely personal, as Louise Bourgeois did with her idiosyncratic sculptures. Agnes Martin combined ordered materiality and individual spirituality to create a third alternative, a painting beyond stylistic programmatics. Author of Minimalism *(1989), a contributing editor of* Artforum *and art critic for the* San Francisco Chronicle, *Baker focuses on a trio of artists whose varied styles, even during the height of Minimalism, point toward the pluralistic avant-garde of the seventies.*

Many artists who began careers in New York late in the fifties had the feeling that they were bringing up the end of the parade. Above all, many felt acutely the peculiar pressure of starting out in the wake of Jackson Pollock, who died in the wreck of his car in 1956, apparently with his best work several years behind him. Pollock personified the possibility of making good America's distance from the ancestral culture of Europe, which could neither be imitated nor fully assimilated. Pollock's big paintings of the early fifties had an American scale and self-sufficiency, but they did not imply obvious next steps. For New York painters coming into their own around 1960, Pollock was almost as large and unanswerable a figure as Picasso had been to Pollock and his generation.

The Color Field painting of Helen Frankenthaler, Morris Louis, Kenneth Noland and others began to be touted as a step beyond the most important work of Pollock, but few young painters believed in it. "I think Pollock's a greater artist than anyone working at the time or since," wrote Donald Judd in 1967, after more than a decade's activity in New York as artist and critic. "The idea that Frankenthaler, Louis, Noland and Olitski form a line of advance from Pollock is ridiculous." Judd (who was born in 1928) painted abstractly all through the late fifties, after receiving an undergraduate degree in philosophy from Columbia and studying intermittently at the Art Students League. He never mimicked Pollock's technique, but tried to make paintings that had the objective intensity he admired in Pollock. Whereas the painting of other so-called Abstract Expressionists, such as Willem de Kooning and Mark Rothko, was identified with their "hands" and therefore with their personal emotions, Pollock literally detached himself from his paint by flinging and dripping it onto the canvas. Judd sought his own route to the combination of artistic power and detachment he saw in Pollock's art. He pursued it first in painting, then in objects that have earned the appellation "sculpture," but which, when they were first made, inhabited a no man's land between mediums. Concurrently, Judd sharpened his thinking and earned a modest income by writing criticism for *Arts* magazine and *Art International*.

Judd's paintings from about the turn of the sixties yearn for concreteness. He mixed sand and wax with his paint to give his surfaces greater density and painted on panels so he could router lines into their surfaces. He built flanges at the edges of his paintings and wedged relief elements into their surfaces, all in an effort to surmount their pictorial character. The formats of his paintings tended to be simple curved or striated patterns of lines grooved into monochromatic surfaces. No matter what he tried, he could not surmount the seemingly arbitrary quality of composition in painting nor the implied emotional tremors of relations between figures and ground. As long as paintings had interior space—a fictive interior of any sort—they seemed ineluctably to evoke the inner lives of artists and spectators, which Judd believed consisted largely of tetherless fantasy. Perhaps it was a "period quality" of abstract painting that Judd struggled with, but quite a few other New York artists—such as Robert Ryman, Brice Marden and Ralph Humphrey—were trying at about the same time either to unmake or to isolate and empty the residual pictorial qualities of abstraction.

The industrially fabricated objects for which Judd has since become famous appear to be worlds away from painting. But in a 1967 article on Pollock for *Arts*, Judd himself hints at some connections. What made Pollock's work unique and epochal, Judd concluded, was that "he used paint and canvas in a new way…This use is one of the most important aspects of Pollock's work, as important as scale and wholeness…It's a different idea of generality, of how a painting is unified. It's a different idea of the disparity between parts or aspects and it's a different idea of sensation…The elements and aspects of Pollock's paintings are polarized rather than amalgamated. The work doesn't have the moderated a priori generality usual in painting. Everything is…specific and independent."

Judd wanted to make objects whose components would be "specific" and "polarized," that would be governed by, and would transmit, a "different idea of sensation" from the generalized notions of vision that most contemporary art—and the spectrum of contemporary culture—tenders. His whole oeuvre since 1965 may be viewed as a

Donald Judd, New York, 1970.
Photo: © Gianfranco Gorgoni.

Donald Judd
Untitled 1965
lacquer paint on aluminum
8 ¼" X 161" X 8 ¼"
Wexner Center for the Arts, The Ohio State University,
Columbus; purchased in part with funds from the
National Endowment for the Arts, 77.24.
Photo: Lynette Molnar.

campaign to undo false equivalences (between objects, perceptions, vantage points, persons) and generalizations that dim and impoverish available reality. Clarifying and giving structure to "the disparity between parts or aspects" of an object—or an ensemble of them—would become one of Judd's artistic principles.

In the early sixties Judd made a number of sculptural constructions himself, but by 1964 he had begun commissioning professional metalworkers to realize his designs for objects, a practice he has followed since. "In the three-dimensional work," he commented in *Arts* in 1965, still distancing himself from painting, "the whole thing is made according to complex purposes, and these are not scattered but asserted by one form…The several limits of painting are no longer present…Obviously, anything in three dimensions can be any shape, regular or irregular, and can have any relation to the wall, floor, ceiling, room, rooms or exterior, or none at all." Clarity of form and purpose have remained Judd's artistic ideals, no matter how many parts a particular work by him may have (some of his serial works are elaborate). For the aesthetics of notional composition and manual performance, he substituted the bald explicitness of geometry and of "one thing after another."

For all their divergences in style and content, there is an affinity between Judd's resort to industrial fabrication and the depersonalized silkscreen, transfer and stencil painting methods of Robert Rauschenberg, Andy Warhol and Roy Lichtenstein. All these artists (and many others) were involved—consciously or not—in rejecting the previous generation's glorification of the artist's hand and individual sensibility. They also rejected—for different reasons—the implications of transcendent meaning in Abstract Expressionist painting. While the Pop artists disparaged the transcendence of a realm of elitist values, Judd, Frank Stella, Carl Andre and Robert Ryman, among others who came to be called Minimalists, rejected the transcendence of rarefied psychological or other metaphysical dimensions in artist or spectator.

To Judd, the art object provided a material form for philosophical discourse. His sculptures do not evoke values and stances but embody them mutely in such a way that the viewer encountering these objects experiences himself as embodying ideas, not in harboring them inwardly, but in his most mundane and unselfconscious comportment and awareness of things. The starkness of an ensemble such as the untitled galvanized iron "stack" from 1966, or the similar aluminum "stacks" from a few years later, may cause the viewer to overlook the work's real claim on his attention. The progression of identical boxlike metal units, suspended from the wall, parallel to each other, at even intervals from floor to ceiling, is a device for recovering the perception of basic facts such as the number and distinctness of things, their separateness from each other and from the viewer's consciousness of them.

In an ideal installation, the intervals between the drawerlike boxes (and between the top and bottom elements and ceiling and floor, respectively) would be identical, so that the empty spaces and geometry of the piece would be "polarized" by their very similarity. Studying one of the "stacks" entails slowly disabusing oneself of the notion that all their components are the same. The adamant character of Judd's sculpture forces the viewer to learn to privilege actual perceptions over ideas (such as that of sameness) that abbreviate awareness and ultimately anesthetize him to the immediacy of existence. The idea of sameness erases the awareness of perceptions as conditioned by one's being a certain height, being floorbound and viewing things inferentially as a consequence. Thus Judd's sculpture can occasion the experience of inference and other mental powers as faculties of the body, as compensations for its limits of size and mobility.

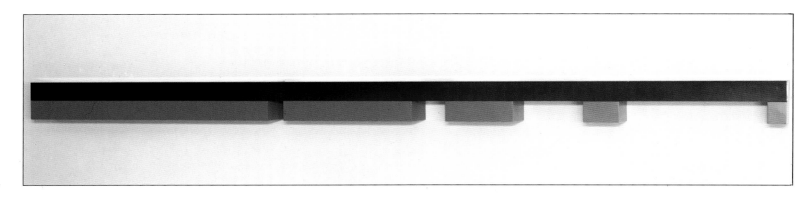

Donald Judd
Untitled 1969
anodized aluminium
114" x 27" x 24", ten units, each unit 6" x 27" x 24"
Walker Art Center, Minneapolis; gift of Mr. and Mrs.
Edmond R. Ruben, 1981.

Number and measure, repetition, variants and systematically changing intervals are common in Judd's work since the mid-sixties. They are not only factors he considers in designing objects of the utmost structural economy; they also discipline the attention of the patient viewer. In its material elegance and severity, Judd's sculpture appears to be about as disengaged as any American art of the postwar period. But his artistic project has been both critical and restorative. His art is a standing rejoinder to the numbing effects of mass production and mass media (that promote fantasies of equivalence between information and experience). It seeks to restore to us (or initiate us in) a taste for the concrete, for lucidity, economy and honesty in moment-to-moment perceptions and dealings with each other. Today this utopian quality of Judd's art is what brands it most obviously as the product of an increasingly discredited modernist sensibility. But despite the conversion of his art to glamour commodity (in which he has participated vigorously), the oppositional posture of his art remains valid. His work still holds up a mirror to the needless deceptiveness, specious differentiation and false promises of American society's material life.

•

Minimalism was a major current in New York art of the sixties and early seventies. But art of every stripe was being made behind the scenes staged by art-world media and institutions. With the rejection of formalist values in art and criticism, beginning late in the seventies, came a new appreciation of artists who had pursued personal visions during the decades when Clement Greenberg's views of the predestined progress of modern art were dominant. (Color Field painting, not Minimal art, was Greenberg's great hope for the future of American art, but in hindsight the two tendencies look equally formalistic.) One of the most admired artists to come in for new appreciation was Louise Bourgeois, who had been working away quietly in New York since she immigrated there following

Louise Bourgeois
The Blind Leading the Blind c. 1947
wood
84" x 88"
Courtesy Robert Miller Gallery, New York.
Becon Collection, Ltd.

her marriage to art historian Robert Goldwater, shortly before the Second World War.

In contrast to American-born artists like Judd, Bourgeois is a survivor of the modern calamities of Europe. Born in France in 1912, she suffered an unsettled early childhood as her mother, with her in tow, tried to follow her father wherever military service took him before and during the First World War. After the war, the family settled and reentered its business of making and restoring tapestries. As a girl, Bourgeois was assigned to draw the designs of portions (usually the bottom edges) of antique tapestries that had rotted away.

In the twenties she was sent to Paris to school; she studied mathematics at the Sorbonne and turned to art soon afterward. Her connections to Parisian modernism were direct: she learned painting from André Lhote, Amédée Ozenfant and Fernand Léger. Forced to live at home with her imperious father, she was still able to explore bohemian Paris and became fluent in English while working as a museum guide to American tourists. This job led to translation projects and her introduction to American art historian Robert Goldwater (1907–73), whom she soon married. With the threat of another world war imminent, she and her new husband moved to New York in 1938, where she joined a growing community of French émigré artists that would include Marcel Duchamp, André Masson, Léger and André Breton.

Ever reluctant to promote her work, Bourgeois exhibited sculpture for the first time in 1949; The Museum of Modern Art (which had showed some of her drawings in 1943) bought a sculpture by her the following year. Exhibition opportunities occurred sporadically over the following two decades.

Bourgeois' sculpture has always been highly personal, recognizably autobiographical in inspiration and often hermetic, even to herself. In the mid-seventies, a new audience for her work emerged, its appreciation tinged with feminist ardor to admit values and

Louise Bourgeois
Fallen Woman 1981
marble
3 ¾" x 4" x 13 ½"
Courtesy Robert Miller Gallery, New York.
Photo: Allan Finkelman.

viewpoints excluded by formalist (and sexist) orthodoxy. Whereas the work of a sculptor like Judd appears in hindsight to have developed almost logically and progressively, Bourgeois' sculpture implies no chronology. A work in wood from the later forties such as *The Blind Leading the Blind* (1949) seems neither to anticipate nor to follow from works of the sixties, such as the plaster *Labyrinthine Tower* (c. 1962), or of the eighties, such as the cast-rubber *Legs* (1986).

Out of context, some of Bourgeois' statements about art make it sound as if she has attitudes in common with Judd: "Art is manipulation without any intervention" or "I am exclusively concerned, at least consciously, with formal perfection" or "All I can find is to repeat and repeat and repeat." However, anyone who looks at Bourgeois' sculpture senses immediately that its references to experience are very different from those of Judd's work. The geometry of Judd's work is strictly controlled; in Bourgeois' work, geometry is casual, molten looking, snapping squarely into shape only where necessary. ("You can push geometry around a bit," Léger had told her in her student days.) In her carvings and bronzes from modeled plaster, Bourgeois lets the energy of the hand (even if it is not always her hand) vibrate; there is no hand in Judd's art. Images come and go in

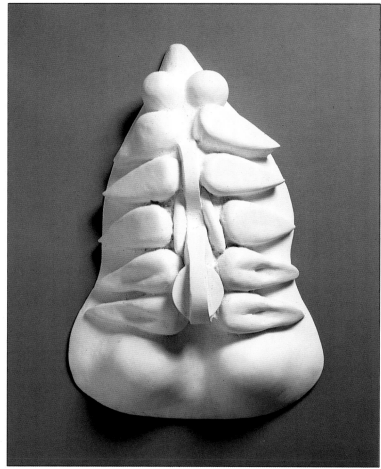

Above left
Louise Bourgeois
Labyrinthine Tower c. 1962
plaster
height: 18"
Courtesy Robert Miller Gallery, New York.
Photo: Peter Bellamy.

Above right
Louise Bourgeois
Torso, Self Portrait 1963–64
bronze, white patina
24 ¾" x 16" x 7 ⅛"
Courtesy Robert Miller Gallery, New York.
Photo: Peter Bellamy.

Bourgeois' work; *Legs* is an unusually economical example. The work consists of two ten-foot-long cylinders of black cast rubber that hang from the ceiling side by side. At the top and for most of their length, they look like "pure" forms, but at the bottom, each cylinder angles and flattens into a slightly pointed, apparently stockinged, foot, like the gently splayed feet in the tapestry designs Bourgeois drew as a child. *Legs* effects a passage from objective to subjective accent in the viewer's mind that seems both comical and magical in its simplicity. It is just that sort of passage and surprise (which Bourgeois often achieves more bluntly) that Judd's art eliminates. Perception is all business in Judd's sculpture and the bodily awareness that it promotes is desexualized, neuter. Bourgeois' sculpture and drawings, on the other hand, are full of reminders that their author is a woman and that artist and viewer alike are inescapably (if also ambiguously) polarized sexually. Female heads occur often in Bourgeois' sculpture as do breastlike, vulval and phallic forms.

"I am not particularly aware [of] or interested in the erotic in my work," Bourgeois says, regarding it as an inevitable byproduct of allowing herself "to follow blindly the images that suggest themselves to me." However, for Bourgeois, even the abstract qualities of sculpture are steeped in psychological meaning in a way they never are for Judd, who reckons everything in terms of external relations. Unlike Bourgeois, he would never aver that "horizontality is a desire to give up, to sleep. Verticality is an attempt to escape. Hanging and floating are states of ambivalence."

There are more images of constraint and defeat than of release in Bourgeois' oeuvre, as I read it. A particularly touching example (literally so in its strong appeal to the fingertips) is the white marble *Fallen Woman* (1981). This object—which could pass for a classic Surrealist artifact of the thirties—is a foot-long pestle whose handle end is capped by a woman's head, looking straight ahead, her hair streaming back as if from a gust of forward motion. The figure's air of surging forward is sadly, weightily contradicted by the smooth, swollen mass of the object's other end, which is vaguely phallic, but can symbolize equally well the inertia of abstraction, stylistic and intellectual.

It is Bourgeois' example, as much as the content of her work that makes her an authoritative figure among women artists of the postwar era. She has worked unstintingly for more than fifty years, without repeating herself, seemingly unswayed by the approbation or indifference of the art establishment. Her work has never degenerated into formula and, as she approaches eighty, shows no loss of force.

•

Critics frequently link Agnes Martin, Bourgeois' exact contemporary, with Minimalism (and thus with Judd, who rejects the Minimalist label as strenuously as anyone). But if Minimalism has any useful meaning, it denotes developments in sculpture—or three-dimensional art—not in painting. There is little or no possibility of mistaking a painting for some other kind of object (though you may try to discredit a work in paint on canvas by refusing to call it "painting"). Judd's art, on the other hand, draws energy from the possibility of its being taken for furniture or objects of uncertain function.

Agnes Martin's painting is formalistic in appearance, but not in spirit, and one of the striking things about it is that its spirit is manifest and significant, rather than fortuitous. Most art that is as understated as hers registers little more than an intellectual posture. It is easy enough to mistake the systematic character of Martin's work for a sign of emotionlessness. Give a painting by her enough time, however, and it will reveal a distinct light, emotional pitch and rhythmic pulse, all carefully but delicately controlled with perceptible clarity of intent.

Martin's work is tangential to Minimalism in its insistence on the physical presence of the art object as the touchstone to any understanding of it. Since the late fifties, when she lived in New York, Martin has made abstract pictures in which ruled pencil lines—or, less frequently, gridded markings in paint—cover the prepared surface of a square canvas. The effective ground of the marks she makes is not the "picture plane" but the physical support of canvas stretched over wood. To see a painting by Martin properly, you have to examine it from various standpoints. Its pattern of pencil lines (if it is drawn upon; some early works are not) may coalesce into a veil or haze at a distance. Up close, you can see the way the graphite wavers, drags and crumbles as it bumps across a gessoed surface. Martin's chosen materials guarantee that minute irregularities will give every ruled line a subtle vibration.

There is an undeniable interiority to most of Martin's paintings, although she never makes it explicit with illusions of depth. Their magic, though, is in the way staves—or a grid of pencil lines or a chord of soft bands of color—appear to levitate the structure that supports them. Martin says, "My paintings have neither objects, nor space, nor time, not anything—no forms. They are light, lightness, about merging, about formlessness breaking down form…You wouldn't think of form by the ocean."

Martin's artistic life has been divided between the city and the desert, an alternation her paintings reflect in tensions between drawn grids and sensations of shimmering light and openness. She was born in Saskatchewan and raised in Vancouver. She came to

Agnes Martin
Falling Blue 1963
oil and pencil on canvas
71 ⅞" x 72"
San Francisco Museum of Modern Art;
gift of Mr. and Mrs. Moses Lasky.
Photo: Don Meyer.

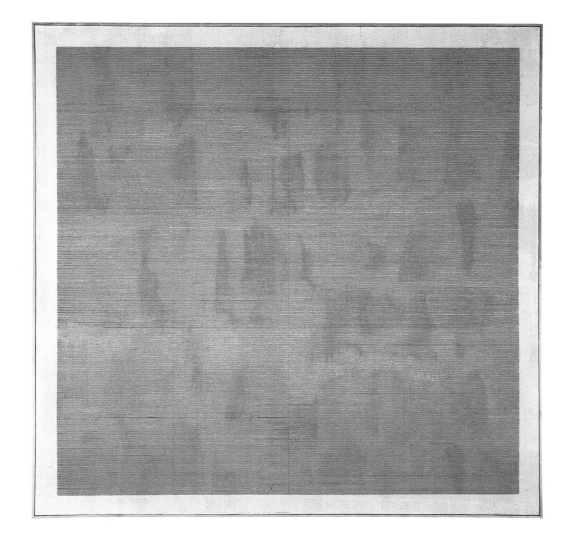

Opposite page, Agnes Martin, Cuba, New Mexico, 1979. Photo: © Gianfranco Gorgoni.

Agnes Martin
White Flower 1960
oil on canvas
71 ⅞" x 72"
Solomon R. Guggenheim Museum, New York; anonymous gift, 1963.
Photo: David Heald.

America in the early thirties and studied at Columbia. In 1954 she moved to New Mexico, where the landscape and light captivated her, compelling her to try to register their effects in images. In the late fifties, she moved back to New York and took up the format of gridded, square, abstract paintings for which she has become famous.

In New York, Martin befriended other painters—notably Jack Youngerman and Ellsworth Kelly—who were also plying an aesthetic of nongestural abstraction. They too, like Judd and the Pop artists active in New York at the time, were in conscious rebellion against the heroics of Abstract Expressionism. Martin seems to have found her own way without ever enlisting in style wars. Memories of nature and a belief in selfless inspiration as the crux of true art have guided her painting from the start. In 1967 she returned to New Mexico and has lived and worked there since. "Nature is like parting a curtain," she says, "you go into it." To recreate that sensation and to celebrate it are the purposes that guide her work.

With the eclipse of modernism, abstract painting is in a distressed condition with respect to its future and its past. Martin appears exempt from this state of affairs, not because she is an established artist (Frank Stella claims to feel the pressure of it), but because the point of her work is not to be abstract. It has subject matter in a sense not countenanced by most abstract painters. "Beauty and happiness and life are all the same and they are pervasive, unattached and abstract and they are our only concern," Martin declared in a lecture. "They are immeasurable, completely lacking in substance. They are perfect and sublime. This is the subject matter of art." It is the subject matter of her art, which tells us that she only appears to be a modernist, because of her work's incidental affinity to Constructivism and early Mondrian. In fact, she is heir to the Luminist tradition in American painting which sees light as the mind of the world. ☐

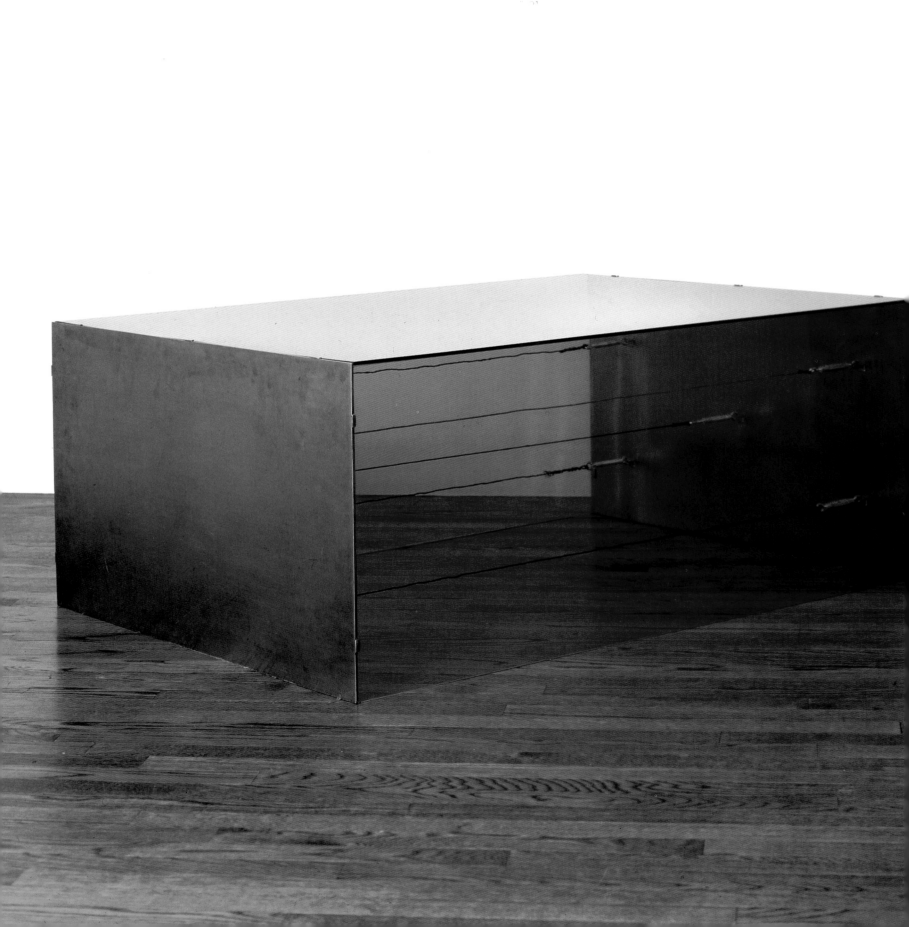

EUROAMERICA
From Minimal Art to Arte Povera

Germano Celant

During the late sixties and early seventies many avant-garde artists rejected the preciousness of art objects and turned from making paintings or sculptural objects to creating unsalable installations and environments. In the United States this tendency is identified most often with process art and earthworks, but similar characteristics appeared internationally, for example, in Italian Arte Povera. Generally speaking, the artists of Arte Povera used a wide variety of nontraditional materials to create fragmented objects and installation-environments; their intentions ranged from employing materials as metaphors to political dissension. Critic, author and curator Germano Celant has been closely associated with Arte Povera, even coining its name. Here, he views the particular development of this movement against the context of opposing and corresponding attitudes found in Minimalism and Conceptualism and in the works of such artists as Joseph Beuys and Robert Smithson.

Germano Celant's essay was translated from the Italian by Joachim Neugroschel.

Minimal Art

In the urban life of New York City filth plays an active part. The city is practically a sewer, its vital rhythm regulated by the daily consumption of objects and refuse, which, day after day, are retained almost anally on the sidewalks and street corners. Nevertheless, the art produced in this territory seems to repress the social impulses toward filth and garbage, supplanting them with a compulsive cleanliness, almost as if it had to observe the protocol of a culture as a puritanical and ethical blunder. According to this vision, art dare not be soiled; art must remain clean and perfect, since it liberates us from the mass of corruption and obscenity that circulates in all the streams of Manhattan. This art permits no excremental contortions because it has to represent an economy unburdened by any hindrance—that is, by mud.

Furthermore, dirt is incompatible with the social order, and since art appears as the maker of symbolic models capable of acquiring social value, art has to criticize, rather than buttress, this concept: art has to plunge the concept into a state of crisis. Thus, if filth is asocial and art sustains a progressive conception, no aesthetic investigation can exalt the display of refuse and disorder; instead, the search will reinforce the belief in rigid and stable values consistent with cleanliness. By singing the praises of junk culture, Pop art became asocial, moving through the territory of evil. Junk culture was challenged and condemned, nothing proving more effective than "thinking about filth."

The sole action favoring those politics is the reaction against them, leading to their elimination. In order to achieve this result, the artwork must return to the uncontaminated, in which forms and materials—presented in their purity of simple volumes and surfaces, of unprocessed woods and metals—are no longer desecrated by the intrusion of consumer materials. Instead, they live autonomously in an undefiled, aseptic world.

The Minimalist religion divides the artistic universe into two categories: things that are subject to being reduced and leveled, and things whose inner disorder and chaos prevent them from suffering that fate. The first group corresponds to innocence and subordination to society; the second group to crisis and disintegration. And since art in America expresses moral judgment, tidiness is the correct evolutionary road, in that it presupposes a plan.

In the early sixties Minimalism, trying to act as the antithesis of Pop and Fluxus, decided to venerate order, rules and norms. Thus, the works of Donald Judd teemed with references to integrity and the perfect whole. In them, the materials of the world, from steel to plexiglass, conform to elementary structures, becoming monolithic entities that tautologically represent the power and independence of a system whose values are limitation and orderliness.

For Judd, the spatial and chromatic autonomy of volumes is total. The pure parallel-epiped rejects any referential value, while the materials introduce the fusion of surface and color into the interior. The outcome is an ensemble of integral entities. This conception of the volumetric phenomenon led Judd to regard sculptural works as totalities constituting autonomous units, which manifest an internal solidarity and obey their own laws. In this way, sculpture functions as a self-determining entity, conditioned entirely by intrinsic relations and by the elements controlling it. By way of proof, sculpture always presents ensembles of separate yet inseparable entities, which mutually delimit and differentiate one another, thereby constituting an indivisible whole. Since these entities are interactive, their interrelationships are multiple and dynamic, and no sculpture is ever closed, for each sculpture continually maintains a dialogue between empty and full. At the same time, the possibilities of position and progression are infinite: the positional arrangement can utilize the three-dimensional and two-dimensional, the vertical and horizontal coordinates, while the progression can be geometric and follow the Fibonacci series. Moreover, the materials making up the whole can vary in thickness, refraction, color, smoothness, transparency and weight.

Donald Judd
Untitled 1966
amber plexiglass and stainless steel
20" x 48" x 34"
Froehlich Collection, Stuttgart, West Germany.
Photo courtesy of Leo Castelli Gallery.

Dan Flavin, New York, 1970. Photo: © Gianfranco Gorgoni.

Hence, Judd's sculpture excludes any hierarchy of full and empty, beginning and end, front and back, above and below, material and immaterial, so that within a given element, the choice is always binary. Therefore, a sculpture will be completely autonomous, and the emphasis on any one factor over another will be due simply to its position in the environment.

Dan Flavin likewise took the cold and rigid given as his starting point. His work aimed at confronting the viewer with the entity of light in order to underscore it as an "iconic" affirmation. Omitting imagination and inventiveness—that is, the participation of what is expressively "dirty"—he concentrated on the isolated phenomenon of light. For Flavin, light was identified with the fluorescent tube, which, for him, became a technological totem whose worldwide availability on all markets made it the perfect example of the nonspatial and the nontemporal.

About 1966 Flavin's fluorescent light, no longer satisfied with its "secondary" role in corners and on walls, began to invade space, becoming intrinsic to architectural passages, actions and motions and the movements of the viewer: as an overriding presence, light pervaded the environment. Light acquired a plural consistency: the light of the tube—a value in its own right—was reflected on walls, on combined and neighboring lights, on the architectural whole. Light created forms and space through the arrangements and the colors employed.

Sol LeWitt worked with "musical scores" of elementary signs, but instead of resorting to the technological icon he was more interested in handmade construction. His works are visual "scores" on two-dimensional and three-dimensional signs, "unconscious and intuitive exercises" in arithmetic, whereby their "performance" is merely a rendering of conceptual processes into volume and surface. In this sense, LeWitt's works are "musical notations" based on the interrelations between concepts and processes, cognitive events that communicate an idea, to which they sacrifice all the intentionality of the material and the subject. It is the idea that gives form and meaning to LeWitt's work, and he labors on the idea, or concept, trying to evacuate as much materiality as possible from the means of expression.

LeWitt calls himself a "musician of concepts and volumes" in quest of an ideal score—a musician who already sees contamination in the mere act of turning idea into practice, and who, with extreme coherence, seeks to negate the visual "evaluation" in favor of a

Sol LeWitt, Gemeentemuseum, The Hague, The Netherlands, 1970. Photo: © Gianfranco Gorgoni.

structural reading. Thus, LeWitt's paintings and his two- and three-dimensional sculptures are formulations of an idea, proceeding according to a mechanical rationalism that admits no chaos or happenstance. Once the idea is formulated, that which follows is beyond all control by the material or the subject. Indeed, the artwork is a conceptual operation that is randomly deposited in a material or a form. However, the object and the trace deriving from it are irrelevant so far as the chosen idea or concept is concerned. In this sense, as LeWitt has said, "even a blind man can make art," because the idea draws the work, and the realization of the idea is nothing but a process of self-visualization through the media that are used.

Hence, an idea with artistic and aesthetic implications is not fundamental to the making of art. The artist need only pick an idea and verify its objective assertion, transcribe it rather than interpret it and "offer it as it presents itself" in order to communicate something that can be communicated only by and with that idea.

In this logical system of conceptual procedure, it is obvious that the investigation is directed toward forms that are noncharacterized, as volumetric and geometric forms, and to materials that are annulled by the noncolors white and black: in their simplicity they are useful in not altering the conceptual "whole," and, with their flatness and insignificance, they tend to concentrate on the intensity of the process.

Conceptualism and Post-Minimalism

According to Lucy Lippard and John Chandler's historical definition, Conceptualism tries to achieve a "dematerialization" of art, which is recognized in the gradual replacement of the object by the idea and the concept. This dematerialization reveals the loss of interest in the formalist evolution of the work and the tension in transforming all material into mental process. The operative assumption, particularly of Conceptualism, was to prefer the philosophical, cognitive process to the materialist approach and to the subjectivism of the artist, who now regarded forms as irrelevant and intrinsically equal. The artist could use any type of form—from the object to the written or spoken word—but he demoted them by exalting the concept, which brooked only a rational linearity that was methodologically precise. Adopting the concept or idea as an operative model, Conceptual art rejected all expressionism of materials and actions by the individual "artist." Any entity foreign to the analysis of the concepts and ideas that give form to art was waved off as less than valid. Thus, the discourse on theoretical process in art became a manifestation of art rather than of critical literature, and art could resort to the printed page, mathematics, numbering, writing, the essay, the book—to any instrument of philosophical and processual communication.

Robert Barry, Lawrence Weiner, Douglas Huebler and Joseph Kosuth formed the original nucleus of Conceptual artists identified in the shows and events organized by Seth Siegelaub in 1968 and 1969. Eventually, the roster of artists classified as Conceptualists expanded to include Hanne Darboven, On Kawara, Jan Dibbets, John Baldessari, Stanley Brouwn, Victor Burgin, Ian Wilson, Hamish Fulton and David Tremlett as well as the Anglo-American group Art & Language, in which Kosuth and Wilson were active participants. A radical Conceptualist direction was followed by the Art & Language group, whose collective ventures were troubled and disjointed; rejecting the use of a dematerializing and ephemeral artistic language, this group proposed the scientific use of concept and politics in art. Art & Language, at least initially, disdained the visual and literary components in order to reduce the conceptual operation to pure philosophy and then to the active political application of the language of art. The reduction to pure concept abolished all interest in the object and in documentation; renouncing aesthetics, Art & Language turned exclusively to language and parlance, in line with a logic that drew on the ultimate speculations of philosophers and linguists, from Wittgenstein to Moore, and then went on to Marx and Lenin. Thus, for both the group and its individual members, books and essays were art, as was discussing educational or esoteric statements on the theme of art.

Among those cited most frequently, Joseph Kosuth seems to have been the greatest extremist in offering problematic directives about the identity of the "art" context. His output since 1965 demonstrates that his focus on use and function eventually wiped out the form of the presentation of the work. Indeed, his discussion on the nature of art proceeded in terms of groups of meaning and not taste or sensitive reaction. The groups of meaning, translated into what Kosuth termed "investigations," revealed all the complex features of the relations between language and art. The definitions making up Kosuth's *First Investigation* initially concerned the concepts of matter/material, such as water or air, and were offered as abstractions of a particular entity, devoid of form and color. Subsequently, the "definitions" were for abstract terms such as "meaning,"

-ism = Gr *-ismós*, often via L *-ismus* or F *-isme*—or both; its conn is abstract; in general, it answers to vv in *-ize* and esp to agents in *-ist*, with their adjj in *-istic*. Its principal manifestations are these: whereas, formed from vv, it indicates action, as in *baptism*, OF *baptesme*, LL from Gr *baptismos*, from *baptizein*, to baptize, formed from nn it indicates the manner of action, as in *despotism*, or the conduct to be expected of the person implied, as in *heroism* or *Micawberism*. Very common too is the conn 'state, condition' (or the fact of being such-and-such), as in *hypnotism* or *barbarism*. Flowing from the general 'action' and 'state' connotations is that of 'doctrine' or 'mental or moral practice or habit', as in *materialism*, or 'adherence to' (a doctrine, a theory), as in *Catholicism*. Hence, 'characteristic, esp a peculiarity', as in *Briticism*. In Med it denotes an abnormal state or condition, consequent upon excess in (the thing denoted by the n implied), as in *alcoholism*.

Joseph Kosuth
'ism' from *The First Investigation* 1966–68
mounted photostat
48" x 48"

"empty," "ism," "time," "universal," "object." That is, they became abstractions of abstractions. In many cases, their presentation showed that linguistic entities commonly used in the language of art have no predefinable characteristic, for the word is not the definition of a single phenomenon but, quite the contrary, the connotation of a class of an undetermined number of meanings. This principle was verified in his 1968 exhibition at the 669 Gallery in Los Angeles: Kosuth exhibited numerous definitions of the word "nothing" that were taken from various dictionaries.

Other conceptual artists reflected on art's physiognomy, on the measurement of its communication structures and what can happen by means of writing, reinvented in the first person by Hanne Darboven, and on the "disorientation" of discussion, by means of which Ian Wilson implemented a mirrorlike reflection concerning the territory of art history and art theory. John Baldessari aimed to disrupt the abstract and pseudoreal iconography of everyday communication. He proceeded as a curator of linguistic strategems that could unmask the fetishized movement of the rhetorical figures sustaining the reproductions of reality. Ultimately, Baldessari struggled against the manipulatory praxis of knowledge through images, as promoted by consumer determinations of the relationship between production and economic expansion. To achieve this analytical goal, Baldessari committed himself to probing the relationship between signifier and signified; he destructured the sign accumulations of the labyrinthine knowledge developed by the media, and he tried to illuminate the hallucinatory system and the method of revealing, on the surface, the occult and fetishistic phenomena of the "myths of today."

In order to expose the functioning of the machines of persuasion and desire rather than bogging down in his own personality and projecting his own individuality—that is, in order to work on the emptiness of languages—Baldessari began to exclude himself. Removing his own centrality and subjectivity, he stopped reflecting himself in his art and, instead, applied a strategy of investigation and attack to the figures of image production. In 1966–68, after completing a cycle of personal and material painting, he launched into an exploration of visual methodology from the outside, by entrusting others with the execution of his pieces. This procedure involved his declaration of externality and loss of self, with the consequent negation of the subject.

The process became most evident in his analysis of the painting vector, construed as a screen with ideas and images flashing across it. The purpose of the white or gray "screens," which present writings or writings paired with associated photographic images, is their informational goal. These paintings are meant to fix an iconic and written duplicate upon the canvas/screen, thereby underscoring the passage of the communicational "figures" outside the personal and subjective order. The artist recedes from these figures, because, as a sign painter, he has others do the lettering and select the photographs, which were not originally taken for artistic purposes. The focus of interest is the fluctuation or irruption on the surface of the art of data that can designate something inside and outside aesthetic perception.

●

The tendency to reduce, to simplify—so dear to the Minimalists—recurred in the generation following Donald Judd, Dan Flavin and Sol LeWitt, but the formal and volumetric rigidities and dogmatisms were now dissolved by the influence of anti-form and process art. The rules of combinations exploded, and materials yielded their value as absolute surfaces or volumes. Instead of producing definite constructions, process artists gathered weights and materials in a "situation," as if the precarious consummation in a room or a meadow were more important than the reductive and geometric modalities. Their installations were characterized by the ephemeral, so that the value of the work was distributed in the chain of effects along the floor and the wall, without remaining autonomous and isolated as in Minimalism. At the same time, these artists valued the elementary materials of latex, cast iron, wood and lead for their lack of security and affirmation of softness rather than for their rigor and hardness; in this way, they stimulated the passage from the intensiveness of Minimalism to the extensiveness of body art and land art.

References to nature became macroscopic in the projects of such artists as Richard Long, Walter De Maria, Robert Smithson and Michael Heizer who conscripted deserts and snowy plains, rocky mountains and the ocean. Indeed, their works necessitated the removal of tons of soil or rocks and are valued in terms of the trucks and Caterpillars mobilized to carry out monumental gestures that marked the earth with mega-hieroglyphs. Land art, in particular, threw down the gauntlet to artistic macroscopy by fusing with ever bigger signs and spaces, almost as if it wanted to vie for the realization of a natural megalopolis that disappeared with the advent of the technologized metropolis. The works that Michael Heizer produced on the earth's crust in Nevada, with *Double Negative,* or with his project of a desert city made up of plains and constructions

EXAMINING PICTURES

FIRST OF ALL, WHAT DO PICTURES CONSIST OF?
WHAT ARE THEY ALL ABOUT?
THERE IS NO END, IN FACT, TO THE NUMBER OF DIF-
FERENT KINDS OF PICTURES.
NATURALLY ARTISTS FROM TIME TO TIME HAVE
STRUGGLED TO ENLARGE ON THESE LIMITATIONS
AND THE HISTORY OF ART IS A SUCCESSION OF
THEIR SUCCESSES AND FAILURES. SEE THE IM-
PRESSIONISTS, THE CUBISTS.

SPACE

MANY ARTISTS HAVE PONDERED OVER THIS PROB-
LEM. THEY HAVE EMPLOYED COLOR TO HELP THEM
CREATE SPACE, LIKE CEZANNE, OR PERSPECTIVE,
LIKE UCCELLO. IN HIS CUBIST PHASE PICASSO
TRIED THE EFFECT OF CUBES. TO ME THIS IS NO
PROBLEM AT ALL.

Robert Smithson
Gravel Mirror with Cracks and Dust 1968
mirrors and gravel: six leaning wall mirrors and six
floor mirrors, each 36" x 36"
36" x 216" x 36"
Estate of Robert Smithson; Courtesy John Weber
Gallery, New York.

Robert Smithson making a "mirror displacement" in
the Yucatan, Mexico, 1969. Photo: Nancy Holt.

of sand and cement, were ventures that would last for decades, that would have endless time, that would be tied to the most advanced technologies, which, however, would create "cathedrals in the desert."

On the other hand, Walter De Maria tried, from the very start, to link up with uncontrolled natural phenomena, such as lightning and earthquakes. He welcomed the experience of risk in order to live a life of sensations and unforeseen eventualities. As early as 1960, De Maria sought a further dimension in natural disasters. And so he confronted the character of the practical and concrete visualization inflicted upon the earth's surface by earthquakes, tornadoes and sand storms. De Maria considers the resulting aesthetic effects "the highest form of art possible to experience."

The incubation of Robert Smithson's earthworks took place internally: not inside the construction of a whole—à la Heizer or De Maria—but inside the confines of a territory. Smithson tackled single sites, transporting his findings from place to place: in his "nonsites," he literally tried to shed light (hence the mirrors and reflections in his "mirror displacements") on the sheer presence of the modality of materials (rock, bitumen, mud). These contain both a past and a future, that which has been and no longer exists. They are disturbing entities, which are proffered in steel containers or mirror containers as "entropic presences," as an energy that escapes but continues to exist. And if the material of the earth is time, the immediate consequence is that time is material. *Spiral Jetty* (1970, at the Great Salt Lake in Utah) recognizes the helical development of taking the passage of material to infinite temporality (the spiral). This is the representation of a coming and going between earth and water, near and far, now and later, in which the plan is open rather than determined. Here, the artist is a messenger and wayfarer on earth.

The signs left on the terrestrial crust thus seem to be hieroglyphs in a natural environment, a meadow or a wasteland, a hill or a riverbed. They are testimonies left by "primitives," who still see nature as a remote space into which human beings can project themselves, as in prehistoric eras, in order to bring forth menhirs of soil and stone.

Arte Povera

American culture identifies with industrial production and the principles of the rationalist creed, is tied to functional spatiality and the absence of decor, practices the use of standard units and sizes and leans toward the approval of formal typologies. Europe, on the other hand, coping with its awareness of how impossible it is to exist in a cosmos based on geometric simplification, on the right angle and the cube, operates within arbitrariness and historical imagination.

Culture and art, which survive by reblending and reabsorbing past and present elements, have plunged into a continuous passage between stratifications and ruins, principles of newness and principles of decomposition. Integrity dissolves in mobile material, which is still incandescent. Here we find the attraction to the insane vectors that zoom off in unplanned directions, taking chaotic routes and upsetting expectations and presuppositions of any order. The source of attraction is the explosion of closed, rigid visions, so that cognition is attained by way of destruction rather than by planning and construction. Vision is actually fed by the magic of reminiscence or recollection, something that reveals a "double," a shadow or specter or enigma. The idea of the new always involves the notion of regeneration, something relying on the transformation of that which already exists. Thus, the iconographic themes cherished by American art change signs. They are the symbolic attributes of an infinite thinking that cannot be paralyzed by the banality of a primary or reductive meaning. Thus, the square or the circle, the line or the cube foster an indefinite existence; they signal the mobility of both mental and physical material.

Indeed, every discovery consists of fragmented elements and historical ruins, imbued with memory and tradition, filled with cracks—the products of human and natural cataclysms. Even while charging into the future, European culture maintains both the sense of the enormous complexity of history and the cognizance of going forward and backward to find a syntax in the crisscross of eras, territories and languages. The flow of energies is preferred to the framing and defining of their structures.

The subject invoked by European art and culture is the nomadic being, who refuses to kowtow to the stability and rigidity of terms. In order to become a subject and acquire a sense of one's own identity, one need not have a role or confine; one simply has to move in the energy field of life, without limits or directions. The same is true in art, where the object becomes "experienced," and not just a *cogito ergo sum*. This assumption of continuous flow derives from an intellectual topography created according to the law of decomposition and downfall, of ruination and history, which, instead of resigning itself to enduring the invasion of "new worlds," tries to inject the morbid enthusiasm for weakness and tragedy. Everything must, in fact, become "mindful of," and the figures and images have to be accepted as residual elements; they designate not an unknown future, but one that is already stored in the memory of the past. European art has thus made up for the wounds inflicted by the new and the different. The ruins of European art and its millennia of devastation have become ecstatic visions and factors that define the future.

Europe is harping on the element of negativity, the segmentation of strength and the blending of the materials or splinters of history, while America is trying to construct a "factory" or a physical and mental mechanism in concrete reality, one regulated by a coherent, functional system in which the machines and apparatuses are systematically inspected and modernized according to the latest technologies. European art, by contrast, lives on a stockpile of time-honored findings and dismembered fragments, which have to be constantly reunited and reassembled in order to lay out a new course. Thus, the reappropriation of history—not its creation—is a continuous project. That is why European "progress" is made up of stupefying blends, ancient and deteriorated materials recycled from the past according to an intuitive and illogical vision. History passes from Dada to metaphysics, from Constructivism to Surrealism, which see contrary and even conflicting universes coexisting, so that life issues from the dialectics and organization of explosion and disorder.

The resulting movement is that of descent and ascent, of the collapse and reappropriation of a history and a spirit that are continuously expiated and purged. That is why European art always seems willing to expel impurities and nightmares, dreams and catastrophic visions—which is how we have to construe the circulation of the "cultural ruins" of Joseph Beuys and Jannis Kounellis, Mario Merz and Anselm Kiefer. Their works perform a therapeutic activity; they are the fruits not so much of a present but of a past that has to be exorcized, with its wicked and accursed contamination. The output of these artists draws strength and energy from the dark and dismal moods of a feverish society tormented by centuries of negation and warfare, plague and suffering. Their art exudes despair and the horror at a loss; it raises buried entities, reabsorbing them in order to produce a different energy. The artists wanted to track down some utterly astounding secret formula that could give them the key for entering a protected existence that is neither laborious nor corroded by history. They too became instruments for purifying sight and touch, and they displayed joy and pleasure, almost as if they had managed to escape a tragic destiny. They all seemed to be bucking the system of disasters and catastrophes, to be forever seeking magical solutions in order to leave the hallucinations of history.

In this way, any object became a phase coalescing love and hate toward reality, whether the object responded to the schemata of Nouveau Réalisme, from Jean Tinguely to Christo, or was represented in its iconic and material ups and downs by Arte Povera, from Luciano Fabro to Giulio Paolini. Angst was induced by the nostalgia for a primordial *anthropos*, an archetypal figuration that could anchor the passing moment. The assemblages appeared as "glorious bodies," able to introject and reabsorb all the possible

Joseph Beuys at home in Düsseldorf, 9 May 1971.
Photo: © Harry Shunk.

histories and vicissitudes of the world. Hence, the absence of compactness and specificity in favor of an inundating dissemination of the meanings of images.

The important thing was a radiant energy in constant motion, the openness toward the other, a kind of love for a sensory restoration that is lost in time. Unlike its American antipodes, European art lives a life that claims to be infinite, because it is continually obsessed with its own rebirth. Actually, if we think of Rebecca Horn or Gilbert and George, European artistic culture might be compared to an enormous house of dreams and nightmares, in which day and night are confused. Every day, surreal mythologies and real dramas consume one another there, and their shadows and figures appear to be made of soot and mercury, broken glass and numbers, decayed materials and fattiness, dandies and proletarians, statue fragments and utterly refined drawings. Here, the boundaries between real and unreal, possible and impossible, sacred and profane, abstract and concrete, holy and abominable, pure and filthy, are unstable and uncertain.

In the early sixties, the movement toward spiritualism and materialism was powerfully attested to in the paintings of Yves Klein and Piero Manzoni, the first artists to seek refuge or liberation in a terminal point, blue or colorlessness, where the drama of a culture is reduced to zero and demonstrates existence. They used repetition, not to affirm the standard, as did the Minimalists, but to make the subject go down in the ocean of nothingness, the upper emptiness or the lower fullness. They accelerated the death of the subject, negating it in the immateriality of cosmic blue and the materiality of earthly breath and excrement. They dethroned the subject from the center of its individuality and personality in order to make it circulate in the empyrean of airy substances and in the bottomless pit of organic refuse. Europeans maintained the priority of the nonsubject, but give it an over- and under-determination, thereby establishing a selected entity (Klein) or a rejected entity (Manzoni) as the antithesis to American indifference and indetermination. Yet they accepted the counteruniverse of repetition and impersonalism in those vague and fluctuating territories that a retreating subjectivity left behind. They still reacted to the implosion of the subject, searching for a celestial and terrestrial surrogate that, purged with Joseph Beuys, once again became potentially explosive, because it was spectrally projected into the desire for the "liberation" of body and mind, history and creativity, politics and pleasure. We can thus state that European artists "dreamed" of a counteruniverse, antithetical to America, the universe of capitalism, the realm of the nonsubject. They still had faith in transgression as the favorite weapon of historical avant-gardes: they thought that its energy could foment the collapse of the ruling power by penetrating its very fibers.

The gist of this practice of objectivity involved a defiance of all the truths. In 1968 and then 1977, this challenge, especially in Europe, expressed a different degree of rebellious creativity, which was able to fluctuate between positive and negative thought, between polarities of relation and revolution, vanguard and rear guard. To understand the recourse to the fragmented and mutating object typical of European art, we must bear in mind that as of 1967, European culture developed a new critical subject, which tended to follow the road of social and intellectual changes: the repoliticizing of Western Europe. This demand was voiced by a generation that wanted the utopia of abolishing all levels of hierarchy and stratification, of order and closed structure. They felt an imperious, urgent need to break loose and fight for equality among all human beings. Their goal was to wipe out the ideological legacies, thereby implementing a true cultural transformation. They critically attacked each mechanism of existence in order to check its defects of direction as well as the rigidity and complexity of its use. In this vast tempest, anything hidden in the age-old depths of the system was carried to the surface. The radical critique of society, in its most advanced industrial phenomena, forged a model of extremist action, based chiefly on the values of poverty and marginalism. These times give birth to street theater and radical architecture, body art and *Arte Povera*; emerging from the tradition of spontaneous creativity, they aimed at blowing up the reasons for current fantasies, exalting their fragments and insane chips. The fantastic and creative events of those years, comparable to the peaceful revolution of 1989 in Eastern Europe, marked an historical watershed: the dogma of neutrality or emotional and physical repression was extirpated, for it was no longer possible to live with boundaries and confines. Nevertheless, the explosion of languages and the toppling of linguistic walls, enabling art objects and behaviors to assume an incredible aesthetic and motoric flexibility, always heeded not only the sensory and physical giveness of materials and actions but also their "historicity."

Every form and every image is a sign charged with symbols and stratifications. The knowledge they contain is the mirror of history in the present. They are enigmas used in both painting and sculpture, from de Chirico to Kounellis, from Duchamp to Beuys. The authority of their presence reinforces the typically European effort to hold back things

Jannis Kounellis
Untitled 1980
propane gas torches attached to a cello, mandolin,
flute, trumpet, drum, violin and trombone
dimensions variable
Collection of Marielle and Paul Mailhot.
Photo: Paolo Mussat Sartor.

and events that possess secrets, keep them on the outskirts of their evanescence, on this side of the threshold beyond which they hurtle into oblivion; and this oblivion is not so much absence pure and simple as the dark presence of night and death. Hence, art is an instrument of memory or, rather, a score on which to inscribe the notes of a history that can be played over and over again.

This regeneration of a dismembered culture forms the basis for the vitality of Arte Povera. In the mid-sixties, when the components of European culture underwent a molecular explosion, enduring the dizziness of collapse and disconnection, artists such as Fabro and Merz, Giovanni Anselmo and Kounellis responded with a visual management of the vertigo. They constructed unbelievable "boilings" of material and wrote a history of the visual metamorphosis. Together with Beuys, they achieved a repertoire of alchemy and esotericism in order to establish a different energy of things, which entered "reality." Thus, Kounellis dealt with the passage from symbolic to real, thereby making that transition a motor of life. His oeuvre was nourished by images and metaphors, from fire to the letters of the alphabet, from wax to musical instruments, because he strove to transform the artist into the great signer of a civilization that has asphyxiated symbols and myths. He added an active and changing dimension to visual culture—the dimension of fire, because he wanted to infuse art with a "hot" and "sensual" condition of life. Moreover, he recovered a condition of multisensory activity, which involved the perception of sound (music), touch (soft materials), taste (symbolic and real foods) and the senses in general, including, of course, sight. Kounellis performed a dance of sensations

that were in perpetual motion; he revived the body of art, which had grown cold in the course of history. He replaced the larval dimension of the static object with the flesh of a visual and tactile mobility. He created the ceremony and the spectacle of hearing.

Merz' compelling need was the same: ceaselessly to renew the image through the grandiloquence of glass and stucco, twigs and soil so that art would be subject to a vital ignition, would move, and incarnate an active and dynamic existence. A shredded and segmented European culture has to recover and reconsolidate: that was Merz' reason for creating the igloos as a coagulation of all principles, from writing to dwelling, from sculpting to painting. The igloo is a turbine for maintaining and radiating energy.

Having agreed to straddle the laceration between past and present, artists, from Marisa Merz to Gilberto Zorio, from Giulio Paolini to Giuseppe Penone, refuse to entrust the solution of their own contradictions to one single form or thought. Instead, they play a "musical score" that is open to determining multiple perspectives. Their goal is to create a work that offers no definitive solution and that does not arrogantly presume to represent something definite; all it has is the extreme difficulty and the extreme pleasure of existing. ☐

Lynda Benglis
Contraband 1969
poured pigmented latex
1" x 108" x 405"
Courtesy Paula Cooper Gallery, New York.
Photo: Fredrik Marsh.

Intruders
Lynda Benglis and Adrian Piper

Lucy R. Lippard

The feminist movement of the late sixties and seventies crucially influenced avant-garde art, opening new lines of inquiry for art making and for critical interpretation. Artists, whether explicitly feminist or not, drew inspiration from feminist critiques of traditional art-world hierarchies. Feminist critics redirected attention toward historical and contemporary women artists and toward previously unexamined aspects of their work. Critic Lucy Lippard shifted her own interests from the formal investigations of Minimal and Conceptual art to feminist and political issues as she began to look at art from the perspective of an engaged social activitist. Here Lippard discusses how feminist strategies affected avant-garde art in the seventies, drawing her particular examples from Lynda Benglis' provocative and decorative work and from Adrian Piper's explorations of self-image and public persona as an African-American woman artist.

About 1970 women artists began to stretch. Their culturally constructed cubicles became too small for the new ideas developing within them, and they began to eye the (illusion of) wide-open spaces in the male-dominated art world. In a process that is still far from complete, they initiated a reverse colonization. The works of Lynda Benglis and Adrian Piper—expansive, intrusive, in very different ways—are metaphors for this larger move toward independence. Benglis' flat latex pieces spread from the center; her polyurethane piles grew voluptuously like rising bread; her layered accretions clawed their way off the walls like science-fictional invaders. Piper's texts and performances—both more intellectual and more potentially violent in terms of cultural change—opened a psycho-social space in which to assert race and gender, hitherto suppressed by "a system of aesthetic values which can be preserved only in isolation from the rest of society, and only by limiting the audience to a highly educated minority."[1]

Benglis and Piper, born in 1941 and 1948, respectively, being women—young women—were both greatly affected by the feminist art movement of the seventies. But neither one, for different reasons, was fully involved in it, and to force both or either into a feminist mold would be an injustice. Although later she counted many of her friends among the Minimalists, Benglis emerged as a painter in the late sixties influenced primarily by such Greenbergian figures as Helen Frankenthaler, Morris Louis, Jules Olitski and Kenneth Noland. In the late sixties, Piper was an early participant in the beginnings of Conceptual art, which constituted a rebellion against Greenbergian premises and social arrogance; Sol LeWitt was the major artist behind her first Conceptual works, but by 1971 she was working in her own territory, which was mined with both race and gender, a domain few others had entered. And, not incidentally, Benglis is a white southerner who has spent most of her adult life making art in New York and California; Piper is a black northerner who is both an artist and a professor of philosophy at Georgetown University; she has lived in New York, Cambridge, Germany, Ann Arbor and Washington, D.C.[2]

A decade lies between the works by Benglis and Piper illustrated here, and it is difficult to write specifically about that decade in the context of art that has little in common and is not "of" the seventies. Benglis' 1969–70 poured paintings and sculptures are the completion of a project begun in and very much the product of the sixties. Piper's 1980 multimedia installation, *Four Intruders Plus Alarm Systems*, anticipated the mainstream's acknowledgment of racism as subject matter worthy of "high art" during the decade we have just survived; like virtually all her work, it also provides a bridge between postmodernism and its antecedents in the Conceptual art of the sixties.

Just as Benglis' poured materials stopped time, the early seventies was a moment of temporary consolidation when sixties' dynamism was "frozen" briefly before dissipating into various mannerisms. This inscrutable "decade," which didn't really begin until the end of the Vietnam war in 1975, is now known as the heyday of "pluralism" and appears in retrospect aesthetically aimless. Art that was radical in form, content or style was, for the most part, cut loose from sixties' support systems and found homes primarily outside the mainstream (in video, performance, film, public or outdoor contexts, and in the feminist and activist art movements), while conservative art, always bolstered by the marketplace, waited for its turn in the eighties. Those treading water were immune to the provocative currents that briefly joined to make 1978–82 a vital outburst in the teeth of the Reagan disaster.

Beginning in 1966, much was made of the notion of "process," of the fusion of finished work with the materials and activities that created it. Benglis has said that her own interest lay in the image rather than the process: "You have to remember that many of the artists who were involved with 'process' were involved with an enclosed deductive system of logic," she recalled. "I've always been involved with the idea of induction in logic, an open-ended system, not a closed system...As information is gathered, as I produce work, a spiral seems to form. Work is the product of information gathered rather than just talk about a closed system."[3] She has acknowledged the influence of Carl Andre, after whom she named a black, piled, triangular polyurethane foam piece, because he

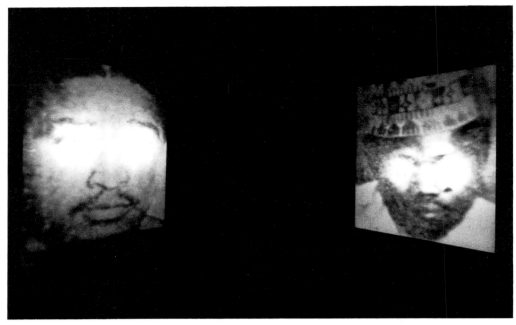

Adrian Piper
Four Intruders Plus Alarm Systems 1980
installation: bounded environment, four silkscreened
light boxes, four audio monologues, audio music
soundtrack
72" (height) x 60" (diameter)
Wexner Center for the Arts, The Ohio State University,
Columbus; purchased in part with funds from the
National Endowment for the Arts, 83.15.
Photo: Fredrik Marsh.

Adrian Piper
Four Intruders Plus Alarm Systems 1980
detail: silkscreened light boxes
Photo courtesy of John Weber Gallery, New York.

"continuously involved himself with very basic, elemental ideas that have always been about both open and closed systems."[4] "Organic yet rigid," as she described it,[5] the 1970 *For Carl Andre* inhabits a corner space; corners and the floor itself were newly discovered sculpture zones in the sixties, and Andre was instrumental in the "horizontalization" process. Benglis has recalled being overwhelmed by his *Lever* in the Jewish Museum in 1966.

In works such as her 1969 *Contraband*—a long thin, multicolored pool of poured latex—Benglis was concerned with the "physicality of an image that was painterly in the Bernard Berenson sense."[6] Her "cosmetic colors" came from pop culture, but the forms were also inspired by nature, by "rock formations, lava formations, coral reefs," organic shapes on a grand scale. She recognized in the latex pours a "mapping quality which was interesting because you could read the color flow from both sides." Ned Rifkin remarked that "they impose an aerial perspective which creates an island phenomenon in terms of scale."[7] "Mapping" was another theme brought to life in the art of the late sixties/early seventies by Robert Smithson, Richard Long, Nancy Graves, Michelle Stuart, Douglas Huebler and Dennis Oppenheim, among others. It offered a sense of micro-macrocosmic omnipotence that permitted at least some of the art's essence to escape from its cultural confines.

In the late sixties, the attitude toward the "precious object" as something suspect and out of touch with the world pervaded advanced art making. Around 1970 this idea—inherent in both dematerialized Conceptual art and ultramaterialized earth art—was merged with feminism's introduction of hitherto taboo content and materials, raising new questions about scale and permanence. Benglis' latex works were begun in 1968–69 at a moment when art and language, "anti-illusion," "anti-form," earth art, process and political activism were on a lot of minds. They evolved from a series of wax paintings inspired by Jasper Johns' work with encaustic. Benglis wanted "to make something very tactile, something that related to the body in some way,"[8] emphasizing material rather than cerebral ideas, and sharing the impetus of another sympathetic alternative to Minimalism called "eccentric abstraction."[9] She was trying to pour wax into more dimensional forms when she saw some little rubber models by Eva Hesse and perceived in latex the same skin-like quality she liked in wax, "a mummified version of painting, as something buried with a dimension that isn't quite perceived upon first glance."[10] This was precisely what attracted Hesse, had already attracted Louise Bourgeois in her latex pieces from the early sixties and was soon to attract many other women artists. Judy Chicago also wrote about the vulnerable "skins" of her airbrushed abstractions about 1970.

The language of the body was the prime vehicle for the burgeoning feminist art, since women artists were well aware of their physical selves as socially determined prisons as well as potential weapons for liberation. Benglis' first poured painting was called *Odalisque (Hey, Hey Frankenthaler)*. It was women's turf. When the mainstream lost interest in process as a "movement," the potentially radical "process-over-product" concept became a feminist issue, finding its way out of abstraction and theory and into performance and socially concerned art.

In the early days of feminist art, individual art practices paved the way for theory; today the reverse is true. In the early seventies, the cooly erotic power of Louise

Bourgeois' work and Eve Hesse's psychologically open-ended, biomorphic/geometric forms provided important models for the visualization of sexuality. These immensely innovative works deeply affected the art of the coming decade, especially art by women, who were first to recognize their extra-formal radicalism.

The only thread between Piper's and Benglis' works that doesn't snap at the slightest pressure is a common, although not consistent, concern with sexuality. In the early seventies, both women made daring feminist persona pieces, using their bodies (but not their lives or autobiographies, as was more common then) to reclaim the representation of women, to transform self into social symbol. As "attractive" young women, both questioned and then restated the history and meaning of physical "attractiveness" in a sexist (and racist) society. They did so, however, in very different ways, which probably affected their trajectories in the art world for the whole decade.

At the same time that Benglis was receiving a good deal of art-world attention for her grand-scale, often "aggressive" (and therefore "unfeminine") poured sculptures, Piper embarked on a very private path, which sometimes, paradoxically, took place in public, in the streets. Deeply involved in a philosophical investigation of self and identity within social contexts, she performed a series of pieces called "Catalysis" that questioned the expectations of aesthetic pleasure in a very postmodern manner and set out to destroy the way that self was perceived by others, thus opening up new potentials for self-definition. She appeared in public (libraries, subways, museums, buses, store-lines) wearing guises or performing activities designed to be repellent physically or psychologically. She doused her clothing in vile-smelling concoctions, blew bubble gum over her face, held monologues with herself, danced to Aretha Franklin's "Respect" or burped excessively, among other things.

Having reversed society's superficial view of her as a good-looking young white woman in the "Catalysis" series, Piper then transformed herself into a handsome, if androgynous, young Afro-Latino male, taking on an alter ego she called "The Mythic Being." Strolling the streets in an Afro wig and shades, she became visibly "of color" (by virtue of assumed class as well as race), her disguise just convincing enough to be puzzling. The self-consciousness that engendered this work was deliberately contagious; it made audiences aware of themselves and their relationship to the art they didn't know they were seeing, transforming the relationship between art and audience into something active rather than passive. Piper herself became "aware of the boundaries of my personality, and how much I intrude myself on other people's realities by introducing this kind of image...When you start realizing that you can do things like that, that you are capable of incorporating all those different things into your realm of experience, there comes a point where you can't be sure whether what you are seeing is of your own making, or whether it is objectively true."[11]

Benglis' poured pieces had announced the sensuous aspect that would enrich almost all of her later work: from the layered wax pieces to the huge, humorously organic reliefs that lunged off the walls, to the glittering, shimmying knot pieces, to the calmer but still sensual recent work. Aside from touches of pop exuberance in color and surface, there was nothing in this considered abstraction to predict the notorious 1974 Artforum "ad"[12] in which Benglis appeared nude, wearing only dark glasses, her body greased and shining, endowed with a giant (double-ended) dildo. It immediately became a cause célèbre, with some of the magazine's own editors (male and female) protesting it as "an object of extreme vulgarity." The hullabaloo was prolonged when it became obvious that Benglis' ad was a companion piece to Robert Morris' more offensive, but less protested, poster of himself in Nazi S-and-M guise.

If Piper's "Catalysis" actions intentionally subtracted from her public acceptability, Benglis' Artforum ad was additive. In a put-on (or take-off) of media stereotypes and role-playing in the art world, she offered a view of herself as a woman with everything—everything needed to Make It (talent being either taken for granted or minimized): a seductive woman's body and the obligatory big prick. (She remarked that "men are more involved with penis envy than women.")[13] She intended to shed the sexual self-consciousness she perceived in the early women's art movement in California, where she was living then, "and the only way I knew how to get rid of it was to mock it...What is porno but a mockery, a kind of tease?"[14] As Angela Carter has pointed out, "pornographers are the enemies of women only because our contemporary ideology of pornography does not encompass the possibility of change, as if we were the slaves of history and not its makers, as if sexual relations were not necessarily an expression of social relations, as if sex itself were an external fact, one as immutable as the weather, creating human practice but never part of it."[15]

The ad is Benglis' best-known foray into satirical eroticism, but it loses something when it is separated from its place in a series of self-portraits/self-advertisements, all of

Lynda Benglis in Greek soldier costume, from an announcement for her exhibition at The Clocktower 6 December 1973–20 January 1974.

Lynda Benglis as "Machorina," from an advertisement for her exhibition at the Paula Cooper Gallery, May 1974.

which mock the role sexuality plays in art commerce, "the way artists use themselves to sell the work,"[16] including liaisons with famous male artists. The series of exhibition announcements of which the *Artforum* ad became the centerpiece was, like Piper's works, an exploration of self-images in which the artist becomes a kind of socially reflective paper doll, influenced, perhaps, by Judy Chicago's earlier "name-change" piece, in which Chicago was photographed in a boxing ring with Arlene Raven as her manager.

The first of Benglis' series was an exhibition announcement in which she appeared dressed in a Greek soldier's "skirt," doubly cross-dressing. The next played on a type of macho southern California sixties art ad in which men were posed with cigar, dog or truck (and sometimes woman). Benglis appeared as "Machorina" (a name she coined for herself) in men's clothes, hair slicked under her hat, looking tough, leaning against her Porsche—the Woman Artist as imitator of men. In an announcement for the same show Benglis appeared as a Betty Grable pinup, nude from the back, peering coyly over her shoulder as her jeans drop over platform shoes—the Woman Artist finding her tradi-tional place. Finally, the dildo piece offered the Woman Artist as true intruder into male territory, not imitator but appropriator of the prime male attribute. "To strike a pose is to strike a threat."[17]

These images "announced" the exhibitions that accompanied them, but they also announced that the relationship between artist and art world was being viewed from a new perspective. "I began to think about who the artist was in relationship to the object/ work," says Benglis.[18] This concern was decidedly part of the sixties/early seventies political climate, in which many artists tried to escape from the art framework, and, failing that, tried to redefine the contexts in which art could be effective. Piper also spent the early seventies trying to see art in a purely relational sense, for what it "does to people." Always working on a radical edge, she was then in fact trying to escape from *all* frameworks, as she told me in 1972. Even though her eccentric public actions were gestures of independence—from the art scene and from female images and roles—Piper also conceded that "a lot of the work I'm doing is being done because I am a paradigm of what the society is."[19] This was a common dilemma around 1970, and one that stimulated an unprecedented scrutiny of the structures within which art and artists existed.

In 1972 Benglis made a videotape entitled *Female Sensibility*, after having been asked by Edit DeAk to define the term for the magazine *Art-Rite*. "I thought at the time, 'it's not the repetition of a doughnut shape, I'm not going to get involved with defining heavy propaganda, it's not this or that, female sensibility could be anything. I'm defined as female, I can't be anything else, everything says so, but how am I to define it in my art? Everything I do defines it naturally.' I began by slightly mocking it, and 'to mock,' in this sense, simply means to allude to femaleness."[20] Initially, she saw video (and perhaps technology in general) as "a big macho game, a big, heroic, Abstract Expressionist, macho sexist game. It's all about territory. How big?" Challenged, she continued to use media to raise the issues of sexual manipulation, as in the 1977 *Amazing Bow Wow*, "about a

Lynda Benglis
For Carl Andre 1970
pigmented polyurethane foam
56 ¼" x 53 ½" x 46 ³⁄₁₆"
Modern Art Museum of Fort Worth; museum
purchase, The Benjamin J. Tillar Memorial Trust.
Photo: David Wharton.

Louise Bourgeois
Noir Veine 1968
black marble
23" x 24" x 27"
Collection of Jerry Gorovoy; courtesy Robert Miller
Gallery, New York.

hermaphroditic dog who can sing and dance," intended as a statement "about repression of humanism using sexuality as a medium. That's what I feel the *Artforum* ad was about, too."[21]

The manipulation and "captivity" of art itself, alienation and manipulation, failures of communication, ostracism, rejection, the ways in which the self is formed by society, the relationship between self and other, have all been Piper's continuing themes since her early self-investigation pieces.[22] During the seventies she could analyze them from several vantage points: her own daily life as a black woman usually taken for a white; her (not necessarily separable) lives as a student, a philosopher, a political person and an artist; and the lived-out fantasy lives as a grotesque or a member of the underclass created in "Catalysis" and "The Mythic Being," in which, as she put it in a 1975 poster piece, "I embody everything you most hate and fear."

By the mid-seventies, "The Mythic Being" had been absorbed into Piper's eerie performer-persona—a sexy dancer, unmistakably female, with long black hair, "white-face" makeup and a thin black mustache. This ambiguously gendered note, combined with the ambivalence of the texts of her performances and posters, led at the end of the decade to the increasingly explicit "Political Self Portraits" (Piper's only truly autobiographical work, dealing in separate pieces with race, class and gender) and to a series of audiovisual installations—*Art for the Artworld Surface Pattern* (1977), *Aspects of a Liberal Dilemma* (1978) and the Wexner Center's *Four Intruders Plus Alarm Systems* (1980).

The 1977 and 1978 works are direct precedents for *Four Intruders* in that they include fictional responses to political art or imagined political imagery. *Art for the Artworld* also utilized a booth for privacy and *Aspects* was installed in a small room of its own, so that the encounter remained intimate. All three works are also related to Piper's indoor performance work since the mid-seventies. Although in the installations she is distanced from the audience, "playwright" rather than performer, *Four Intruders* maintains the directness of performance art, the confrontational quality that many art audiences, accustomed to control over their relationship to the art object, still find disturbing. They can't miss the presence of the artist behind her portrait surrogates.

Four Intruders is a circular black booth, with a curved vestibule leading to a dark space illuminated only by four silkscreened light boxes; photographic portraits of four black men leap from the walls; four audio monologues and a music soundtrack assail the viewer, who is presumably alone in this small space. The piece was inspired by Piper's experiences of racism in academia, by association with people "so smart in their respective fields, yet so very provincial and tasteless in all other areas of life. As elitists each of whom violated all of *my* elitist assumptions about the 'intellectual aristocracy,' i.e., the implicit connection between education and courtesy, cultivation, sensitivity, integrity, honesty, etc., they fascinated and repelled me. I tried to, but couldn't, crack the fears, fantasies and stereotypes they projected onto me."[23]

These encounters forced Piper to consider racism anew and to deal with the fact that even within liberal circles she was seen as "the racist's nightmare, the obscenity of miscegenation...a reminder that segregation is impotent; a living embodiment of sexual desire that penetrates racial barriers and reproduces itself...I represent the loathsome possibility that everyone is 'tainted' by black ancestry: If someone can look and sound like me and still be black, who is unimpeachably white?" She and others of mixed race become "unwilling witnesses to the forms racism takes when racists believe there are no black people present...Each of these responses—fear, fantasy, suspicion, anger, confusion, ignorance—obstructs my self-transcendence, my ability to lose myself temporarily in the other, in the world, in abstract ideas. These are the barriers my art practice reflects."[24]

Piper has said that she wants to "hold up for scrutiny the rationalizations about world problems that my audiences hold."[25] *Four Intruders* is about offense and defense mechanisms. The "intruders" are not the black men whose faces we see as we enter, but the white audience peering at them. The four audiotaped monologues represent a range of audience responses: the informed liberal, the offended ignoramus, the hip wannabe (or "appropriator"), the outright racist. The voices are not "acted." Patently fake and didactic, they are at the same time too real, too close to the bone for white viewers who have almost inevitably harbored at least some of the sentiments displayed:

> ...I'm antagonized by the hostility of this piece. Not all blacks are like that...Some of my best friends are black...I can understand black anger because I'm angry too...It's not my responsibility, it's not my fault...To be quite honest, I don't like blacks...They're all immoral, all animals...If they're having a bad time it's a basic defect in character...

Adrian Piper
Self-portrait Exaggerating My Negroid Features 1981
pencil on paper
9" x 12"
Photo courtesy of John Weber Gallery, New York.

Adrian Piper
Aspects of the Liberal Dilemma 1978
installation with audiotape and photograph
detail: photograph, 18" x 18"
Photo courtesy of John Weber Gallery, New York.

Dear Friend,
   I am black.
   I am sure you did not realize this when you made/laughed at/agreed with that racist remark. In the past, I have attempted to alert white people to my racial identity in advance. Unfortunately, this invariably causes them to react to me as pushy, manipulative, or socially inappropriate. Therefore, my policy is to assume that white people do not make these remarks, even when they believe there are no black people present, and to distribute this card when they do.
   I regret any discomfort my presence is causing you, just as I am sure you regret the discomfort your racism is causing me.
                                        Sincerely yours,
                                        Adrian Margaret Smith Piper

Adrian Piper
My Calling Card #1 1986
card for guerrilla performance
2" x 3 ½"
Photo courtesy of John Weber Gallery, New York.

But behind these critical, outsider voices, are those of the subversive insiders—the almost inaudible lyrics of the satirical chorus of "Night People" by the musical group War, ominous whispers, unfamiliar rhythms. These voices were later embodied in the drawn black figures that silently invade the opulent pages of *The New York Times* in Piper's "Vanilla Nightmares" series of the late eighties. There the threats are overtly sexual as well as political; the nude black "intruders" have sex and revolution on their minds. Taken as a group with the 1986 *My Calling Card (#1)*—a "reactive guerrilla performance" in which Piper hands a printed card to people at social occasions when she hears a racist remark; the card announces, "I am black…"—these works are remedies to social ills, wrenching but healing potions that can be taken only by the brave. This is art as philosophical action, socially responsible as well as morally rational.

The myths and stereotypes of black and female sexuality, the culture of sexuality and a melancholic desire on both sides of the color line, is a subtext in much of Piper's work. She tries to make sense (for us) of the legacy of destruction—wrought by slavery, rape, forced miscegenation, lynchings and psychological mutilations—that has formed the lives of both African-Americans and European-Americans in the United States. Piper's work is rare in its intensity, in an art scene where it is chic to be diffident about even the most crucial issues. Placing herself in the dangerous middleground (if it's no man's land, it must be woman's land), she insists on her own estrangement as a metaphor for ours. She demands that we look at society under the skin, "in depth," that we understand that "we" are the mirror images of "them" and that only the separations and divisions are backwards. By representing herself she challenges the representations society has made of her as a woman, a black, a "tragic mulatto." Like Benglis in her 1974 gender series, she demands that we look at ourselves in unaccustomed, often violent, frameworks, acknowledging the roles of power and desire in daily and political life.

At that crucial moment when the sixties gave way to the disappointing and disappointed seventies, neither Benglis nor Piper settled for fixed views of themselves, or of others like them. Their ideological self-representations, or what Craig Owens has called "strategies of mimetic rivalry,"[26] changed the terms of "difference" by offering mirror-readings of the master narrative that determined what art was in the sixties. For better and worse, nothing has been the same since. Both women have made art that functions as an "alarm system," calling attention to a reciprocal process. Every time people with whom we live—in the personal and public senses—redefine themselves, we respond involuntarily by our own reevaluations, as James Baldwin pointed out in the sixties:

> So where we are now is that a whole country of people believe I'm a "nigger," and I *don't*, and the battle's on! Because if I am not what I've been told I am, then it means that *you're* not what you thought you were either! And that is the crisis.[27] □

Sigmar Polke
Menschkin 1972
oil on fabric
39 ½" x 31 ½"
Collection of Elaine and Werner Dannheiser.
Photo: Fredrik Marsh.

"Give Up Painting" or the Politics of Art
A West German Abstract

Walter Grasskamp

Traumatized by material and spiritual devastation in mid-century, German art experienced a striking revitalization during the sixties and seventies. Influenced by the anarchic actions of the performance-oriented Fluxus group and the political activism of Joseph Beuys, artists such as Sigmar Polke, Georg Baselitz, Gerhard Richter, Jörg Immendorff and Anselm Kiefer challenged the postwar generation's apolitical and abstract Informalism. In the following essay, art historian and critic Walter Grasskamp outlines the resurgence of avant-garde West German art in the context of divided "German/German" (West and East) social and political history. Given the strong postwar ties between the United States and West Germany, German art was bound to have a strong impact on the avant-garde in America—perhaps even stronger than in Europe—contributing to revived interests in expressionistic and figurative painting and to renewed awareness of international developments.

Walter Grasskamp's essay was translated from the German by Joachim Neugroschel.

The Fight over Postwar Abstraction

In May 1985, on the occasion of the fortieth anniversary of Germany's surrender, Günter Grass gave a speech at the West Berlin Academy of the Arts. Titling his lecture "The Gift of Freedom," Grass summed up his view of how the West Germans had, or rather had not, come to terms with the defeat of National Socialism. When it was printed in *Die Zeit*, a leading West German weekly, Grass' speech triggered a brief, but vehement discussion. With several derogatory remarks, the writer had deliberately "broken a taboo" in rebuking postwar West German art for contributing to the suppression of all memory of the National Socialist terror and the war:

> When I arrived in Berlin as a young sculptor in January 1953, the arts were in danger of drifting off into total noncommitment...As little as possible was to be recognized of all the ugliness that we thought we had happily transcended. Ciphers, yes. Ornaments, of course. Plus materials and structures galore, pure form. But nothing too blunt, no image that would cause distress. No Dix, no Kirchner, no Beckmann forced the experiences of horror upon the canvas.[1]

It is certainly a curious feature of German art history that the profoundly shocking experience of the First World War was central to a large number of works by artists including Max Beckmann, George Grosz, Otto Dix, Ernst Ludwig Kirchner, Wilhelm Lehmbruck and Ludwig Meidner, while, on the other hand, the Second World War had almost no creative impact on West German artists; at most, it affected some who are considered second-rate: for instance, Rudolf Schlichter, Werner Heldt and Heinz Trökes.[2] Postwar painting in West Germany, as Günter Grass aptly charged, has been predominantly abstract. Nevertheless, one could disagree with his evaluation by pointing out that postwar abstraction should not necessarily be construed as an utterance of noncommitment and the blocking of history; abstraction can also be regarded as epitomizing the freedom of modernism—a freedom that the National Socialists denied to German artists for such a long time.[3] One of the major art critics in the Federal Republic of West Germany, Eduard Beaucamp of *Frankfurter Allgemeine Zeitung*, settled the conflict in Solomonic style by affirming that Grass' rebuke should really be aimed not at the goals of the abstract artists, but at the reception of their works.[4]

The End of Abstraction

Until the sixties abstract styles monopolized the official image of West German art, both at home and abroad, at the Documenta exhibitions in Kassel (which, in 1959, actually hailed abstraction as the language of the entire world) and at the Venice and São Paulo biennales. Ernst Wilhelm Nay, Hann Trier, Georg Meistermann, Emil Schumacher, Fred Thieler, Bernard Schultze, K. H. R. Sonderborg, Joseph Fassbender, Julius Bissier, K. O. Goetz, Gerhard Hoehme, Theodor Werner, Fritz Winter—these were the better-known representatives of West German abstraction. During the sixties a few of them taught at art academies in West Berlin, Kassel, Karlsruhe or Düsseldorf. However, not all the students were well-behaved adepts who believed in Informalism—the style of spontaneous abstraction then most prevalent—as the ultimate advance in the history of art, for during that period not only political conditions but also aesthetic conventions were shattered.

Two paintings, by artists who eventually became renowned, indeed world famous, can be seen as exemplifying those turbulent years: *Hört auf zu malen* (Give up painting, 1966) by Jörg Immendorff and *Moderne Kunst* (Modern art, 1968) by Sigmar Polke. Using different approaches—expressive and high-handed versus posterlike and ironic—both artists made it clear that a new generation was intent on refusing allegiance to the abstraction of Informalism. Polke and Immendorff were by no means the first artists to

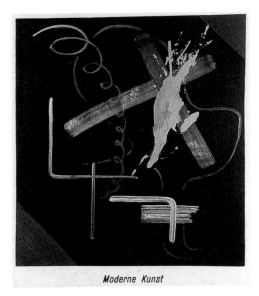

Moderne Kunst

Sigmar Polke
Moderne Kunst 1968
acrylic on canvas
59 ¹/₁₆" x 49 ³/₁₆"
Private Collection, Berlin.

Jörg Immendorff
Hört auf zu malen 1966
oil on canvas
53 ⅛" x 53 ⅛"
Stedelijk Van Abbemuseum,
Eindhoven, The Netherlands.

defect from this style. Back in the late fifties, Günther Uecker, Heinz Mack and Otto Piene, forming the Zero Group in Düsseldorf, had experimented with light and material in order to get away from monochromism and Informalism. In 1960 they were joined, if only for a brief moment, by a young artist who was just completing his apprenticeship under the abstract painter Fritz Winter in Kassel and who had, like Immendorff and Polke, resolved to give up painting: twenty-four-year-old Hans Haacke. Yet the two paintings by Polke and Immendorff brought the stylistic conflict of the early sixties to a head, paradoxically through painterly expression. They confronted an avant-garde art that had quickly become academic, and two of whose representatives, Gerhard Hoehme and K. O. Goetz, had been Polke's teachers. Immendorff, by contrast, had chosen a mentor who seemed to be overcoming Informalism: Joseph Beuys.

The Aesthetics of Revolt

Beuys was not as yet the charismatic catalyst of a "new concept of art" or "social sculpture." During the mid-sixties, he had students of vastly different temperaments: Blinky Palermo, Norbert Tadeusz, Imi Knoebel and Reiner Ruthenbeck, among them. Sigmar Polke had also attended his courses as an onlooker. Having become professor of sculpture at the Düsseldorf Staatliche Kunstakademie in 1961, Beuys initially tried to hitch up with an art movement that was then causing a sensation in the Rhineland: Fluxus.

During the early sixties the Rhineland between Wiesbaden (where George Maciunas was a draftsman with the United States Army in 1960), Wuppertal (Galerie Parnass), Cologne (Atelier Mary Bauermeister) and Düsseldorf (Galerie Jean-Pierre Wilhelm) had become a center of Fluxus and other artistic experiments. Nam June Paik and Karlheinz Stockhausen were revolutionizing what had previously been considered music; their mentor John Cage presented concerts; Benjamin Patterson and David Tudor performed; international Fluxus vagabonds such as Tomas Schmit, Dick Higgins, Wolf Vostell and Alison Knowles teamed up for public performances and events.

In 1963 Beuys took part, for the first time, in a Fluxus function, one that he himself organized at the Düsseldorf Academy: *Festum Fluxorum Fluxus*. Along with Schmit, Vostell and Paik, the participants included Emmett Williams, Frank Trowbridge, Arthur Köpcke, Bengt af Klintberg, Daniel Spoerri and George Maciunas. In Beuys, the Fluxus movement now had its first professor—a bridgehead in an institution that embodied just about everything that Fluxus was attacking: specialization, professionalization, isolation, personal artistic "penmanship," anticreative regimentation, production for the marketplace and academicism. Thus, Beuys was already openly defying the academy (a conflict that eventually culminated in his dismissal in 1972).

In 1964 Beuys was the involuntary focus of a spectacular Fluxus action at the Technical Institute of Aachen. It took place on the Twentieth of July, a West German holiday commemorating the abortive attempt on Adolf Hitler's life in 1944 and the subsequent execution of the resistance fighters who were involved. Enraged at the actions of the Fluxus group (which on this occasion included Tomas Schmit, Wolf Vostell, Stanley Brouwn, Bazon Brock, Eric Andersen, Henning Christiansen, Robert Filliou, Ludwig Gosewitz, Arthur Köpcke and Emmett Williams), a number of students finally charged on stage. A container of nitric acid had been placed there for a Beuys action, and in the confusion, a few drops of the acid were splashed on one student's socks and trousers. The student, wanting revenge, punched Beuys in the face, right on stage. Beuys' evidently spontaneous reaction—a pose with crucifix in his left hand, his right arm stretching in a Nazi salute, blood on his mouth and chin—became a frequently reproduced incunabulum of the Beuys myth.[5] (That same year brought Beuys his first showing at the Documenta exhibition in Kassel. This was the third Documenta; Beuys' work was given increasing prominence at subsequent Documenta exhibitions until and including the eighth one, which took place in 1987, a year after his death.) Then in 1965 in Wuppertal, the legendary *Twenty-Four Hour Happening* became a stunning high point of the German Fluxus movement. Nonetheless, Beuys was gradually separating from the group, absorbed in his highly independent actions but without forfeiting his public reputation as one of the leading Fluxus artists (an assessment with which not all the founding Fluxus artists concurred).

In retrospect, Fluxus was like an aesthetic curtain raiser to the student uprisings that followed just a few years later, like a preformed artistic version of the students' activism (which, however, was not adopted by the protest movement). Why didn't the rebelling students in Berlin and Frankfurt discover and venerate Beuys, Vostell and George Maciunas as their artists—instead of, at best, John Heartfield and George Grosz? Why was there no broad symbiosis of political and artistic activism, since the enemies pictured by the student movement were at least partially congruent with those pictured by Fluxus? The answer is simple if one looks at the documents of the Fluxus period. Fluxus was an elite matter, and its artistic revolution could not be directly translated into the milieu and

Five vitrines containing objects and multiples by Joseph Beuys from the collection of Lucio Amelio, Naples, Italy. Photo: Fredrik Marsh.

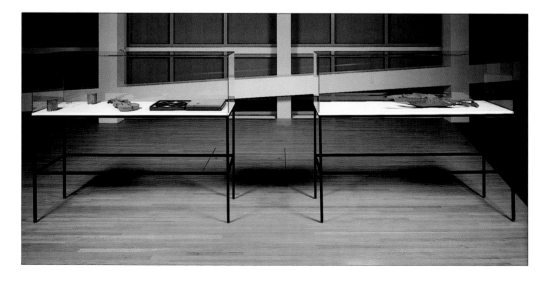

Joseph Beuys, Fluxus event, Aachen, 20 July 1964,
Photo: © Heinrich Riebesehl.

Joseph Beuys, *Twenty-Four Hour Happening,* 1965.
Photo: © Heinrich Riebesehl.

language of the students who now stormed forth with sit-ins and demonstrations to create a short-lived culture of protest. Furthermore, the students' protests were aesthetically undemanding; in any case, the students were uninterested in current "bourgeois" art, which, in their eyes, included everything that was linked to the art market or that made elitist claims.

The Politicization of Beuys

The student movement had a deep impact on several artists, Beuys in particular. In rapid succession, he adopted forms of political organization as fields of artistic work: in 1967 he founded the "German Student Party"; in 1970 the "Organization of Non-Voters/Free Referendums"; finally, in 1971 the "Organization for Direct Democracy through Referendums." These were marginal groups: on a political level, they were taken seriously by, at most, their few members. It was not his activities in these organizations, however, that contributed to the academy's dismissal of the irksome professor. What happened was that Beuys, ignoring an internal academy decision to limit student enrollment (*numerus clausus*), had permitted rejected applicants to attend his class. Nevertheless, his ouster in 1972 brought him some welcome publicity as a figure to be reckoned with in current politics. A photograph that showed Beuys cheerfully leaving the academy, flanked by an "honor guard" of policemen, supplied further blatant evidence of his special mission—and this evidence was frequently cited.

In 1973 Beuys founded the "Free International School for Creativity and Interdisciplinary Research," the last of the "mailbox companies" he established. Beuys, more than any other artist, devoted himself to activism, symbolic political understanding and the carefree anarchism that were propagated by the student revolt—unprofessionally but with a powerful effect on the public. No small number of observers wondered if it was precisely this public effect that interested Beuys, the missionizing marathon orator.

Beuys' cooperation with the ecological movement of the Greens in the late seventies finally seemed to produce the longed-for synthesis between art and politics: in 1979 Beuys was the party's candidate in the European parliament election. Nonetheless, the artist's charisma, which was now reaching its zenith in the art world, could not be translated into the distrustful and even antiartistic milieu of this ecological offshoot of the student movement. A short time later, the alliance came to an abrupt end when the Greens refused to let Beuys run for office in the German parliament. Beuys may have declared in 1985, "I hereby renounce art," but his claim to a leading political role was always based on artistic pose and fiction. As a politician, Beuys the shaman, the internationally renowned top-flight artist, remained a phantom by his own grace.

"To Do What Has To Be Done"

Beuys' student Jörg Immendorff was one of those artists whose self-conception was permanently "rattled" (as the term went) by the politicization of the sixties. The reproach of "escapism" and "bourgeois aestheticism" induced many art students in Immendorff's generation to give up their "individualistic, subjectivistic" art, temporarily or permanently. The protest movement wanted them to switch their majors to "more socially relevant" subjects, especially pedagogy; painting was not considered a politically meaningful activity. In 1985 Beuys struck the same note with his statement "the mistake already begins when you set out to buy stretchers and canvas."

Like no other member of his generation, Immendorff made this conflict the theme of his art, with a sometimes oppressively self-tormenting resoluteness. His early ironic and posterlike paintings referred to the situation of the academy student and "Beuys knight"; next came the anarchistic actions of *Lidl-Akademie* (1968–69), inspired by Chris Reinecke and Immendorff; and then *Rechenschaftsberichte* (Statements of Accounts, 1972), in which he zeroed in on a new role as artist, partially as art teacher in a *hauptschule* (approximately equivalent to an American junior high school). Immendorff's devotion to various local civic initiatives and, last but not least, his membership in a Maoist splinter party testified to the naïve sincerity of his political commitment—a sincerity that is now often greeted with suspicion. A shattering insight into the mentality of those years is still provided by his 1973 book *Hier und Jetzt: Das tun, was zu tun ist* (Here and now: To do what has to be done); this was a chaotic yet emphatic attempt at defining an artistic position in terms of a radical political engagement.[6] Like Bernd Koberling, who also was on the verge of abandoning painting altogether because of Maoist group pressure, Immendorff ultimately remained true to art. Indeed, his panoramic, richly allusive, by now almost relaxed ironic oeuvre has remained loyal to contemporary German/German history and to the artist's role.

Sigmar Polke, Bonn, 1984. Photo: Franz Fischer, courtesy of Galerie Klein, Bonn.

"Higher Beings Command"

Sigmar Polke, while no less politically aware than Immendorff, never pledged his painting to the student movement nor to any of its dogmatic spinoffs. During those years, his work gently poked fun at abstraction in a series of ironic reprises. His showpiece *Moderne Kunst* was framed by other paintings that looked like wily caricatures of the random and arbitrary nature of abstract painting, an art that had overestimated and overstimulated the value of subjectivity and spontaneity. Polke also took hefty pot shots at Minimalism and Conceptualism. For this artist, the incipient commodification of contemporary art (in 1967 Cologne was the site of the world's first fair devoted to current art) must have been as cogent a proof of the artistic crisis as the breakneck looting of all available sources of inspiration by the innovation mania of modernism. With *Langeweileschleife* (Boredom loop, 1969) and *Wiederbelebungsversuch an Bambusstangen* (Revival attempt on bamboo canes, 1967), Polke provided seemingly casual yet striking metaphors for the artistic situation. *Kartoffelhaus* (Potato house, 1967), his famous sculptural construction stocked with fresh potatoes, was accompanied by a text, supposedly co-authored with Friedrich W. Heubach, that explicitly addressed the problem of inspiration, but in a grotesque refraction that was typical of Polke in those days. His flirtation with "higher beings," who supposedly told him how and what to paint, also falls within the purview of this topic: *Höhere Wesen befahlen: Rechte obere Ecke schwarz malen!* (Higher beings command: Paint the upper right-hand corner black!, 1969).

Despite his political reserve, Polke was one of the most important political painters of the sixties if one considers his "grid pictures," which he based chiefly on printed newspaper photos, enlarging them and preserving their dotted screen patterns. Polke borrowed his pictorial ideas from the media, keeping the traces of the printing blocks as clues to the origins of his themes. By and large, such clichés also made up his contents: with a crafty dejá vu effect, simple wares and plain scenes appealed to the standardized consciousness of those West German consumers of goods and media who had just enjoyed the "economic miracle" of an unexpected postwar boom and prosperity: the *Wirtschaftswunder*.

During the seventies Polke became the second most important and influential model, after Beuys, for the subsequent generation of artists. His retrospective in 1976, curated by Benjamin H. D. Buchloh and mounted in Eindhoven, Tübingen and Düsseldorf, displayed the oeuvre of an artist who appeared less and less in public. While Polke's works of the sixties made him famous, his reputation was not consistently justified by his output during the seventies, particularly since he began to exploit—even grandstand with—the visual materials of the world of media and commodities, the very materials that he had once spoofed. Then, in the early eighties, Polke made a triumphal comeback at the seventh Documenta and at the *Zeitgeist* exhibition, where his paintings indicated that his sensitivity to the material character of colors had assumed alchemistic features.

The Indifferent

By comparison with Polke and Immendorff, Gerhard Richter, who had studied with Polke under Hoehme and Goetz during the sixties, seems to have been completely apolitical. When the Berlin Wall was erected in 1961, Richter had moved from East Germany to Düsseldorf. Trained as a craftsman of painting and photography according to the standards of Socialist Realism, Richter, after settling in the West, pursued a second course of studies, that of modernism. In his paintings, Richter, who was born in 1932 and, like all émigrés, was a late bloomer, seemed quite unfazed by the political turmoil of the sixties. In a highly concentrated manner, he swiftly covered all the stages of modern painting.

> I follow no aims, no system, no direction. I have no program, no style, no message. I care nothing about professional problems, work themes, variations to the point of mastery. I flee all specific commitment, I don't know what I'm after, I'm inconsistent, indifferent, passive. I like vagueness, rambling and constant uncertainty. Other characteristics lead to achievement, promotion, success; in any case, they're obsolete as ideologies, views, notions, names for something.[7]

That was how Richter summed himself up at the end of the sixties. Like Polke's "grid pictures," Richter's blurry paintings offer a continuity of style in what is otherwise an intricate and multifaceted oeuvre.

People suspected, however, that the wealth of gray and gaudy, abstract and figurative, decorative and irritating paintings camouflaged a discreet but nevertheless intense drama in Richter's studio and that the posture of the arrogant and indifferent artist concealed a brooding and vulnerable loner. Those suspicions were nourished by certain

Sigmar Polke
Untitled 1971
acrylic and chalk on cloth
51 ¾" x 61"
Collection of Bette Ziegler.
Photo: Zindman/Fremont.

interviews and especially by the 1987 publication of some of Richter's journals. Thus, it came as a complete surprise when, in 1989, he painted a series of portraits of the leading figures in the Red Army Faction, the left-wing terrorist group that, during the early seventies, had helped to wreck the few liberalizing successes attained by the student movement. The title of Richter's exhibition was *October 18, 1977*—the date of the never fully explained suicides of the group's leading members in the high-security ward of a prison that had been built specifically for them. Richter's show confronted a political trauma of recent West German history—a trauma that still cannot be publicly discussed or properly tackled without resentment.

"A New Type"

In 1981, at Düsseldorf's Kunsthalle, Jürgen Harten installed an exhibition that juxtaposed the works of Gerhard Richter with those of Georg Baselitz. This constellation could not have looked immediately plausible to many connoisseurs of postwar German art—for what was the common denominator between these two so disparate artists? It could scarcely be their origins in East Germany, which Baselitz had left in 1956 at the age of eighteen and Richter in 1961 at the age of twenty-eight. After all, they shared this fate with several other prominent representatives of postwar West German art: Sigmar Polke, Gotthard Graubner, Günther Uecker, Eugen Schönebeck, A.R. Penck, Blinky Palermo and Markus Lüpertz all had come West as adolescents or adults. Could the link between Richter and Baselitz have been the fact that both of them stuck to painting without following its traditions—one artist vagabonding through styles, the other painting upside down? Was it their discernible love-hate relationship with the narrative aspect of painting, their struggle with subject matter, which they wished neither to eliminate nor to build on? Or was it their Informalist training, which Baselitz had completed under Hann Trier in West Berlin and Richter under Goetz in Düsseldorf?

In any case, Baselitz, unlike Richter, had always avoided abstraction. In 1969 he had rigorously defined and delimited his oeuvre by reversing the motifs of his paintings. His work includes various painting styles, as does Richter's, but these do not manifest themselves simultaneously, enjoying equal rights, as they do in Richter's work; instead they occur in various stages of his artistic development. In West Germany, the painters who, like Baselitz, lived in West Berlin for a time—Hödicke, Koberling, Lüpertz, Schönebeck—were noticed much later than the major artists of the Rhineland, and Baselitz started off with a group of works that were long ignored. These were known as variations on the theme of "A New Type." In Baselitz's archaic and grandiloquent formulation, the problems of the artist's role were tied to the experience of war, represented by a devastated land and burning houses, as if they were victims of the Thirty Years' War. Tools from the sphere of agrarian labor contrast with the viewer's metropolitan and industrialized world, sunken flags look like signals of defeat. The constantly recurring figure of the towering loner, identified as an artist by his props, is also a border crosser, who enters the picture by smashing through a wall. The burning house can thus also function as a metaphor for a lost homeland. It was hardly a coincidence that when Baselitz settled in the West, he took the name of his hometown as his pseudonym. In these Baselitz paintings, the postwar German/German destiny has assumed the contours of an individual drama, like the vast cataclysmic war, through whose smoking ashes the "barricaded" artist seems to be roaming.

Scorched Earth

Baselitz had left the theme of connections between artistic biography and postwar German history by the end of the sixties, but in 1973 he found a successor in Anselm Kiefer, who was seven years his junior. Kiefer had attended a provincial academy in southern Germany, and it wasn't until 1970, his final year at school, that he occasionally visited Joseph Beuys in Düsseldorf. Kiefer then settled down in the south German provinces, where Baselitz had also painted for a few years. Baselitz recommended Kiefer to his dealer, Michael Werner, who had once had a gallery in Berlin but by then had opened a new gallery in Cologne, and in 1973 Werner gave Kiefer a solo exhibition. In 1980 Baselitz and Kiefer were the West German representatives at the Venice Biennale, which launched their international reputations.

Anselm Kiefer
Malen=Verbrennen (Painting=Burning) 1974
oil on burlap
86 ⅝" x 118 ⅛"
Collection of Jerry and Emily Spiegel,
Kings Point, New York.

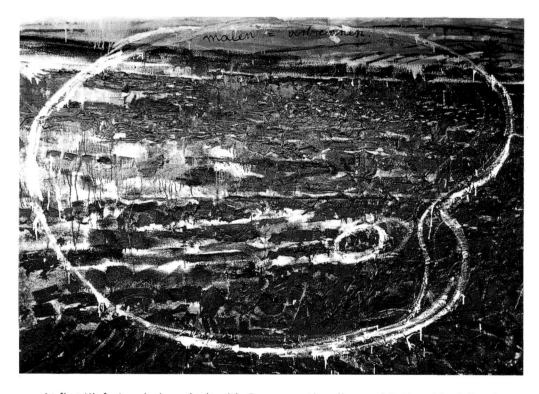

At first Kiefer's paintings dealt with German nationalism and National Socialism in a manner that could be extremely misleading and even eccentric, but during the seventies and early eighties he moved on to examine more closely and thoroughly the "adulterated legacy" of the National Socialist blend of German traditions. His paintings were a tremendous, almost violent analysis of German hubris, virtually a daily psychotherapy in which an individual worked through the guilt of an entire nation. Kiefer was the first artist who dared to overrate himself so thoroughly as to tackle a theme for which modern painting seemed to have found no legitimate approach. Kiefer was rebuked for painterly eclecticism; his sources were traced back to the poster demolitions of Nouveau Réalisme and the central perspective of an obsolete pictorial conception, to the chalk drawings of Beuys and the German chauvinism of woodcuts, to the material aesthetics of Arte Povera and the impasto pigment battles of a sportive Informalism. In fact, half-finished canvases in Kiefer's studio look like poetic, suggestive, and first-rate products of Informalism. Some artists of the fifties and sixties would probably have given their eye teeth just to pull off such paintings. For Kiefer, they are intermediary phases, rough forms, from which the real painting has to be hauled out, squeezed out. Could the abstract and Informal painting of the fifties and sixties have been such a necessary intermediate phase in the evolution of pictures that come close to German history and reality? ☐

Gilbert and George
The Queue 1978
95" x 79"
Collection of Robert J. Dodds III.
Photo courtesy of the artists.

Ways To Be

Carter Ratcliff

After several decades of successive (if inevitably overlapping), relatively cohesive art movements, defining the avant-garde became particularly complex in the late sixties. Critic and author Carter Ratcliff discusses various strands of what had become a very tangled skein: video sculpture, earthworks, performance art, "new image" painting, autobiographical objects. New areas of art making blossomed in the increasingly eclectic—or pluralistic—avant-garde of the late sixties and early seventies as an apparently monolithic American culture began to break into distinct factions over issues such as the Vietnam War and civil rights. The mixture in the art world was decidedly international: the German Joseph Beuys, the Korean Nam June Paik, the English team of Gilbert and George and such Americans as sculptor Robert Smithson and painter Susan Rothenberg spoke to international audiences as like-minded attitudes coalesced on a global rather than national scale.

The passage of time has expanded the meaning of a work like Nam June Paik's *TV Buddha*. When it was new, in 1974, this piece looked like another in a series of the artist's affronts to the severe, self-contained styles that dominated the sixties and still retained much of their authority in the following decade. *TV Buddha* is particularly well calculated to disquiet a Minimalist sensibility. Minimalism was a search for what Donald Judd called "the specific object," the artwork that is plainly and undeniably itself and nothing but itself. By deliberate contrast, Paik's Buddha is both its statuesque self and an image on the television monitor it faces. Or maybe, in our era, the image on the screen is the primary presence and the statue is secondary. *TV Buddha* denies the self-evident unity that the Minimalists tried to establish with simple geometric form. However, the piece presents a less obvious kind of unity, one that also appears in works such as Judd's horizontal "progression" *Untitled* (1965).

Across the front of Judd's sculpture stretches a pattern of solids and voids. As curved protrusions diminish in width, the empty spaces between them grow proportionately larger. To trace the narrowing of voids is to watch solids grow wider. Because a left-to-right reading seems just as legitimate as a right-to-left reading, the eye feels itself caught in an endless loop. In Paik's *TV Buddha*, an analogous loop joins the statue seated on the floor to its image on the screen. I'm not suggesting that we revise our definition of Minimalism to include Paik's art. Still, he shares with artists such as Judd, Sol LeWitt and Robert Morris a predilection for closed systems.

Substituting a flame for an electronic image, Paik's *Candle TV* (1975) suggests that television is not just a means of getting the news and being entertained. It also provides social focus, like the hearth or occasional bonfire of earlier times. With these speculations, Paik gravitated into the neighborhood of the visionary Marshall McLuhan, who talked of television and "the global village." Paik's affinities with McLuhan far removed him from the Minimalists, who made it a matter of official policy to expunge social commentary—indeed, commentary of any sort—from their art. Judd's "specific object" does not acknowledge what the Surrealist Paul Eluard called the "physics of poetry." Paik's objects do.

Paik has reinvented Surrealism's technique of poetic discontinuity for the electronic age, yet the metaphoric nature of his art does not prevent him from employing devices usually considered Minimalist—*Candle TV*, for example, is a precisely symmetrical object; his installation pieces are as serial as Sol LeWitt's; and, as we've noted, *TV Buddha* sends the mind on a loop as securely closed as the one the eye follows through Judd's "progression" sculptures. Paik looks like an artist determined to provide Minimalism with social vision—and a sense of play.

Dispensing with canvas in the late sixties, Lynda Benglis poured tinted polyurethane directly on the floor. Her solidified puddles look like the work of a sculptor whose chief ancestor figure is a painter—Jackson Pollock. Splashed, dripped and poured, these thin objects are action sculptures. They suggest geological events, the quick flow of lava or the soil's slow sedimentation. When form thickens, metaphor turns biological. Heaped in a corner, *For Carl Andre* (1970) attains the bulk and, with it, the bodily presence of a creature that is decidedly not human but not entirely alien, either.

Since the early seventies Benglis has worked with gauze, wire screenings, spangles and other, mostly unorthodox, materials. In recent years she has cast wall sculptures in bronze, covering some of them with gold leaf. Even when made with these traditional methods and materials, Benglis' works inhabit the present with the immediacy of animate things—startling flowers or invertebrate animals in odd, even alarming forms. Early in her career, a quirky, organic energy spread her polyurethane pieces across the floor. Exerting its evolutionary pressures, that same energy generated the crisply ribbed bodies of her recent works and then, still restless, it tied those bodies in elegantly writhing knots.

The late sixties was a frantically busy time. As Lynda Benglis displaced action painting from canvas to floor, Robert Smithson reinvented it at the scale of the Western landscape. Like a splash of Jackson Pollock's Duco enamel, Smithson's *Spiral Jetty* (1970) is the track of a gesture in a space understood as unlimited. Pollock gestured with his hand and arm. To make his forms, Smithson directed earth-moving equipment. Thus he mechanized a kind of action that, in the myth of Pollock, was quintessentially natural. According to that myth, only a surge of bodily energy could generate authentic art. Having looked hard at Jasper Johns' detachment and the assembly-line procedures of Andy Warhol, Smithson disagreed. Physical gesture, he argued, is no more natural than the workings of a mechanical device. If art is to have a public presence, why not borrow the methods of road builders and architectural contractors? Only with the machinery that had formed—and deformed—the present-day landscape could one make pertinent art, Smithson claimed.

During the mid-sixties he fabricated from metal and mirrored glass sculptures as quirky as Judd's and Morris' works from that period are regular. By the end of the decade, Smithson was incorporating detritus from urban landscapes into pieces he called "nonsites," among them *Gravel Mirror with Cracks and Dust*, a sprawling sculpture that originally appeared in a nonsite exhibition in 1968. Its six mirrors line the gallery wall, their lower edges resting on the floor, where six more mirrors lie, abutting their vertical counterparts. Along this glass-line meeting of wall and floor, gravel has been dumped with enough force to crack the horizontal mirrors. Reflecting the random shape of the gravel heaps and the cracks they made, the vertical mirrors establish symmetry. Yet the look of randomness persists, mocking the Minimalist axiom that symmetry enforces order.

Toward the end of the sixties Robert Morris and Carl Andre, who also had seemed an obsessive grid maker in the mathematical compositions of his earlier fire-brick sculptures, exhibited scatter pieces as disorderly as any of Smithson's gravel and mirror works. Within a few seasons, Sol LeWitt had permitted random patterns into his wall drawings. Styles evolve under many pressures, most of them undetectable. Surely, though, we can be certain that Smithson's skepticism helped undermine confidence in Minimalist geometry.

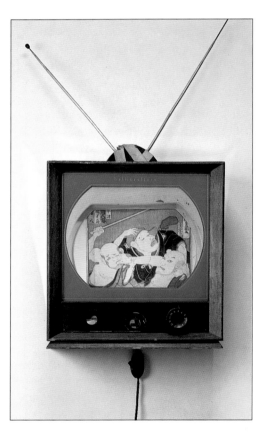

Nam June Paik
18th Century TV late 1960s
vintage wood TV cabinet with antique oriental scroll, aerial, electric light and stand, masking tape
17 ¾" x 15 ¾" x 7"; aerial height: 18"
Collection of Peter and Barbara Moore.
Photo: Fredrik Marsh.

Nam June Paik
TV Chair 1968
standard metal-frame chair, lucite seat, plastic backing, suspended TV set
30" x 20" x 20"
Collection of Allan Kaprow.
Photo: Fredrik Marsh.

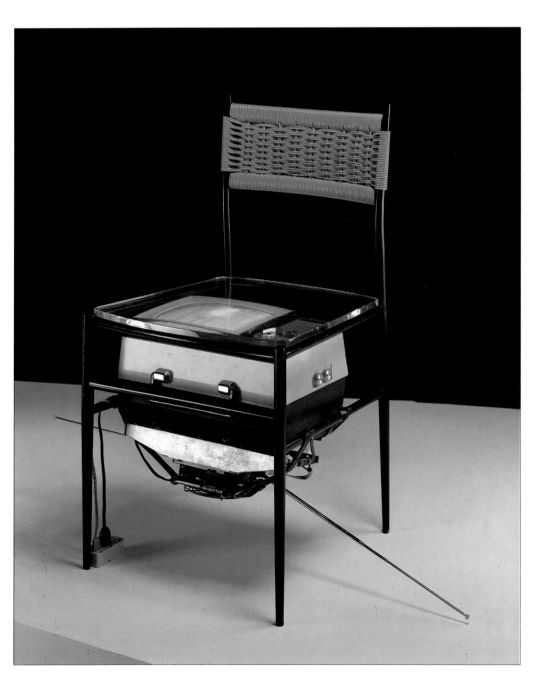

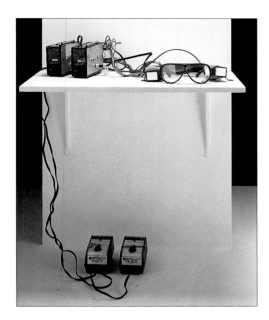

Nam June Paik
TV Glasses 1971
Reconstruction by the artist
mixed media
dimensions variable
Collection of the artist.
Photo: Fredrik Marsh.

Andre later returned to straight lines and sharply defined angles. Judd never abandoned them. Yet after the sixties no one pretended that Euclidean clarity provides enduring solutions to problems of form.

Agnes Martin's luminous canvases from the sixties are sometimes associated with Minimalism. One understands why. Her images are linear, sparse and repetitive. Yet there is nothing impersonal about them, no air of industrial fabrication. Eye and hand determine the intervals of her patterns. Her closest links are to Barnett Newman, Mark Rothko and other painters of that first postwar generation. Like them, she intimates boundless space with imagery related only arbitrarily to the edges of the canvas. No master concept enforces closure, as in Judd's *Untitled* (1965) or a serial sculpture by Sol LeWitt. Feeling, not concept, drives Martin's art. She cultivates a pensive ecstasy, a contemplative sublime. Wide open, her canvases intimate infinity—and, by the way, call into question the neat labels and closed pattern of analysis we so often rely upon when we try to make sense of art.

Standard accounts divide American art of the sixties into three parts—Pop art, Color Field painting and Minimalism. But if one forgoes the comforts of this cliché, the sixties reveal themselves as an unbounded, eclectic sprawl, in which—as one example—the seeming certainties of Judd's Minimalist sculpture fought to hold their own against the doubts advanced by Smithson's ironic antisculpture. Such eclecticism reached far into the next decade. Long evident on the American and international scene, stylistic independence often seemed willful during the seventies. In 1971 Joe Zucker replaced brush strokes with cotton balls soaked in rhoplex and tinted with acrylics. Wrapping simple geometric forms with wire and rope, Jackie Winsor turned anonymous Minimal sculptures into obsessively personal fetishes. Susan Rothenberg violated monochrome canvases with images of horses.

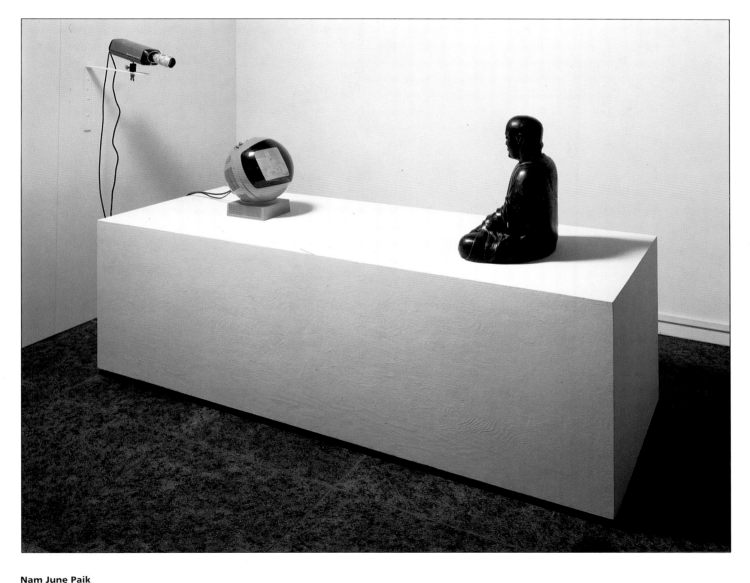

Nam June Paik
TV Buddha 1974
2-part video installation with wooden, 18th-century
Buddha, camera, monitor
64" x 86" x 32"
Stedelijk Museum, Amsterdam, The Netherlands.
Photo: Fredrik Marsh.

Denounced as regressive, Rothenberg offered no theoretical defense, no explanatory manifesto. When asked for a catalogue statement, she would sometimes remain mute. Never has she said why she chose to make pictures of horses. Reluctantly she acknowledged that the large Xs reaching across her early canvases have Minimalist origins. They bring a degree of abstraction, of the arbitrary, to works that run the risk of looking like illustrations of a sentimental subject. Stretched taut, each X seems to enforce a rule requiring the horse to stand—or to gallop—in silhouette.

These creatures never turn their heads toward us. If they did, there would be no gaze directed outward, for they have no eyes. Rothenberg's horses are oddly absent, or one could say that, despite appearances, her paintings are abstract. One finds the vitality of works like *Sienna Dos Equis* (1974) in the dense, heavily worked textures of their pigments. By the end of the seventies, the pressure of the artist's ruminative, quietly driven hand had broken her horses into fragments. Skeletal heads floated free of bodies. In *Blue Frontal* (1978) a pair of detached legs make a gawkily circular pattern. Letting the flesh fall away from these body parts, Rothenberg made configurations from giant bones. From these motifs others slowly evolved, and her images accrued weighty but elusive meanings. The Minimalists hoped that with impersonal, regularized form they could impose a degree of uniformity on their audience's response. Rothenberg's enigmatic art makes only one demand: that the viewer's reaction be thoroughly idiosyncratic.

In the photographs that art-world publications sometimes require, Rothenberg looks like a reluctant sitter. She seems to distrust the camera because it functions at a distance from its subjects, unlike this artist, who works and reworks her canvases with myopic intensity. We too must get close to the image, so that vision can work its way into the grain of the paint. This is a private process that no public persona would illuminate, so Rothenberg has been content to present the art world with a blurred and enigmatic image of herself. By contrast, Gilbert and George have not merely given their public image a sharp focus. They have made that image the center of their art.

Upon graduating from St. Martin's School of Art, London, in 1967, Gilbert and George dubbed themselves "the human sculptors" and proclaimed that every object they presented—whether drawing, photo-piece or booklet filled with writing—was sculpture. So was everything they did—"walking sometimes, reading rarely, eating often…drawing occasionally, talking lightly…greeting politely and waiting until the day breaks," as they wrote in 1970. Of course Gilbert and George are also sculptures, the products of their own sculptural efforts. Early in their joint careers they would sometimes assume a pose in a public place and hold it for hours, their hands and faces covered with metallic pigments that gave them the look of objects cast in bronze. Since the late sixties they have worn the same uniform: white shirt and sober tie, slightly outmoded suit, sturdy and sensible shoes. Just as invariably, their manners have been formal, considerate and rigorously detached. Blending art and life by iron-willed fiat, Gilbert and George did away with their private selves. Even when, in the mid-seventies, they played the part of public drunks they maintained a propriety that might be called statuesque. They have always faced the world as if they were monuments, not people.

From their "drunken" period came photo-pieces that show Gilbert and George in all the stages of inebriation, from bright chattiness to squalid stupor. Neatly framed but scattered over walls in tipsy patterns, these works upset the serene order established earlier by photo-pieces that show "the human sculptors" amid nature, striking poses in London parks and strolling down country lanes. After drunkenness came the deep melancholy of photo-pieces showing the artists in dreary, unfinished interiors. Gathered

Gilbert and George, *The Singing Sculpture*, 1971.
Photo: © Fred W. McDarrah.

Gilbert and George
Taxi 1978
95 ¼" x 74 ⅜"
The Arthur and Carol Goldberg Collection.
Photo courtesy of the artists.

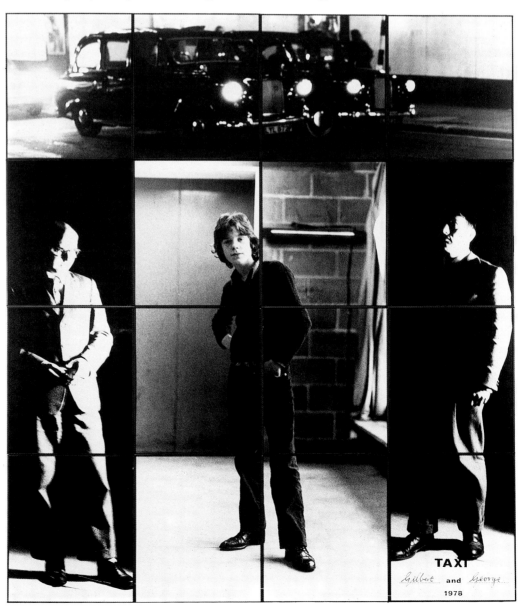

Gilbert and George
Lick 1977
95" x 79"
Collection of Martin Sklar.
Photo courtesy of the artists.

Opposite top
Susan Rothenberg
Siena Dos Equis 1974
acrylic and tempera on canvas
144" x 274"
Private collection; courtesy Sperone Westwater,
New York.
Photo: Fredrik Marsh.

Opposite bottom
Susan Rothenberg
Blue Frontal 1978
acrylic, flashe and tempera on canvas
77" x 88 ½"
Private collection; courtesy Sperone Westwater,
New York.
Photo: Dorothy Zeidman.

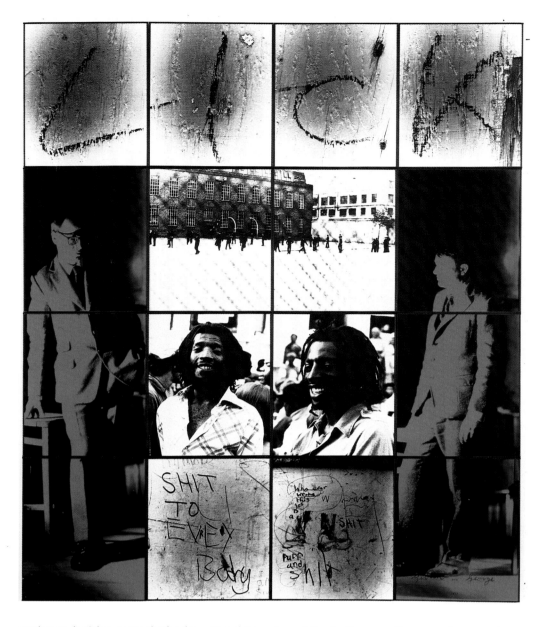

under such titles as *Dark Shadow*, *Dead Boards* and *Dusty Corners*, these works seem to be imprisoned by the gridwork of black frames enclosing their black-and-white images. In 1976 images of London and its denizens began to appear within the grid, alternating with the inevitable pictures of Gilbert and George. A bright red, transparent dye spread over some photos. By the end of the decade, faces, buildings, bits of graffiti had begun to reach from frame to frame. Though the grid persisted, it let violent, often directionless currents of modern life flow at will through such works as *The Queue* (1978), *Taxi* (1978) and *Lick* (1977).

Pictured full-length or in close-up, Gilbert and George appear in the margins of these pieces. Perhaps they are witnesses to the glum, bitter, frenzied misery that surrounds them, yet their gazes don't seem to focus on anything in particular. The artists are pensive, as if thoughts of the city and its sorrows had driven their attention inward. Nonetheless, they are still "the human sculptors," public presences with a monumental air. Their awkward postures and downcast gazes charge the surrounding images with a peculiar urgency. In these works from the late seventies Gilbert and George look like allegorical figures of conscience. They invite us not only to look but to think and to reckon up the significance of what we see. If the world is thus, "the human sculptors" imply, it could be otherwise. Obliquely but powerfully, a utopian impulse animates their art.

This utopian impulse is easier to see in the ecstatic spirituality of Gilbert and George's works of the eighties, especially their mural-sized exhortations to see the oneness of all life. Yet even as drunks, they wanted to redeem and to be redeemed. They have always striven to be more conscious of "the universal self," which, in their view, is the source of individual personalities. They dedicate themselves tirelessly to what they call "the substance of life and its indwelling forces." And they hope that their efforts to understand and to celebrate life will gain an exemplary strength from the public, statuesque nature of their being. Gilbert and George propose a new mode of existence, and that is why I call their art utopian.

Granted, one cannot not extract from their images and pronouncements a systematic utopia of the kind proposed by the visionaries of the European prewar avant-garde—

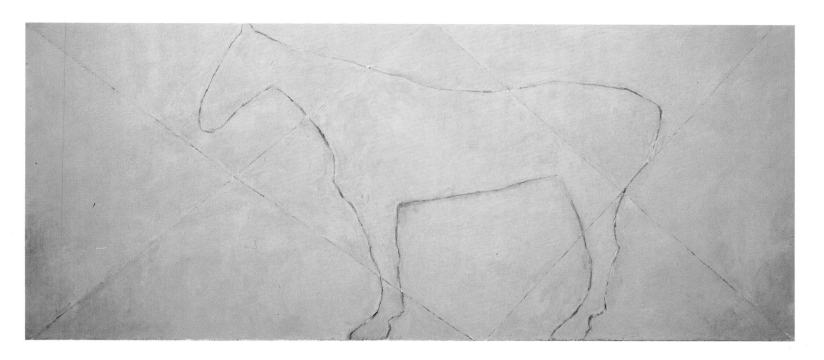

Joseph Beuys, *Twenty-Four Hour Happening*, 1965.
Photo: © Heinrich Riebesehl.

Le Corbusier, for example, was not content merely to design buildings. He also imagined a Radiant City so harmonious in form and function, he claimed, that it would produce a new and better variety of citizen. Piet Mondrian and his colleagues of de Stijl tried to impose an impersonal clarity on painting and sculpture, architecture and city planning. Purged of idiosyncrasy, artworks and buildings could raise individuals above the constraints of their individuality—or so the movement's polemicists argued. In de Stijl's city of the future, people would be integral parts of a smoothly running metropolitan machine. Programmatic visions like these did not survive the Second World War, yet visionary artists are rife in our era.

To register the utopian impulses of postwar art, we must construe utopia not as a rigid program for an ideal society but as a predilection, often only half-conscious, to resist the main thrust of society as it is. Two activities are characteristically modern: gathering hard, empirical data and seeking success in the marketplace (often by the application of data). The artist who lets speculative thought usurp the privileged place of empirical investigation is utopian. So is the artist who insists that we calculate success by some measure other than conformity to the demands of the marketplace. Empiricism and commerce reduce the self to a manipulable detail in a large, abstract pattern, so any art that insists on the singularity of selves, on the irreducibility of the individual, has at least some flavor of utopia—not of Corbusier's or Mondrian's kind but of the only kind that we find plausible now. In our time, we must look for utopia in the model of the self that an artist's work proposes. How does the artist suggest that we live our lives, and what world does that suggestion imply?

Opposite from the grand spectacle of Gilbert and George's photo-pieces are Susan Rothenberg's elusive, inward paintings. As Gilbert and George's art asserts no inward concerns, Rothenberg's projects no public persona. In short, they and she have nothing in common—save that each proposes a way to be. Gently snared by the nuances of Rothenberg's paintings, the viewer's sensibility shuts in on itself. To examine her art is to reflect on one's own perceptions and feelings. By encouraging this reflection, her work argues—implicitly, of course—that the elaboration of the self is a primary good. A corollary to this argument concludes that the best of all possible worlds is the one that most vigorously promotes this good, this essential benefit. Rothenberg gives no sign of believing that her art will bring that sort of world into being. Still, her art suggests how it would feel to live in it.

The late Joseph Beuy's elaborate programs of political and economic improvement gave him a resemblance to an avant-garde utopia from the prewar era. A teacher not only to his students at the Düsseldorf Academy but to the world, Beuys put us under an obligation to extract lessons from his art. This is not easy, for his methods blended a Pied Piper's glamour with the obscurities of a tribal shaman. He did not, after all, work out the sort of utopian detail that fills the writings of Mondrian, Theo van Doesburg and other members of de Stijl. The blackboards he covered with notations during his lectures are prized as much for the quality of his hand as for any utopian prescriptions that can be deciphered from their chalky tangles.

Like Gilbert and George, Beuys made his public persona his chief image. Dressed like an old-fashioned rural worker, his gaze beaming intently from under the brim of his fedora, Beuys personified a Europe that advances optimistically while maintaining contact with a myth of its pastoral origins. He made himself an allegorical figure of community in a time when we routinely suppose that the technological advance can only reduce social structures to fragments. Animal fat and felt, materials with which Beuys layered and swaddled so many inanimate and mechanical objects, became his aesthetic property. Both are organic, both conserve warmth. Symbolically, they confer life on objects that we usually see as dead, or at least as deadening, for they are mechanical.

Ever since the onset of the Industrial Revolution, visionaries have warned that machines mechanize those who work with them. Now, electronic equipment generates the same fear: humans will lose their humanity to their tools. Beuys wanted the energies of transformation to run in the opposite direction. His art implies a world in which each of us can make the shamanistic gesture that removes the alien aura from objects. In a world like that, we would make only the most agreeable gestures toward one another. We would feel our closeness to animals, the source of fat and felt. Further, our respect for their environment—which, of course, is ours as well—would increase. The Beuysian utopia is Eden-like.

Robert Smithson was a dystopian. From the urban landscape he drew detritus and photographic evidence of decay, arranging these to suggest that the present is a dreary, as opposed to a dramatic, inferno. With his earthworks, Smithson raised his infernal vision to a geological scale. In the desert and at ocean's edge, he built forms to be unbuilt, a particle at a time, by the forces of entropy. Invoking the universe's eventual return to chaos, he suggested that utopian impulses are absurd. One can, at most, be conscious that a principle of disintegration is built into the structure of matter. Art is good, in Smithson's view, if it encourages that consciousness. If not, it is merely a distraction. Maybe his sculptures and earthworks imply an ironic utopia, a world inhabited only by those who face the future with no delusions about what it can be made to promise.

I said at the outset that Nam June Paik shares certain devices with the Minimalists— symmetry, serial progression, closed loops of form and imagery. Though Donald Judd has explicitly rejected utopian programs like de Stijl's, his work proposes an ideal of order, and so does sculpture by the other Minimalists. The clarity of their forms encourages an analytical response. In Paik's art, formal clarities prompt the viewer to look beyond the shapes of objects to the meanings of symbols—to decipher his equation of candle and television screen, for example, or to note the way his *TV Glasses* (1971) change the terms of seeing and being seen. "TV has attacked us all our lives; now we are hitting back!" the artists has said, though his counterattack is hardly violent. With disjunctions and displacements, he catches in webs of metaphor a medium that usually reduces us to passive receptivity. Paik jokes with TV, a utopian practice suggesting that someday television and its audience might share power equally. For Paik, that utopian future has already arrived. □

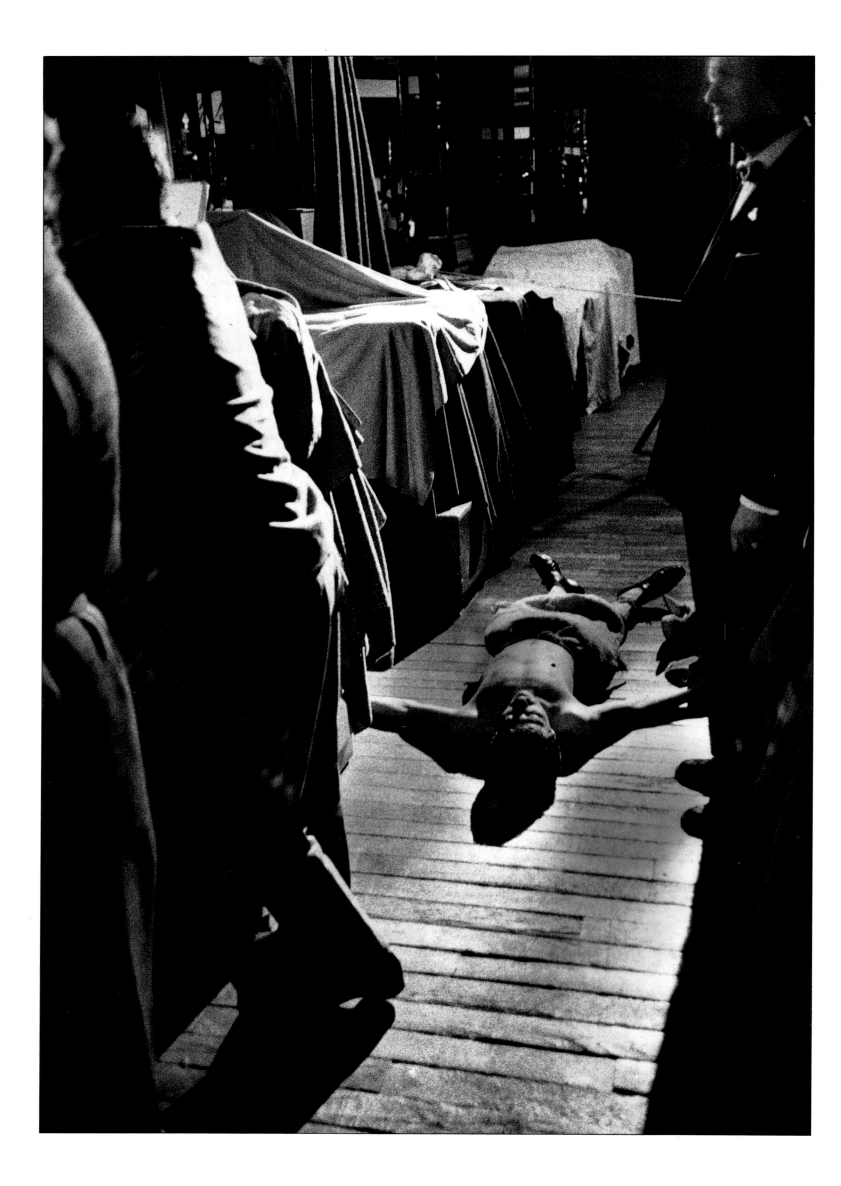

Bon Marché

Allan Kaprow

Allan Kaprow is credited with having named an entirely new art form with his 18 Happenings in 6 Parts (1961), one noted example of live art staged by visual artists during the early sixties. Although the term "Happening" finally expired of overuse, the idea of performance art became one of the most influential avant-garde inventions of the decade; performance has continued to attract numerous artists as an independent genre and to affect developments in avant-garde dance and theater. The notion of multidisciplinary interactions had been sporadically enticing earlier in the century, notably at educational communities such as the Bauhaus and Black Mountain College, but Kaprow's activities showed that performance art could yield something different indeed. Here, Kaprow contributes an essay describing the genesis and reception of one Happening, a time-capsule document originally written in 1963 that demonstrates the heady energy of performance art in its formative period.

In the summer of 1963 Brian O'Doherty, who was then working at the *New York Times*, asked me to do a piece for the newspaper on one of my first European Happenings, which had just taken place in Paris. I wrote the following story but it was judged too long, and I replaced it with a shorter account of a subsequent event I did in Edinburgh. The text of the Paris Happening was filed away and remained unpublished—until now. As I look it over twenty-six years later, there are wonderful differences of style and subject matter in that event compared with what I do today. Back then my work was a mix of Kerouac and dime-store surrealism; now it is plain and without urgency. Then it was wildly romantic; the current work is flat-footed. The artistic background in 1963 was European modernism and American Pop; today art has been left behind, and instead I wonder how many steps it takes to wear a hole in my shoe.

But outside of the art world the early sixties was a time of crisis. Cold War tactics intensified. Nuclear development proliferated, along with conventional arms build-up. Scientists warned of radiation dangers and of acid rain and pollution from unchecked technology that were destroying the earth. Violence marked Third World nations' bids for independence, as one leader after another was overthrown. Apartheid in South Africa and the civil rights movement in America fueled social unrest and dominated the news. The United States cut all ties with Cuba, and Russian missiles were revealed on the island. The Berlin Wall was built as fact and symbol of ideological incompatibility. Vietnam became the focus of East-West conflict and would soon erupt into a full-fledged, disastrous war. Civilian protests grew and joined forces with civil rights activism. Campuses here and abroad became scenes of political opposition. President John F. Kennedy was assassinated in Dallas.

Only the frightening side of that time is pictured in the above description. It doesn't contain a word of the more positive, even heady, aspects of the sixties: Elvis Presley, the Beatles, the youth movement, the sexual revolution, and above all the vivid belief then in the Promised Land, a dream that has seduced three-hundred years of Western progress. There would be, someday, a modern world fit to live in. It was implicit. But it was exactly this conviction that lay at the heart of the outrage expressed by young people against military and political conflicts, and especially against social injustice. They believed the world could be better, as they'd been told by their parents and teachers, but they also believed that the world's aged leaders were throwing that chance away. It was simple, and it was probably true. But there was very little practical sense of the hard and complicated task of bringing about change.

It was this unstable world that framed the new arts of that time. Artists became concerned with whether and how their art related to the times. Some would become politicized and would devise a fresh kind of activism, using the mass media and performative techniques such as sit-ins and marches. Others, not overtly political in their work, turned dramatically away from formalist modernism and toward the literal materials and spaces of everyday life. What all these artists shared was a powerful interest in the real world where so much that was crucial was taking place. And out of this context, *Bon Marché* was conceived. (In fact, the Algerian independence controversy was in full force then, and plastic bombs were a commonplace in Paris.) Here follows the text of the 1963 article, with only a few repetitive phrases and sentences removed.

Allan Kaprow's *Bon Marché*, Paris, 7 July 1963.
Photo: © Harry Shunk.

Above and below, Allan Kaprow during *Bon Marché*.
Photo: © Harry Shunk.

Bon Marché was the final offering of the Théâtre des Nations' annual summer festival, to which I and other Americans (Erick Hawkins, Jean Erdman, Kenneth Dewey) were invited. The title means "cheap" or "budget-priced" and was taken from the name of the well-known Paris department store where the Happening was performed on three successive evenings. Its theme was suggested by the daytime activities of the store and by the morguelike, shrouded appearance the store took on after the closing hour. I sensed in the ritual exchange of packages for money, and in the nighttime aisles of cloth-covered merchandise and mannequins, an inevitable circularity of imagery.

I was advised by the Théâtre des Nations that "the French public would never come to a store for a performance, much less pay money for it," and therefore it would be best if I met them first at the Recamier theater a few blocks away from the Bon Marché. I did this and took the opportunity to give a short talk. I said (through a translator) that we came to the theater to leave the theater, that we were not an audience but had a part in the work to come, which was then outlined along with its general idea. Some aspects of the Happening were to be known beforehand, some not. After repeating the instructions and cues, we left on foot for the department store. Here's what happened.

Arriving at main stairway of store (Théâtre des Nations and Bon Marché officials plus cops waiting there, a "reception" of sorts) everybody's given a white, paper-wrapped package tied with a string. (They don't know it contains a two-pound rock.) Once upstairs, holding on to packages, they wander around spooky, quiet aisles. On five counters, far from one another, pale bulbs over each, attendants sit staring blankly beside their exhibits. Over PA system lady's impersonal voice announces, in French, weather (clear) and time zones around the world. In between these facts, she recommends purchase of bread, plastic film, plastic pool, soap, rope, washing machine, TV, jam, paper, coat, umbrella, wine, chair, table and rocks, all sold at Bon Marché. (Part of this info transcribed by listening to store's daily blurb.)

Voice finishes. Exhibits demonstrated. Washing machine wrapped and unwrapped with heavy tarpaulin and rope. Crumpled paper stuffed in, pulled out. Light switched off and then on. Zombie-type salesman. Repeated. Little mouse guy, sitting in wire shopping cart together with tall, white, gawky paper construction, is lifted onto counter by thin, sensitive Abe Lincoln figure, where third man in oversize coat wraps him up (supermarket style) in plastic film and clothesline, puts him back in cart. Coat man blows a foghorn, takes off coat while Abe L. blasts on police whistle as he pushes cart through crowd. Returns after awhile, repeats. Sparkling TV set under beach umbrella, nice gal watching program for time, covers it with burlap, turns on bulb under umbrella, sits, thinks, turns off bulb, uncovers TV again, watches. Repeated from time to time. Other gal (health-food type) at table with loaves of bread, cuts slices, puts jam on some, eats, smiles. Different gal, standing still in blue kiddy-pool, looking like bride, clothes on, covered with plastic film, is sudsed up with Lux Flakes by bearded attendant. She clicks like machine.

People help themselves to bread and jam (bread gal smiling to herself), start to ask demonstrators the important question, "You got the bread?" Reason is, one of them has 50 NF (New Francs, $10) and will give it to person who asks at right time and in right tone of voice. For fifteen or twenty minutes, all questions ignored.

At same time, and randomly, efficient madame (tight girdle) drags cot with sheets, blanket and pillow through aisles, making and unmaking it, getting into it occasionally. Shirtless workman, gunnysack apron on, rolls huge truck tire around crowd. When some nice visitor takes it over, he crawls painfully on belly under everybody's legs, making quiet motor sounds. Photographers shoot flashguns, these answered by cap pistols. Mad-dog man rushes in on all fours (like guard dogs at night) two or three times, covered with rags and packages, howls explosively, disappears fast. Also, couple of visitors get into act, howl and set up own booths among merchandise, sell swiped bread, each other. One older lady, dumped feet up into display of dry goods, lies that way, not moving, for rest of Happening. Idle conversations. Everything aimless. Slow collapse of focus. Crowd much too large. Almost lose it one night.

Then someone gets the bread! It's given by kiddy-pool attendant, sleeves rolled up, arms covered with soap suds, in exchange for white package. Person yells I'VE GOT THE BREAD! Crowd cheers, bravos, claps. Other attendants turn out lights over counters, actions all stop, crowd presses toward winner's counter. Spotlight on now, bright, hard circle of idiotic importance, Lux Bride standing there in pretty blue pool, no longer clicking. Winner helped onto counter, shows crowd the bread (it's a long baguette with 50 NF bills sticking out of it like lettuce). Waves of cheering again. A folding chair is opened for him, bottle of wine uncorked, cup poured. He drinks, a little embarrassed.

The other demonstrators, meanwhile, press their way through the crowd, pardon-me's, excuse-me's, reach counter, are also poured wine. They toast winner (more cheers), wander off a few steps, and collapse. Some people try to get at the wine but are refused.

Soap man suddenly gets terrible look on face, and booms out in French, LADIES AND GENTLEMEN. OPEN YOUR PACKAGES! Sounds of tearing paper, exclamations, and everybody finds stones. He takes swig from bottle, pours remainder over head of bride, opens three more bottles, pours these, methodically, bloodily, rivers of red soap running down plastic, gal clicking again. Crowd gasps, mocks, indignant (French sin to mix wine and soap, I guess). Soap man hesitates, takes a drink, reels slowly, staggers, drops in slow motion, sliding over edge of counter to floor. Hush.

Now over PA, advertising voice again, saying, LADIES AND GENTLE-MEN, THE TIME IS (whatever time it actually is), PLEASE PLACE YOUR STONES IN THE POOL AND LEAVE AS YOU ENTERED. I REPEAT, THE TIME IS…Quiet exiting. Last person out is prize winner with baguette.

What was the response to the Happening? The answer, hinted at in the preceding, can properly be divided among three groups: cultural institutions as sponsors; the public as consumer; and the press, purportedly representing either or both of these, as quasi-official judges. Each of these responded at different times according to its interest, that is, either before or during the preparation, at the Happening, or afterwards. Altogether, I was forewarned, the French would be less kindly disposed to my work than Americans.

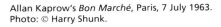

Allan Kaprow's *Bon Marché*, Paris, 7 July 1963.
Photo: © Harry Shunk.

Allan Kaprow during *Bon Marché*.
Photo: © Harry Shunk.

Actually, reaction was similar to that in the United States.

The Théâtre des Nations, a prestigious enterprise with a year-round program of offerings brought from all over the world, is partly supported by the French government and partly by UNESCO. Its invitation to me was very warm. But soon afterward, its administrators changed their minds. Our contractual agreement was ignored, they tried to persuade me to conventionalize my work and, failing to succeed in that, did approach the Bon Marché as I had requested, but then did not follow through with necessary communications and support. Deliberate indifference was followed by the full weight of bureaucratic opposition. Weeks of precious time elapsed. Finally, it was clear that there would be no Happening as things were going, that the Théâtre des Nations, having invested practically nothing in me, could easily explain away a cancellation as a casualty of "unusually difficult circumstances." It was now more than an artistic challenge: it was, as the French say, "a matter of honor." So friends and I moved on our own with scarcely three days left before performance time. Seeing officials and technicians at the Bon Marché, rounding up and rehearsing performers, total strangers amongst them, scrambling hysterically all over Paris for materials, growling at each other, we at least made it under the line with literally minutes to spare. A real melodrama!

By contrast, the other institution, the department store, was at first cautious. An old and conservative establishment (actually a Paris landmark) with close business ties to the Church, it was considered by artistic circles the last place on earth to agree to a Happening on its premises. As we have been taught by our history books, there, obviously, was the "enemy," the heart of bourgeoisie. But after some meetings in which I described exactly what I would do, they agreed. And once committed, the store's officials were cooperative, generous with time and material, and not a little encouraging.

During the Happening, the crowd was a familiar one. It was composed largely of professional avant-gardists with tongues-ready-to-go-in-cheeks, the rich slumming a little, some curiosity seekers (tourists in Paris from God knows where) and a number of young artists, actors and writers. A very few were moved by what took place, a number of others would think about it afterwards, a sprinkling of rebel-types would go off with a new battle cry, but most of them did not like it, and nearly all found it hard to enter into its spirit. Gallic resistance is more cutting than American sullenness or near-violence, but at the core, the Frenchman responded like the New Yorker did back in 1958. Lacking any tradition of his own with which to (typically) compare it unfavorably, he was reduced simply to a "person." At the conclusion he left, uncertain of himself and of me.

Practically nothing of this was reported by the press. French journalism, when it is hostile, becomes cool. Unlike those days of the past when critics were incensed and cried scandal in lengthy columns over anything different, today's commentators are polite but uninterested or are at least too blasé to ask the artist if they do not understand something. There is undoubtedly more of this shown to an American coming with his wares than to a French artist, especially in view of the feverish efforts of the de Gaulle-Malraux [André Malraux, Minister of Culture] administration to prove Paris' unabated cultural superiority. Thus, aside from a preperformance interview which friends struggled to get for me in *Arts*, only *Figaro* printed a small notice of the work; it was nasty enough to damn me but too quiet to do me any good. So far as I know, the other papers and magazines simply ignored the Happening.

This, of course, reflected the attitude of the Théâtre des Nations (which also represents Malraux), but not quite the ambivalence of a public that, in spite of its reserve, came in large enough numbers to be turned away. And it certainly did not account for the dignified conduct of the Bon Marché, for its unexpected agreement to the project and for the most unusual thing of all: that a publicly attended work of art was inspired by and created in a famous landmark of Paris. Eliminating Allan Kaprow entirely, this is still news in anyone's city. But the Bon Marché looks not at all like the Louvre, and the Happening seemed not at all like art, and the combination of the two explains everything.

The whole story, as I said, is quite familiar. The press in the United States was so identical in attitude and style some years ago that it needs no further comment. Those cultural institutions in this country which have extended invitations to me have almost invariably recoiled in embarrassment or anger because they failed to sufficiently inform themselves of what they were inviting. Big Business, now emerging as a major sponsor of the vanguard arts, appears in my experience to be easier to approach, less constipated with artistic prejudices than the intelligentsia and therefore potentially a new pressure upon art to confront. The public, though it has been less than effusive and is sometimes hostile, always seems to come back in growing numbers. I have no quarrel with it. It will soon cease to be the traditional art public in favor of a smaller "special interest" group, one which will actively participate in the work, not just attend it.

Happenings are being composed in growing numbers throughout the world. But because of their extreme brevity, their improvising dependence on particular performance space, the often perishable nature of their materials and the relatively small groups of people who can manage to take part in them, their creators know rather little in any detail about one another, though they do know, increasingly, *of* one another. Probably for this reason, Happenings, to judge from the scant information available, currently display a marked variety of approaches.

For instance, while in Paris, I received kind assistance from the Ileana Sonnabend Gallery and from Jean-Jacques Lebel, who participated in *Bon Marché* and who has been active producing Happenings in France. Although I have not seen any of Lebel's recent events, we discussed them and examined photos, and it is apparent that, in contrast to what I see as my "rough ritual" style, his style is more surreal, erotic and sometimes political in overtone and intent. While he and I were in agreement over the need to break down as many traditional barriers as possible—those that divide the arts, that separate the arts from the spectator or listener and that prevent art and life from mixing—our work is quite different; and these differences reflect some of the basic contrasts between the cultures of our respective home grounds. I gather that it is similarly so in Amsterdam, Stockholm and Osaka.

I do not wish to make an argument for nationalism in the arts. If for no other reason, that would be isolating and thus fatal. What I do find refreshing about Lebel's position and, say, Wolf Vostell's in Cologne, which is equally German, is that both are *distinct*. It is a quality that is present in spite of the fact that we are in touch, personally and via the press. This is not due to the greater individuality of Happening-makers; it is simply a fortunate consequence of the kind of work we do.

In a time when communication systems and air travel are efficient and easy to take advantage of, the established arts are becoming alarmingly homogenized as they are becoming widely disseminated. The "international style" prevailing in modern painting, sculpture, architecture and music is so clearly lacking in vitality, that it is evident that large-scale uniformity deadens professional responsibility while giving one the seductive impression of being simultaneously universal and *au courant*.

I once thought nostalgically of the good old days when artists starved and were left alone to create marvels of inner revelation. Today, while most artists are still starving from their art (though they've acquired the good sense to get regular jobs in order to eat), the critics' cameras and their news columns permit the public and other artists to enjoy the spectacle. I considered this perverse and perhaps half-consciously yearned for that past I knew only through books.

But publicity in the widest sense is very much here to stay; you cannot both seek it to spread knowledge of your work and tell it to go away when it appears to be destroying your privacy of vision. This is an unfortunate dilemma shared by the majority of our contemporaries, but it will have to be met head-on. I have no doubt that eventually, many will make positive use of the techniques of Madison Avenue, the mobility of the jet-age and the atmosphere of the marketplace. The mass media, printing presses, computers and speed are really quite amoral: we can do with them what we wish. If we destroy people with them and agree to be destroyed, it is simply our fault.

For the difficult present, however, the Happening appears to be one art that can sustain public curiosity with relative impunity, because the *work itself* cannot be mass-communicated. Moreover, so far, Happenings, once presented, are not repeated. Even an account such as the foregoing is nothing like a magazine reproduction or an LP record, stamped out by the thousands. The framework of the event is written out, but there is still a wide margin of mystery about what it actually felt like to *be there*. No more than "red" can be described to a blind man can that experience be conveyed, or even filmed, accurately. For the time being, the Happening seems incapable of easy standardization, and if the day arrives when it, too, is faced with that problem, I believe it could figure out a way to make TV dinners into something astonishing. □

Nam June Paik and Charlotte Moorman performing
their version of John Cage's *26'1.1499" for a String
Player*, 1965. Photo: © Fred W. McDarrah.

American Dance and Performance Art
The Sixties and Seventies

Sally Banes

Interdisciplinary explorations melding art, dance, music and theater occurred on several fronts in the avant-garde of the sixties: Happenings, Fluxus events and the collaborations of experimental choreographers and visual artists at the Judson Dance Theater. Antiprofessional, anti–high art and fiercely nonjudgmental, the Judson group, in particular, served as a training ground for the choreographers who have shaped postmodern dance. In the following essay, critic and historian Sally Banes traces the changing concerns of vanguard choreographers over the past thirty years. Placing developments in dance against the cultural landscape, Banes notes the significance of feminism and other social movements for performing artists, suggesting another link to the visual arts, film and video.

The topography of avant-garde dance and performance art over the last three decades has at times seemed to represent areas as utterly distinct as three separate continents. How, for instance, could Simone Forti's deliberately infantile dancers of the early sixties—clad in casual clothing, spending long periods of time hauling themselves up along a wooden incline by means of knotted ropes or pulling each other around on careening rickety wagons—have anything to do with, say, Stephen Petronio's svelte, sophisticated, hard-edged and fashion-designed troupe, pulling off star turns to avant-pop orchestration? What do the ragman-poets and balloon-studded Venuses of Claes Oldenburg's Happenings have to do with the ultra-high-tech androgyny of Laurie Anderson's musical spectacles? Yet looking back from the turn of a new decade, it is possible to see the past thirty years as in many ways connected, if not united.

The Sixties: Blurring Boundaries and the Effervescent Body

The sixties may be divided into two parts. The early sixties, a time of official consensus, was nevertheless marked by pockets of dissent—from the civil rights movement to the birth of SDS to the avant-garde arts arena. By the later sixties, when the social fabric publicly unraveled, dance and performance became especially powerful sites of social and cultural protest and alternative cultural community building. Buoyed by an expanding economy, the fine arts in America were democratized during this decade, although in different ways for different strata. For instance, mainstream theater, opera and dance began to be widely broadcast to middle-class audiences over television, while Happenings were eventually appropriated in the late sixties by the mass counterculture, in the form of be-ins and political demonstrations. Images of a vigorous, pleasurable and abundant American popular culture also were appropriated by the avant-garde. Moreover, the economic and political strength of the American body politic—even as it underwent the ravages of the Vietnam War and racial conflict—produced a cultural discourse of bodily power. That is, if in the eighties we were obsessed by the rhetoric of morbidity—from AIDS to computer viruses to horror novels—in the sixties our culture everywhere sang the body effervescent: invulnerable, overflowing, loosely bounded, unpretentious, increasingly "natural."[1]

Both parts of the decade saw the proliferation of interdisciplinary activities and the emergence of new, cross-media genres, partly influenced by the partnership of John Cage and Merce Cunningham, whose works were a crucial part of the sixties arts scene. Happenings, Fluxus and expanded cinema characterized the early sixties, and guerrilla theater and various participatory events (from environmental theater to political rallies, be-ins, rock festivals), the later sixties. The refusal to respect conventional boundaries between media was a hallmark of sixties art, which makes criticism and history sorted out by medium difficult.

One might try to classify a work by the genetic method: if a dancer made it, it was a dance; if a composer made it, it was music. Yet, especially during the early sixties, there were dances made by visual artists and composers as well as by dancers, films made by choreographers, performances by poets and visual artists, and all manner of indefinable events by people who were already defining themselves as unclassifiable intermedia artists. So if a work was not immediately identifiable by measuring how much recognizable dancing, acting, painting, sculpture, poetry, film or music it had in it, one might have to think of it as a dance if it was presented by the Judson Dance Theater; as drama if it took place at Caffe Cino or Cafe La Mama; as a Happening if it was announced as such and performed at a gallery or in an outdoor environment or some other unusual non-performance space.

For instance, Simone Forti, trained as a dancer, forsook the typical taut, muscular dancer's movements for a playful, improvisatory, comfortable stance.[2] Her dances, such as *Slant Board* (1961) and *Rollers* (1960), described above, were often structured as rule games or children's playground pastimes. They were also presented in places and ways unconventional for dance—in an art gallery, as part of a program of Happenings; or in a loft, as part of a series of avant-garde music concerts and performances. Forti drew the activity of the choreographer into visual art venues and formats, conferring on the dance artist a more serious art-world status.[3]

Yvonne Rainer, a choreographer who began as an actress, trained as a dancer and eventually (in the seventies) moved into narrative performance art and then feature filmmaking, incorporated verbal texts and ordinary movements into her dances from the start. As a choreographer, Rainer was above all fascinated by the body, in all its unabashed material concreteness. As she put it:

> If my rage at the impoverishment of ideas, narcissism, and disguised sexual exhibitionism of most dancing can be considered puritan moralizing, it is also true that I love the body—its actual weight, mass, and unenhanced physicality. It is my overall concern to reveal people as they are engaged in various kinds of activities—alone, with each other, with objects—and to weight the quality of the human body toward that of objects and away from the superstylization of the dancer. Interaction and cooperation on the one hand; substantiality and inertia on the other…My body remains the enduring reality.[4]

Rainer's *We Shall Run* (1963) was paradigmatic of the early sixties, encapsulating the spirit not only of the Judson Dance Theater cooperative venture, but indeed of the entire downtown arts scene in Greenwich Village. In it, a group of twelve people, dancers and nondancers, simply ran, in leaderless, shifting groups that coagulated, split off and rejoined, according to complicated floor patterns, to music by Berlioz. Simplicity and grandeur met in an ethos of egalitarian community. Rainer's evening-length *Terrain* explored a broad range of bodily movements and bodily states, from play to love to ballet to sleep and death. By 1966, her *Trio A* was another model, for a rigorously analytic approach to phrasing and movement invention that would permeate the mood of the seventies.[5]

Other members of the Judson Dance Theater workshop—Steve Paxton, Trisha Brown, Deborah Hay, Lucinda Childs, Elaine Summers, Fred Herko and many other dancers; visual artists Carolee Schneemann, Robert Morris, Robert Rauschenberg, Alex Hay; composers Philip Corner, Malcolm Goldstein, James Tenney, John Herbert McDowell—also explored in their dances the pervasive issues of community, equality, freedom, play and the "resurrection of the body."[6] And part of the way those liberating, somatic themes were expressed was in the very loosening of boundaries—among art forms, between performer and spectator and between life and art.

These themes also permeated the two new intermedia genres that emerged during this period: the Happenings of the late fifties and early sixties by such artists as Claes Oldenburg, Allan Kaprow, Robert Whitman, Jim Dine and Red Grooms;[7] and the Fluxus

Lucinda Childs in *Carnation*, 1964. Photo: © Peter Moore.

Right, Yvonne Rainer's *We Shall Run* performed at the Wadsworth Atheneum, Hartford, Connecticut, 1965. Photo: © Peter Moore.

Yvonne Rainer's *Trio A* performed at the Judson Flag Show, 1970. Photo: © Peter Moore.

events that flowered in New York in 1963, masterminded by George Maciunas, with numerous participants, including La Monte Young, George Brecht, Dick Higgins, Alison Knowles, Robert Watts, Yoko Ono and Nam June Paik.[8] Most often Happenings were flamboyant multisensory and multilayered spectacles of abundance, while Fluxus events were spare, compact and wry. For example, in Whitman's Happening *Flower* (1963), women spray-painted multicolored stripes on the walls and seemed transformed into flowers as they lifted satin petals of various hues from their skirts and a film showed a woman sleeping, moving restlessly in her bed linens like a seed about to sprout. In Watts' Fluxus event *f/h trace* (1963), a formally dressed musician, carrying a french horn, leaned over and dropped rice, ball bearings, ping-pong balls and other objects from the bell of the instrument. Happenings and Fluxus performances were at opposite ends of the theatrical spectrum stylistically (one might compare the first to Surrealism and the second to Dada performance), yet they shared certain biases of the period. The writings of both Fluxus and Happenings practitioners made explicit their democratic anti–high art stance; their use of everyday actions and objects celebrated the egalitarian values of amateurism; and their refusal to respect genre boundaries exemplified their antispecialist pluralism. Both movements appropriated folk and popular art as means to undercut high art, professionalism and specialization. And both also reflected an early postmodern awareness of the historicity of their position as heirs to an avant-garde tradition.

In the late sixties (which, as I see it, ended in 1973, brought to a close by the combined pressures of the oil crisis and Watergate) much avant-garde dance, if not explicitly political, implicitly reflected the social extremes and mobilizations of the day. Yvonne Rainer's *WAR* (1970) was clearly an activist dance, as was her piece for the Judson Flag Show (an exhibition protesting an artist's arrest for desecrating the flag), in which several dancers wore nothing but the flag as they danced her *Trio A*. Steve Paxton's *Collaboration with Wintersoldier* (1971) and performances by such groups as Bread and Puppet Theater and San Francisco Mime Troupe were also overt protests. At the same time metaphors for community participation, censorship, war and intervention appeared in numerous works: Deborah Hay's dances for entire conclaves of performers, such as her *Deborah Hay with a Large Group Outdoors* (1969) and her participatory Circle Dances; Steve Paxton's pieces for crowds, such as *Satisfyin Lover* (1967), for anywhere from thirty to eighty-four, as he put it, "any old bodies of our any old lives...in ordinary everyday who cares postural splendor,"[9] and his *Beautiful Lecture* (1968) and *Intravenous Lecture* (1970); Meredith Monk's large-scale images, such as *Juice* (1969) with eight-five performers. And various improvisational collectives—from the Grand Union to the women's

159

group Natural History of the American Dancer to the international network of the form, founded by Paxton, of Contact Improvisation—created vital images of democracy, freedom and cooperation, and even, in the case of Contact Improvisation, formed an alternative socio-political culture.

The Seventies: Separation and Specialization

With the oil crisis, the revelations of Watergate, the end of the Vietnam War, the decimation of the Black Power movement and the breakup of the New Left, the mood of the United States in the seventies was suddenly considerably more sober, down-to-earth and ascetic, causing changes along many fronts of the culture. Although avant-garde art by no means represented official culture, it participated in the drift of American society in that much of it retreated from an activist stance and turned toward formalist explorations. Medium-oriented, such explorations inevitably led to the sifting apart of the various media that since the late fifties and early sixties had intermingled. As in other arenas of American life, there was now a premium on professionalism, and both artists and spectators tended to specialize in one genre or another—especially since the New York art world, still the postwar international center, had expanded so enormously that cross-fertilization no longer seemed logistically possible. A major exception to the retreat from political themes was the outcropping of feminist performance art, especially rich on the West Coast, that sprang out of the one political movement that made significant gains in the seventies.[10]

The development of the improvisatory group Grand Union, which spanned the late sixties and early seventies, is perhaps emblematic of the shift. In its early phases the Grand Union functioned as a political collective both implicitly, through works that addressed issues of leadership and control, and explicitly: the group presented one 1971 performance as a benefit for the Committee to Defend the Black Panthers. By 1976, when the group split up, its events were no less catalytic but were more concerned with exploring the theatrical conventions of performance, particularly in regard to dance of all kinds.[11] When Lucinda Childs returned to choreography in 1973 after a five-year hiatus, her work also reflected changed aesthetics; for the next five years, she would pursue a course of rigorously pristine dancemaking—as in *Calico Mingling* (1973) or *Congeries on Edges for 20 Obliques* (1975)—in which the dancers traced out geometrical, repetitive shapes in silence, their feet beating out both aural and visual patterns with the simplest of walking, striding, hopping or skipping steps.[12]

Opposite page, Meredith Monk's *Juice (Part I)* performed at the Solomon R. Guggenheim Museum, 1969. Photo: © Peter Moore.

The Grand Union in a performance to benefit the Committee to Defend the Black Panthers, 1971. Photo: © Peter Moore.

Trisha Brown performing *Accumulation with Talking plus Water Motor* (1979) at the Wexner Center for the Arts, 1989. Photo: Kevin Fitzsimons.

Works such as these, or Trisha Brown's *Accumulation* pieces (based on stringing movements together according to mathematical progressions) or David Gordon's *Times Four* (1975) or Douglas Dunn's *Gestures in Red* (1975) were analytic, programmatic investigations of the dance medium, building on the far-ranging, permissive rule-breaking of the sixties but narrowing the field of inquiry to dance as an art of bodily motion. They were analogous in their aims and structures to the work of such Minimalist composers as Steve Reich and Philip Glass and such Minimalist visual artists as Sol LeWitt and Mel Bochner, as well as to the rigorous conceptual and body works by performance artists such as Chris Burden and Vito Acconci. But these dances nevertheless operated in a separate arena from the other arts, refusing to share the stage with anything that might distract from their almost scientific scrutiny of the body and its anti-illusionist workings.

If the reigning ethic of the sixties was play, that of the seventies was work. The dance studio became a laboratory and operating theater where experiments were assiduously carried out and periodically shown to the public. By 1975, when Michael Kirby published a special issue of *The Drama Review* devoted to postmodern dance, he proposed the following definition of the genre:

> In the theory of post-modern dance, the choreographer does not apply visual standards to the work. The view is an interior one: movement is not pre-selected for its characteristics but results from certain decisions, goals, plans, schemes, rules, concepts, or problems. Whatever actual movement occurs during the performance is acceptable as long as the limiting and controlling principles are adhered to.[13]

If this kind of dancing now sounds dry and academic—and if, in the hands of second-generation epigones, it often became so—experiencing it at the time decidedly was not. Brown's dances were antic and sensuous; Childs' were marvels of crystalline beauty; Gordon's were wittily reflexive, weaving narrative contexts through pure movement invention; Dunn's showed a warmly eccentric elegance. The strikingly intelligent structures these choreographers explored were matched by a new kind of bodily grace.

While the analytic postmodern dance I have been describing dominated the avant-garde of the seventies, another strain—metaphoric, or metaphysical postmodern dance—emerged from many of the same concerns and strategies. Asceticism led in one direction to Minimalism; in another, to devotional expression. The interest in non-Western culture—the heritage of Cage, but also of an American culture resituating itself in world power relations—led to an appreciation of the spiritual, healing and social functions of dance in other cultures, as well as to familiarity with non-Western movement techniques, such as Tai Chi Chuan and Aikido. The works of Meredith Monk, Deborah Hay, Barbara Dilley, Laura Dean and Andy deGroat fall into this category, as do Kenneth King's use of dances as metaphors for technology, information and power systems, and the mind itself. Both Monk and King were involved in multimedia expression, creating small-scale spectacles. Their works, and also Robert Wilson's anomalous large-scale performance art spectacles, extended the interdisciplinarity of the sixties and prefigured that of the eighties.

The Eighties: Postmodern Pleasures

When Lucinda Childs presented *Dance* at the Brooklyn Academy of Music in 1979, it was clear that avant-garde dance had once again changed its course. In this, Childs' first piece for a large proscenium theater, the juxtaposition of three Minimalists' work (Childs', LeWitt's and Glass') produced a "maximalist" combustion. The eighties were ushered in, not only by this work and similar large-scale collaborations by sixties and seventies artists but also by the arrival of a new generation—choreographers such as Bill T. Jones and Arnie Zane, Wendy Perron, Jim Self, Molissa Fenley, Johanna Boyce and Karole Armitage; and performance artists such as Laurie Anderson, Stuart Sherman, Paul Zaloom, Spalding Gray and Eric Bogosian. These pioneers from the new generation—and those too many to name who've come after—have married technical virtuosity (partly a product of the power-driven, greed-and-glitter ethos of the Reagan-era imperium) to a postmodernist appropriation of pop culture and historical styles. The "post-modern" dance that Kirby described in the seventies—analytic, formalist and in many ways modernist in the Greenbergian sense—gave way to the more broadly held notion of postmodernism across the arts.[14] What Charles Jencks in architecture has called the "doubly coded" aesthetic (entertaining to the general public, while making historical reference for the cognoscenti) had perhaps only been tackled previously in dance by Twyla Tharp.[15] But now, in the eighties, postmodernist allusion began to permeate avant-garde dance and performance art.

Molissa Fenley in *State of Darkness* (1988). Photo: Jack Mitchel, courtesy of the artist.

Laurie Anderson performing at the Wexner Center for the Arts, 1989. Photo: Kevin Fitzsimons.

Right, The Japanese Butoh company Sankai Juku in *Unetsu (The Egg Stands Out of Curiosity)*. Photo: Philippe Pierre.

By the late eighties, "Serious Fun"—the title of the summer series of dance and performance art at Lincoln Center's Alice Tully Hall—was the name of the game. But the international offerings, from Japanese Butoh to German Tanztheater, at the BAM Next Wave Festival and other dance venues and the multicultural productions, from American Indian dancing to Creole performance, at Jacob's Pillow Dance Festival reflected the geographic decentralization in the art world and a cultural realignment in the United States. The corporate shift in world economies and rapidly changing American demographics are part of the postmodern era. And their mark on our cultural production may prove to be the sign of the nineties.

A sense of play, an interpenetration of words and text, a consciousness of historicity and of multiple cultural strata and an awareness of interdisciplinary plenitude (this time realized not in terms of antispecialist practioners but through the collaborations of teams of specialists) have returned, and the close analysis of the medium continues in a new vein. So although the dances and performance art of the eighties—with their ornamentation, multiple layers of sensory input, fascination with narrative and sign systems, and both historical and political sophistication—appear quite disparate from their forebears, these qualities themselves may be seen as the flowering, in a different socio-economic soil, of seeds planted in earlier decades. □

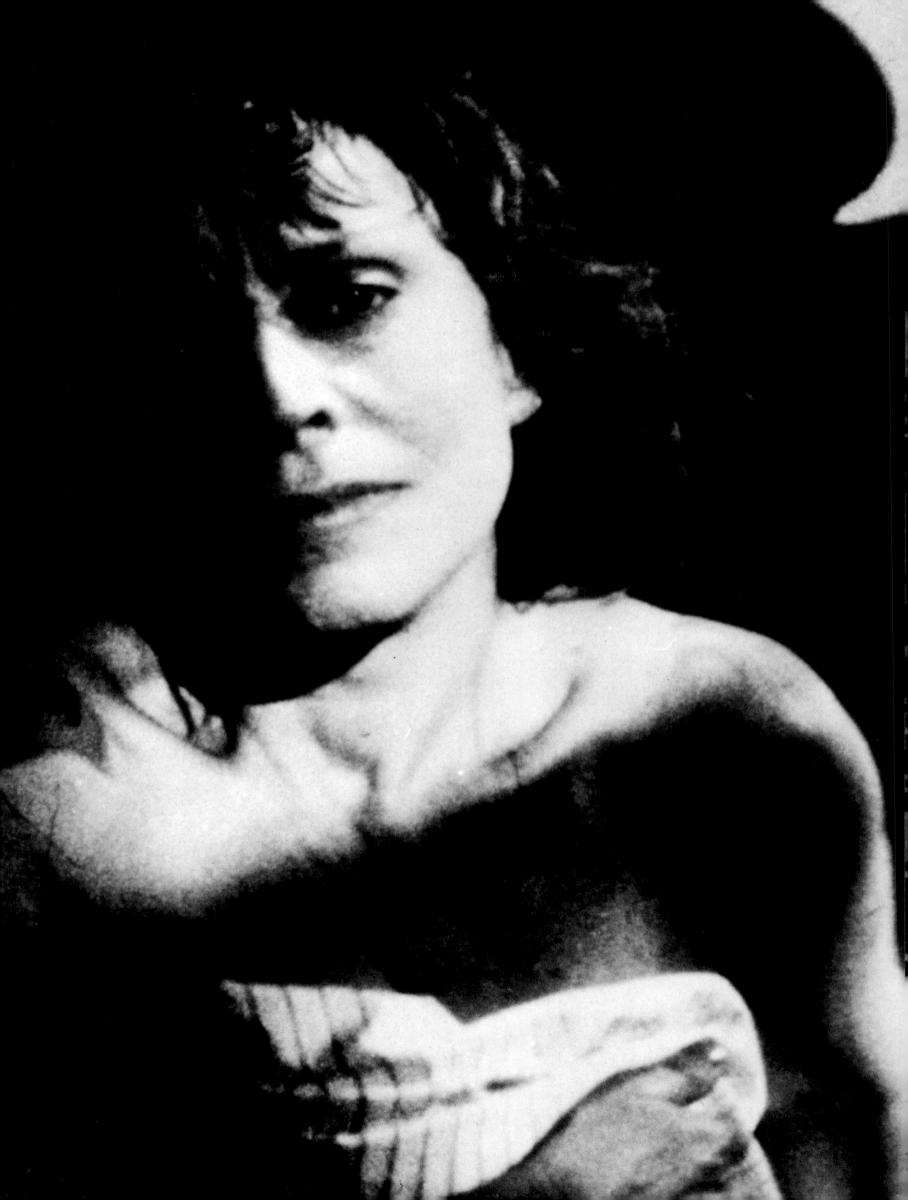

Don't Look Back
Film and Video From Then to Now

B. Ruby Rich

*Avant-garde visual and media arts inter-
sected in the evolution of video as a
gallery- or museum-exhibited art form
during the late sixties and seventies, but
independent film and video also produced
innovations in other areas, as critic and
curator B. Ruby Rich notes in the following
essay. Politically motivated film- and
videomakers employed new technologies
and new distribution networks to counter
the prejudices and omissions left by
previous traditions of film and television.
Multicultural concerns and political
strategies produced new fields of inquiry
and new approaches to existing genres,
paralleling and extending similar developments in other disciplines.*

The approach of a new century, the start of a decade, the opening of a new arts center,
these are the sorts of symbolic moments that give rise to grand pronouncements and
carry the danger of grandiosity for anyone who tries to rise to the occasion. It is sobering,
amidst all the hoopla of fin-de-siècle prophecy now being touted by a press that has long
since forsaken its more serious responsibilities, to note that the millennium will soon
change only for those who profess a belief in one particular Western religion that names
this moment 1991. For Jews, this year is 5751. For the Chinese, it's 4689. For Arabs, it's the
year 1411. Ethnocentrism is alive and well in the midst of all the rhetoric professing an
allegiance to multiculturalism.

Besides that, it's obvious that any clean-cut delineation of epochs is an impossibility,
each millennium—or decade—containing hints of the one before or after. In trying to fix
upon the evolution of film and video in the past twenty years, then, inevitably the sixties
and the nineties edge their way into the frame. It turns out that retrospection is as risky
an art as prophecy, and just as suspect, however teasingly the slo-mo (if video) or time-
lapse (if film) of the backward gaze may seem to offer certainty.

It should come as no shock that independent film and video in the United States have
been no more independent of the political and economic determinants of the period
than any other sector of the arts. From its euphoric heyday in the late sixties, independent film has moved inexorably toward being a part (albeit specialized) of the very
industry that it first rebelled against. Video, meanwhile, has spent a lot of time trying to
keep pace with its own machinery. More recently, though, it has grown and broadened,
assuming that very mantle of potential film once carried, and it is poised to go even
further.

In the period under consideration here, then, the determining factor for film has
been a changing economy and for video, a changing technology. Both fields have undergone pronounced change, in terms consistent with what has happened to society as a
whole: the commercialization of daily life, the disenfranchisement of whole communities,
the faltering of values inconsistent with the maximization of profits and, finally, the
beginnings of a reawakening and the empowerment of artists of color, of values and
traditions and aesthetics apart from the mainstream, white-male-Anglo universe.

Act One: Antiwar, Postwar

Both independent film and video had their heydays, if not their origins, in the
turbulent times of sixties counterculture.[1] There were always two distinct camps: the
galleries and the streets.[2] In the art world, the emphasis was on the decommodification
of the object, a direction that led video into the areas of Conceptualism and obsessions
with new technology, and that led film into a break with the perceived commodity core
of cinema—narrative itself–and the development of Structuralist filmmaking. Where the
focus was on the streets, there was all the documentary righting-the-wrongs activity that
the development of lightweight synch-sound 16mm rigs and video portapaks could make
possible. As the seventies got underway, a few artists, such as Yvonne Rainer, even tried
to combine political and art-world goals. Film and video were players within a broader
terrain of alternative cultural production that included an active alternative-press
movement, music, art and political organizing.

Many expected that the evolution from the sixties to the seventies would be just
that, a continuation along the same route. But it's instructive, in this regard, to remember
that 1971 marked the opening in New York City of Anthology Film Archives, founded as a
veritable museum of the flickering image and an enshrinement of so-called Structuralist
and formalist film as a canon of true value.[3] The absence or near-absence of women,
blacks, Latinos and our ilk from the pantheon was to be taken as a mere byproduct of
aesthetic rectitude. In this, Anthology was merely continuing a trajectory that had begun
earlier. Carolee Schneemann, whose *Fuses* (1967) redefined sexual imagery from the
feminine viewpoint, complained for the next ten years of her infantilization in the macho

Yvonne Rainer's *Privilege* (1990).

world of formalist filmmaking. And artist Mary Kelly recently commented retrospectively on the limitations of Minimalism, noting that it had always struck her as resembling nothing more than "a vessel waiting to be filled."

Unfortunately, in the monastic environment of the avant-garde cinema, avoidance of commerce soon became synonymous with a condescension toward audience and an orthodoxy of production that stifled the development of any populist second generation. The formalist movement became its own cul-de-sac and ran out of steam as the seventies wound down, only to find itself superseded over the course of the decade by one or the other of its twin nemeses: documentary, which became the emblem of the seventies, or narrative, due to emerge as emblematic of the eighties. The gods that Anthology had come to bury would reemerge from the ashes and define the decades that formalist film had sought to own, just as surely as the diversity of producers exiled by the pantheon would come to dominate the world of independent film and video, producing its most interesting work.

Video in those days was a technology and a strategy. It was new, new, new. And it was tech-intensive, the boy-toy of its day. Video was guys with Volkswagen vans and homemade synthesizers. Video was a vision of pure art pulses, visionary transponders looking for converts. Video was also the newest art object, merchandised by the Castelli gallery, which put half-inch machines into the hands of Conceptual artists and started a tradition, sparking the hope that video could attain the salable-object status that film had never managed to grasp. It was also the antitech pyrotechnics of Ant Farm and its far less Conceptual, more material riposte to capitalist largesse. And video was the legions of conscripts, women as well as men, intent on realizing a global univision, using cameras in the service of (if not always, if ever, quite in the hands of) the disenfranchised. Community video took off with a vengeance, creating truly grass-roots bases for what was still a phenomenally centralized medium in its above-ground guise of network and, yes, public television.

If the decade of the seventies could be described in any unitary way, it might be because of the reinvigoration and reinvention of documentary in the hands of new technologies and new practitioners: women, blacks, Latinos, Asians, native Americans. In each case, the movements of the late sixties and early seventies provided the political necessity and creative impetus for the transformation of documentary into a culturally specific mechanism with its own aesthetic strategies and thematic emphases. *Black Journal*, a public television program, and *Yo Soy Joaquín*, often regarded as the first Chicano independent film, had provided examples at the close of the sixties; other projects such as *Realidades*, a Puerto Rican public television program, furthered these goals in the seventies. Today we know that none of these accomplishments was without struggle: the producers of *Black Journal* had to go on strike to get a black executive producer, and the public television station agreed to institute *Realidades* only after an on-air takeover of its studio during pledge week.[4]

It was the era of engaged political documentaries focused on the here-and-now: *Antonia*, *Word Is Out*, *Harlan County, USA*. New Day Films was established to distribute

Carolee Schneemann's *Fuses* (1967). Photo courtesy of the artist.

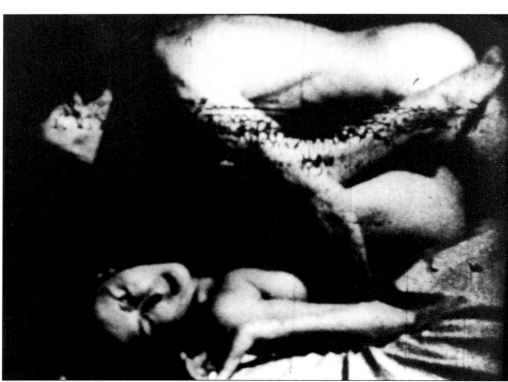

the emerging feminist documentaries. New money from the Independent Documentary Fund and the Corporation for Public Broadcasting let longer (one-hour or feature) documentaries be made and shown. Revisionist documentaries became the rage, as films including *Union Maids*, *The War At Home*, *The Wobblies* and *Chicana* told the history that had been left out of earlier books and movies. New makers with new stories to tell began to proliferate, traditions to develop, communities of response to form. With hindsight, the seventies can be seen as one big archaeological salvage mission, scrambling to document whole cultures before the dam broke and the floodwaters of neoconservatism rushed in to drown them.

Still, the obligation to represent an entire community and its history with every work became burdensome to some filmmakers as the decade progressed. Some began to rebel against the documentary style of talking heads and first-person testimony that was becoming formulaic, while others stayed the course or entered it late, committed to giving voice to the long-silent, the still-unspoken. Documentary makers began to look to the past for their cinematic material, a trend that would reach fruition in the early eighties with the films that won the National Endowment for the Humanities jackpot and could buy up archival footage. Other filmmakers began to experiment even further with the documentary form, testing its elasticity and probing its fictive corollaries. Still others moved on to narrative, which had quietly, almost clandestinely, been gathering strength throughout the decade.

Mark Rappaport's *Imposters* (1979).

Act Two: Prewar, Postmodern

The late seventies and early eighties were fruitful years for independent film in the United States. Breakthroughs in documentary were made at the level both of representation and of that which was being represented. At the same time, a large number of artists began to defect to fiction from documentary, in both short and feature formats, and younger artists sidestepped the documentary altogether. The Independent Feature Project and its annual Independent Feature Market first appeared, and filmmakers began to imagine the theatrical possibilities (read: audiences and money) inherent in the fiction feature form.

Early in the seventies, filmmakers such as Yvonne Rainer and Mark Rappaport had begun to redefine narrative from the avant-garde end of the spectrum, freeing it from commercial imperatives and allowing it to float free of genre expectations (and, not incidentally, exposing the bankruptcy of the Structuralist trajectory). Meanwhile, filmmakers with a loyalty to particular communities began to picture those communities on the screen, in fiction rather than *vérité* terms. The seeds for this development had been planted much earlier, when UCLA started its Ethno-Communications program in 1968.[5] As the seventies moved on, an extraordinary group of black filmmakers graduated to the big screen. In 1976 and 1977 Haile Gerima's *Bush Mama*, Larry Clark's *Passing Through* and, most notably, Charles Burnett's *Killer Of Sheep* sent out a signal of what was to come: an unprecedented dramatic-feature movement was a'birthing.

Charles Burnett's *Killer of Sheep* (1978).

167

If the spirit of the eighties had its roots in these initiatives, the decade itself actually must be said to have opened ahead of schedule. In 1979, a landmark year, the currents of the seventies and eighties mingled in a number of events that would stand out retrospectively. The Alternative Cinema Conference was held that year, marking the first national gathering of kindred souls who saw film and video linked to social issues. It was the founding year of the Film Fund, a moment which turned out to mark—as the opening of Anthology had done eight years earlier—a time of struggle rather than triumph for the kind of filmmaking (in this case social-issue documentary) it was dedicated to championing. It was the debut year of the Independent Feature Project, which would turn out to be a fulcrum in the transition from documentary to fiction-feature emphasis. And it was a year when dramatic filmmaking, as signaled already by the NYC avant-garde rebels and the UCLA grads, began to expand. In 1979 Robert Young made *Alambrista!*, Lourdes Portillo directed *After The Earthquake* and Michelle Citron challenged documentary conventions with *Daughter Rite*. It was the year in which regional independent features emerged in force, among them *Gal Young'Un*, *Northern Lights* and *The Whole Shootin' Match*—all deliberately produced outside the established centers in New York and California. By 1980, a company called First Run Features would be founded to develop the theatrical market for independent features. It was also in this era, this "window of opportunity," that permanent mechanisms and institutions were founded: Cine Accion in San Francisco, the Black Filmmaker Foundation in New York. Women Make Movies became a distribution company, Visual Communications became a production force.

At this stage of development of the dramatic film, there was little hierarchy between short and long formats. Everyone was just feeling their way, every film was a contribution, every year a doubling of production: 1981 brought *Zoot Suit*; 1982 brought *Illusions* and *Ashes And Embers*; 1983, *El Norte* and *Committed*; 1984, *Born In Flames*, and so on. Documentary filmmakers saw the trend and switched to features, too. After *Atomic Cafe* hit the jackpot in 1982, *Las Madres: The Mothers of the Plaza de Mayo*, *The Times Of Harvey Milk*, *Dark Circle*, *Seeing Red*, *Sherman's March*, *When The Mountains Tremble* and other feature-length documentary films all found theatrical or semitheatrical release and broad audiences.

It was an exciting time, and once again prophets figured the future would bring just more of the same. But something a bit different was going on. New funding and development entities emerged to address the dramatic feature-film sector more directly than public agencies could or would do, with the Sundance Institute and American Playhouse becoming prestigious imprimaturs. Budgets grew larger. Public funds, meanwhile, shrank under the Reagan regime. Independent filmmaking in the public sector faced an economy of scarcity, from which it suffers just as badly today. Investment, not grant funding, became the key to production. And predictably, not surprisingly, the proportion of women and makers of color began to shrink. When expenses go up, something called risk—and how to avoid it—enters the picture as a forceful presence.

Then, in 1986, a young, fresh-out-of-film-school filmmaker by the name of Spike Lee used grant money to make his first feature, *She's Gotta Have It*. The film was bought for a lot of money for its time, and it made money. All of a sudden, black independents turned into good business. Hollywood, addressing a changing economy and structure itself, began to bank on the new talents growing up outside its borders. And independent filmmakers, some of them fresh out of film school, others further along in their careers and frustrated with low-budget existence, began to reverse the aims of their field. Independent film had originally been the province of people who wanted no part of Hollywood; now, a hell of a lot of them wanted nothing more than to go there (and have, ever since).

The implications, causes and consequences of this reversal are complex. First, it is important to remember that 1991 ushers in the eleventh year of Republican rule in the United States, characterized first by alternating neglect and hostility to the arts and more recently by full-fledged attack. The erosion of public television's commitment to alternative voices, the politicization of the National Endowment for the Humanities and—even before the recent Jesse Helms drama—the stagnation of funding for the National Endowment for the Arts, which reduced its funding below its own past inflation-adjusted levels, all have contributed to a drying-up of support for filmmakers trying to work outside of commercial channels.[6]

At the same time, Hollywood has been changing, too. Its supremacy was eroded by massive technological change; adjustments had to be made to the arrival of home-video markets and the expansion of cable television. The Hollywood studios and the new "mini-major" distributors that were giving them a run for their money began to comprehend the implications of "narrow casting" as a market strategy. As a result, opportunities for entry into the Hollywood system increased. The growth of cable and of independent film itself, together with the generational changes in Hollywood and the arrival of both Ted Turner and the Fox network opened new creative terrain inside commercial movies and television. Genre and style rigidity were no longer operative, making innovative work increasingly possible in both areas.

The feature film movement, which had begun as an alternative response to what was on the screens, became after a decade of development deeply contradictory. Annual events like the Sundance U.S. Film Festival make the contradictions evident, as low-budget independents brush shoulders with Hollywood-bent colleagues and as acquisition reps seek out the next product likely to break the bank (the biggest, recently, being *sex, lies and videotape,* a film that could succeed at being acclaimed as new because it was so thoroughly traditional, made by a filmmaker who affirmed in interviews that he didn't consider himself part of any movement). In Park City, Utah, site of Sundance's annual festival, the contradictions and occasional consonances between originality and market-ability are easily observed.[7]

If the independent sector began to be what it had never been—an R&D camp for mainstream production and distribution—there were still alternatives to this particular form of market commodification, continuations from the past and presentiments of what is still to come. To track present and future directions, then, it's helpful to look at the video sector as well as at recent documentary developments in film.

Act Three: Fusion and the Future

Video had a decidedly different trajectory from film throughout this period. Video costs did not escalate to the degree that film costs did, nor were funding cutbacks the rule—since video had never had access to the Corporation for Public Broadcasting and NEH budgets that film did. The shrinkage experienced in video had to do with the demise of such facilities as the Experimental Television Lab, which had been established at WNET in New York City, the temporary suspension of support (due to changes of emphasis) from the Rockefeller Foundation in the early to mid-eighties and the need to keep up with constantly changing formats. On the other hand, video distribution improved through-out the seventies and eighties. The Video Data Bank, for instance, founded in Chicago in the mid-seventies, became a major player in the field, opening new markets, raising the profile of video and expanding the boundaries of video work taken seriously.

Shu Lea Cheang. Photo: © Lona Foote.

Video's history in the eighties consisted of an ever-evolving set of responses to ever-evolving technologies. When high-priced technologies arrived—in the form of engi-neered studios, computerized visual effects, one-inch masters, etc.—then on-line pro-grams evolved to provide artists with low-cost access. Work produced within this context could easily enter into the museum and gallery world, finding widespread acceptance and sales in European museums and festivals as well as within the United States. Video installation work, produced to high-end production specifications, succeeded in attract-ing full commodity status within the art world. Landmark points in the eighties were the Whitney Museum's retrospective of Nam June Paik's work (the first major U.S. museum show dedicated to a single video artist), The Museum of Modern Art's tribute to video artist Bill Viola and the Carnegie Museum's ambitious video-installation exhibition. Works by such artists as Mary Lucier, Juan Downey, Gary Hill, Joan Logue, Shalom Gorewitz, Dan Reeves, Rita Myers and others began to form a canon. Video art had established itself as legitimate.

While work concerned primarily with formal aesthetic values found wider accep-tance, other artists were exploring different tendencies that had been gathering momen-tum within the video world: appropriation and narrative.[8] Ever since works such as Dara Birnbaum's *Wonder Woman* had thrown video straight into an explosive collusion-confrontation with the broadcast world at the close of the seventies, video artists had been mining television, not to ape its example but to play in the sandbox of quotation as critique, fashioning a kind of reflexivity particular to the medium. In the mid-eighties Joan Braderman's *Joan Does Dynasty,* for instance, merged this style of network-raiding with explicit social commentary and media theory; Braderman literally inserted herself into the site of contention. Indeed, as video became more sophisticated theoretically, narrative strategies began to be fully explored—not in the purely dramatic direction pursued by many filmmakers in this period, but rather in a more interdynamic mode, drawing from documentary and experimental vocabularies as well. Works by Braderman as well as by Martha Rosler, Steve Fagin, Vanalyne Green, Shu Lea Cheang, Cecilia Condit, Marlon Riggs, Sherry Milner and Ernie Larsen and others have laid the foundations for major narrative developments in the nineties. Meanwhile, work in documentary has begun to evolve a video vernacular through such works as *The Mexican Tapes, The Politics of Hunger* and *Inside Life Outside,* which all elaborate distinctive models of engagement.

Tom Kalin's *They are lost to vision altogether* (1988).
Photo: Ellen Spiro.

As the ceiling on costs inched higher (all the way up to 1" at this writing), video simultaneously returned to its origins via the development of Video-8 and the low-cost return to basics that it offered. At the same time, the evolution of cable and the evolution of grass-roots video production came to a meeting point, with the opening of community cable facilities that offered access to community producers, often on more sophisticated equipment than most nonprofit facilities could muster on their own. Projects such as the Deep Dish national satellite feed of community-based video production and Paper Tiger Television's ongoing media critiques illustrated the impact that this sector could have once distribution problems were solved.

The potential of video as a medium to carry on and further a mandate once assumed solely by film—the elaboration of formal strategies and means of production that could advance the evolution of the medium as well as advance if not action, then at least dialogue, on social problems and political organization—has been made clear most explicitly by the response to the AIDS crisis of the late eighties.[9] In this instance, video artists have responded to a particular social crisis through the immediate deployment of equipment, invention of aesthetic approach, and creation of new and effective distribution networks. There has been no hierarchy of form, no exclusionary kinship system of artists, no correct-line bastion of orthodoxy.

Whether assigned to Stashu Kybartas, Tom Kalin, Ellen Spiro or Jean Carlomusto, AIDS video has a collective strength of presence. Work has built on other work; video has been a player within a social movement and at the same time has taken this movement's concerns as the material for making art. Elegy, testimony, meditation, investigation and intervention have each defined a number of works. Aesthetic strategies that had been elaborated for their own sake by video artists in the past now find a concrete application to a particular cause. Artists have in general avoided the ad-hoc, campaign-based functionalism that so often undermined the art/politics collaborations of the past, opting instead for an aesthetics of invention.

The relative cheapness of engaged video production is crucial at a time when most nonprofit production must still be characterized as suffering from the economy of scarcity. This economy has further advanced video's propensity for experimentation and the speed of production essential to its effectiveness. The unique conditions that have contributed to the explosion of interesting video work on the subject of AIDS do not end here, as they point to the likelihood of dramatic evolution and reengagement in the video future. The fusion of aesthetic invention with political engagement around AIDS

Yvonne Rainer's *Privilege* (1990).

provides a model to build upon across genre lines, applicable to other issues and communities of need.

Film and video have had markedly different histories in the past two decades, often for the reasons of technology and economy that I've identified as so determining. In addition, however, it might be noted here that the eighties witnessed the bifurcation of video artists from film artists on the basis of training. Increasingly, filmmakers came out of film schools that came to provide traditional professional training in the wake of the free-for-all autodidacticism characteristic of the field in the sixties and early seventies. Video artists, on the other hand, tended to come out of the schools and progressive liberal arts colleges. Filmmakers more and more came to join a tradition, video artists to subvert one. Television models such as MTV may have accelerated the rapid turnover of video vocabulary that made the medium a more elastic one. Yet the more fundamental determinant has been the training itself: that of specialization (film) versus exploration (video), a response to the medium that has privileged interaction (video) over mastery (film), a career path of tracking (film) via self-selection (video). Throughout this period, certain filmmakers have managed to reinvigorate the old "avant-garde" tradition—notably Su Friedrich and Todd Haynes—by jumping the old genre fences that separated formal devices from narrative and documentary approaches. However, they've been the exception in a field increasingly fossilized and lacking in the invention and genre mutability that has made video so interesting in the corresponding period.

In film, the narrative trajectory that has continued uninterrupted since the seventies is in need of revival, to expand its thematic borders and retool its stylistic options. Neither can be accomplished without a broadening of the ranks of its practitioners. Such recent releases as Charles Lane's *Sidewalk Stories* and Charles Burnett's *To Sleep with Anger*, both crossover films by uncompromising independents who secured mainstream distribution, suggest that less commercialized approaches can once again find favor. Similarly, Yvonne Rainer's first-time inclusion in the New York Film Festival with *Privilege*—an experimental feature dealing with menopause and nuclear annihilation—is a reminder that narrative film can survive and prosper outside the theatrical circuit. As the work of these filmmakers and others like them should testify, dramatic feature film can only fulfill its initial alternative promise if makers pay attention to the issues at the forefront of our lives at this moment (rather than retreating, as so many have done, into a tired and opportunistic replay of already-acceptable cliché or, at best, work that is timeless by virtue of being irrelevant to this particular historical juncture).

Meanwhile, documentary film is at a critical crossroads. A decade of funding cutbacks, the shrinking of the short-film market, and a long-standing aesthetic cul-de-sac have all taken their toll. Recent forward movement has come in the form of feature-length theatrical documentaries (a trend present since the early seventies when filmmakers like the late lamented Emile DeAntonio pioneered the form) that have updated documentary by giving it a narrative spin. Jill Godmilow's *Far From Poland*, Erroll Morris' *The Thin Blue Line*, Nick Broomfield's *Driving Me Crazy* and Michael Moore's *Roger And Me* all employ narrative strategies in an effort to move documentary beyond genre predictability.

This is a positive trend, but one that bears careful watching given the infotainment drift of network news television. After all, what these four films have in common is their elevation of the filmmaker to the role of star. First out, ahead of the pack, Godmilow pictured herself in the bathtub when martial law denied her access to Poles—and started a trend. Morris' version of the Randall Adams case got coverage in the op-ed sections of the newspaper rather than the film pages, and Morris made himself as much of an attraction as his documentary's subjects. Broomfield got his document of a show-biz disaster publicized via his own lethal persona ("if he filmed your wedding, you'd get a divorce"). And Moore put himself in virtually every shot of his General Motors documentary, only to get knocked by Vincent Canby, who explained that the filmmaker might have missed an Oscar nomination due to his "loudmouth" behavior. This is the state of documentary, post-Grenada, post-Panama, post-Nicaraguan elections, post-Berlin Wall: at a time when the U.S. press virtually prints State Department releases as news, when the press is routinely excluded from capers like Panama and Noriega never gets heard from at all, when the savings and loan scandals get shushed and a key Supreme Court nominee tries to succeed by just keeping mum, we're told that *Roger And Me* shouldn't get an Academy Award because it didn't tell the truth, the whole truth (in order), and nothing but the truth. Such is the double standard applied to news and documentary.

Fusion of documentary material with dramatic structure suggests one future direction for the genre, but it is likely that documentary in general is due for a renaissance. Documentary film practitioners such as Deborah Shaffer, Lourdes Portillo, Jacqueline Shearer, Loni Ding, Bill Jersey, Christine Choy and Renee Tajima, Tony Buba, Barbara

Trinh T. Minh-ha.

Kopple and Louis Massiah have persevered in hard times and have been joined by such new arrivals as Robby Henson and Amy Harrison. Now, they stand ready both to further the evolution of the genre and to inherit the attention of audiences starved for a re-tooled nonfiction form, one that delivers the kind of analysis and context no longer possible in the mass media. At the same time, work by filmmakers such as Trinh T. Minh-ha indicates how far from traditional representation the documentary can be taken and still reveal important truths.

Documentary in the seventies and eighties tended to fall into a trap of registering itself in only two keys—outrage or irony. Now, documentary makers need to rewrite the genre for a new decade (dependent, of course, on changes in the funding situation) and redefine the term "nonfiction" in the process.[10] They need to revive the essay form and help the citizens of this country—the most brainwashed populace in modern history—recover the means to think critically.

It's a fusion kind of time. As work reflects, more and more, an engagement with both past and present, as artists struggle to integrate theatrical with nontheatrical strategies, as different financial structures empower different styles and practitioners, as evolving popular vernaculars (from MTV to rap music) challenge the nonprofit sector to accentuate its contemporaneity without abandoning its soul, then the independent film and video work of the nineties has a chance at redressing its limitations and exceeding its achievements to date.

If this is to happen, multiculturalism and diversity should not be taken as idle, if pro forma, points of recognition. Critics have made a minor industry out of defining and quarreling over "postmodernism," without ever seeming to notice that the term itself annexes for white culture strategies that the disenfranchised have been employing all along as a method of survival and resistance—appropriation, irony, pastiche. These strategies have as much to do with Chicano low-riders, black rap, lesbian butch/femme and gay camp, as with the current art-world and literary strategies that have been deemed significant by virtue of their de-ethnicization.

A true postmodernism for the nineties is ready to emerge, one that pulls together the finest attributes of independent film and video while retaining a healthy skepticism regarding both mediums' sacred truths. A fusion approach that permits both invention and diversity without tying practitioners to outmoded traditions is most likely to permit the kind of exploration necessary at this point. But if artists are to create truly valuable work, then their ties to communities and to the body politic must first be strengthened and reaffirmed, at the level of inspiration, motivation, and audience reception. Artists must find the way back to what Toni Cade Bambara has called their "authenticating audience." In a time of fragmentation, even atomization, of society into disconnected and unconnected individuals, it is precisely this *connection* that heals and teaches. Only the reinscription of the artist into society can conjure up the power so necessary to the creation of films and videotapes for the nineties.

After all, at a time when media genius sometimes seems to be the sole prerogative of ad agencies and electoral campaigns, there is lots to be done.

Epilogue

Between the initial writing and imminent publication of this perspective on the past two decades, the terms of debate have been displaced entirely by the raging battle over the National Endowment for the Arts and the legitimacy of public funding for the arts. It is relevant, then, to note that virtually none of the history which I have taken such pains to trace could possibly have come about in the absence of an active program of public funding. Nor is it conceivable that any such trajectory will continue without such a program.

That said, it's important to note that public funding in the United States has most often proceeded without the benefit of any articulated funding *policy* in effect, leaving its methods and beneficiaries vulnerable to the very sort of attack now in progress. It must also be said that the marked isolation of artists from communities of support (apart from the art world and academia) has facilitated their infantilization and the scapegoating of their work, just as the lack of a shared vernacular between artist and public has made "public" art in this same period fraught with misunderstanding and mutual recriminations.

Political pressure and censorship have come late to museum directors, photographers, performers and visual artists, by comparison with the attacks on filmmakers and film exhibitors that have seasoned this part of the field for so long. Amos Vogel's Cinema 16 faced down the censors in the fifties and sixties, while the New York Film Festival weathered storms of censorship and protest for several decades (right up to the Christian right's organizing against Godard's *Hail Mary*). In the eighties, the Guadalupe Cultural Center was red-baited by a local San Antonio politician for its film festival, while New York City's Film Forum had to hire a round-the-clock security guard to counter threats against a Cuban film series. The New York State Council on the Arts was itself attacked by the *New York Post* in front-page headlines in 1987 (with the funding of a "pro-Sandinista" film one of the charges) and compelled to appear before an unusual joint hearing of the state legislature in Albany to defend its actions. Even Hollywood studios were not immune, as the assault on Martin Scorsese's *The Last Temptation of Christ* demonstrated all too forcefully.

Today, some of our most vigorous and hopeful work in film and video is the stuff of which restrictions are shaped. Filmmakers and video artists have already retreated in mass from the barricades of meaning-formation so missing in the commercially shaped media of our time. If they, and those who exhibit their work, retreat further, then the fabled marketplace will indeed become the sole arbiter of our souls. This is no time to close ranks, hunker into the bunkers, trust no one, take no prisoners. It is a time, rather, to take to heart the role that film and video can play in a society under siege, one in which basic values and assumptions are under revision. It is a time for the notion of service to reenter the lexicon of the arts, and for filmmakers and video artists to turn their cameras back on the world; American society surely needs the images, stories, and resonances, both intellectual and emotional, that they can bring. Finally, it is a time to reaffirm diversity, multiculturalist practices, and multivocal strategies in the face of an attack that would reposition culture as univocal and authoritarian, grounded in restrictions rather than imaginations.

Film and video, more than the other arts, still retain their link to a popular sphere. May the artists of the nineties fulfill that promise—and its burden. ☐

NEW WORKS FOR NEW SPACES

Into the Nineties

Construction of the original station no. 14 for Tadashi
Kawamata's *Sidewalk in Columbus, Ohio* (which was
destroyed and subsequently rebuilt). Photo: Mika.

New Works for New Spaces
Into the Nineties

New Works for New Spaces, the third section of *Breakthroughs*, brings the consideration of the avant-garde up to the present by documenting—in interviews, illustrations and artists' pages—"new works," artworks completed, for the most part, in 1990. The visual artists' projects discussed in the first thirteen interviews were created or chosen for a specific "new space," the Wexner Center for the Arts in Columbus, Ohio. Regarded together, these projects reveal the varied preoccupations of artists working in the visual, performing and media arts as the eighties turned into the nineties. Identifying characteristics that might be common to the avant-garde of the moment requires a willful disregard of surface differences that initially seem overwhelming. The selection of artists echoes the polyphony of voices comprising the multiculturalism and internationalism of contemporary art—extending, in this case, beyond the transatlantic axis of the United States and Western Europe to include Magdalena Abakanowicz from Poland and Tadashi Kawamata from Japan. The visual arts projects range from a sound installation by Christian Marclay to a marble sculpture by Fortuyn/O'Brien to a habitation system for moths by Ann Hamilton. Nonetheless, as one reads through the interviews and studies the artists' pages, some shared subjects and strategies become apparent.

Politically engaged commentary, already mentioned by several authors in this book as a recurrent concern since the late sixties, figures as a foreground or background interest in the work of Barbara Kruger and Gretchen Bender among the visual artists, Bill T. Jones among the performing artists, and Tom Kalin and Julie Zando among the filmmakers and video artists. Less explicit references to social and political conditions also can be discerned in several visual artists' suggestions of the tensions provoked by human interventions in the natural environment.

Another expansive area of common ground derives from shared predilections for elaboration, narration, eclectic (and often historical) references and content beyond formal explorations. These attributes, all tendencies associated with the urge to put back into art the qualities modernism had eliminated, loomed large in the consciousness of the art world during the late seventies and early eighties. Particularly apparent in Neo-Expressionist painting, such characteristics transcended that style's brief but intense outburst of activity, persisting as part of the common language of postmodernism. Since many of the artists interviewed on the following pages developed their approaches to art during this period, it is hardly surprising to find such interests well represented. Among other works, Malcolm Cochran's content-laden architectural constructions, Fortuyn/O'Brien's sensuous and mysterious objects and, in other disciplines, Steve Fagin's investigations of B-movie sources and Spalding Gray's of narrative structures draw from this well.

But the chronology of art rarely proceeds in neat, decade-long segments, and not all the ideas current in the art world at the beginning of the nineties have their roots in the eighties. Several of the artists—Joseph Kosuth, Sol LeWitt, Chris Burden, Magdalena Abakanowicz—began their careers in the sixties and seventies and carry layers of earlier concerns into their current work. Among the performing artists, Trisha Brown stands in an analogous position, providing in her career glimpses of changing directions in dance and of continuities and shifts in her own interests. Other artists and works connect with those discussed in previous sections of the book in thought-provoking ways. Gretchen Bender, whose fascination with television involves communication strategies as well as content and technology, updates the Pop artists' earlier investigations of mass culture and Nam June Paik's more formal explorations of video. Gilberto Zorio, in his interest in materials with transformative potential, continues a line of inquiry that attracted Jannis Kounellis and Piero Manzoni.

New Works for New Spaces also introduces significant areas of artistic activity that have figured only incidentally, if at all, in the previous sections, thus filling out the composite picture of the avant-garde. Debates about the possibilities of public art, for example, have engaged numerous artists. Here, projects by several artists cover a range of contemporary approaches to public art: continuations of, or breaks with, the tradition of public monuments. LeWitt reinvents the monument as a demonstration of logic in *Tower,* and Fortuyn/O'Brien proposes an model of public art for intimate contemplation in *Marble Public.* Kruger addresses her audience in familiar, advertising-based terms, adopting the format as well as the language of public communication; the projects documented with her interview include works exhibited on outdoor billboards as well as in gallery settings. Kawamata seeks to engender community interaction with his work, making it public in use and meaning as well as in placement; without working in specifically public places, Hamilton adopts similar approaches to community involvement.

The concept of the "installation," often temporary in duration and intended for a single viewing situation, also has played a significant role in the avant-garde's continuing redefinition of art. Whether presenting their installations as collections of assorted objects grouped to create an environment or as more unified gestures of intervention in architectural spaces or natural landscapes, artists who work in this format challenge basic assumptions regarding art's status as salable commodity. For those, such as Robert Irwin, who developed the ideas of installation art during the late sixties and seventies, this rebuke to conventional definitions was one of the form's prime attractions. In more recent years the concept of the installation has been internalized as a given. It's become almost as elastic a category as painting or sculpture, an approach that can be chosen at will and used as a means to other ends.

At least in the sense that they were created, with one or two exceptions, specifically for the Wexner Center exhibition *New Works for New Spaces,* the visual artworks documented here fit into the category of installation art. Yet of the artists interviewed in the following pages, perhaps only two, Hamilton and Kawamata, incorporate the ephemerality of installation art as a critical component in their work. Many of the artists, however, embrace another element of installation art: heightened awareness of site, of the places in which art is presented and for which it may be designed. Context—compounded of physical characteristics, historical associations, iconography and contemporary uses—continues to be a significant concern even as artists choose different aspects of context to explore. In their Wexner Center projects some, such as MICA-TV, responded primarily to the building's theoretical foundation; others, such as Chris Burden and Christian Marclay, to its physical facts. Still others chose to investigate this site's identity in other ways: as part of a university and an urban community, or as an art museum with all that implies. The aspects of the Wexner Center's context the artists chose to address and to ignore provide clear signals of the issues and ideas that intrigue the contemporary avant-garde.

Ann Bremner

MICA -TV filming the *Inbetween*. Photo: Jo Hall, courtesy of The Ohio State University Office of Communications.

Construction of Sol LeWitt's *Tower*.
Photo: Kevin Fitzsimons, courtesy of The Ohio State
University Office of Communications.

Ann Hamilton's *dominion* during construction.
Photo: Jo Hall, courtesy of The Ohio State University
Office of Communications.

179

Collecting Culture
Paradoxes and Curiosities

Patricia C. Phillips

The redefinitions characteristic of avant-garde art in the past decades have not been confined to art's materials, categories and messages. Art museums also have reevaluated their traditional identities as storehouses of historical and timeless objects. Some museums, as Patrica C. Phillips notes in the following essay, have begun to regard their facilities not as "shrines" for their collections but as "laboratories": forums for the creation, as well as the display, of new artworks. This shift in self-identification has shaped museum design and been critical for the institutionalization of avant-garde ideas: museums as "laboratories" are able to embrace art forms such as performance and installation that developed outside of, and even in opposition to, the mainstream. Phillips, who teaches in the environmental design program at Parsons School of Design in New York, has written extensively on connections between art, site and architecture. Her discussions of installation art and museum design and her specific analysis of the Wexner Center's architecture establish a common background for the artists' interviews that follow her essay.

[The collection's] function is not the restoration of context of origin but rather the creation of a new context, a context standing in a metaphorical, rather than a contiguous, relation to the world of everyday life...The collection presents a hermetic world; to have a representative collection is to have both the minimum and the complete number of elements necessary for an autonomous world—a world which is both full and singular.

Susan Stewart

In 1964, four years before he died, Marcel Duchamp concluded that he believed in the artist but had decided that art was a mirage. Duchamp's words have a haunting resonance; in fact, his long, creative life was a prophecy of the strange, rapid changes that have occurred in the deployment and perception of art in the twentieth century. The philosophical cataclysms in art that Duchamp's work frequently presaged involved fundamental questions and issues of the art object and the transformative role of the artist. The essence of the object was no longer so confidently discovered in its material and formal characteristics or in its enduring qualities; the fact that it had occurred, the circumstances of its manifestation, became preeminent issues. Art could be the trace of a developing idea—something both singular and serial.

In the twentieth century there also has been consideration of the "how long" of art. How is ephemerality measured—or valued? What do we make of art that is not only new but short-lived, purposefully impermanent? The first documented collectors of art in the thirteenth and fourteenth centuries acquired hard-sought antiquities, objects often appreciated not so much for embodied ideas or aesthetic qualities but for their tenacious presence in a world accustomed to inevitable decay. It was not until the sixteenth century that a few exceptional collectors began to assemble works that were new, recently created. The authority of age was not diminished, but it was joined by other motivations and passions of the collector.

Whether composed of the new or old, the collection has always been determined and driven by the supposed infallibility of the object. The object had survived and would endure in its protected state; what's more, its importance (value) normally would appreciate over the years. The conventions and assumptions of the collection remain intact in the late twentieth century but there now is an unmistakable irony, at times a remarkable dispassion, in the act of acquisition. Duchamp and other artists in the past fifty years have intensified the immediate significance of a situation: the ordinariness of the object, the often mercurial character of art. Frequently the forms of art not only register but actually embody the transient, transformative qualities. For some, the contemporary collection is less a gathering of coveted objects than an assemblage of intentions, instructions and ephemera.

> ...the collection offers example rather than sample, metaphor rather than metonymy. The collection does not displace attention to the past; rather, the past is at the service of the collection...The collection replaces history with *classification*, with order beyond the realm of temporality. In the collection, time is not something to be restored to an origin; rather, all time is made simultaneous or synchronous within the collection's world.[1]

Contemporary art—and architecture—documents the mutability that surrounds our lives; often the methods employ profound philosophical changes as well as new techniques required to record a relative state. Installation art registers the restless temporality of the contemporary condition. It calls for an enhanced but generally short-lived commitment to site, a dependence on environmental contingencies, in order to make an art of shifting indeterminacy rather than absolute resolution. The installation is

Eisenman/Trott Architects, *Wexner Center for the Arts* (1989). View from lower lobby. Photo: Kevin Fitzsimons, courtesy of The Ohio State University Office of Communications.

phenomenological: influenced by time and circumstance, the potency of ideas and the fallibility of objects. Its inherent adjustability challenges the less resilient institutions of culture and politics. The times have asked for and allowed the emergence of the installation because it is ephemeral, unfixed and heterogeneous.

This is a challenging time to write about art. There are so many ambient conditions that affect and influence it. Art is often so short-lived, so conditional, that viewing it is like coming to terms with a sensation, a memory or fast-flying thought. In the here-today-gone-tomorrow world of contemporaneous ideas, the critic frequently writes about an object or installation that has disappeared—extinguished like an ordinary event or a single day. Less frequently, the critic writes about art as a speculation waiting for realization. The relationship between critic and subject has changed in this century. The writer does not stalk the object; subject and critic circle each other, ever-moving.

This is a challenging time to write about art and a difficult time of perpetual unrest in which to make a courageous building for art. The program for the museum or art center expresses this flux as well as the extremities and uncertainties of the art world. The art museum has become programmatically sophisticated; the list of required spaces and functions is daunting and often disenchanting. The new facilities are required to provide not only the usual spaces for display, observation and study of art but also areas for growing museum administrations, educational and research activities and immense storage requirements as well as prominent places for commercial activities. The museum shop and restaurant get premium locations these days. In the past twenty years, hundreds of cities and communities throughout the world have launched museum projects—either new buildings or ambitious additions to existing centers. The museum has reemerged as a monument to civic pride and cultural vitality.

With all that has become fast and fixed about "the new museum," there is confusion—or at least many points of view—about the relation between the building and the public, between the building and the art it temporarily or permanently contains. While there continue to be two predominant typological strategies, these represent poles that leave a wide horizon of possibilities to wander. The traditional, historically sanctioned museum or art center program envisions the building as a sanctuary: a calculated sequence of contemplative, sanctified spaces where viewers can quietly, thoughtfully and methodically study art. Circulation may provide several itineraries or a single, well-plotted course, but the experience is meant to be different—an elevated, extraordinary moment distinct from the commonplace. The museum functions as a rarefied environment.

With the completion in 1978 of the Pompidou Centre at Beaubourg in Paris by architects Renzo Piano and Richard Rogers, another vision of the museum became a physical fact. The Pompidou Centre was an open factory: a manipulable, raucous, unregulated atmosphere in which to encounter art. Its internal arrangement was almost always under change, huge signs announced the smorgasbord of exhibits, noise and perpetual activity were the normal—and only—course. Most architecture imperfectly satisfies its program and Piano and Roger's spectacular building is no exception, but its intentions and provocations remain influential. If art registered the maelstrom of life, the building for art would be the vortex—the center for chaos, the site of sensation.

In the new pageant of notable art centers, there is now the Wexner Center for the Arts at The Ohio State University. The center, first unveiled in fall 1989, continued to mark its inauguration for over a year with a trinity of exhibitions providing a rite of initiation for the young building. The Wexner Center was built by a collaboration of architects; Peter Eisenman from New York and Richard Trott from Columbus created Eisenman/Trott Architects, Inc. in order to pull off this logistical and architectural tour de force.

> Perhaps the main service which a museum can perform for its visitors is to arrange displays which stimulate curiosity. Paradoxically, it does not have to be what the professionals would call 'a good museum' in order to achieve this. Most of the eighteenth century collections were, in the modern sense of the term, very bad museums. Their owners made little attempt to set out the items attractively or to explain them in any way. That they existed and had been brought together was sufficient to produce a sense of wonder, the excitement of having been brought into contact with the unknown.[2]

On the typological expanse of museum design, the Wexner Center is a new tangent, an axis that nearly breaks off from its genealogical spine. But it hangs by a thread, neither completely faithful nor heretical, neither securely connected nor entirely disengaged. Its tenuous relation to building type, public expectation and tradition makes it an anxious endeavor for the architect and an unfamiliar experience for the public. That it is

Eisenman/Trott Architects, *Wexner Center for the Arts* (1989). Interior of the circulation ramp. Photo: Kevin Fitzsimons, courtesy of The Ohio State University Office of Communications.

Eisenman/Trott Architects, *Wexner Center for the Arts* (1989). Aerial view. Photo: Kevin Fitzsimons, courtesy of The Ohio State University Office of Communications.

new territory is one reason the building seems like a rebel without a cause, a complex apparatus without purpose. The Wexner Center desires to be both a shrine and a laboratory, both monumental and maverick. Time and art will influence but not resolve these conflicts.

> The collection is a form of art as play, a form involving the reframing of objects within a world of attention and manipulation of context.[3]

The Eisenman/Trott building is about the potency and idiosyncrasy of the collection and the always unique motivations of the impassioned collectors who have influenced the understanding of art. But in this case the architect is the collector, a gatherer of contemporary ideas rather than objects. The Wexner Center is an architectural cabinet of curiosities whose wide-ranging, mysteriously related contents reflect the intellectual passions and preoccupations of the designer. Eisenman is an architect who collects ideas from many places; he is drawn to some for their urgency and currency and to others for their constancy, less vulnerable to winds of change and whims of taste. His collection of ideas has been influenced by shifting psychological strategies and cultural theories, by local and universal grids and by the more predictable configurations of architectural typography and form.

In this opportunity-of-a-lifetime building, the architect displayed the entire collection of ideas and impulses that has driven his discursive, intellectually demanding work. It is a collection that can easily overwhelm; the experience asks for a pioneering independence, an excitement for the unusual. It is up to the viewers and artists who will do their own work and reside temporarily at the center to sort out this curio cabinet, to either discover what the pieces mean to each other or to enjoy or ignore the building's unsettling elements or demands. People may either match the building's rigorous, imperfect strategies with their own systems of order and equilibrium, or they may push the experience to a reckless state to uncover the dark, unrestrained character of the architecture.

The intentions and systems that generated the Wexner Center have been well documented by the architects and a willing press. An important genesis for the building was an inconsistency—an incompatibility between campus and city. There are many differences, sources of strife that can occur between a college and its surrounding community; there are always cultural, territorial and political quarrels. Eisenman chose to look at this city-campus breach abstractly. The grid of the city of Columbus aligns with the plat system first used in the early nineteenth century to map an unruly, undeveloped frontier. The Ohio State campus followed another drum and the rhythms of topography and university iconography. Designed by the office of landscape architect Frederick Law Olmsted, the campus alignment slips apart from the city plan. The two grids skew by a scant twelve and one-quarter degrees. This potentially forgettable idea and barely observable fact had a significance for the architect that provided a beginning for the building. The inconsistency of the two grids generated a building of discrepant forms; the building follows one, then the other and sometimes neither grid, and the result is an environment of complex and residual spaces and surfaces.

What is it about a grid? What does it contain and release at the same time? It remains interesting because it is so ubiquitous, habitual, accessible—and so susceptible to violation. It is both dogmatic and imperfect in almost every application. The platting of the American continent in the nineteenth century was a practical and philosophical way to manage the sublimity of the wilderness. To place a grid on the unknown and unexplored was part of the mania for freshness, opportunity, invention and, if lucky, prosperity. The question of Eisenman's preoccupation with the grid is a far more challenging thought than the physical fact of the grid at the Wexner Center.

The Wexner Center is like a vast, spatial puzzle. One can wander through the building studying column grids, trying to distinguish structural from formal elements, walking with head down to unravel restlessly changing floor patterns, materials, colors and textures. But with enough time and patience the building's mystery can be solved. The moment of solution would be disturbingly conclusive if there were not other reasons to be in the building, to care about and question the architecture. Decoding its compositional complexities may help "to get" the building, but the process does not lead the mind to the dimensional possibilities of the architecture. The real conundrum is a mania for systems that, in the end, provide no answers but enhance the sense of the random. The grid, seen as a register of desire, does not imprison the composition, dominate the space nor dictate experience. In the Wexner Center, the grid is a device to unleash, rather than control, the intellect.

People don't simply build in order to put a roof over their heads, they don't build in order to render homage. The act of building is an act of honour rendered, and the tragedy is that of knowing who or what is the addressee of this gift...Today we don't know the destination of building...[4]

The center must be overcome to be fully, freely experienced. Part of seeing and working with the building is the acceptance of its fallibility—that it neither follows a previous standard nor offers a definitive new one. It is as much about a singular vision as about a new proposition for the display and production of art. The building does not discourage or disdain art; it is simply a private, notational collection of the architect made into a built, brilliant fact. It is a magnificent, self-possessed environment. The point is to see it as nothing more or less:

> Freed from the restriction of collective style, the artist discovered he could create a style in the image of his own personality. The art of the twentieth century has no collective style, not because it has divorced itself from contemporary society but because it is part of it. And here we are with our hard-earned freedom. Walls are crumbling around us and we are terrified by the endless vistas and the responsibility of an infinite choice. It is this terror of the new freedom which removed the familiar signposts from the roads that make many of us wish to turn the clock back and recover the security of yesterday's dogma.[5]

Eisenman/Trott Architects, *Wexner Center for the Arts* (1989). View of south façade.
Photo: © ARTOG/D.G. Olshavsky.

As the third of three inaugural exhibitions, the Wexner Center's curators invited an eclectic group of artists to do projects and installations that somehow responded to this brave new world. *New Works for New Spaces: Into the Nineties* suggested the building's future in many ways. As an introduction of the Wexner Center's artist-in-residence program, it set a tone of strained, volatile and lively domesticity. Given the range of artists selected, the exhibition implied not the proper place of the artist in this building but some of the possible roles that might emerge in this kind of off-center collaboration.

There will be artists—now and in the future—such as Gretchen Bender, whose work is about the everywhere and the nowhere of contemporary culture, who may choose to virtually overlook the building. Her work is about the nonspecific quality of all sites, the placelessness required of and produced by media saturation. She took on the Wexner Center site by dismissing its challenging peculiarities. If Bender was interested in the anonymity of the building, artists including Sol LeWitt chose to avoid the building for other reasons. LeWitt's independent, detached structure—a tall tower of cinder blocks in an adjacent pedestrian walkway—was a proposition on how people use and make sense of systems. LeWitt's systemic analysis suggested an alternative that set a debate with the Wexner Center. It required a pulling away that severed the coexistence of two prevailing visions. Art and architecture served as counterpoints to each other.

A number of artists saw the building as a big toy—an instrument alternately menacing, frustrating and stimulating. Christian Marclay used the outdoor white grid that stitches the space between the Wexner Center and the older Mershon Auditorium as a sound machine that released an assault of clanging, banging noise on the hour. Chris Burden's crenellation of the reinvented brick towers that recall the armory once on the Wexner Center's site used the nostalgic architectural scenography on hand to develop another game of imagery and associations of the fortifications built for art. Barbara Kruger's smart, aggressive images invaded the entire building through strategic occupation, engaging the space in a great battle of spirited wills. Joseph Kosuth's installation of a neon-lit Walter Benjamin quotation on a beam cut through two galleries to remark on the habits of optical perception and architecture, on the implications of convention in the Wexner Center's exaggerated nonconformity.

Other artists worked in particular spaces of the building like temporary viruses occupying cells in some large organism. Malcolm Cochran's passion for the commonplace, for the beauty and irony in ordinary things, produced a full echo of life in the Wexner Center's almost maddening, precious atmosphere. Sculptors Gilberto Zorio and Magdalena Abakanowicz simply, elegantly inserted sensual, expressive and raw presences within the building's pristine environment. The obvious contrast of sensibilities in this site required no other rationalization. And Fortuyn/O'Brien's placement of two marble chairs in an outdoor, walled wedge of space adjacent to the Wexner Center's primary entrance made an awkward residual space an anxious garden of contemplation and estrangement.

The first museums were part of large precincts that included libraries and other cultural facilities. It was not until the sixteenth century that the museum first became an independent enterprise with a clearly segregated structure. Ann Hamilton and Tadashi Kawamata saw the Wexner Center as a small part of a larger center of intellectual and civic life. Hamilton worked closely with an entomologist at Ohio State to create a habitat for thousands of moths in the building. The painstaking preliminary research was guided and aided by the human and intellectual resources of the contemporary university. Hamilton introduced what she described as a "liquid chaos"—the inherent energy of life cycles—into the Wexner Center's stillness. Kawamata placed restless, unruly wood installations against the building's facade and through its exterior passageways and positioned small guerrilla projects at additional sites across and beyond the campus. Both artists invoked the interdependency of building site, campus and city.

Video artists Carole Ann Klonarides and Michael Owen (MICA-TV) visited the Wexner Center to film and produce a Gothic tale inspired by its many "dead" spaces, which served as locations for a mysterious narrative. The artists were intrigued by the curious corners, the ungainly passages that occur in an intellectual deployment of architectural form.

Many of the artists chose to work with what is unremarkable about the building, to create static in the atmosphere of the structure, to dismiss its obvious, aggressive physical challenges. Others sought and identified connections—whether seen as areas of accord or conflict—between the architecture and their own artistic predilections. Most were intellectually intrigued by the Wexner Center but found the terms of Eisenman's environment—the art-architecture discourse the building suggests—too strident to circumscribe their own aesthetic inquiries. Instead they chose to disengage their work from the building's sculptural and systemic authority, to pursue more independent, ongoing investigations. Acceptance or rejection of the architectural philosophy remained incidental to individual aesthetic objectives. The artists' responses could suggest retreat or escape from the Eisenman/Trott building; their avoidance and, in some cases, disinterest in the physical facts of the architecture could denote a despair often felt in difficult, oppressive circumstances. But the investigations are of another sort, the inquiries of a different kind, than the architect has brought to the building. In many cases they are skeptical—not about the building as it is but about what it can become.

Eisenman/Trott Architects, *Wexner Center for the Arts* (1989). Interior view.
Photo: © ARTOG/D.G. Olshavsky.

All architecture is a form of mind control and it is the inhabitants' consciousness of this manipulation which influences the nature and extent of domination. The Wexner Center is a marvelous place for collaboration, but this complex, variable process will unfold over time as viewers and artists circumvent or subvert the commanding presence of the building, the particular collaboration to which it appeals, in order to discover a new method of inventive cooperation. It is the test of the artist to get beyond what is clearly provided by the architecture—to construct fresh questions rather than to answer the obvious ones the building can command.

We have inherited two dominant models for the museum: the shrine and the laboratory. The Wexner Center is serene, stern and untouchable, but its oddities call for riotous, devoted experimentation. The building's strength and energy are not in its fidelity to intellectual and architectonic systems but in its curious imperfections, strange excesses, marvelous inconsistencies and memorable spaces. This architectural cabinet of curiosities invites a parade of other systems that will temporarily reorder and, over time, define the Wexner Center.

> First, how long is ephemeral?…In art the ephemeral stands for greatness and dignity. All works should attempt to be ephemeral. This should be their ambition…It is to accept our limitations, our sparse knowledge, our period…It is also to accept that neither duration nor quantity are synonymous with quality. It's to accept that a stroke of lightning can be impressed upon our memory just as strongly as a pyramid.[6]

The ephemeral is surprisingly invasive; it leaves a residue. The requirements and restraints of the building are both unusual and daunting, but art has a long legacy of disobeying prevailing standards. Whether the subversion is quiet or boisterous, we should expect nothing less here—of all places. □

Magdalena Abakanowicz
Winged Trunk 1989
wood and iron
Courtesy of Marlborough Gallery, New York.
Photo: Fredrik Marsh.

Magdalena Abakanowicz

Claudia Gould

Magdalena Abakanowicz's poignant sculptures testify to the persistent strength of expressionistic tendencies in vanguard art, particularly in Europe. One of the few contemporary Eastern European artists to have attained an international reputation, Abakanowicz began her career as a weaver and first gained respect for her innovations as a fiber artist. In the Alterations series she began in the seventies, Abakanowicz composed haunting installations of anonymous and fragmented figurative forms (among them the well-known Heads, Backs and Seated Figures) that she constructed in multiples by pressing string, burlap and other fibers into plaster molds. The evocative humanism of these works struck a powerful chord with American artists and audiences in the eighties, as interests in figurative representation and emotional content again came to the forefront of avant-garde investigations. Born in Falenty, Poland in 1930, Abakanowicz studied at the School of Fine Arts in Warsaw, where she continues to live and work.

At Abakanowicz's request, the documentation of her Winged Trunk (1989) is accompanied here by a brief essay rather than an interview.

I first met Magdalena Abakanowicz in the spring of 1988 in Warsaw, Poland. She took me straight from the airport to her house in the country, a small log cabin near a man-made lake and a forest. As we walked around the lake, she told me about a group of works she had just begun. She explained that she had received permission from the government to collect fallen trees and cut down dead ones in the nearby forest, and she spoke with excitement and anticipation about using nature in a new way in her work. The tree trunks Abakanowicz harvested from the woods became the basis for her War Games.

Previously Abakanowicz had been reluctant to use wood in her work, because she saw it as a material already finished and complete in its own identity. She began the War Games after recognizing metaphorical connections between tree forms and the body: the core of a tree trunk as a spine, severed tree branches as amputated limbs. The tree trunks of the War Games series maintain their natural identity but build on what the artist sees as their "corporeality."

Slashed by a semicircular iron blade and bound by burlap and rope, Winged Trunk is an unsettling sculpture, evocative of wounds tended yet still painful. The blade penetrating the trunk suggests violations—the rape of the land, the rape of an individual, the amputation of body parts—but the "winged" of the title suggests the possibility of flight and transcendence. With both fragility and strength implicit in its materials and form, Winged Trunk also conveys the dual identity of victim and survivor that Abakanowicz expressed in her figurative Alterations. In the War Games as in the earlier series, she comments eloquently on the vulnerability of nature and human life and the resilience necessary for survival.

Abakanowicz selected Winged Trunk, a work not previously exhibited, as her response to the Wexner Center building and site. Not site-specific in any usual sense, the sculpture nonetheless draws attention to contrasts between its own rough-hewn appearance and the polish of its architectural surroundings. Juxtaposed against the systematic logic and technological sophistication of the Eisenman/Trott building, the humanistic expressionism of Abakanowicz's Winged Trunk stands as one artist's defiant confirmation of a very different aesthetic. □

Winged Trunk 1989
detail
Photo: Fredrik Marsh.

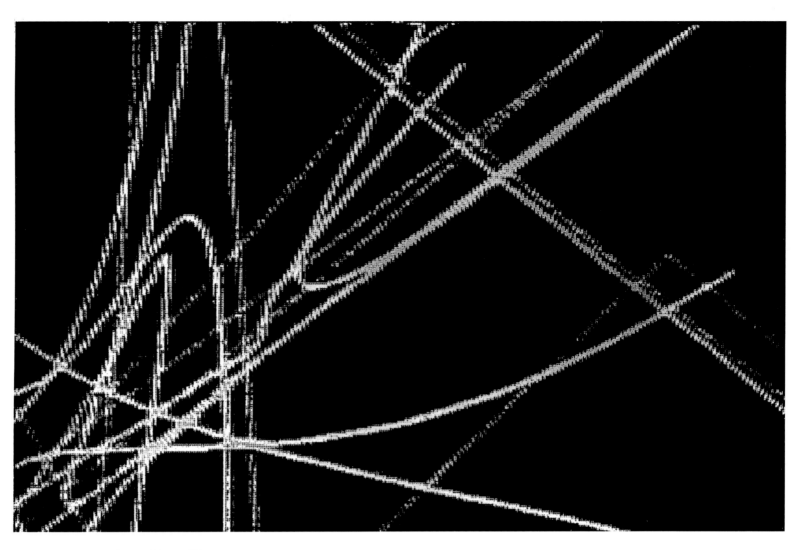

Aggressive Witness–Active Participant 1990
detail: still from videotape
Photo courtesy of the artist.

Gretchen Bender
Aggressive Witness–Active Participant 1990
multi-monitor installation with videotape, live
television and sound
detail: television monitors with texts
Commissioned by the Wexner Center for the Arts;
collection of the artist.
Photos: Fredrik Marsh.

Gretchen Bender

Social and political commentary, recurring themes in the seventies and eighties, continue to engage artists such as Gretchen Bender. Among the first artists to formulate such critiques in the language of television, Bender brings a new technological sophistication to the avant-garde's ongoing investigations of popular culture. She takes her creative strategies as well as her content from television and appropriates its manipulations as well as its images. In her media environments and "electronic theater" presentations, she questions and disrupts the conventionally passive process of "watching TV." Born in Seaford, Delaware in 1951, Bender received a B.F.A. from the University of North Carolina at Chapel Hill in 1972 and moved to New York City in 1980. Since the early eighties she has exhibited at The Kitchen and Nature Morte Gallery in New York and in numerous group shows in the United States and Europe including the Whitney Museum's 1989 exhibition Image World. Bender was interviewed by Sarah Rogers-Lafferty.

Sarah Rogers-Lafferty: What are you focusing on for your Wexner Center project?

Gretchen Bender: The installation consists of twelve television monitors. Eight are set to different broadcast channels. Simple phrases in boldface type adhere to the front of these screens so that the TV images are seen through the texts. The eight phrases are:

LESBIAN AND GAY RIGHTS
BODY OWNERSHIP
LIVING WITH THE POOR
DEATH SQUAD BUDGET
NUCLEAR WARHEADS
NO CRITICISM
PUBLIC MEMORY
CLASS, RACE, GENDER

The four other screens show abstract, black-and-white patterns: computer-generated grids that seem to "breathe" and then splinter, apparently spontaneously, and then revert back to grids. Each monitor with an abstract pattern is flanked by ones with texts.

One challenge the work poses is how to go beyond simply depicting an environment. All my work with television, in installations and performances, uses multiple TV screens to present different aspects of an issue as conflicting images and conflicting content simultaneously. By looking at multiple screens, viewers start to see how we're talking to ourselves and manipulating ourselves. I want to get people to look at television with greater awareness and to recognize that what they see, even on the news, is in many ways as artificial and controlled as the abstract patterns I'm using here.

The phrases on the screens address the contemporary socio-political situation by referring to specific issues and to the ways we think about those issues. They're like catalysts that might "jump start" the critical consciousness of viewers. I want to infiltrate the face of TV with these catalysts, to melt into and provoke and radicalize every image that's shown—every football game, every little girl, every cat-food commercial, every drug bust—with thoughts about "body ownership" or "living with the poor" or whichever phrase is on that screen. I'm also focusing on the seduction of the abstract, its evocativeness, and the need to tie it to the external psyche represented by television. I want the abstract to be accountable for its sensuous mask.

SRL: Do you think art can effect social change?

GB: This work is an attempt to see what I can do to actively influence viewers' actions, but I know the project will come across as my art, my opinion, my propaganda. The viewers can decide that it's my art, and take it or leave it. Still, I would like my work to remind viewers that they—that we all—have a voice in societal decisions, that we decide what to consume and produce and that we have a responsibility to live with our choices. I'd like to think that the work could possibly influence viewers to activate themselves, to actually do something like call their congresspeople or write to their senators. So I'm trying to incorporate something very difficult.

SRL: Will you be trying to provoke this response by the physical orientation of the monitors in the gallery space, or are you going to leave that as straightforward as possible?

GB: I am going to have a fairly simple installation that may counter the artiness of the building's postmodern architecture so that the impact of the work will come from what is on the televisions, from the confrontations and conflicts that occur between the images and words on different monitors.

SRL: What about the sound for the installation?

Above and opposite
Aggressive Witness–Active Participant 1990
installation views
Photo: Fredrik Marsh.

GB: There's an electronic soundtrack designed by Stuart Argabright that intensifies a kind of postindustrial sighing. It's rather sci-fi, like biogenetic fly sounds or maggots munching, and I think it accentuates the sense of a controlling grid that underlies even the seemingly random spontaneity of television.

SRL: Do you think the media is a buffer to reality?

GB: I think it's a very complicated buffer, because it operates in part as a way we deceive ourselves into a political calm, while we also seem to be trying to address socio-political issues obliquely. I feel I have to connect viewers with the fact that they participate, as I participate, in the agenda of this culture. Too often we feel detached from it, and maybe television and film make us feel like we're doing something when we really aren't doing very much except trying to calm ourselves.

SRL: And to break through that buffer, you're really making public art?

GB: I hope so. I'm trying to use things that we all see as my source material, as the foundation of this work, without bringing any esoteric aesthetic sensibility to it. I use the techniques that the audience already knows from mass culture. I want to bring viewers toward issues that multiply their resonances and dissonances within our mass-media, "televisual" reality. To hold the contradictions of seduction and alienation simultaneously should allow the viewer a sharper interaction with the TV text pieces.

SRL: Why is this project particularly appropriate for the Wexner Center?

GB: As an art center at a university, the Wexner Center offers its community of students a forum for supplanting clichés, which is also what I intend to do. In many ways the work I do strains against the ivory tower, the ivory tower of the university and the ivory tower of the museum. The challenge of this work is to introduce into the museum context a sense of actuality too often absent there. And the elaborateness and complexity of the Wexner Center's architecture may make the clash with media culture seem even greater. Both the project itself and its placement at the center represent and build on contradictions.

The "breathing" grid image could be looked at as a metaphor for the grids that determine and control the building as well as for the electronic pixel grid of the television

Aggressive Witness–Active Participant 1990
detail: television monitors with texts
Photos: Fredrik Marsh.

screen, but I didn't really worry about making my project appropriate for the architecture in its content—the ideas and issues are common to all my work. Still, after several visits, I've thought a lot about the architecture. The building is so clearly a reflection of the architects' ideas that it's already established its content as well as its form, unlike a more neutral museum space that waits for the art to fill in the content. Here content is a fait accompli, and artists have to be ready to use guerrilla tactics to sneak their content in around the meaning that the building already has or to subvert its messages with their own. In some ways that parallels the situation I face in using television.

SRL: Why is television so vital to you?

GB: We live in motion, and television connects us with that motion. Film has been called the art form of the twentieth century, but TV represents the cultural life we inhabit. When I first came to New York in 1980, I was interested in art as signs and as scanned information rather than as contemplative, modernist objects, and I worked with appropriated art reproductions and popular advertisements. It seemed that most of the artists who were working with mass media were still using—getting their information and their images from—newspapers and magazines, and I wondered why television wasn't in the art world. Video figured prominently in the art world in the seventies; in the eighties it became ghettoized. In the nineties television is being reinvented through computers. I thought TV could work well with the Brechtian idea of entertaining and revealing or critiquing at the same time: you try to go to the edge of seduction yet remain aware that you're being seduced.

If TV is the major metaphor of our visual experience it's essential to challenge the alienation and passivity that the television industry produces. The work I've done using television fights this disconnection aggressively by reminding us of our socio-political condition. At the same time my work can present liberating associations formed in the imagination of viewers. I set up an interactive viewing situation where what viewers see can trigger individual revelations that access their own imaginations. Instead of accepting the neutralizing passivity of watching TV my work attempts to translate it into a more complex experience that can encompass political thought and imagination. ☐

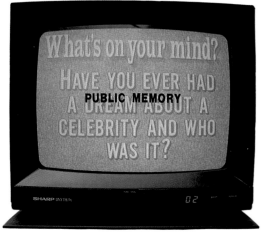

Chris Burden

Chris Burden's restless experimentation has continued without stagnation or repetition since the early seventies, when his explorations of performance art and video helped map these new territories. His early body art projects tested his endurance with disconcerting, often self-punitive actions; his more recent works transpose themes of aggression and defense to sculptural and installation formats. The thread connecting Burden's diverse oeuvre is anxiety—he makes uneasy art for an uneasy age, addressing issues of power and control in contemporary society. Born in Boston in 1946, Burden studied architecture and science as well as art while an undergraduate; he received a B.A. from Pomona College in 1969 and a M.F.A. from the University of California at Irvine in 1971, performing Five Day Locker Piece for his master's-thesis exhibition. Burden continues to live and work in California. Since 1978 he has taught at the University of California at Los Angeles. Burden was interviewed by Claudia Gould.

Claudia Gould: For your project at the Wexner Center you are adding crenellations to several of the building's towers. Can you tell me about how your ideas developed?

Chris Burden: Well, I was just trying to do my job here, which was to make an artwork in response to the building, but it's a trick to figure out what your response is. I visited the Wexner Center a couple of times, and I had some other impulses, but I finally decided to backtrack to my first impression—that there was something wrong and unnerving about the towers. I could deal with the interior mishmash—the grids and everything—but the towers bothered me.

After I had read about the building and seen pictures of the old armory, I could see what the towers were supposed to represent—the echo of the armory. Still, I felt as if the towers had been smoothed over, as if they had been put into a computer and the computer couldn't handle the crenellations because it just didn't have the capability of doing that. It's as if Peter Eisenman was trying to deny the decorative nature of what he had done by building the towers.

CG: So, to you, the towers seem decorative, even superfluous?

CB: Well, superfluous may be too strong a word. I can understand how Eisenman thinks of them as a very important part of this project. But they're so generic. It wasn't clear to me exactly what they were. They could be smokestacks for some bizarre, evil industry. Then you look at pictures of the old armory and you say, "Oh, yes." But why aren't the towers crenellated? That would be my question.

CG: And what you are doing is bringing the towers back to how they originally were in the armory, as if that had been part of the Eisenman-Trott design?

CB: Right. The idea of the crenellations is that they will look like they have always been part of the building. Or, maybe, people will look at them and think "Gee, they finally finished the towers."

CG: That's interesting since Eisenman intends for the building to look like it's always evolving—it's a building forever becoming a building. By adding the crenellations you're closing a question that the architects purposely left open.

CB: When I kept coming back here and walking around and studying the building—particularly looking from the northeast corner—one of the things I thought about was how I might be able to return the building to its "Ideal" state as if it were a pure architectural model before the real life blemishes began to appear, as if it were an untouched Minimal sculpture. You can see the building as a beautiful, minimal, clean box, but then there are all the practical imperfections—lightning rods and rivets and gutter spouts and stains, things like that. One of my ideas was to simply remove or hide those things and clean the building up so that it would just become this pure white slab. Nobody would have noticed it, but it would be different.

CG: Now you're adding things instead, but the project still may be almost invisible.

CB: Except that the towers will feel more right than they do now. Psychologically, in people's psyches, they will read as more correct, and they will be less noticeable because they will fit.

CG: They won't be as ambiguous.

CB: Right.

CG: Historically, towers and crenellations in architecture have been associated with military defenses. Was this part of what drew you to thinking about using these features in your project? I know you collect military toys, and a number of your recent works—*Reason for the Neutron Bomb* (1979), *A Tale of Two Cities* (1981), *All the Submarines of the United States of America* (1987)—address contemporary military issues.

The Wexner Castle 1990
detail
Photo: Kevin Fitzsimons, courtesy of The Ohio State University Office of Communications.

193

CB: I think you see more of a connection than I do. Towers and crenellations have been decorative—rather than functional as defenses—for a long, long time. As soon as artillery started being effective—and a cannon could shoot up at a tower and knock it down—the military rationale was gone. What's interesting to me is that crenellations have been purely decorative since medieval times, but they were still being incorporated into architecture, like on the towers of the old armory at Ohio State. By building towers but eliminating the crenellations, an iconic symbol of a building's essential purpose as protective shelter, Eisenman is denying this function. Yet he would *never* leave the roof off a building or leave the glass out of the window panes. Either you go all the way, or you don't do it at all.

I do have a little article on crenellations from a military magazine I bought four or five years ago. Because I'm interested in making military models, I mentally filed the article away, and when I started thinking about the Wexner Center towers I remembered specifically that I had the magazine.

I'm interested in architecture too, although I don't think I want to be an architect. My *A Tale of Two Cities*, which has two cities at war with each other, is architectural in some sense. Now I'm working on another piece, *Pizza City*, which is like a wedge—it's about thirty feet long—taken out of a make-believe city. For two or three years I've been collecting miniature buildings in the smallest model train scale, where the scale ratio is 1: 220. The smaller the scale the more area you can represent. The buildings are very detailed, and I've found all kinds of eclectic architecture—a Swiss chalet, Tudor houses, Japanese, whatever I can get my hands on—that fits the scale. The city is going to be a potpourri of cultures. Whenever I have the time, I move the buildings around and look at the little scenes, which end up being destroyed because right now I'm basically just playing.

People ask me what it's about…I live in a city of—I don't know—however many million Los Angeles' population is now, and in everybody's mind's eye the city is this thing, this object with a center and outskirts. They carry a romantic, nostalgic vision of what a city is or should be. The reality has nothing to do with it, but you are able to tolerate the reality because of the fantasy of a city you have in your mind's eye. I'm not designing specific buildings here, but I am working with architecture—or maybe it's city planning.

CG: The works you've been describing are very elaborate and complex, while much of your early work and your work in performance was quite minimalistic.

CB: I was trained as a Minimal sculptor—Ronald Bladen and Donald Judd were my heroes. It's funny—now we see Minimalism as rather passé, but when I was first in college everybody was pouring bronze and making heads and carving. Then, when the new professors came in, everything changed: no more clay, no more casting, clean off the tables and okay, everybody, make a cube, a perfect cube. I found that really refreshing.

Pretty soon, I started making some really big works outside—one of them was two hundred feet long. Just to work on it, I had to walk two hundred feet from end to end. I was trying to distill the essence of sculpture as opposed to two-dimensional art. That was Minimalist logic, to get to the essence of things. I started understanding that, for me, one of the essential things about sculpture was the way it forced viewers to move. That was the essence of sculpture—never mind what you were looking at—physically it forced viewers to move. In graduate school I did a whole series that involved objects I'd made specifically for viewers to move and interact with. The problem was that people would see them and say "Oh, wow, that's beautiful sculpture," when the object wasn't the sculpture—you using it was the sculpture. People would see the objects as sculpture and not use them unless they were instructed to. The objects were tailored for my body though, and if you were taller or shorter they didn't work so well.

CG: How did you become involved with performance?

CB: When I was getting ready for my M.F.A. show, I'd go over and look at the space—like I did here. It was a big, converted classroom building and off to one side was a bank of lockers. I kept thinking of making a box and being in a box in the space, and it finally occurred to me that I didn't have to make a box: there were boxes—the lockers—right there. That was a breakthrough for me, to realize that I didn't have to make the box. I could use a preexisting box and go into it, *be* art by being in it, and come out and not have to make a box to be in. That's how I started doing performances—it seemed to solve so many problems.

A lot of people began doing performances in the sixties and early seventies—Vito Acconci, William Wegman, Tom Marioni. I think we saw performance as a way to make art that we had control of, which may have been naïve on our part. But it came out of a

The Wexner Castle 1990
installation view of south façade
Photo: Kevin Fitzsimons.

kind of antimaterialist reaction against the gross commercialism that was happening in the art world and in American culture.

CG: In a quite different sense, your project for the towers might also seem antimaterialistic, because of its disappearing act, the way it may become almost invisible. It combines, or draws from, both the more conceptual or minimalistic slant of your performance work and the military and architectural interests you've developed more recently—even if these are secondary layers over your immediate response to the building.

CB: I think the towers bothered me as a sculptor because they were so obviously fake sculpture, if I may be so bold as to use the word. There is always offense when architects start making sculpture. Maybe architects get offended when artists start making architecture, so I am opening myself up there a little. I'm not saying that there shouldn't be a crossover, that the categories are rigid. Artists and architects are close in some ways, especially sculptors and architects. Architecture has to straddle two sides of the fence: great architecture becomes art but architecture still has a client and still has to function. Art doesn't need to have a functional purpose and so can deal more comfortably with ambiguity.

If the towers were really sculptures, they wouldn't need the crenellations on top. But then if they were sculptures I couldn't do the project, could I?

CG: Maybe that's a liberty that Eisenman has given you because he is an architect rather than a sculptor.

CB: There's the question of "Is the building art?" or "Is it a building?" I guess architecture can be both, and I'm sure Eisenman had that in mind. Actually, I'm rather surprised that this is all going to happen. I hope the crenellations stay there forever. □

Malcolm Cochran
Western Movie 1990
16mm film, coin-operated horses, lead, wood, theater
seats; transparency of Frederic Edwin Church's *Niagara*
(Corcoran Gallery of Art)
Commissioned by the Wexner Center for the Arts;
collection of the artist.
Photo: Fredrik Marsh.

Malcolm Cochran

Malcolm Cochran shares the fascination with recycled objects that has made assemblage common currency throughout the postwar decades. Deploying mechanical cast-offs in architectural constructions, he infuses the ephemeral format of installation art with monumentality and evocations of the past. His seemingly unrelated objects often reveal unexpected connections and imply narrative possibilities if not explicit narratives. Sound and movement energize his monumental stages and often suggest unseen human presences. Born in 1948 in Pittsburgh, Cochran received his B.A. in 1971 from Wesleyan University and his M.F.A. in 1973 from Cranbrook Academy of Art. From 1974 to 1986 he lived in New Hampshire, combining his career as an artist with employment as a curator and exhibition designer at Dartmouth College's Hood Museum of Art. Since 1987 he has taught at The Ohio State University in Columbus. His numerous commissions include projects for Artpark in Lewiston, New York and for Socrates Sculpture Park in New York City; he has exhibited extensively in New England and the Midwest as well as at P.S. 1 in New York City and in the recent traveling exhibition Awards in the Visual Arts 9. *Cochran was interviewed by Robert Stearns.*

Robert Stearns: How does *Western Movie*, your project for *New Works for New Spaces*, fit into the development of your work?

Malcolm Cochran: *Western Movie* shares some characteristics with a couple of my recent constructions—*Song without Words (for Amy Beach)* (1987), *Bridge of Sighs* (1989) and *In Maine* (1990)—because it too recycles castoff mechanical objects in an architectural setting. In those pieces, I was interested in unlocking the metaphorical potential I see in everyday appliances: oscillating fans, vacuum cleaners, the insides of refrigerators. In *Western Movie*, I'm using the coin-operated horses you find in shopping malls throughout America. I was drawn to them because they are somehow both heroic and pathetic. There are also links between this work and my first site piece, *Dream of Arcadia*, which I did in 1981 at Artpark in Lewiston, New York. *Dream of Arcadia* was suggested by Thomas Cole's Hudson River School painting of the same name. *Western Movie* has Frederic Edwin Church's 1857 painting *Niagara* as its jumping-off point.

RS: Can you tell me about your response to the Wexner Center? For the exhibition, we asked you to respond to the building in one way or another—formally, structurally, emotionally.

MC: I admire, maybe from a distance, the thoroughness of the thinking behind the building. When I walk through it, I can appreciate the interlocking of the various grids and the layering. It's like an intricate puzzle taken to an extreme, all the way down to the floor tiles and all the way up to the ceiling. The finishes are gorgeous. The care and craftsmanship that went into the building, particularly the floors, do a lot to make the logic warmer, to humanize the space.

At the same time, it's as if the logic is carried out to an illogical extreme. For me, an artist creating a work in and for the building, the biggest problem is that there is no relief from the imposition of that logic. It doesn't ever stop: the obsessive attention to detail carries through to every single facet of the surface and space. I don't deny Peter Eisenman the desire or the right to play—to impose his ideas and interests. But I wish that he had said "Okay, I'm going to play here and you go play there." Despite the professed democracy of the building—the idea of it being an open-ended structure—it strikes me as very authoritarian. It's anything but an open building.

RS: Did your response to the building affect the choice of a location for your project?

MC: It's easier to do something unconventional in a conventional space, and it's easier to play off a foil that is essentially neutral. On my first or second walk through the building I noticed Gallery A, the space I am using, as the building's most conventional gallery in its lighting and proportions, and that's why I was attracted to it.

Another part of my response in the project comes from the "insider's" perspective I have as part of this community. I came to teach at Ohio State in January 1987, while the building was under construction, and when I think about the Wexner Center, I think about the building and the program together. It's exciting for a university to make such a strong commitment to art that is new and experimental. In *Western Movie*, I am responding to the Wexner Center's program as much as to the qualities of the building itself.

RS: How do you see your ideas for *Western Movie* as a response to the program?

MC: Since the Wexner Center is dedicated to late twentieth-century art, to Contemporary Art with capital letters, the unexpected in this situation would be to do something absolutely not contemporary. I liked the idea of putting into this space a work that has, at least as a starting point, a key painting from the nineteenth century. The references to movies and theatrical situations are also, at least in part, a response to the Center's multidisciplinary mission.

RS: What attracted you to Church's painting, and how are you using it?

MC: Both Niagara Falls itself and Church's painting of it are key icons for America: for the power, resources and promise of the New World. A friend who was studying the Hudson River School introduced me to the painting fifteen years ago. Since I've been thinking about this piece, I have been reading David C. Huntington's *The Landscapes of Frederic Edwin Church: Vision of an American Era*, and it has helped me remember why the painting was so significant and revolutionary in its day. Huntington calls Niagara Falls "the national Mecca in the Era of Manifest Destiny" and "the most 'suggestive' natural spectacle in the New World." He also describes it as "a million water incidents, each with its own peculiar cause and effect." One of the remarkable things about Church's painting is the way he pulls you into the picture so convincingly—there's nothing between you and the water at the top of the falls. The proportions were also unusual for its time, since Church stretched the width of a traditional easel painting to capture the sweeping curve of the falls.

I'm using a projection of the painting as a backdrop for the whole piece, and I'm layering the image with film footage of the falls I shot this summer. There will be a number of projectors using a combination of still and moving imagery. Since I have never worked with film before, I am getting help from Bruce Thompson, the manager of the labs in the photography and cinema department here. I hope I can layer the image of the falls so that at some points the water will appear to be moving, almost as if the painting was pulled away to reveal the actual falls. I'm going to stretch the proportions of the painting even more, so that the image becomes almost cinemascopic. It will stretch forty-six feet from side to side and sixteen feet from floor to ceiling, across a curved wall I have designed for the west side of the gallery.

I'm not sure where the idea of projecting the image came from, but maybe, sub-consciously, it started with the square of light projected on the west wall of Gallery A during the Antenna Theater project last autumn.

RS: I remember that—the square of light stood as a reference to the "perfect" abstract painting. What happens in front of your projection?

MC: That's where the mechanical horses will be. I began thinking about those horses as a final, popularized derivation of the concept Church portrays—the promise of the New World, the frontier—and the irony that this image has become something you put a

Frederic Edwin Church
Niagara 1857
oil on canvas, 42 ½" x 90 ½"
The Corcoran Gallery of Art, Washington, D.C.,
Gallery Fund Purchase, 1876.
© Corcoran Gallery of Art.

Western Movie 1990
Photo: Fredrik Marsh.

 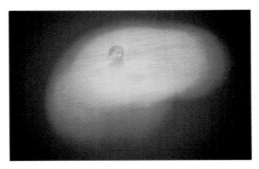 

Western Movie 1990
details: film and slide projections
Photos: Fredrik Marsh.

quarter in outside of Odd Lots department stores. I want to juxtapose the two visions, the high culture icon and the lowest-common-denominator one, the painter's image of natural grandeur as a symbol of the New World and the popular image that has been passed down through the whole genre of the Western—in literature, movies, television—to end up as a children's ride.

What I am hoping to create is a stampede of the horses, the kind of stampede I remember from cowboy-and-Indian movies, where you see the horses from slightly above and clustered together so that their movement creates almost a wave. I've found a company in Kentucky, Robinson Kiddie Rides, where I can get the horses, and I have thirteen coming by the end of the week. I think I'm going to cover them with lead, so that their carnival or honky-tonk aspect is not what you key into immediately. I want them to appear powerful, darker and more ominous.

RS: And the horses will be moving?

MC: I think they'll all be moving all the time. Formally, the rocking motion of the horses will parallel and reinforce the rush of the water's current in the projected images. I'm also interested in suggesting the implications of power and Manifest Destiny gone awry, and I think the profusion of motion and noise in the piece—from the horses, the moving images, the projectors—will convey that quality of being out of control.

RS: Are you planning to incorporate the noise of the water? Have you recorded the sound of the falls—either separately or as part of the film footage?

Above and opposite
Western Movie 1990
details and installation views
Photos: Fredrik Marsh.

MC: I haven't recorded the falls, so it will be like a silent movie with the sound provided by the whir of the projectors and the grinding, squeaking noises of the horses' mechanisms. I'm not going to mask those sounds, and I'm not going to hide the projectors, either. They'll be in plain view on top of the east wall of the gallery.

RS: A moment ago you mentioned the projected image as a backdrop, and you're heightening the theatrical connotations by the way you plan to modify the gallery space.

MC: I want to put viewers into a theatrical setting, where they can watch the—literal and figurative—movie unfold. When Church's *Niagara* was first shown, people flocked to see it, almost as a replacement for going to the falls or as if they were going to the theater. The painting became a performance. By adding the film footage of the falls, I'm making the painting into a movie too, and the horses have their own connections to the movie imagery.

Across the gallery from the projected image, I'm going to build a pitched platform or ramp—that's where the viewers will be. The gallery will be quite dark with the light coming from the projectors, like in a movie theater. There will even be a few theater seats where people can sit and watch. This ramp will also refer to scenic overlooks where you view a natural landscape—like the falls—outdoors. I want that sense of unsure footing, the vertigo of looking over the edge, Church conveyed in the painting. On another level, my ramped structure will play off the ramped floors Eisenman used throughout the building.

RS: The connection between the curved west wall and the curve of the Horseshoe Falls in the projected image also will establish a strong formal relationship with the curved edge of the viewing platform.

MC: The curves will answer one another to form an ellipse, and that's part of my formal response to the architecture. I'm imposing curves on the rectilinear space. I didn't consciously decide to oppose the building's grids with a compositional system based on elliptical forms, but the ellipses will be more interesting because they play against the grid as a foil.

Niagara Falls as an image for America was bigger than life, is bigger than life still. I want this to be bigger than life too—like in Cinemascope—with the curves of the wall and the platform and the energy of the moving horses in the center. At the same time, I am interested in establishing a darker side in the piece, a sense of things going out of control and of pathos from the horses running constantly but going nowhere. As a counterpoint, I'm considering projecting a film loop of a single child swimming in a corner of the painting's image. It will be the only element that appears to move from left to right, against the current—a reference to individual action and maintaining equilibrium. I hope it all adds up to something that is not just a spectacle but is spectacular, awe-inspiring and a bit terrifying. □

Fortuyn/O'Brien

For many artists the reconsideration of sculpture in the postmodern, and post-Minimal, era has involved investigations of functional and decorative modes through references to architecture and domestic furnishings. The Dutch collaborative team Fortuyn/O'Brien has explored intersections of architecture, furniture and sculpture in installations that question the autonomy of art objects and draw on a wealth of historical references. Their approach to these concerns is subjective, however, and their objects are expressive rather than mutely decorative. Much of Fortuyn/O'Brien's work, whether for interior or exterior settings, addresses the concept of the garden: a place where nature encounters human intervention. Robert O'Brien and Irene Fortuyn began working together as Fortuyn/O'Brien in 1983; their collaborative works subsequently have been exhibited throughout Europe and in the United States and Canada. O'Brien died in 1988, but Fortuyn continues to work and exhibit under the collaborative logo of Fortuyn/O'Brien. Fortuyn, who was born in 1959, lives in Amsterdam. She was interviewed by Claudia Gould.

Claudia Gould: As your contribution to *New Works for New Spaces*, you placed two marble chairs in a courtyard adjacent to the building. Perhaps we could begin by talking about why you chose this site and then talk about why you made these chairs.

Irene Fortuyn: When I came to the Eisenman building, I thought it was a very curious building, but I also saw that it addresses something that has been on my mind and in the works that I have been making. It addresses the idea of "what is the object and what is the subject?" You walk into this building and there are no exhibition spaces, so I couldn't imagine an object on display there. The whole building is like a corridor or a tunnel that you walk through, and at the end there is light. There never seems to be an actual room, a finite space. The building denies the difference between subject and object, which I find interesting because that denial becomes a work in itself.

CG: Yes, the building is always in a state of transition. When I interviewed Fortuyn/O'Brien in 1986, you said:

> A bottle looks like a bottle because it relates to our memories of bottles. Our purpose in shifting meanings is to make it impossible to say what a bottle is. If you combine elements so that neither predominates, they become invisible.

So you've worked with the the identities and illusions of objects for a long time. In a way, Peter Eisenman also explores similar issues.

IF: He uses architecture and we use objects, but that may be the same thing. We are both really addressing the question "what is an object?" Or, in the architectural sense, "what is a building?"—what is the inside, what is the outside, where does it start, where does it stop?

CG: And this building has no clear center, no clear front or back—you can't find or identify one front door, for instance.

IF: Yes, and there is no inside and no outside. It's a complete reversal. As I thought about making a work in response to the building, I was looking for an ambiguous space, even within the ambiguity of the architecture as a whole. What I found was this strange, little theaterlike space that is half outside and half inside. It took exactly the position of a non-space. You look at it from the inside through a glass wall, and it is outside. But if you look at it the other way around, from the outside, it's like looking in the window.

CG: The space you chose is very hermetic and insular, protected and yet vulnerable. These are also qualities Fortuyn/O'Brien has always embraced.

IF: Yes, it is hermetic. At the same time, it is open in its point of view. I wasn't looking for a space where a work could exist most "easily"—a space where at least you would have a bit of a straight angle and some white walls. I was looking for a position where what is happening with the architecture, even its ambiguity, is most evident. I like the inside/outside quality of this space, but I also like it because it has to do with the theater. Is a work in this space looking out from on stage or is it in the place of the audience? It can take the role of spectator or actor and then reverse the two. And similar reversals affect the roles of spectator and object in the museum. What I like about this building is that you can't escape it. You become part of it—it envelopes you, and there are no spaces, there are no rooms, you keep on wandering.

CG: It's difficult to fit a typical, normal exhibition into the building's unusual spaces, so it makes us rethink our notions of what exhibitions are and can be, it challenges us as curators and it also challenges you as an artist working at the center.

Fortuyn/O'Brien
Marble Public 1990
marble
detail
Commissioned by the Wexner Center for the Arts; collection of the artist.
Photo: Fredrik Marsh.

Right and opposite
Fortuyn/O'Brien
Marble Public 1990
marble
Commissioned by the Wexner Center for the Arts;
collection of the artist.
Photos: Fredrik Marsh.

Marble Public 1990
installation view looking east
Photo: Kevin Fitzsimons.

IF: I like that strange position because it is not safe. I don't want to make a work or an object or a thing that you can look at in one safe, conventional way. I'm just not interested in that anymore.

CG: Can we switch the topic to the objects you are installing? You have used similar chairs in your work for several years now. What makes these chairs different?

IF: Chairs have been in the work many times but it actually has never been about those chairs, although there is a metaphorical quality: two persons, two chairs, two positions. This time, there really aren't any chairs. What you actually see is the modeled drapery. There are no chairs, but there is recognition. There's also the reversal involved in the hermetic positioning and then the title, *Marble Public*.

CG: And what does *Marble Public* mean?

IF: Marble is the material and public is what they are. They are looking at you and you are looking at them. The chairs are on the stage, but, at the same time, they are in a position from where you look, from where you talk, from where you sit and confront the world, in the theater, at a film, at a table, in a discussion. And from there, you look at the world. So it's *Marble Public*. I see this work as having similar concepts to those of the architecture—just as the building is always in the process of becoming a building…

CG: The chair is always about to become a chair?

IF: Yes, but it's also a stone which is about to become something. First there is the stone, and you take something away and there's the fabric, and if you could take away more it would become a chair.

CG: This work also conveys a poignant sense of memory—maybe of a grandmother's attic or of a vacant house, where the people have gone away and covered their furniture with white cloths. Then, too, the marble of the chairs is very sensual as it shows the folds of the fabric. There's an impression of sensuality and also of absence. But why two chairs?

IF: One chair makes one object. With two, one reflects the other. That's the escape from having the separate positions of the spectator and the object. Because the chairs are together, they already have a rapport between them. If you have only one, you have one spectator against an object. Three chairs make a multitude. Two is always intimate. If there were more, say ten, it would become a group.

CG: And that follows the idea that Fortuyn/O'Brien has always had of duality? That it's one looking at the other, the reflection of a reflection, two people working together?

IF: Yes, but working together with two people was also about how you could escape from the confines of your own being into something bigger than yourself. I have lived that and it is still there, and on the other hand, it is impossible to do it again.

CG: What do you mean? Do you want to explain that a little bit more?

IF: No. Because I think we—Fortuyn/O'Brien—also succeeded in not being too much of a person. That is why some things have not changed that much, because the work still goes on. There is no reason to now say, "Okay, I'll use one chair." The story that the chairs tell is not always the same story, although they are the same chairs. They come from the same chair. But the story in the work, and the position the chairs take is different each time.

   I have a story to tell you. On the day you came to visit me in Forte de Marmi, it was raining very hard, almost like a tropical rain. I opened all the windows in the bathroom and sat in the bath. And it was almost as if you could not see, because it rained so much that the rain was stronger than the day. So it was as if the day disappeared.

CG: Because the rain took over the day?

IF: Yes, the rain made the day disappear. There was just no day. There was rain. And this is what I think happens with strong emotions. They are so strong and they are just there. I mean, they don't ask any questions but exist in opposition to fixed ideas, to petty details, to all those bourgeois, bureaucratic things. I still feel that is the biggest enemy, and solitude comes from there. It's not that the rain is so strong—that's okay, that's fine, because we can all deal with that, we can all deal with strong emotions because we were built for that, but we were not built for mediocrity.

CG: Is that why you are an artist?

IF: No, but I look for that. I want to find it. I am looking for those moments in the work. What I am trying to say is not that I like the rain to take over the day but that I want to make work that is like the rain. I want to make work which has this possibility, this capability of being something against this mediocrity, this frightening, lonely life. And I don't want to make work just to have an exhibition or just to please anybody else. That just makes the work smaller—because it can't rain like that everyday.

CG: You and I have often discussed the abyss, an engulfing void in which one can search endlessly for the essential simplicity in complex situations. When you say "the rain made the day disappear," it's like that, so basic and yet mystifying.

IF: Yes. It's very simple and at the same time it's the only thing. ☐

Ann Hamilton

As much an orchestrator of events as a maker of objects, Ann Hamilton stresses the significance of process and collaboration in her temporary environmental tableaux. She embraces the ephemeral through her frequent choice of organic materials as well as through her work's temporary duration; her projects are site-specific not only in formal configurations but in associative references to the context of their sites. She often incorporates animal or human presences in her projects, introducing aspects of performance art into the installation format and continuing the interdisciplinary melding of categories so evident in the postwar avant-garde. Born in Lima, Ohio, in 1956, Hamilton grew up in Columbus; she received a B.F.A. in 1979 from the University of Kansas and an M.F.A. in 1985 from Yale University. Since 1985 she has lived in California and has taught at the University of California at Santa Barbara. She has exhibited extensively in California and New York as well as elsewhere in the United States and Canada and participated in the recent traveling exhibition Awards in the Visual Arts 9. Hamilton was interviewed by Sarah Rogers-Lafferty.

Ann Hamilton
dominion 1990
corn cobs, corn husks, corn meal, paper, bassinet, fabric, wood and moths
details
Commissioned by the Wexner Center for the Arts; collection of the artist.
Photos: Fredrik Marsh.

Sarah Rogers-Lafferty: You saw the Wexner Center very early on and at different stages of construction, even before you were invited to participate in the show. What was your response at that point to the space, aesthetically and also as a place for art?

Ann Hamilton: That it was incredibly cold, that the surfaces were hard. The spaces didn't have much to do with human scale, and the volumes were diagrammatic. I felt there were interesting spaces being made, but how in the world would you work with them? I felt that from the very beginning—and approaching these initial responses is obviously what the commission is about. These rooms have so much presence that, whether you want to or not, they force you into collaborating, not just with the architecture but with everything in the context of the site.

SRL: Do you usually go into a space for the first time and wait for some kind of visceral response?

AH: I wait for an emotion or a feeling, often beginning with a very general hunch that leads both toward an abstract, analytic train of associations and thoughts, and toward very specific materials and processes. Usually it is something ambiguous that can't be "named" as either this or that—something abstract enough and yet specific enough to work with. If I can keep going back to that core thing, to that initial hunch, then that's what will make the piece work. When projects become more intellectualized—when they move too far out of my stomach—I don't learn as much doing them and I don't take as many risks.

SRL: So, here you are, responding to a building that is very "intellectual" and based on words in terms of explaining itself and its reason for being.

AH: I think the building is as much about the space itself as it is about the words that surround it. Much of my work is a way to approach the gap between language and experience, between the factual description of a situation and the perception of a situation. Too often we operate from the assumption that if you can wrap something up in words it meets the experience of the thing. But it doesn't. My work attempts to articulate the gap between the two and to expose the inadequacy of our reliance on the codification and quantification embedded in our habits of language. I want to make a place for those things that cannot be stated but can be known in other ways.

This is why my work is so based on the senses, an aspect that wasn't even conscious at first—it was accidental. I would choose materials or elements that refer to systems I'm interested in, but it was only in working that the relationship would unfold and I would become conscious of why the choices were important. I always think I'm doing one thing and then I find out I'm doing something else. It's what I am not controlling that makes the work.

The danger of working this way is that it easily can be dismissed, like the intuitive, as romantic and sentimental. But I think it is important to acknowledge that what has come to be considered sentimental often is something we are afraid to look at. We are an incredibly self-conscious species, and if you make a place where some of that drops away, where you can simply respond to what is around you, it's enough.

SRL: Is this why you make installations, temporary tableaux, instead of objects?

AH: Yes. An installation surrounds you, absorbs you into it. You are part of it the minute you step in—it can get closer to breaking down the separation between you-the-viewer and it-the-object. In an installation, an object only has meaning as a part of a series of relationships in the skin of the surroundings. You become implicated as an agent in the relationships that make the work. It's like the interior/exterior condition we live with in our bodies—the skin creates illusions of separation, but it's a permeable membrane that goes both ways. An object on its own is always outside you.

This page and opposite
dominion 1990
details and installation views
Photos: Fredrik Marsh.

Ann Hamilton during installation of *dominion*.
Photo: Jo Hall.

Also, the scale of making installations involves a level of collaboration with other people and a commitment in time that takes it out of the studio and into daily life. Making installations is a living process, and I am concerned with the whole cycle of the pieces—from the first phone inquiries to where the various parts are dispersed at the end.

SRL: At the Wexner Center, you're working in, and with, a building based on a system which you feel is foreign and hostile to how you approach your life and your art making. How are you stepping through that?

AH: I'm responding not only to the building, but also to Columbus, which is where I was raised. It's my home—and that gives me an emotional connection to the site which the other artists might not feel. At first, the building made me very mad because I felt it stood for so many ideas I don't believe in and has qualities I fight in myself. Initially I understood that the interior spaces were derived from an exterior system. I believe so much in the importance of the interior that my first response was that the architects had done a really selfish thing—used a series of systems as ends in themselves.

SRL: Yet the ironic link between you and Peter Eisenman is your reliance on systems.

AH: As I've worked with the building, I've come to appreciate the thoroughness and the obsessiveness of the systems and have realized how much that relates to the obsessiveness in my work. You often react most strongly to something that makes you recognize your own habits.

The overwhelming experience of the building's systems is the grid. It's a man-made construct—and I'm more interested in systems that question the hierarchies in which man is always at the center. Initially, I wanted to defile the building. I wanted to bring something in that, in its chaos or transgression, would be stronger than the grid because, as useful as a grid is, it's a system we use to contain and control what we can't know. That led me to think about water and materials that would flood the building or ooze mud through it. But I didn't want to just react, and I think those initial responses were very reactionary.

SRL: Unlike in your other projects?

AH: Yes, and that was new to me. But then I switched the question: instead of thinking about what I didn't like about the building, I started thinking about what I felt it needed. I started thinking about something that would not have a heavy-handed presence, imposing one system over another, but would create a more invisible presence that worked against the building's system by working with it. I thought about the airspace, the volume, the light in the building. Ohio is actually on a major migration route for birds, so I started thinking about birds and about how the gallery could be linked with that system. Practically and ethically, you're not going to be able to take wild birds and funnel them through this space. But that began a process of thinking as I realized I wanted to bring in a system based not on a grid but on the cycles of living systems.

SRL: This site was once farmland, and your installation will use corn from land the university still farms. Does the agricultural imagery you are using here connect with the idea you mentioned earlier, that you are responding to this site as part of your "home"?

AH: Concepts and processes of tending and cultivating run throughout my work—this is how installations become, for me, lived relationships. Although I was raised in the suburbs, I do link ideas of home with agriculture. I am very close to my family, and I always seem to be restored when I go home. In my mind, these things align with notions of agriculture as something which involves taking time and going through cyclical processes, paying attention to the fact that human lives are linked to natural systems, as perverted as the relationship sometimes may be.

At one point, I considered using food in this piece. I thought about getting all the organic food waste from all the food preparation areas at Ohio State and having that funneled through a composting system in the gallery. I thought, here's a real system that you can't ignore—and it can't easily become a picture because the smell would invade the space. But that idea just didn't seem to have the emotional complexity or depth of feeling I wanted.

Through a circuitous route of associations, moths entered the piece. I began reading about moths and their different stages, and my thoughts began to focus on reproduction with all its connotations. Moths appealed to me because they are very much household creatures, without the exotic and romantic qualities of butterflies. They also can be pests to agricultural products and production, and that fact began to link up with the corn.

SRL: I thought moths were useful in agriculture.

AH: They're good for certain things, but in the larval stage some kinds can do incredible damage to crops, partly because of the way we practice agriculture now. Dr. Dana Wrensch, an entomologist at Ohio State, has done some research about the kinds of moths I should use because I need some that are active during the day. Graduate students will be involved in tending them so that the piece can work with the university system in another way.

And the corn…corn figures in so many of my memories from growing up—"knee-high by the Fourth of July" and all that. Corn is also a crop that exists, at least as we know it, only through cultivation and tending, because the seeds are harvested and so it doesn't seed itself naturally. I decided that there was a relationship I was interested in—tending something traditionally seen as a pest in a room containing a food, corn, which wouldn't exist if it wasn't for a process of cultivation. The piece began to form around the perversity of creating and tending these two adversarial systems, and in this relationship, it reflects my interest in how culture produces nature.

SRL: And you're going to include a human presence in the gallery, as you've sometimes done in the past?

AH: Yes, there will be a person in the piece. Actually, there will be a series of individuals in the gallery, one at a time. They will be engaged in unraveling a length of fabric that extends from the bassinet where the moth pupas will incubate.

There hasn't been that human presence in the last two installations, and I have missed the ongoing life this brings to the work. It completes the cycle and introduces another level of change. One of my first responses to the building was my desire to introduce a human scale and to make room for the subjective within the rigidity of the grid. As predictable as the role of the "image tender" may be, each day and each person is different. Much of my work has been concerned with acknowledging and making primary individual experiences, memories and desires. This is how we each subjectively know the world and the systems we live within. Bringing a person into the center of the diminishing perspective of the room places the individual at the center of the work, but not in a position of domination. The action of slowly, arduously unraveling the grid of the fabric locates the person in a position of living within, rather than over, the system of corn and moths. This is tied up with the title of the installation, *dominion*, that which dominates. It is meant as a question. □

dominion 1990
installation view from south entrance
Photo: Fredrik Marsh.

Tadashi Kawamata

The internationalism of the contemporary avant-garde extends beyond Europe and North America, as Tadashi Kawamata's career illustrates. One of several Japanese artists to attract international critical attention in the eighties, Kawamata has exhibited not only in his native Japan but in Australia and Brazil and throughout Europe and North America. Kawamata's temporary wooden constructions refute distinctions between sculptural object and architectural space: some of his projects fill and transform interior rooms, others envelop and extend from buildings' exteriors. He has created constructions for discotheques, restaurants, shops and other untraditional venues. By choosing to work in such locales and to invite community interaction with his work, Kawamata proposes alternatives to art's conventional role in public spaces. Born in 1953 in Hokkaido, Kawamata attended Tokyo National University of Fine Arts and Music. He presently divides his time between Tokyo, Japan, and Amiens, France. Kawamata was interviewed by Robert Stearns.

Tadashi Kawamata
Sidewalk in Columbus, Ohio 1990
lumber
station no. 2
Commissioned by the Wexner Center for the Arts; collection of the artist.
Photo: Fredrik Marsh.

Opposite page
Sidewalk in Columbus, Ohio 1990
station no. 10.
Photos: Kevin Fitzsimons; Fredrik Marsh (inset).

Robert Stearns: A few years ago in another interview, you said you were first interested in painting and then focused on the structure of the paintings.

Tadashi Kawamata: My initial interest was in the physical construction of the canvas. The structures of the painting, the wooden material of the stretcher bars, seemed more interesting than the flat surface of the painting. This was a point of departure, of exploration. But even more, I found it interesting to consider the painting within the space of the studio. It wasn't just the painting itself and the physical construction of the painting that intrigued me but also the painting as a physical object within the space.

As I continued this exploration, I became interested in constructing space. I found that if you put a large enough canvas on the wall, the distinction between the wall and the canvas disappears—the canvas *becomes* the wall. If you put the canvas on the floor, it becomes the floor.

RS: So, for you, the work itself cannot be separated from the site or surrounding space?

TK: Yes, it is indivisible. I take my material from the particular space and the problems that particular space presents to me.

RS: You have stated that you don't create to exhibit but rather exhibit to create—that you begin the creative planning once an exhibition has been arranged.

TK: I begin with the "order," when you put in your order for an exhibition. Before that I have absolutely nothing in my mind—it's absolutely blank until I am presented with the order, and then I fill the order. I am using the double meaning of "order": something that you demand from somebody as well as the arrangement of elements that meets a certain demand.

RS: For you, are different spaces easier or harder to work with?

TK: Again, I wait for the request. Then I begin to focus, though not immediately on the specific work that I'm going to produce. I begin to consider the space itself and its requirements, its utility, the kinds of people who are going to come to it, the positioning of the building and the space it occupies. In other words, I begin with a general concept, the situation, the sociological condition of the place and its relationship with the audience and me, the artist.

RS: Several of your works—the project for the Japanese Pavilion at the Venice Biennale in 1982 and *Destroyed Church* in Kassel at Documenta in 1987—have been expressively extroverted, appearing to explode outward from public structures. Others—the project at the Takara House apartment in Tokyo in 1982—have been located in private, internal spaces not traditionally used for art. Are you interested in continuing to explore these two very different kinds of space?

TK: Some places have a great historical significance; others are neutral. They have no special presence or history. In my earlier works, I used neutral spaces and was very much interested in them. The Takara House project was one example and *By Land* (1979) was another. At that time, I was more interested in the conditions of the particular location than in any historical connections.

When I was first working in Tokyo, in the neutral spaces, the materials themselves didn't have much meaning. When I worked inside a house that was made of wood, there wasn't much difference between that wood and the wood I was using in my own projects. The first thing I confronted when I went to Europe was the use of very different building materials, stone and so on. The Biennale and Documenta gave me an opportunity to work in a historical setting, where the structures had significant social activity in them before I was there.

Sidewalk in Columbus, Ohio 1990
top, station no. 1
above, station no. 4
right, station no. 3
Photos: Fredrik Marsh.

RS: When you say "materials," do you mean the materials of the built environment that you're going to work with?

TK: Yes. Let's say masonry, brick, whatever. There is no real significance in bringing wood into a wood environment, where the building material is wood and my material is wood, since there's no contrast. That doesn't have a meaning in the work. So I always use the same material for my work. I used the same material—wood—over and over again in Tokyo before I went abroad. When I went abroad, I saw no meaning or reason to bring the same materials to the new environment.

RS: Do you mean the same kind of materials or exactly the same boards?

TK: I had done that in Japan. But when I began to work in other places I felt that I should use the materials that were there, that were native to that environment. So I began finding materials, but I still used wood. Since my work is temporary and I want the site to be exactly as it was before, wood is the most natural material to use, natural in both meanings of the word.

RS: So, wood is "ecological"?

TK: It's soft. I wanted to build something simple, crude, almost like child's play. In contrast to some big industrial sculpture that's created with machines and elaborate technology, I want something that has the feel of my hands on it. Something immediate. For me, wood is most appropriate.

RS: To what degree do you design the work, and how much do you let the material itself determine its ultimate form? Do you totally preconceive a piece? Or do you leave some aspects of the final result to chance?

Sidewalk in Columbus, Ohio 1990
top, station nos. 5
above, station no. 6
Photos: Fredrik Marsh.

TK: I put together a design. I do work with models, but only up to a certain point. It's a means of warming up the project through the drawings and the maquettes. And then, when I get into the actual space, I allow my feelings and instincts to take over. The conditions of the moment exert an influence, too. For example, I might expect my assistant to be able to do something, and the assistant can't do it or doesn't show up or it rains. The viewers might even change the piece after I have finished.

RS: Vandalism?

TK: If you want to call it that!

RS: What do you think of those kinds of external forces?

TK: Once, while I was making a work, a typhoon came and blew about half of it down. But the way the typhoon changed the structure was just right. I really liked it, so I built on that.

RS: Even when you have a specific intention, you believe that a typhoon might improve, so to speak, on what you're doing?

TK: Of course. But I don't want to feel that what I do happens just by accident. I make specific plans, and I organize all of the schedules. Still, something might be missing. I also consider vandalism in the category of natural forces. It's part of the way my work relates to the conditions of the neighborhood or the area where it is shown. My work continues to change with these reactions. So my work is endless, in that way. Both very temporary and yet also endless. Temporary means endless. And ongoing, perhaps. Temporary and ongoing. We say that to destroy actually means to change the form. It's a precondition for the creation of something new.

RS: While that statement could sound like essential Asian philosophy, I also hear echoes of Hegelian dialectics. Is your view as much Western as Eastern?

TK: Yes. All too often, everything Japanese is explained in the West in terms of Buddhism and Shintoism and the tea ceremony.

RS: The exotic, picturesque Japan.

TK: Exactly. Everybody comes up with this interpretation. I don't think it's very interesting to be viewed in that way. It's clichéd. Perhaps it's more neocolonial. Instead of talking about countries, it would be more meaningful to discuss artists creating within the environment of certain cities. I'm an artist in Tokyo. How I deal with the space and the conditions in Tokyo forms my art, just as Parisian artists' work is formed by the environment of Paris, and New York artists are influenced by the environment of New York.

New York is an interesting example because people come from all over the world. There is every language, every tradition, every type of food. And yet, when people come and live and work in New York, they also develop a common language. People who live in great cities have two different identities: one is their identity as whatever group they come from and the other is their identity within that city. The interactions of identities form the particular character of the place, and that becomes the energy of the city. I want to take in that energy and re-create from it. I try to express this in my own work.

Sidewalk in Columbus, Ohio 1990
left to right, station nos. 7, 8 and 9
Photos: Fredrik Marsh.

Sidewalk in Columbus, Ohio 1990
station no. 10
Photo: Fredrik Marsh.

I find materials from that environment and use them to make something which interacts with the environment and grows out of that particular place.

RS: Any place? There is a big difference between New York and Columbus. How important for you is that fractious energy of New York? Is the more subdued energy of Columbus also interesting?

TK: I am interested in all types. What interests me in any place is that kind of struggle or contradiction going on within it. I am not interested in a controlled environment where everyone is the same and where everyone follows the same rules. This is prevalent in Japan but not in Columbus. People are here for many different reasons.

RS: Let's talk about the Wexner Center.

TK: I wouldn't call this a building, not in the normal sense. There are spaces and passageways. It reminds me of descending into the Times Square subway station. There are areas and spaces that you notice while you're walking, that are overhead, or below or behind fences. You see them while you're moving through the space. Your motion through the space is very important.

In that way, the Wexner Center feels like it's still under construction. It looks like scaffolding.

RS: Intentionally. That is as the architects describe it. And the intention of that scaffold is to give a sense both of "having been" and "going to be," past and future. Does this relate to how you view your work as being temporary and also endless?

TK: It is very similar to what I've been thinking about. The Wexner Center encompasses historical buildings as well—there are the references to the demolished armory, and the two flanking theaters also beome part of the site even though they are in great contrast stylistically. So, it may be very difficult for me to create a work for this space.

RS: Because you may feel that what you do may be superfluous?

TK: To break anything down here or to add anything wouldn't really add meaning to the site. So I think I will consider working first with the grid of the city, and then the building as it extends into the city and into the surrounding campus environment, and to work somehow with the extension of these lines and spaces and the tension and energy they create. That's my first idea, anyway. This is very definitely not a neutral space!

I don't believe I will create something inside the building because of that. I think I will work outside the building, in the tension between it and its surrounding community. I am thinking not in terms of making one monumental structure and placing it in one place but, rather, of making a series of structures around and extending from the building's axes. If this were the usual type of art museum, in a self-contained building, then it might make more sense to build one work inside it. But this place is using the spaces in between, and I also want to create something that builds on a sense of connections. □

On the tactile s de there is no counterpart to contemplation on   optical side.

Tactile appr   tion is accomplished not so much by atte   as by habit. As

As regards architecture   habit determines to a large extent even opti   ception.

Joseph Kosuth

The ideas of Conceptual art that Joseph Kosuth defined in the mid-sixties have gained renewed influence in recent years as challenges to art's commodity status and interests in language have once again engaged a new generation of artists. Kosuth himself has continued his explorations of language and meaning, although his recent works—such as those involving quotations from Sigmund Freud, Ludwig Wittgenstein and Walter Benjamin—are more elaborate and complex than his first investigations of the sixties. In those early works Kosuth examined individual words and concepts; subsequently he has focused on the linguistic, philosophical and organizational systems through which information is conveyed. Since the beginning of his career, Kosuth has presented some projects as billboards or as neon texts: using the format of commercial signs to investigate the ideas of linguistic ones. Born in Toledo, Ohio, in 1945, Kosuth studied at the Cleveland Institute of Art and in Paris before moving to New York City to attend the School of Visual Arts in 1965; he later studied anthropology and philosophy at the New School for Social Research. Kosuth presently divides his time between New York and Europe. He was interviewed by Antonella Soldaini.

Antonella Soldaini: Your project for the Wexner Center's exhibition *New Works for New Spaces* consists of a neon text attached to a beam that passes between two galleries. Can you describe this more precisely?

Joseph Kosuth: The text says: "On the tactile side there is no counterpoint to contemplation on the optical side. Tactile appropriation is accomplished not so much by attention as by habit. As regards architecture, habit determines to a large extent even optical reception." The quotation is from Walter Benjamin.

One reason I use 'borrowed' texts is because I like to avoid the idea that you have in one artwork, isolated, a kind of model or microcosm of the world and something that reconstructs a total world in itself—a 'masterpiece', a centered view. An example would be abstract painting, which continues, in many ways, the tradition in which we see the artwork as a window to another world; it's a habituated way of seeing that creates a fictive space. Art is no longer at the service of religion, but the trace of taught fiction remains. We still get the simple scripture of a particular belief. But even when painting became abstract we were still habituated to a learned psychological approach—to canvases, to artworks, even to sculpture—organized as a certain fictive space. Anyway, the whole idea of this kind of organization of an artwork is something I felt I had to somehow disrupt in my work. *All* material—now *outside* of belief—is borrowed, or 'ready-made', be it textual or pictorial. That has also meant that in art, language is always there—whether words or pictures are used—but texts cut themselves from the traditional authority of pictorial art. And language is a very important model for understanding how our culture works, an understanding that cannot avoid being a political one as well.

AS: When you talk about making a work that doesn't want to create a definitive reality, aren't you dealing with some of the issues addressed by Peter Eisenman in architecture?

JK: That is true. I think a lot of the issues I am discussing here are certainly ones I would imagine that Mr. Eisenman is familiar with, too, as he attempts to avoid certain traditional problems of architecture by the de-centering of the building. But theory aside, our practices necessitate important differences. I actually got a letter once from Peter Eisenman, some years ago in the late sixties, in which he described his activity as "conceptual architecture." He wanted an exchange of views, which, regrettably, I didn't pursue.

AS: How do you see your work interacting with that of other artists in the adjacent galleries?

JK: I don't care too much about what else is happening specifically in the room. It's fine for this work if the gallery goes along doing the business of being an exhibition space. The work, of course, reflects on the architecture. But that it can do that, and the *way* that it does that also reflect on the practice of art. The comparison of my work with a context provided by other works in the vicinity, I suppose, aids in making that point.

AS: Why did you decide to work with the specific element of the beam, an element that stays up in the ceiling? It's as if you are trying to avoid touching the ground. Is there some specific reason for this?

JK: The reason I chose the beam is to keep the work architectural in terms of its base, so to speak, rather than just being an artwork hanging on a wall. When you are walking through a building, at any specific floor you are on, it is very easy to naturalize that. And we also tend to naturalize gallery space a lot, and we are used to a certain environment for art. So by putting the work up in the air in this case, it is much more embedded in the architecture—as a specific part of it. Moreover, you are removed a bit from it, and it's outside of your direct body experience. What we have with the beam really is a slice of the architecture. So that the work just articulates it, in a sort of pseudo-formal way, just as a visual underscore to something also visual, and it then reflects back on the context that it's articulating.

Joseph Kosuth
'Ex Libris, Columbus (for W.B.)' 1990
neon
Commissioned by the Wexner Center for the Arts;
collection of the artist.
Photos: Fredrik Marsh.

221

AS: What interests you about working in an architectural context?

JK: To work with architecture is nicely problematic, because it provides an opportunity to take the shape of the place—which means to work with the context of the place—that invites one. Architecture in this way becomes a given, becomes the syntax that provides the specificity of *that* particular work. And so, for me, part of the work is a relation between what I include and what I cancel; the location of doors and windows become other aspects of the cancellation and the other kinds of removals, for example, with some works. So that one could see how these forms create meanings, on whatever level—whether it is on the level of letters that construct words and so meanings, or the level of the kinds of meanings that this syntax of the architecture provides. In any case, there are lots of levels and lots of interrelations, and that provides a rich context to work with.

AS: Is this the first project where you are dealing directly with architecture?

JK: No, 'Zero & Not' (1985) very much dealt with architecture, in this syntactic sense. The final version of this work was completed in 1989 in Vienna, where the Sigmund Freud Museum invited me to use Freud's former apartment—adjacent to the museum, which is located in Freud's former office—for an installation. When I found myself working in the room where Freud did his dreaming for thirty-some years, I decided that this was a good place to stop with Freud. But related to this work is one I did in Franfurt in 1989, when I was invited to participate in an outdoor exhibition that was held in the center of the city with site-specific works in most cases. Because it was Frankfurt—location of the Frankfurt School—I decided it would be interesting, if I was working with architecture, to consider Walter Benjamin as a work source. He is someone important to me, someone whom I respected a lot. As I was discussing earlier, 'quotation', which has been basic to my work since the sixties, is an aspect of all work—either consciously or naïvely. It's important to me to use it intentionally and critically. The other element, of course, is context: since one is really working with meaning, context is central to the working process.

AS: How are the contexts of the Frankfurt and the Wexner Center projects different?

JK: In Frankfurt, my work is on the street, on the façade of two city government buildings, constructed in the thirties. The architecture itself is more generalized in terms of its context, but it is very much a part of where it is. What is excellent about the possibility of doing the project at the Wexner Center is that the architecture makes its presence very much known. In this case, my attempt is to show how as artists we can also layer another level of meaning on that architecture. As an architect, Mr. Eisenman can appropriate certain aspects of artistic practice in the building. But the moment he does that, the architecture shows that its process is a naturalizing process. Since we live in an urban landscape, the building will always be part of 'nature'. But my presence in the work, the presence of the artist, will always be different. Marcel Duchamp was once asked what the difference was between architecture and sculpture. He thought a moment and said "plumbing." I bet Mr. Eisenman would have loved to leave out the bathrooms here.

AS: How has your work changed and developed since the beginning of your artistic career?

JK: Well, because of the larger process it was part of, those changes were themselves instructive. The meaning of the whole work is continually formed and reformed by the temporality of a particular given situation in relation to its accumulated history. I think my work has transformed itself with consistency. Of course that's lousy for 'market identification' (some still call it style), but at least *I'm* still having fun and doing something I can respect. I want the meaning of my work to have a cultural life independent of fashion. One can manage to continue working. I think it remains possible for us to develop a certain critical awareness of what we *don't* want, even if the world seems to want it at a particular moment. Throughout the seventies, we began to simply experience our own institutionalization as representatives of a certain kind of work. Since we saw our work itself as a kind of institutional critique, that was a bit of a shock. And when a lot of the values, really a whole body of ideas, were rejected in the eighties, it certainly had a salutary effect. At a certain point, if one works long enough, these changes become part of what one works with—sort of another 'material', instead of a threat.

AS: Today things seem changed. Just recently there was a large show of Conceptual art in Paris, and it traveled to Madrid, Hamburg and Montreal. Do you think this signals a rejection of the invasion of painting experienced during the eighties?

'*Ex Libris, Columbus (for W.B.)*' 1990
detail: exterior view
Photo: Fredrik Marsh.

JK: Absolutely, although some form of painting will obviously linger for decades; its history is simply too rich and the tradition too strong for it to actually disappear overnight. As for being relevant or authentic, yes, it would appear to be over. What they did during the eighties was to devalue all the values, as historically perceived, of painting. They brought about the deconstruction (to put it positively) of painting even faster than we could have. They made a kind of caricature of—and in the process demystified—what was still in the market as a sort of presumed standard of quality and value, in spite of the scarcity based on aura. Transavantguardia, Schnabel and all the rest represented the entropic spin-down of *that* conception of art.

But what the Paris show (*L'Art conceptuel, une perspective*) underscored—revealed really—is how the market accelerated a kind of crisis in art criticism. Much of the catalogue gives up any attempt to provide an accurate historical accounting of an art movement. Instead, you get briefs for art-market factions. Benjamin Buchloh, in a surprising act of self-demystification, notably abused the presumed moment for historical objectivity to show us how personal ambition and political moralism get along together quite comfortably. Rather depressingly, it seems where there were once insights there are now only endorsements, and if you are an art historian you can rewrite the history in aid of your candidates. It's the craft of history as practiced by the Chinese Communist party. No noble struggle here though, just careerism for me and my pals. Anyway, those of us who actually lived that history—such as Seth Siegelaub and myself—demanded and received catalogue space to at least register our dissent from such blatant falsification. Mr. Buchloh's disciples have been scurrying around trying to put the best spin on this scandal, but it's there and it's pretty plain. It's unfair—artists are always being criticized for 'policing their own history,' but tell me what we are supposed to do with dishonest cops? I mean, here it's a critical desert, and we just found out that the priest of the oasis is *selling* the water.

AS: How do you define the role of the artist today?

JK: The whole point, I think, is to understand that what artists do is to make meaning, and with that comes a political responsibility to understand how cultural mechanisms work, how such questions are part of what an artist works with and not simply that he or she plays with forms or techniques. That art is not simply a kind of neutral tool, sometimes decorative or not, sometimes filled with 'political content' or not—Mr. Haacke notwithstanding. It would be a mistake to think our only choice, for art, is between expensive decoration and conservative illustration—be it in the employ of a laudable mission or not. That there is emerging a valid role for art as a kind of post-philosophical activity seems, to me at least, quite clear. Whether the vulgar pragmatism of a market-fueled discourse would perceive art within such a perspective is yet another thing. It's really up to the artists to change the level of the conversation. □

Barbara Kruger
Why Are You Here? 1990
silkscreen on paper
Commissioned by the Wexner Center for the Arts;
collection of the artist.
Photo: Fredrik Marsh.

Barbara Kruger

Barbara Kruger treats appropriation, a common technique in the avant-garde art of the eighties, as a means to political ends. Her photomontages with text overlays borrow from popular culture to examine and critique the power hierarchies of contemporary society. She often draws on the devices of advertising, presenting her work in billboard format and sometimes actually on billboards, matchbooks or in other advertisement locations. Born in 1945 in Newark, New Jersey, Kruger presently lives and works in New York. She attended Syracuse University and Parsons School of Design and then worked as a commercial graphic designer and photo-editor for more than fifteen years. She exhibited abstract paintings and combinations of painting and fiber art in the early and mid-seventies and developed her photomontage approach, influenced in part by her earlier career in design, by the early eighties. Kruger was interviewed by Sarah Rogers-Lafferty.

Sarah Rogers-Lafferty: What was your initial response to seeing the Wexner Center?

Barbara Kruger: My immediate response to the building was influenced by the fact that I have lived in Columbus, and so my response was less to the building per se than to the site and the city. I taught at Ohio State in 1977, and this was the second time I had been back to Columbus. There was no way that I could minimize my reaction to a whole city and turn it into a reaction to an objet d'art, a piece of architecture. My first response was to the economy of Columbus, how it seems to have changed and apparently for the better. It's probably one of the few places in the country where that is the case. I noticed how the main streets around the campus felt pretty much the same, with similar stores or refills of the stores that had been there. The building did alter the entry to the campus from the main street—it changed the perspective of the entry completely.

I found that what interested me most about the building was how, whether consciously or not, it seemed to disregard the conventional needs of esthetic exposition and exhibition in that those conventions have to do with a certain luxuriousness of walls— white walls, lots of them. I was also interested that there were so few conventional gallery spaces. Perhaps if I were an artist doing another kind of work that would have been disconcerting to me. But because I really don't care whether those spaces are there and I like to make do with whatever is there, I found it a very exciting, good space to work in. I see it as a place where words and pictures can make a difference, just like a billboard space. This is a terrific environment for making, for presenting different voices.

SRL: It's an arena.

BK: That's right. It's a spectacle of effects of some kind. But my interest is not in reproducing spectacles as they are in the world today. I don't aim to diffuse meaning and to totally break down any concept of meaning. We know that's already happened. But how can we reinvest events with meanings, knowing that we exist within and are constructed and contained by that spectacle?

SRL: What's the next step in your process of doing a project in the context of this show?

BK: I should say that what's terrific about the environment, again, is not just the building. It is on the campus of one of the largest state universities in the entire country. That's what adds spice to the brew for me. A lot of the people who will come into the space are at a very formative time in their lives. Frequently, they have a very tenuous relationship to the idea of culture. What is it that people feel or think they're supposed to feel when they go to a museum, a so-called museum space? What I see and have always felt is intimidation on a certain level. People don't know why they are there except to affiliate with "high culcha," to get cultured. This space offers a chance to talk about commonalities of experience I have with my spectators. I don't want them to feel that they need a graduate degree to understand what I'm doing, I want to think that I can "reach out and touch someone."

SRL: During your site visit, you selected three locations inside the building that function as markers through the interior space.

BK: They follow a kind of quasi-narrative path. There is an episodic quality to the presentation. I like the idea that it will be fragmented and episodic rather than constituted as one whole thing. The idea of the fragmentation also is carried off outside the structure.

SRL: Do you know what ideas, what issues, you'll be addressing in the project?

BK: I really can't say precisely. Basically, I tend to loiter on the same old corners where sex meets money when it approaches power. It's like a fork in the road.

Barbara Kruger
What Makes History While It Does Business? 1990
silkscreen on paper
Commissioned by the Wexner Center for the Arts;
collection of the artist.
Photo: Fredrik Marsh.

Barbara Kruger
Whose Body Is a Battleground? 1990
silkscreen on paper
Commissioned by the Wexner Center for the Arts;
collection of the artist.
Photo: Fredrik Marsh.

Above and opposite
Barbara Kruger
Your Body Is a Battleground 1990
silkscreen on paper
Commissioned by the Wexner Center for the Arts;
collection of the artist.
Photo: Fredrik Marsh.

SRL: But the context of the university might veer that a bit?

BK: College is a formative time in young people's lives. I like the idea that this museum is a place where people will go without necessarily saying "Well, I'm going to the museum today." Instead, it's a part of campus life, a place where people may loiter and hang out. Especially because it's so close to the main street, it's accessible to people who might just have fifteen minutes to kill and think that they want to run somewhere before class. I really like that power.

SRL: Do you see the texts of the work as your propaganda or as critical analysis?

BK: I don't know what propaganda means anymore. I think it would be different if we were in Lithuania or Estonia, but we're talking about America and you have to think what that word, "propaganda," means. Is Peter Jennings propaganda? Are The Simpsons propaganda? I mean, how do words and pictures work? How do they influence people? "Propaganda" to me is a word that just doesn't have that much resonance in American society or Western capitalist society right now. It has more to do with the constancy and effectiveness of being bombarded by that sort of circuitry of pictures and words. I hope to displace the conventions of that bombardment a little bit. I do not have deluded utopian assumptions about what I can do or whether I can compete with television—it would be ridiculous to think that. But one does make one's suggestions, and I'm just trying to ask questions or make suggestions. Instead of saying how things are, I might suggest how things might be. I could say that I'm involved in a series of attempts to displace things, to change people's minds, to make them think a little bit.

SRL: Although you often have addressed women's issues in your work, do you think your approach has become more visceral and overt in the last several years? I'm thinking particularly of the works in your 1989 exhibition at the Mary Boone Gallery.

BK: I can't say that the recent work has been more involved with women's issues, because I can't think of any moment when I wasn't totally involved in how one is defined and produced as a woman in this culture. The show you mentioned came at a time when, here in New York, there was this apex of trials and public spectacles having to do with the battering of the body and the battering of women's bodies. The works in that show were not just about women's bodies, though that was very much on my mind, but they were very much about the body: the body of sex, the body of illness, the body of vanity, the body of humiliation. One showed a picture of a man holding out an apple captioned

"The marriage of murder and suicide"; it had to do with the conflation of utopian notions of romance and real experiences of familial violence. Another was a picture of an autopsied woman lying on a table with a doctor holding her heart; its text read "no radio," which makes an analogy to a car having its radio stolen. And yet a number of male critics just didn't get it. Nowhere in their critical writing did they mention "feminism" or "the female body" or issues of gender. The word "body" did not come up at all.

SRL: And that's one of the major issues that runs throughout the work, whether it's the physical body or the body used as a metaphor for other ideas. Do you think these thoughts might also figure in your projects for the Wexner Center?

BK: I think it's likely. In many artists' work right now there seems to be a real grounding, consciously and unconsciously, in the vulnerability and finiteness of our bodies. We have to be aware of the fact that we're living in a time of epidemic. □

Sol LeWitt

Antonella Soldaini

Sol LeWitt's interest in the impersonal logic of mathematical systems helped define the avant-garde aesthetics of Minimal and Conceptual art in the sixties, and his work forms a significant link between the two movements. His open, white-painted, cubic modules from the sixties share the austerity and pristine simplicity of Minimal objects; his emphasis on artwork as a materialization of ideas recalls the intellectual basis of Conceptual art. LeWitt has continued to base his artistic vocabulary on serial concepts but has applied his ideas to a wide range of two- and three-dimensional media. Born in Hartford, Connecticut, in 1928, LeWitt graduated from Syracuse University in 1949 and subsequently settled in New York City. His first solo show there came in 1965; retrospectives of his work have been held at the San Francisco Museum of Art in 1974, The Museum of Modern Art, New York, in 1978 and the Stedelijk Museum, Amsterdam in 1984. He presently divides his time between Chester, Connecticut, and Spoleto, Italy.

At LeWitt's request, the documentation of his Tower *(1990) is accompanied here by a brief description rather than an interview.*

Built of industrial concrete blocks, Sol LeWitt's *Tower* (1990) is governed by a simple principle of arithmetical progression involving the numbers one through eight. The sculpture consists of eight related, geometric components arranged vertically as the tiers, or stages, of a tower. The first component in LeWitt's series, and so the first level of the tower, is eight blocks wide and one block high. Each subsequent stage decreases one block in width and increases one block in height; the final stage is one block wide and eight blocks high. Each tier follows the same determining rule: the sum of horizontal and vertical blocks on the façade of each stage equals nine.

Although constructed from homogeneous modules—concrete blocks—the eight stages remain distinct, and LeWitt avoids tedium through subtle variations in each component level. Differences in size and proportion unfold gradually from tier to tier but build a strong cumulative effect. The sculpture's broad, horizontal base maintains contact with the ground; its sequence of increasingly vertical stages urges the eye upward in a steady, rhythmic movement from base to summit.

LeWitt chose to place his sculpture outside the Wexner Center building, in the middle of a long avenue that flanks the north side of the architectural complex. By electing to locate his sculpture at one of the points furthest from the center, LeWitt might seem to want to keep as far away as he can from any contact with the Eisenman/Trott building. Yet comparison of building and sculpture reveals intriguing parallels and contrasts. Both LeWitt and Peter Eisenman derive their forms from mathematical applications, though LeWitt demonstrates a single system, and Eisenman manipulates several systems in complex layers. *Tower* develops in a clear progression of strictly ordered, geometric tiers. The building unfolds in a succession of seemingly fragmented and disjointed spaces where varied stylistic codes (among them the Minimalism of the "scaffold," which might recall LeWitt's own early work, and the historicizing romanticism of the towers) collide without mediating transition. LeWitt's rigorous logic is immediately apparent in *Tower*: the system behind the sculpture leaves no room for superfluous play. Eisenman's no-less-rigorous logic seems camouflaged in the Wexner Center: variations in construction materials, for example, initially appear unpredictable even though they too derive from a governing mathematical system, the architect's reliance on grids. The clarity of LeWitt's sculpture provides a counterpoint to the complication of Eisenman's architecture.

LeWitt's *Tower* asserts itself as a steady point in space with its insistent centrality and self-contained monumentality. The sculpture translates the serial and geometric vocabulary of LeWitt's well-known open cubes into something closed and solid with the weighty monumentality of traditional public statuary. In this seemingly permanent yet ephemeral outdoor "monument," LeWitt questions traditional assumptions regarding public art—such as the conventional relationship of plinth and sculptural object. In the sculpture's progression of tiers, each level becomes the plinth for the next level's nonobjective form. *Tower* functions as a demonstration of LeWitt's artistic principles, a site-specific counterpoint to the Wexner Center's architecture and a more general comment on the conventions of public monuments. □

Sol LeWitt
Tower 1990
concrete blocks and mortar
Commissioned by the Wexner Center for the Arts;
collection of the artist.
Photo: Fredrik Marsh.

Christian Marclay

Drawing on the examples of Happenings and Fluxus events from the sixties and Conceptual art from the seventies, many avant-garde artists have made sound as significant a feature in their work as form, color or texture. Some create objects that make sounds; others create works that are perceivable only as sounds. Still others incorporate sounds in multimedia installations and performances. Christian Marclay investigates sound and sound-making devices—phonograph records, speakers, audiotape—in sculptural objects and installations and in solo and collaborative performances. His work reflects the connections and interactions between visual artists and vanguard musicians that have been particularly frequent and influential for interdisciplinary explorations since the eighties. Born in 1955 in Geneva, Switzerland, Marclay attended the Massachusetts College of Art in the late seventies. Since moving to New York City in 1980 he has exhibited and performed throughout the United States and Europe. Marclay was interviewed by Claudia Gould.

Christian Marclay
The Clock 1990
aluminum clamps, mechanical strikers and timer
Commissioned by the Wexner Center for the Arts;
collection of the artist.
Photo: Fredrik Marsh.

Claudia Gould: Your project for the Wexner Center is a sound installation located in a walkway along the building's east façade, the area that we often refer to as the "scaffolding." How does this work represent your response to the building and why did you choose this site? I have the feeling that you don't like the building.

Christian Marclay: My first impression of the building was negative—I didn't like it, and I still don't like it. When I first came to look at the building I spent quite a while there, and by the end of the day I still didn't know what I was going to do. As I left, I found myself hitting the scaffolding with my keys as I was walking along, but what I really wanted to do was to kick it or something. I think that was the spark that got me started. The initial idea was to kick something in disagreement. The giant grid structure made me think of a cage and of the alienation produced by so much totalitarian architecture. I was thinking of prisoners hitting secret codes on heating pipes to communicate from cell to cell or banging in unison on bars as a sign of protest. These are ways to communicate. The scaffold does not communicate with the rest of the building. It is an appendage to the building that serves no structural purpose, and so it is mute. If it does communicate, it is only the way a sign communicates, a sign or rather a signature, saying Peter Eisenman/ Wexner Center for the Arts. It struck me as a large signature on an otherwise anonymous building hidden between two older structures. Everyone will remember the building because of its decorative scaffolding. It also makes a great photo opportunity!

CG: Why did you choose to draw attention to this particular site if you find the scaffolding so alienating?

CM: Because it is the most visible element of the architecture and the least functional. I'm not saying that the scaffold is alienating in itself but rather that it makes reference to a type of alienating modernist architecture, the way a skeleton refers to a body. I see the scaffold as an image of a white skeleton, a giant rib cage. The building refers to structure in a nostalgic way. Inside the building, beams and columns protrude everywhere, blocking gallery space or ending in a staircase or cut off in midair. But they are fake, like a Hollywood set. When you knock on them they sound hollow—they're only sheet rock and plaster, and they're not connected to the outdoor scaffold/skeleton. It self-consciously recalls a past when columns had to be taken into account esthetically because they were a structural necessity. This structure doesn't require them—the beams and columns, and the towers as well, are here as reminders of an architecture limited by material and function. Limited, that is, if one agrees with Eisenman that function is a limitation. I don't believe it has to be. The combination of the deconstructed towers and this three-dimensional grid reminds me of an eighteenth-century folly, a sham ruin, a romantic reminder of the destructive power of time.

CG: Why do you employ sound or make reference to sound in all your work, from the performances to the tangible visual pieces?

CM: Sound interests me because it is elusive, or should I say, it was elusive. Recording technology has turned sound into a material, because recording allows sound to be repeated. Magnetic tapes, phonograph records and, now, compact discs make the reproduction and stockpiling of sounds possible. Repetition is not a necessity when looking at a static art object, a painting or sculpture that is there as long as you want to look at it. Sound recordings are time-based, more like films that you can look at over and over. But with film you can stop the flow of time and you get a still frame. With sound, you can't stop time, you can only repeat it. The present is instantly relegated to the past. So sound remains more elusive. It is also more abstract, maybe even more spiritual.

CG: Often your music is very loud, but your visual work is much softer and more subtle. Could you talk about that in connection to the Wexner Center project?

CM: In my performances, I like the music to become very physical. Loudness doesn't just

Above and opposite, Christian Marclay during installation of *The Clock*.
Photo: Kevin Fitzsimons, courtesy of The Ohio State University Office of Communications.

affect your sense of hearing, it also affects your whole body. Your whole body starts to vibrate. That's what I like about loudness. But all aspects of sound interest me, so I can use something very quiet, something very loud, something without sound, something about sound. *Tape Fall* (1989) was a very quiet piece, very meditative. The Wexner piece is nonvisual, practically invisible, but it is audible. I'm using an intermittent sound that is loud, irritating, maybe alarming. People will be wondering what the hell is going on. Is it closing time? Is it a fire alarm, an earthquake? It might sound like workers drilling holes in the scaffolding, and that might even please the architect, as he wanted his building to feel unfinished, continually under construction. At night when the building is quiet, the occasional wanderer will be very surprised, maybe even frightened.

CG: What are you using to make this noise?

CM: I'm using bell mechanisms—the type used in fire alarms and school bells. They have been adapted so that instead of striking a gong or bell they will be hitting the metal beams of the scaffolding. I'm going to spread twenty-five of them throughout the metal scaffolding and connect them to a timer. Time and sound are the installation's main components. A slow rhythm marking the hours will ring in time with the other bells on the campus. There's a large clock on the side of Mershon Auditorium, a building close to the scaffold, and the sound will relate to it and to the chimes from Orton Hall that can be heard all over the campus. The University and the Wexner Center are structured institutions. The classification of knowledge and culture is at ease with a clock mechanism—it depends on it. Repetition also implies a power structure. If the installation underlines this power structure or power rhythm, it also offsets it by triggering an alarm, a signal of panic—noise as disorder.

The scaffolding will become a giant noisemaker. I won't try to tune the sound or to set an original ringing pattern within each event. If noise is a threat and music a reassurance, I want this piece to be noisy. I won't try to reassure listeners with a composition—the only structure the sound will have is determined by the clock. Time is the composer. I won't know until the mechanisms are installed how much noise, and what kind of noise, the installation really will make. The beams will generate their true natural tones and overtones. Maybe it will even sound musical, but that will be incidental.

CG: Is the idea of disturbance something you aim for? Many of your performances—*Mosaic* (1987) for example—stress the imperfections of sound. Are you attempting to annoy listeners?

CM: No, my intention is not to annoy. I'm more interested in the idea of disturbance as a way to destabilize habits, to change perceptions. And I think it's the destabilizing that annoys people rather than the noise itself. In my performances, I don't just let the record play by itself. I interfere, I do something else with it, I change things around to create a new music. I want to break the illusion that recordings present. When you hear a scratch or a skipping loop, you can't be fooled into believing that you are listening to live music. You are reminded that it's only a mechanical reproduction. Records are precious objects because of the history they preserve, and like books they are saved for posterity. They must be handled with care and protected from scratches and dust. They are fragile, so we respect them and use them carefully. In my performances, I destroy, I scratch, I act against the fragility of the record in order to free the music from it's captivity.

CG: In *Record without a Cover* (1985) you made explicit that this piece of posterity was intended to be scratched and abused.

CM: I didn't want to publish a finished composition but rather one open to changes, to accidents. In a sense, it's the perfect record because its imperfections will never offend the music. It's a living record. I am revealing the musical properties that the record has built into itself. It is music for the record and about the record. It's all about that object, this precious and delicate object. Time and abuse leave marks on it and I take advantage of that weakness.

CG: At the same time, you create this weakness, you entrap it.

CM: The surface noise, the pops and crackles, all those unwanted sounds, occur with time. I don't reject them, I use them to my benefit, value them and enjoy them. This sound patina has a great expressive quality. It is an aural expression of the passing of time. The record is supposed to be a stable reproduction of time, but it is not. Time and sound become elusive again through the mechanical failure. Technology captures sound and stamps it on these discs. They then begin lives of their own. Within those lives, technological cracks—defects—occur. That's when it gets interesting for me, when technology fails. That's when I feel the possibility for expression. ☐

This page and opposite
MICA-TV
The Inbetween 1990
videotape
Commissioned by the Wexner Center for the Arts;
collection of the artist.
Photos: © MICA-TV 1990.

MICA-TV
Carole Ann Klonarides and Michael Owen

Many contemporary video artists have re-thought the objective ideals of the documentary tradition, analyzing its possiblities for engaged or subjective commentary. In their MICA-TV tapes Michael Owen and Carole Klonarides go beyond providing comments about or information on other artists' works. They instead involve the subjects of their documentaries in active collaborations that often take the collaborating artist's own work as a point of departure. Klonarides, an artist and independent curator, and Owen, an independent film and video producer, have worked together as MICA-TV since 1980. They have shown their work in art venues as well as on television. Carole Ann Klonarides and Michael Owen were interviewed by Sarah Rogers-Lafferty.

Sarah Rogers-Lafferty: What is MICA-TV?

Carole Ann Klonarides: The name is an acronym for Michael and Carole Ann. We are a collaborative video production team formed in 1980 to pursue an alternative to television. We particularly wanted to explore a creative reinterpretation of how art and arts are depicted in the media. At that time, video art was mirroring the Conceptual and Minimal ideas of the seventies. We were interested in using television as an influence along with the ideas of artists who were also using the media environment as their source. We wanted to collaborate with these artists to create a hybrid, a new kind of art documentary—video art that could be broadcast on television.

SRL: How do you select artists to work with and how do you begin a project?

CAK: We have an appreciation and understanding of the artist's work prior to making the tape. Together Michael and I start to translate the ideas in the artist's work into something that could be made as a video. Then we approach the artist and propose our ideas. Cindy Sherman, the first artist we worked with, really wanted to be involved on all levels. She helped write the script, she brought her own costumes, she brought the slides for the backgrounds and she acted in the tape. The video became a three-dimensional Sherman B-movie still, while also being informative about the artist. John Torreano was very interested in having hands-on involvement with the video technology. But when we first approached him, he didn't quite know what his participation would be. We knew he'd be great on camera. Because his work used imagery of diamonds and galaxies as a metaphor for the value of knowledge, we thought it would be interesting to do a think-and-do-type children's educational video. For the fifties generation, that would be like the old TV show "Watch Mr. Wizard." John made a great Mr. Art World Wizard!

I think in every tape we do there's a new video problem for us to resolve. In *Art World Wizard* (1986) we had to appropriate the look of early kinescope television, and John had the opportunity to use a Quantel Paintbox [a computer image-manipulation system], which enabled him to create the video galaxy.

SRL: Your tapes deal with artists using the vocabulary and stylistics of television, and yet they're screened in an art setting, not on television.

CAK: Not originally. At first we had screenings in artists' lofts and invited people who work in television and people we knew in the art community. The videos were also shown on cable art programs.

SRL: What were the initial responses to the pieces?

Michael Owen: I think most of the feedback we got was that the videos were very "digestible," as art goes, for the nonart public. We copied the idiom of lay television. But because we mimic real television the question "is it art or commercial television?" kept coming up. And, in terms of authorship, there was difficulty with the idea of a collaboration—our own and then with a third party.

SRL: *Cascade* (1987) is a very different type of project. You involved three other collaborators to create a tape that mimics a vertical urban landscape.

MO: The idea was to make something that was a continuous landscape.

CAK: We began thinking that the way one looks at video could be approached as a problem or an idea. Because television is a horizontal medium, we thought it would be interesting to do a vertical read. After we had this idea, three artists immediately came to mind: Dan Graham, who uses urban architecture as a subject in his sculpture, photography and video; Dike Blair, who paints in a vertical format using layering techniques and "media(land)scapes" that exist in advertising; and Christian Marclay, an artist, composer and performer who manipulates records from eclectic musical genres (jazz, rock, pop, classical), creating a "generic" composition when performed. So we approached them about working with us.

SRL: Do you use special editing equipment or computers?

MO: In this case we used a remote-controlled camera mount that enabled us to shoot 360 degrees in any location. This was a fairly new piece of equipment, and we suggested a unique use for it. We were able to be creative while getting support from the commercial video industry.

SRL: Let's talk about the Wexner Center project, which also has involved many steps. When you came to Columbus, what did you think about the building? How did your ideas for the project develop?

MO: We had read a lot about the building before visiting, and, in many ways, that made it difficult to visualize the space and what it has to offer. Once we were there, we realized how photogenic the site is. One could make several tapes there, and each would look different. I wasn't surprised by that, but it was a challenge to come to terms with the space and focus in on one point of view. Since that visit, I think we've come full circle. In trying to come to terms with our approach to the subject, we went back to reading about Peter Eisenman's theories to establish a distance again and get back to the original intent of the architecture.

SRL: You were trying to understand what the building was architecturally?

MO: The building is a manifestation of Eisenman's theories, but it's also a space that's going to have to be dealt with. At the time of our site visit, we were very seriously investigating the possibility of doing an installation, because we had been working with the artist Andrea Blum in a project to incorporate *Cascade* into an installation. Also, the idea of doing an interactive videodisc that could be part of an installation was intriguing. What became very clear to me is that the building would overpower anything but an excruciatingly expensive and large-scale installation. The space is too intimidating at that level to do a piece that referred to architecture—it would be dwarfed by the space.

Right and opposite
MICA-TV
The Inbetween 1990
videotape
Commissioned by the Wexner Center for the Arts; collection of the artist.
Photos: © MICA-TV 1990.

CAK: I'm sure everyone is going to be dealing with, or trying to deal with, the monumentality of the space.

MO: When we came back to New York, we started thinking in terms of a single-channel piece.

CAK: I did a Video-8 walk-through of the space. While looking through the camera I noticed, as Michael just said, that the space is very photogenic—almost as if it were made to be photographed rather than experienced. We didn't just want to make a beautiful document of the building. We realized our collaborator is the creator of this building, and we've got to get beyond the photographic qualities and really get into the theories and ideas that created the building—and then go beyond that. We now know that the building isn't going to function in the way people want it to function, it isn't going to house art. One of the things that interested us was how you can get beyond function.

First we discussed the idea of changing the building into something else. Michael reworked the notion that it's a perfect setting for a sci-fi adventure or a futuristic story involving the building. I think you can say images of destruction and violence came to mind amid this perfection.

SRL: You wanted to mess it up.

CAK: I felt that science fiction was not the right approach because it dealt so much with the future. I was interested in dealing with the past in a way that wouldn't be nostalgic or sentimental, even incorporating some sort of narrative or story. So then we began to discuss the idea of working with a writer and trying to use fiction, a Gothic-type story, which we felt would be very appropriate for the building. We had never worked with a writer. We started by going to Eisenman's architectural offices, and his archivist Judy Geib selected some writings she thought would be appropriate for our project. One was a treatise by William Gass, the writer. It was very helpful as an exercise to see how writing can be something else, much like Eisenman's building is not just a building.

SRL: At this point, given that you're still in the process/idea phase, what is your fantasy of what the project will end up being?

MO: Right now I have two realities. There's the part of me that's coming up with many different creative scenarios and then there's the producer part, realizing that, come August, we will have an important production coming down with a tight budget.

Personally, I would like to pursue the narrative end. I would take Eisenman's building and shoot it in a way that is not seen in the magazines but would still make it read clearly as an Eisenman building. Then, in the tape, I would have something going on that is a hybrid of different kinds of popular fiction.

CAK: In the same way that Eisenman wanted to realize an actual building that embodied his theories about architecture, I'd like to make a video that stands on its own and does not compromise the subject, in this case the building and its creator. It's challenging to try to create a video that will be something new in the definition of what's being created in video but that also will be entertaining to a television public that may never see the building or comprehend Eisenman's theories.

SRL: Your piece, probably unlike anyone else's in the show, will still be able to exist in its completeness after the show is over.

CAK: But like everyone else, we're still dependent upon a context and an audience. And as long as the building is received and talked about, the tape will have its own life but be enriched by that experience. What will end up happening—as has happened with all of our collaborative works—is that as the careers of the artists unfold and their ideas become general information the tapes will take on a new life and become something else.

SRL: They're moments in time.

CAK: They're unique. They straddle so many different categories: they're not just art any more, they're not just documentaries. There are layers of information and meaning there, and that is what interests us. □

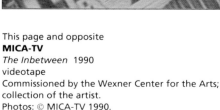

This page and opposite
MICA-TV
The Inbetween 1990
videotape
Commissioned by the Wexner Center for the Arts;
collection of the artist.
Photos: © MICA-TV 1990.

The Inbetween 1990
installation view
Photo: Fredrik Marsh.

Gilberto Zorio
La Sedia di Marzio (Marzio's chair) 1988
metal, compressor, plastic, rubber, copper and water
Courtesy, Sonnabend Gallery, New York.
Photo: Fredrik Marsh.

Gilberto Zorio

Italian sculptor Gilberto Zorio first received critical attention as one of the artists associated with Arte Povera, and his work reflects that movement's radically inclusive attitude toward materials. Zorio joins recycled objects, such as old canoes, with plastics and other contemporary materials, making his works evocative of both the humanistic past and the postindustrial present. He is fascinated, as are many of the Arte Povera artists, by materials with potential for transformation: he sometimes uses substances that are sensitive to light, heat or humidity in order to render changes over time visible and evident. In other sculptures he incorporates activating devices that add another kind of temporal dimension to his work. Born in 1944 in Sagliano Micca, Italy, Zorio studied painting at the Accademia di Belle Arti in Turin in the sixties. He lives and works in Turin, where he has taught at the Liceo Artistica since 1971. Zorio was interviewed by Antonella Soldaini.

The interview was translated from the Italian by Charles Klopp.

La Sedia di Marzio (Marzio's chair) 1988
detail
Photo: Fredrik Marsh.

Antonella Soldaini: What did you think the first time you visited the Wexner Center? What effect did it have on you?

Gilberto Zorio: Not entirely positive, I would have to say, though the positive aspects of contemporary architecture don't register on me very quickly. Contemporary buildings always seem to belong to the political system. So they are always on the offensive and—no matter what the system itself may be—they are always trying to increase that system's prestige.

AS: How do you view the inclusion of your own work in an aggressive architectural structure like the Wexner Center?

GZ: I create my work, set it up, and that's it. All things considered, I have always been an indifferent person and, in the end, I am indifferent to architecture too, even if I like it. If my art gets along well with the architecture as a whole, fine. If it clashes, better still.

AS: So it doesn't make any difference to you if your sculpture is put in a white cube, as contemporary gallery spaces are sometimes described, or in some completely different space—a baroque drawing room, for example?

GZ: I don't believe in harmonious placement. If it happens, it happens by chance. If I were to worry about harmonious placement, I would run the risk of creating decoration instead of art. But I am convinced that architectural space and works of art can get along fine if they can manage to titillate each other. In the final analysis, the whole matter of the relationship between the architectural space and the work of art is just a demagogic problem. There was a lot of talk in the sixties, seventies and eighties about rapport with space—it was important, but it shouldn't be made into an enormous problem. An artwork's power has nothing to do with the space where it's placed.

If you really want to talk about architectural spaces, the most exciting space of all for me is the Guggenheim Museum in New York. The Guggenheim is sculpture, not architecture. It's like the inside of a vase. It's the craziest space there is and a big and authentically stimulating space as well.

AS: When critics talk about the Wexner Center, they often compare it to the Guggenheim precisely because of its strong personality and expressive force. Do you agree with this?

GZ: The Wexner Center reminds me a little of a Minimal sculpture. It's been sliced up almost like a piece of cake and I don't think it has anything to do with Frank Lloyd Wright's genius at the Guggenheim. As far as I'm concerned, his space is the only one that's really crazy.

AS: Do you think that in the future the Wexner Center might be viewed with the same astonishment that greets the Guggenheim today?

GZ: Maybe so. Who knows? Twenty years from now it might not be anything but ruins. There are millions of things that can be done with architectural structures of this kind. Often, however, they just wear you out, turning into vast machines that sap your strength in inhuman ways. Maybe it's better after all to have a white cube whose only function is to contain artistic quality and that in time becomes a temple. The more artistic quality that passes through it, the nobler the space. But white cube or not, the difficult part is to get the space to soak up the artistic quality.

AS: How do you feel about being part of this show, with a dozen very different artists participating with you?

GZ: It's obvious that I will have to interact with them. When you work on a show like this one, you have to be concerned with the others, whether you like their work or not. I hope I won't cause any trouble. My work is a sign, a live signal that continues to develop all on its own.

AS: How did you begin your artistic career? What other artists influenced your work? Often, when you talk about yourself, memories crop up about southern Italy.

GZ: For me the south represents childhood and the intensity of early life.

AS: When did you come to Turin?

GZ: In 1956 after a stay in the Molise. But I was born in the north, in Piedmont, in a town called Sagliano Micca. I went to art school in Turin. Even as a a little boy I loved to go to art shows. Ever since I was a child, I wanted to be an artist. This might have been because my mother was an artist and I was fascinated with her art supplies. I used to play with her putty, glass and wax the way other children played with soccer balls. But it was only in the early sixties that I came into contact with works by Lucio Fontana, Alberto Burri, Fausto Melotti, Enrico Castellani, Michelangelo Pistoletto, Roy Lichtenstein, Louise Nevelson, Robert Rauschenberg and many, many others. Meeting the gallery owner and "talent hunter" Gian Enzo Sperone was an important moment for me. The roster of Sperone's shows from the sixties and seventies is still dazzling. It was wonderful to meet artists of my own and other generations: Giuseppe Penone, Giovanni Anselmo, Pietro Gilardi, Emilio Prini, Alighiero Boetti, Pier Paolo Calzolari, Pino Pascali, Jannis Kounellis, Richard Long, Jan Dibbets. I also met Mario Merz, who at that time was no longer a young man, and the perennially youthful Michelangelo Pistoletto. It was also stimulating to get to know the two young critics Tommaso Trini and Germano Celant. In 1967, when I had already had a one-man show, which Trini organized at Sperone's, Celant decided to organize a group exhibition called *Arte Povera*. Although the artists involved were all very different personalities, we continued to show together until 1972. Later, we also exhibited together in Paris, in *Identite italienne* of 1981, and in Turin, in *Dall'Arte Povera ad Oggi* of 1984. Germano has sketched the history of this movement in several publications, so this is just a brief account of those times and of the people who were and still are following the same path as I am.

AS: In just a few words, can you describe what the Arte Povera artists have in common?

GZ: I would say the quality of the work, its staying power. For the first time in the history of twentieth-century art there are artists who have been working at the top of their form for twenty-five years. I find this extraordinary. Even during the dark times, the "years of lead" at the end of the seventies, when other images were in the public eye, even then we did not stop creating powerful works of art. The fact that today we can speak of Arte Povera and that we are still on the scene is simply extraordinary. Everything has changed, including political systems, but no one has lost his way on the road to Damascus. On the contrary, we have invented new roads whose ends are not yet in sight.

AS: Your work features several recurrent forms or symbolic figures, among them the star, the javelin and the canoe. What do they mean to you?

GZ: The star is an abstract image of mankind for me, an image of the imagination. It is also a universal image found in all cultures. The canoe exemplifies the desire to travel. Trips are knowledge, and the more you know, the more you are able to fend off death. The canoe and the javelin are similar in that they share the same shape. Both of them are connected with space and attempt to attain what cannot be reached. The javelin is a basic tool that even today has not lost its importance. Its concern is extension: extending the head, the thought, the arm. The javelin soars and strikes its unique, compact target. The canoe floats on the water and bears its oarsmen like an enormous javelin on a voyage across the water. I love canoes because of the traveling they have done. I think of them as filled with adventures. The canoes I buy are always used. I find them down at the banks of the Po and buy them when others are ready to throw them away.

AS: Why do you cover some of your canoes with rubber?

GZ: Because I want to eliminate the colors underneath. I always change the canoes by cutting them up or covering them with something. In this way, I transport them into the world of art. An old canoe is like a crucible that has contributed a great deal to art but becomes too fragile for further use just when it reaches its maximum potential. That's when I buy it and bring it over into the world of art. That's the thing about canoes. They mustn't be burned. They are loaded with memories, with extraordinary, dramatic images full of suggestions for the future and mustn't be destroyed.

La Canoa di Columbus (The Columbus canoe) 1990
detail
Photo: Fredrik Marsh.

Gilberto Zorio
La Canoa di Columbus (The Columbus canoe) 1990
fiberglass, canoe, motor, one timer, one lamp, two
copper tubes, six metal bars and one transformer
Commissioned by the Wexner Center for the Arts,
collection of the artist.
Photo: Fredrik Marsh.

AS: The two works in this show are connected by a timer-activated siren that sounds at certain intervals.

GZ: In this instance the two sculptures work in tandem. They are able to call out to each other by means of the siren, which is nothing more than exasperation invading space. The siren is an exaggerated sign of the phenomenon of compression. In this work, the air is sucked in, compressed, run through tubes and then released into the water. It's air, wind, that makes the noise.

AS: It seems to me that the idea of transformation is central to your artistic activity. When you use words like "reaction" or "process," I think about your interest in magic, alchemy and the culture of the cabala.

GZ: I often think I would like to be a shaman. What really interests me is seeing "energy." The idea of arriving at an exaggerated equilibrium intrigues me. The unknown fascinates me. I like to set off reactions, initiate a process that will lead to the creation of emotional tension. My work always contains an element of the unknown. Here, the siren is surprising, completely unexpected. I never know exactly how to begin a work, let alone how it is going to end up. It's always a wrench for me to have my work exhibited. The work tears itself away and ceases to be an object for contemplation. I become the one who looks at it in surprise. The work has been transformed and now draws its nourishment from different sources. I love to look at something that seems perfectly apparent even if you cannot figure out where it is heading, because the future is a dangerous and—why not?—revolutionary unknown. □

Trisha Brown Company performing *Foray Forêt* (1990)
at the Wexner Center for the Arts. Photo: Will Shively.

Trisha Brown
An Informal Performance

Through her work as a dancer and choreographer, Trisha Brown has played a seminal role in contemporary performing arts for the past three decades. A founding member of the innovative Judson Dance Theater group in the early sixties and the improvisational collective the Grand Union in the seventies, she participated in many formative moments of postmodern dance. In the comments that follow, Brown traces her own career from her early work as an "outlaw" in New York's interdisciplinary avant-garde to her ever-visionary ideas for future activities and projects.

Brown's comments touch on many aspects of her choreography and on the evolution of several specific works—from The Floor of the Forest *(1970) to* Foray Forêt *(1990). The latter composition, which had its United States premier at the Wexner Center on 1 November 1990, was commissioned by the Lyons International Dance Festival in association with the Wexner Center for the Arts at The Ohio State University, Walker Art Center, Minneapolis, Jacob's Pillow Dance Festival, Massachusetts and Cal Performances at the University of California, Berkeley.*

The presentation transcribed here (from a performance by the Trisha Brown Company at the Wexner Center on 31 October 1990) included four works from the company's early years, revived to mark the group's twentieth anniversary in 1990, followed by comments from Brown and a question-and-answer period with the audience. Brown's comments are identified with her initials; questions from the audience are marked with a **Q**.

Born in 1936 in Aberdeen, Washington, Trisha Brown studied dance at Mills College and during summer sessions at Connecticut College. After graduating from Mills, she taught for two years at Reed College, where she became interested in improvisation as a teaching technique and began to develop her own movement vocabulary. Although her training at Mills stressed the modern dance techniques of Martha Graham and Louis Horst, Brown soon came into contact with other models. A summer workshop with Ann Halprin, the West Coast–based dancer and teacher, reinforced her interest in improvisation and introduced her to Halprin's concerns with nonstylized, vernacular movements often based on everyday tasks. At Halprin's workshop, Brown met Yvonne Rainer and Simone Forti, whom she encountered again after coming to New York City. There, in 1961, she became a student at the Merce Cunningham studio and attended Robert Dunn's influential composition class with many of the dancers and other artists who soon coalesced into the Judson Dance Theater. After presenting her work with this group and independently during the sixties, Brown formed her own company in 1970.

Brown's work reflects both continuing interests—in improvisation and structure, in the effects of weight and gravity on movement, in language and other organizing systems—and stylistic shifts: from gamelike improvisations through formal explorations of movement to sensuous theatrical collaborations. In the "equipment dances" she created beginning in the late sixties Brown expanded the parameters of the dance stage to include walls, floors and other unusual indoor and outdoor locales. In the *Accumulations* that followed in the seventies she employed serial techniques to research and organize the possibilities of movement itself and then to combine movement with other elements such as spoken commentary. The humor and inventiveness Brown brought to her work with the Grand Union, also in the seventies, were key ingredients in the collective's performances. Since the late seventies, she has worked in collaboration with visual artists such as Robert Rauschenberg, Donald Judd and Nancy Graves and with composers such as Robert Ashley and Laurie Anderson, mounting performances that explore, exploit and expand the conventions of both dance and theater. As Brown notes in the following comments, her dances seem to develop in "cycles" as she works through the implications of each problem she sets herself.

Trisha Brown: *The Floor of the Forest* (1970) was first presented suspended at eye level in a large loft space in SoHo in New York. The audience was given no clue about what to do or about where the "front" was. They circled it and bent down to see the dancers below and stretched up to see them when they were on top. In my mind the audience's movement became a secondary dance around the grid. Its second performance was at NYU a few years later. I suspended the grid overhead and had a full-scale rummage sale going on below. So what you had was the horizontal dressers and the vertical dressers, those torn between bargain and art, and then a final circle way out in the back observing the full effect.

The piece falls into the category of "equipment dances," a term someone coined for a number of my works, including the ones with dancers walking down the side of a building or walking on a wall. For me these works are like dance machines that reduced the number of choices of what one did in making a dance—something that's very useful when you're not working in a classical form and are confronted with a thousand choices and wish to make them not arbitrary and reduce them to the least number possible. When walking down the side of the building, the dancer started at the top of the building and walked—could have done something else, but walked—and the dance was over when the dancer got to the bottom. That to me was like a little dance machine, as was *The Floor of the Forest*, and, in fact, in looking at the *Accumulations* tonight, I think

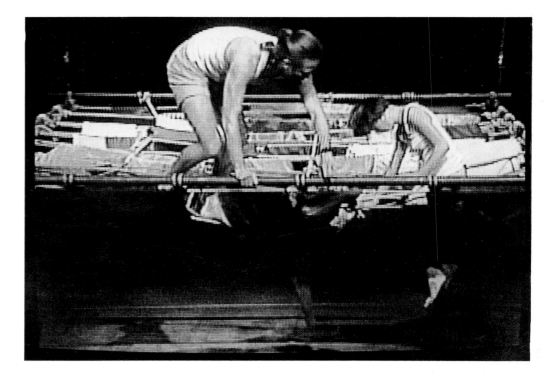

they are too. I also thought of all these pieces as objects—since they were performed in galleries and museums, the audience could walk around them and observe them as such.

I included the *Leaning Duets* (1970) tonight because I like looking at them but also because they are centrally concerned with weight and with language, two elements that I went on to develop in my work and that continue to figure in my work today.

Then we have the *Accumulation* (1971) with, or to, the Grateful Dead's "Uncle John's Band." This was its second performance. From the original four-and-a-half-minute version with music it developed into a fifty-five-minute version in silence and through that into an entire cycle of *Accumulation* pieces, the *Group Primary* being an example. *Group Primary Accumulation* (1973) is a dance in which I put myself, us all, down on the floor on our backs in order to free the legs, to remove their obligation to support the upper body and to give them equal status with the arms in movement potential. What else can I tell you about it? Why don't you ask me a few questions?

Q: How many times has *Group Primary Accumulation* been done, and do the people who move the dancers do different things with them every time?

TB: The *Primary Accumulation* has been done many, many times and in many different incarnations. It was done on rafts, four rafts set free in a lake, in Minneapolis in 1973, and on the Hudson River in 1989. I wanted to have a natural phenomenon make the decisions about where the dance was going and what the spatial relationships between the dancers would be, so I used the tide or the current. It's also been performed in Central Park, in the plaza of the McGraw-Hill building, on a beach in Staten Island—many, many times. The original version was without carriers, but they entered the piece early on. David Gordon and Douglas Dunn were the first carriers, and I was told "Don't you dare have men carrying women around like that!" But they're quite heavy, you know, it's quite difficult to carry a moving body around like that, and so...I have added a woman carrier. I hadn't done the carrier version in many years—I don't know how long it's been.

Q: Did the carriers decide spontaneously where to put the other performers or did you give them directions?

TB: I left it up to them to decide what those configurations would be. I asked them to work with the architecture. And that's a problem in a small space with two intersecting grids such as this. We discussed their choices before the program and I concurred with their decisions.

Q: The fact that the dancers are in synch all the time, is that the result of their extensive training, or are you really tapping something else, like some kind of breathing cycle, to have them locked into each other? Just at what level does the synchronization occur?

TB: (to dancers) Does someone want to answer that?

A: All those levels. Sometimes a movement will have a natural rhythm just by virtue of the length of your arm and the kind of joint action you use. And also, we've done it a lot together and discussed rhythmic choices: it's as if we fall into a groove with it.

Trisha Brown performing *Accumulation* (1971) at the Wexner Center for the Arts, 1990. Photo still from videotape courtesy of The Ohio State University Office of Communications.

TB: These pieces actually are the bridge between my working as an outlaw in downtown Manhattan, very involved in the visual arts, and then my making the decision to go back into movement and gesture, and wishing to find a way of moving which is nonfunctional and nondecorative. The *Accumulations* began that investigation of [demonstrating gestures] "Is this okay?" "This is okay; is this okay?" "Is this okay?" in a very methodical way. In fact, I did it with this piece: "If this is okay, then this must be okay," "If these are okay, this is okay." I began very carefully repeating those gestures and integrating them into the whole circular pattern of accumulating and building up a lexicon of movements.

Q: What were the instructions you gave to the dancers in *The Floor of the Forest*?

TB: For *The Floor of the Forest*, the instructions are to sight an article of clothing you would like to put on, traverse the grid to it and dress into it in the most natural, efficient way that you can, given the fact that you have to always support your weight.

Q: Do the dancers have to change clothes a set number of times?

TB: No, that would be determined by the dancers and the duration of the performance. I actually don't know how long the first performances lasted. But the work wasn't intended to be seen by an audience sitting as spectators in a proscenium situation. Originally the audience had an activity too: selecting ways of viewing the work. And that being absent, I made it fifteen minutes long.

Q: Were you asked to present it in this form or did you choose not to have us walk around?

TB: Well, these seats are as close to permanent as you can get. It's a conflict because audiences are not really used to sitting on pillows, which is what we used to do. You picked up a pillow at the door and dusted it off and took it to your place of choice and sat there uncomfortably for a long period of time. So, what can I say? It was a practical decision.

Q: What do you see as the continuity in your work over the past twenty years? Where do you see the work going at this point?

TB: I'm overwhelmed with the distance, and this work seems to be from thirty years or fifty years ago instead of twenty. I know that the early work feeds into what we do now in the demeanor of the dancers, in the concern with weight, certainly, and in its openness, willingness to include error and other accidental events in the choreography.

Trisha Brown Company performing *Group Primary Accumulation* (1973) at the Wexner Center for the Arts, 1990. Photo still from videotape courtesy of The Ohio State University Office of Communications.

Another connection is probably in looking at the dance as a sculpture of the body or paired bodies, using dancers as sculptures or as objects in space. That has come back into the work recently. I work with the idea of "geometrizing" the body and making a drawing with, or on, the dancers. In the opening men's duet of *Newark (1987)* it was as if my eye was a pencil directing the bodies through a continuum of shape and form—leaving some of them tipped over upside-down and then, at a signal some many seconds later, shifting only a quarter turn to another view. So another connection is taking the time to look at the body as it is, shaping it and really taking the time to look. *Newark* is probably the most highly combustible, intricate, power-structured dance I've ever seen in my life. *Foray Forêt* (1990), which I've just recently completed, is at the opposite end of the spectrum: it works in a metaphor of slowness and softness and stillness. It "revs up" but it's pulled back down. And those pieces are linked to the earlier work too, through my central notion about how movement is organized, working with the vertical of the spine, the horizontal of the arms and the legs and all the subdivisions of that. And perhaps that is related to the grid in *The Floor of the Forest* and the human body weaving its way through it.

What is going to happen in the future? I'm making a second part to *Astral Convertible*, which premiered in 1989, and it's quite interesting to come back to a work that is fully organized and thought out and have the opportunity to take it back apart and think about it further. But I have dreams about the piece that follows—which is what I do to keep from feeling terrified about what I'm doing right now. It's really too big to articulate to you, but I hope to work in the theater with light and sound. That sounds truly vague, I know, but I've never really gotten my hands on theater equipment, and I can do that now with the production supervisor we have, Spencer Brown. He has a great appetite to experiment in the theater, and I'm looking forward to that hands-on involvement as well.

Q: How would you explain your creative process? Is it very different for each piece?

TB: Yes, each piece is a reality unto itself, but they come in cycles. There are certain facts that relate to a group of pieces—like the equipment dances or the *Accumulations*. *Foray Forêt* is different from all other pieces in that I have built into it an opportunity to reorganize it after the fact of its premiere. It's built in sections, it's modular, it can come apart and go back together in other ways, so that I can make a new section for it and add, delete, whatever. But how do I develop those sections prior to that? I always make the dancing first, yards and yards of dancing, like material you would buy at the store if you were going to make a new dress. After that has been established and everybody in the company knows all of the phrases of the dance, then we come into a period when we mix it and figure out how things will go together. And then there is the experimental period where many, many things are tried and formed and merged.

Q: How do you think about collaboration, for example with Robert Rauschenberg in *Set and Reset* (1983), which I saw last year?

Trisha Brown demonstrating gestures during "The Early Years—In Celebration of Her 20th Anniversary," an informal performance at the Wexner Center for the Arts, 1990. Photo still from videotape courtesy of The Ohio State University Office of Communications.

TB: The way I collaborate is I tell my fellow people what it is I intend to do as best I know it, and I start working on it, and I show them the rough draft of the material, and they enter in as soon as they can with ideas and tapes or whatever to get into a linked path with me.

Q: I also was thinking about *Set and Reset* when you were talking about nondecorative movement and wondering how that relates to the use of the sets.

TB: In fact, the dancing in *Set and Reset* comes around the outside edges of the floor, and it really is nondecorative, if you know the way the movement was designed. Then it goes into the mix. Honing the dancers into very refined instruments of choice making, learning the movement so that we all know it, and then taking a set of instructions— "keep it simple," "act on instinct," "work with visibility and invisibility"—and pooling your impulses simultaneously in short increments and memorizing it, that's how we built *Set and Reset*. Once you go into that overlay, and especially with the subtext of "act on instinct," you get all kinds of things happening that are outside the confines of the original, rigorously organized material. In fact, *Set and Reset* was the first time that humor was really an element in the work. Sabotage, high jinks, exuberance, those kinds of things, showed up in the work. I couldn't keep them out of the work.

Q: Could you talk a little bit about your first contact and collaborations with Robert Rauschenberg?

TB: I was a scholarship student at the Merce Cunningham studio in 1961, and my job was to answer the telephone. And this fellow would call, and he said his name was Robert Rauschenberg. I was very shy at that time, but I had a good sense of humor, and I had the greatest conversations on those phone calls. His initial participation with the Judson Dance Theater a few years later involved assisting us with technical problems, lighting and such things. He had that skill, having traveled with Merce Cunningham as his technical supervisor.

His first dance I knew about was *Pelican*, which was performed in 1963 at a roller-skating rink in Washington, D. C. He and Alex Hay were on roller skates with huge parachute-like umbrellas on their backs, and Carolyn Brown was in gray sweat pants and a sweat shirt and *en pointe*. I named that dance, he said he needed a title…All these memories intermix, and I can remember, for instance, a dinner party where you arrived at Bob's house and he came to the door on roller skates and you risked your life while he skated you down to the other end of the loft in his arms. So all of this is mixed. Those were the days and that's why I'm so emotional: the work you have seen tonight is very much of that time.

Q: How is the art community now different than the way it was then?

TB: I can speak of New York because that's where I was. There were fewer people and it was possible to live and work on not very much money. My first apartment's rent was fifteen dollars a month. It was a society of abundance and there was much left over, and it was very possible for artists to find materials on the street and construct extraordinary works, as you know. And it also was possible to find furniture or a crate of apples, I don't know—it was a simple time. Large lofts were available and cheap, and people made huge paintings because of it, huge dance because of it. Conversation was about artwork and about moral issues. People wore overalls and said "How is your work going?" when they met you on the street. A lot of people left town during that period of the sixties, during the time I was there, and they went out and moved to communes, so there were departures and returns. But primarily, it was that I knew everybody, that's the thing, I knew every dancer and I knew every visual artist and sculptor in New York, it seemed. Now— you know what it's like now. ☐

Spalding Gray
Talking about Talking

John Howell

Spalding Gray examines the landscape of contemporary popular culture, blending personal memory and social comment, fact and fiction, the outrageous and the commonplace with striking resonance. Emerging from the experimental theater movement of the New York avant-garde, Gray has become recognized as a mass-media celebrity and an experimental artist accessible to popular audiences. The thirteen monologues he has performed since 1979 define a distinctive art form poised somewhere between scripted theater, or stand-up comedy, and non-narrative performance art.

In the following interview, Gray shares his thoughts on talking in general and on talking in his monologues. He describes audience reactions to his monologues and the creative processes behind them and behind Monster in a Box, *his latest solo performance, in particular. Gray first performed* Monster in a Box *at New York's Performing Garage in March 1990; a subsequent tour brought the monologue to the Wexner Center in September 1990. Gray was interviewed in New York by John Howell.*

Born in 1941 in Providence, Rhode Island, Spalding Gray spent his childhood in the town of Barrington and became interested in theater while a teenage boarding-school student. He graduated from Boston's Emerson College in 1965 and spent the next two years acting in summer stock theaters in New England and New York State and at the Alley Theater in Houston. Soon disillusioned with conventional theater, he left for several months in Mexico in 1967, discovering on his return that his mother had committed suicide during his absence. Gray moved to New York in the late sixties and joined Richard Schechner's experimental theater company the Performance Group, performing in company productions of Sam Shepard's *The Tooth of Crime* and Bertolt Brecht's *Mother Courage and Her Children*. In 1975 Gray and actress/director Elizabeth LeComte founded the Wooster Group, another experimental ensemble. The Wooster Group's first three pieces—collectively known as *Three Places in Rhode Island* (1975–78)—drew extensively on Gray's memories of his childhood, his family, his mother's suicide and his acting ambitions. Contributing to the group's explorations of collaged, nonlinear narrative, Gray began to develop the style of melded autobiography and commentary characteristic of his monologues.

He performed his first monologue, *Sex and Death to the Age 14*, in 1979 at the Performing Garage, the small SoHo theater that was (and is) also the Wooster Group's permanent home base. For the next several years he continued to work with the Wooster Group, developed additional monologues—including *Booze, Cars and College Girls* (1979) and *A Personal History of the American Theater* (1981)—and pursued other acting projects. His experiences acting on location in Roland Joffe's 1984 film *The Killing Fields*, became the basis for his Obie award-winning monologue *Swimming to Cambodia* (1985), subsequently filmed by Jonathan Demme. More recently he returned to a more conventional theatrical role, the Stage Manager in Lincoln Center Theater's 1988 revival of Thornton Wilder's *Our Town*. Directed by Gregory Mosher at the Lyceum Theater on Broadway, the play was shown on the PBS television program "Great Performances" in 1989.

Gray's monologues have received increasing mainstream and popular recognition since 1986, when he performed *Terrors of Pleasure* (his monologue about home owning) at Lincoln Center, and 1987, when Demme's film was released. Yet his celebrity has not overtly affected the sparse and intimate tone of his performances. Sitting behind a small desk, he uses only a few props, such as the mock book of *Monster in a Box* (1990). Avoiding elaborate theatrical effects, Gray continues to rely on his words, gestures and inflections—the talking he describes in this interview.

John Howell: You've talked a lot about talking—where would you like to start talking about talking?

Spalding Gray: Actually, I haven't talked a lot about talking. There is something I do now, which I am calling *An Evening with Spalding Gray* (1989), that grew out of a piece called *The Personal History of American Theater* (1981), but instead of performing using cards with play names to prompt the monologue I simply stand with a microphone on stage and trace the process. That is, I trace how I came into this autobiographical, poetic, journalistic mode, from the first play I was in right through to the two groups I've worked with, the Performance Group and the Wooster Group, and on to my appearing on Broadway in *Our Town*. And there's lots of stuff left out, of course, so then I do questions and answers or questions and responses. That's where the talking about talking comes in because it is more reflective about the work. In time, it probably will become a book, working from tape transcriptions. It's a nice blend of anecdotes and storytelling as a form of communicating stuff orally that is constantly lost now because there's not a whole lot

Spalding Gray performing *Monster in a Box* at the Performing Garage, March 1990. Photo: © Paula Court.

of literature on the greatest movement in theater in America, the experimental theater.

As far as definitions go about talking, I don't like storyteller. Storyteller, when it is not applied to a novelist or a short-story writer, usually rings of folktales. And storytellers rarely move into the first person and say, "This is what I was going through, this is what I was thinking, this happened to me." So I don't like to align myself with storytelling because I'm doing something different. I don't like monologuist, it sounds a little like anthropologist—a bit academic. So people say, what are you? They're usually the ones who are defining that—the press and the people who are writing. But I say the best definition that I ever heard—besides my own, which is poetic journalist—came from a ten-year-old girl. Because I didn't see her with her parents and I wondered why she'd come to my show, I asked what brought her there, and she said, "My dad told me I had to come and see the talking man."

JH: When you think about talking, you think about America and its blizzard of talk shows and interviews, and it makes you wonder if there isn't something culturally specific about our form of talking as theater. We have a plethora of media here. We have a population that doesn't take time to read and thinks that speaking is a quick form of communication. Is there something in the American psyche that makes us blabby?

SG: The question about Americans as blabbers is a good one, but it's something I haven't really thought about. I don't ever like to generalize or speculate about what's going on outside of myself. But I'm trying to figure out the difference between the way that I work and the way someone like Howard Stern, a radio "shock jock," does. Take Howard Stern or Mike Feder on WBAI here in New York. Both talk show hosts are extremes, from the right and the left, of spontaneous, undigested chatter. I don't think they spend a lot of time hearing the talk or reflecting on it. I work much more by listening back to the tapes and I'm much more conscious about the choice of tapes, of editing, and the choice of words, which is more formal. But why Americans are blabbers…

JH: You know, you meet someone on an airplane and in five minutes they're talking away, telling you everything.

SG: Drives me crazy. I can't stand that. I'm trying to be private when I'm not talking because I talk so much for my shows. I was in Jerusalem interviewing the audience, and I interviewed a philosophy teacher who had grown up in Los Angeles, and now he's over there and is about to marry a New York woman. He just kept saying, "Americans, they make themselves up. They invent themselves every morning."

I think a lot of the American need to talk has to do with the size of the country, the lack of roots and history, not having a clear identification. And I think a lot of the need to make yourself up is manifested through chatter about self. In Israel, it might start with the self, but it would quickly move to politics. What is American, good God, I don't know America. I know Los Angeles. I know New York, and that's what I mean about the size of it—it's a series of feudal states: your drug state in Miami, your political center in Washington, your capitalistic center in New York, your image center in LA, and then they spread out and affect the rest of the country through television.

JH: So there is some kind of ache to fill up this empty place? Our great poets and writers have been oral types from Whitman to the Beats.

SG: Robert Lowell is another example of that, as an autobiographical poet. I heard a record of his, one of the last recordings of a reading, and he would introduce each poem and tell what lead up to the poem. All the vignettes in between were more interesting than—or equally as interesting as—the poetry.

JH: What's the difference between writing and talking for you? I've heard people talk of you as a performing actor because they're aware of some kind of written process behind the monologues.

SG: The written process is odd and interesting because none of the monologues are written. What happens is that I do keep a small journal now. I did keep a diary but now it is really just the slightest reminder of details, notes of what someone said or a certain phrase, so I keep it in my mind. The monologues are ongoing oral journals of my life. That's not to claim that my life is more interesting than other lives, it just happens to be the process that I am working with. At times it is more interesting. At times it's less so, depending on whose it's being compared to. I always hope that the critics can realize that so they don't say "Oh, it's a new Spalding Gray monologue" as in Lily Tomlin or Jackie Mason. But the monologues aren't written out, I just use notebooks for details so that I am actually experiencing what I am talking about while I tell it. That's quite different from scripted acts or entertainment bits or whatever.

JH: How do you justify your emphasis on the personal?

SG: I have to stay with the personal because I have to trust that the personal is the political. I can only prove it by, in Jerusalem, for example, when I was interviewing the audience, asking "What did you have for breakfast? How did you get here? Who drove, What did you think about while driving? What did you talk about while driving?" and go right for that and talk about it. That's where I get grounded in the details of personal living.

JH: Doesn't this direction also come out of the experimental theater idea that said we've had enough of the scene classes, of these classic reinterpretations? That said we need a stronger personal connection with what we're doing and seeing, with an emphasis on the process of doing so rather than on the subject?

SG: Yes, I think that twenty- or thirty-year history of experimental theater has had an enormous effect on all the arts.

JH: Tell me about your latest monologue, the one you performed at the Wexner Center. How do any of these ideas we've just discussed apply to it?

SG: Well, it leads us back to writing. It's an odd form of writing because I'm working from an outline of serendipitous events. The new monologue, *Monster in a Box*, is based on all the interruptions of *Impossible Vacation*, the book I've been writing for Knopf.

JH: So there's the book, which spawned the monologue.

SG: And now there are new interruptions which have come up that are so big to me that I can't let them go—there's another monologue growing out of the book as gestalt. There's the prop book on stage with me bound like an S-and-M prop, and I'm referring to it all the time. And I'm telling about what's happening in the book and the story that interrupts it. It's a piece that people can relate to because it's about procrastination and indecision and the temptation to live more than to reflect. It's a tricky thing going on in this monologue. At the same time I'm talking, the audience can be aware that I'm not writing the book because I'm talking to them about not writing it. So the whole process of being in front of them is another escape from writing the book.

The point that I'm trying to make is that I make an outline of things, that's all. I line up the way things happen. I'm using my memory as structure, historical memory as structure. The way I remember events is mine—I'm not claiming that that's the way they occurred. But I don't think I'm consciously distorting them. I make an outline from them and I have told the stories to friends in bits and pieces, so it's not to say that they're not rehearsed at parties and situations. Then I tape record it and then I listen and start to see the form. That's where the fiction comes in—rearranging events to make the piece structurally sounder, to make it more dramatic and to condense time.

JH: Are there any particular books, any particular talkers who have been models?

SG: No. It's intuitive in a way that pleases me. But influences—certainly Ram Dass' early stories about going to India and finding his guru. I've always thought he was as good or better a storyteller than he was a spiritual man. Of course, the autobiographical poets, Thomas Wolfe as a writer and John Cage.

JH: If you really work with memory, doesn't that mean each performance is different?

SG: In, say, *Monster in a Box* I'm just acting one word or phrase on the outline to guide me. It could be "House with a View," "K.O. is My Assistant," "Earthquakes," "Hollywood Lunches." Those are four categories that could take twenty minutes to perform from that one page of outline. As soon as I see that word it triggers a film in me—a memory film— that's what I'm describing. Each time I'm trying to corral the best description and the important thing about that is that it's plastic, it's fluid. So that every night it is both finished and a rewrite—every night refers back to the past night too, and not just to the original memory but to the memory film that's developed in the performance. And two things about that make it important for me. One is I've been trying to work with this book, writing this novel, and I resent the straight-jacket linear business of print where you have to settle on the way a line is going to line up. I have been thinking in the book about my father, say, as an example, and summering in Rhode Island. And I'm having four or five clear, vivid memories of my father in those summers and I want to write about those memories without bridging them, without saying, "This happened, this happened, this happened." They appear to me as on a wheel, not lined up, because I don't see them lined up. They are four memories that are spinning in my head that don't have a relation-ship to linear time. I can spin those in my monologue if I'm doing a monologue about my father; I can spin that wheel differently and I can remember differently every night. It is linear in the way that it progresses that evening, but finally it isn't linear because I can change it constantly. It's not that I'm changing the material. People ask me about how much I improvise but I'm only changing the structure until it feels good to me. Whereas in the book I fall into this straight-jacket situation of making a choice, which I hate. Other people may like the finality of choosing.

The other thing I wanted to say is that by not having a text prewritten, memorized, it appears fresh to the audience every time, as though I'm speaking it for the first time—besides acting, I am remembering for the first time in front of them. It's subtle. It's like when you try to go to sleep, you get in bed and you assume you are going to sleep but you don't know how you are going to do it. You only do it by relaxing and letting go. It's the same with sitting down at a table. I assume I'm going to remember the stories that I want that night but there is no proof of it because it hasn't been memorized, its an inner text. It doesn't exist outside of myself, whereas the traditional actor takes a text, memorizes it and has to find all sorts of Method or Stanislavskian ways to pretend that they don't know the text to make it fresh. So it's the difference between being on a track and bushwhacking—and that's part of why my monologues aren't prewritten.

JH: Do people in your audiences believe your stories?

SG: No, they don't. That's what's odd. A large percentage of them doubt them. When I am in social situations afterwards I have the most outrageous questions. I'm working in the new monologue with a prop of the book on stage and a woman afterwards at a party will say, "We loved it, you're not really writing a book, are you?"

JH: Where does that response come from?

SG: It comes from thinking that everything in a play or a book is fiction, a naïve concept that comes from people who think that when they go into a theater they're going to another planet. I think that is why I insist these stories are the truth or a form of truth. Jonathan Demme was resistant to me bringing that up and wanted to cut it from the film of *Swimming to Cambodia*.

JH: Cut what part?

SG: The part where I stop and say, "I'm telling you the truth: every story here tonight is the truth except for the banana hitting the wall." So that sets up something that's going to come, that the audience watches for, a history in the room of a banana hitting a wall—it's a game in the room, it unites us. So then I tell the story of the banana and the people who remember the reference clap and laugh, so it's both an intellectual recognition and an obscenity. Jonathan didn't want that in the film. I'm a Godardian and a Brechtian at heart. I always have been fans of the two of them, ever since I learned how to look into the audience's eyes and not be hidden on stage. I wanted that in *Swimming to Cambodia*, and I fought for it. It's really important for those questions to be in there.

JH: There is a big, deep, wide strain in American arts, from Whitman's S*ong of Myself* to Rauschenberg's *Bed,* in which he painted on his quilt, that says you cannot err on the side of truth. Americans seem to have this insatiable thirst for truth, for personal exposure.

SC: Exactly. As you say this I think two things about it: one is a new thought and one is an old thought. The new thought is, I've been thinking about America because I want to do a monologue about the idealism, the idealistic concepts of democracy I grew up with in Barrington, Rhode Island, versus the reality of the situation now. I think that a lot of that need for the artist to go to the truth comes out of the schizoid state created between the original forefathers' ideas of democracy and how they have evolved into such a corporate greed structure that runs governments. I think one thing it comes out of is the need to equate truth with idealism.

The other thing, for me, is my growing up in New England, where everything is shuffled under. This sets some people off, others it doesn't. I can remember how important it was for me to say to people that my mother killed herself because in the obituary it never stated that and it was rumored by certain people that she died of cancer. I think that that's where my need for truth came from.

JH: That's another appeal in your work for the average person, isn't it? They can relate vicariously to your experiences because they've had experiences like yours—relationships, deaths, whatever—and they've not quite acknowledged the truths of them, either to themselves or to the people they feel it was important to acknowledge them to.

SG: That's why I've always felt that the monologues were dialogues. I never felt that they were so painful and so demanding that people couldn't reflect at the same time about their own lives. Particularly the original monologue, *Sex and Death to the Age 14* (1979). I mean, what does it have to do with? The death of goldfish and masturbation. As people are listening they are recognizing associations and that's a form of interaction.

JH: Theoretically, as long as you're alive you can never run out of material, true?

SG: Yes. What I know is that if I want to do it, the map is there. I've never enjoyed maps because I've never had them. I came into what I'm doing by chance and evolved it by serendipity. So I always like to think that it may evolve to something else, but it probably will go on right up to the end. And then even continue beyond death—though that would require the right medium for the right message. But I probably will end up doing an oral journal right to the end. □

Bill T. Jones/Arnie Zane & Co. performing *The Last Supper at Uncle Tom's Cabin/The Promised Land*. (1990). Photo: © 1991 Martha Swope, courtesy Martha Swope Associates/Carol Rosegg.

Bill T. Jones

Preparing *The Last Supper at Uncle Tom's Cabin*

Elizabeth Zimmer

In his own works and in his collaborations with the late Arnie Zane, choreographer Bill T. Jones has helped establish the eclectic conventions of contemporary postmodern dance in movement vocabulary, narrative subjects and sources, decor and sound—both music and spoken text. As Elizabeth Zimmer notes in her biographical introduction to the following interview, Jones' work with a racially and physically diverse, multigenerational group of dancers has served as a model for changing standards regarding exclusivity in dance.

Zimmer's interview with Jones focuses on the genesis of The Last Supper at Uncle Tom's Cabin/The Promised Land, *a multimedia theatrical composition that explores issues of racism, homophobia, feminism, loss and faith. Commissioned by a consortium of sponsors—including Hancher Auditorium at The University of Iowa, Jacob's Pillow Dance Festival, Walker Art Center, UCLA and Cal Performances—the completed work had its world premiere in November 1990 at the Brooklyn Academy of Music's Next Wave Festival, following a series of in-progress performances in 1990. In February 1991* The Last Supper at Uncle Tom's Cabin/The Promised Land *was presented at the Wexner Center with partial funding support from Arts Midwest. Presently dance critic for the* Los Angeles Herald Examiner *and a frequent contributor to* The Village Voice *and* Dance Magazine, *Zimmer previously worked with Jones and Zane on the 1989 publication* Body Against Body: The Dance and Other Collaborations of Bill T. Jones & Arnie Zane.

Bill T. Jones was born on 15 February 1952, to Estella and Augustus Jones, migrant farm workers in New York's upstate Steuben County. The tenth of twelve children, he numbers his mother and several sisters among his collaborators in dance works that have grown to include songs, conversation and text from novels and plays. He studied theater and dance at the State University of New York at Binghamton, and his teachers, notably Percival Borde and Pearl Primus, urged him to take his substantial talent to New York to be "finished" by Alvin Ailey. But he fell in love with Arnie Zane, and soon thereafter the two men left Binghamton.

Jones is tall, eloquent, serious and rooted in African-American religious traditions. Zane, who succumbed to AIDS on 30 March 1988, was short and frenetic, a visual artist, the son of an Italian Catholic immigrant and a Jew. When he died, just shy of his fortieth birthday, he and Bill T. Jones had been lovers and partners in life and art for more than seventeen years. Early in their relationship, they lived and worked in Amsterdam, where the things that made them marginal in North America—their homosexuality, their interracial union, their engagement with the arts—were more generally accepted. Jones urged Zane, then a practicing photographer, to experiment with movement. They returned to upstate New York and encountered Lois Welk at a contact improvisation workshop. Contact improvisation, a movement form that stresses physical interdependence, trust and a sharing of weight, proved the ideal medium to lure Arnie Zane onto the studio floor and, it turned out, into a productive collaboration with Jones, Welk and other artists. The three, in Welk's words, "improvised [their] way to a bonding" and soon formed the American Dance Asylum in Binghamton.

For five years, from 1974 to 1979, the American Dance Asylum made and produced nearly a dozen dances annually while also offering evening classes. They were influenced by many experimental dance artists of the seventies, from Daniel Nagrin to Yvonne Rainer and other members of the Grand Union. They listened to jazz, thought a lot about improvisational relationships, developed their technique, expanded their knowledge of experimental film and music and brought other experimental performers to the building they had bought in Binghamton. Eventually, Jones and Zane opted to make rather than produce art, sold their building and began showing work in Manhattan. In 1979 they bought a small house in Valley Cottage, an hour north of New York City, and began the trilogy of *Monkey Run Road* (1979), *Blauvelt Mountain* (1980) and *Valley Cottage* (1981) that first brought them international critical acclaim.

The aesthetics of the two men were at odds in many ways. Jones' impulse was to expose his thoughts and feelings, confronting and challenging an audience, and Zane's tendency was to retreat behind a camera, constructing opaque visual landscapes. The resulting creative friction produced a hydra-headed ensemble, formalized as Bill T. Jones/Arnie Zane & Co. in 1982, which presented works the two artists made separately and together. Individually and in the company, Jones and Zane often also worked in collaboration with other gifted artists, including visual artists Robert Longo and Keith Haring, video artist Gretchen Bender, fashion designer Willi Smith, drummer Max Roach, composer Peter Gordon and choreographer Johanna Boyce.

Since Zane's death, Jones has had to find his way anew, rediscovering the personal voice that for so long had been blended with his partner's. In the past few years, he and his ensemble have branched out. Jones began directing operas in Europe and won his third New York Dance and Performance Award ("Bessie") for *D-Man in the Waters* in 1989.

Jones' thirteen-member ensemble, bonded by shared experiences of loss and triumph, includes black, white, Asian and Hispanic dancers. Individual members may be thin or fat, old or young, gay or straight. Forty-five years separate the oldest dancer from the youngest, and the largest is more than twice as heavy as the smallest. Viewed together, they represent a universe both historical and transcendent; they are, like their leader, full of peace and contradictions, and they seem to take great pleasure in their jobs. For the production of *The Last Supper at Uncle Tom's Cabin* the company has been augmented by actor R. Justice Allen, Minneapolitans John and Sage Cowles and an auxilliary dance corps recruited at almost every stop of the tour.

Jones is an artist in his prime, wrestling with subjects worthy of his talent and intelligence. In *The Last Supper at Uncle Tom's Cabin,* he has made a genuinely original, genuinely American work of contemporary art, fusing his impeccable theatrical sense with texts seminal to any discussion of contemporary race relations. He offers visual irony, textual deconstruction and a passion for human equality and justice. His insights, expressed in movement, take the breath away.

What follows is the product of two interviews conducted during the summer of 1990. Because they engage the same material—the genesis and work process of the new piece—they are presented here as a seamless whole.

Elizabeth Zimmer: *The Last Supper at Uncle Tom's Cabin* makes direct use of images and conceits about American Negroes which have been formally taboo in liberal society for a long time. On a shelf in your living room are a number of "collectibles" which represent stereotypes of black people long held by whites. Why do you have them?

Bill T. Jones: The choreographer Ed Mock has a collection of Aunt Jemima cookie jars. I've seen these memorabilia in the homes of very chic, young, upwardly mobile black people. There's something we recognize in them, something bitter, funny, horrible. I've thought we should be collecting them. They're our Masada: "Never again." There's a bit of humor in it, too. Because I have such a direct link to the old South—my mother was born in Georgia, her mother was a sharecropper—the era the memorabilia represents is not so exotic or implausible to me.

Arnie Zane and I enjoyed a synergism for so long that he could vicariously experience this. He could see the tragic humor in them, as he did in the circumstances of blackness, without having to sacrifice his own identity. His daydream of a gigantic black opera singer, Jessye Norman, on an ice floe was the genesis of *The Last Supper at Uncle Tom's Cabin*. The first time he mentioned it to me was late in 1987. He died soon after, but not before getting a commitment from Harvey Lichtenstein to produce the piece at the Brooklyn Academy of Music. I was left with the title and had to think what each part of it meant.

Bill T. Jones/Arnie Zane & Co. performing *The Last Supper at Uncle Tom's Cabin/The Promised Land.* (1990). Photo: © 1991 Martha Swope, courtesy Martha Swope Associates/Carol Rosegg.

Bill T. Jones/Arnie Zane & Co. performing *The Last Supper at Uncle Tom's Cabin/The Promised Land.* (1990). Photo: © 1991 Martha Swope, courtesy Martha Swope Associates/Carol Rosegg.

EZ: How and why does the work use Harriet Beecher Stowe's novel?

BTJ: I've been called an Uncle Tom a lot, and I wanted to set the record straight. Nobody knows the story now. Let's see who he was in the book. Uncle Tom is such an incredible part of our Western consciousness, the epitome of the American liberal impulse with all its hypocrisy, inconsistency, idealism. It's something most people think they know, and it deserves to be examined on a much deeper level.

There are problems with the way Stowe depicts the people she was meaning to uplift. Andrea Wood, a new [black] member of the company from Philadelphia, said that *Uncle Tom's Cabin* made her angry. She immediately felt that it had very little to do with the reality of slavery. She saw the Eliza character from a feminist point of view, as representing docile and maternal womanhood.

If Harriet Beecher Stowe had had her way, Eliza wouldn't have run away from slavery. She had a kind master and mistress, but they were threatening her boy. Eliza was a quadroon; her values were the same as those of a nineteenth-century white woman. The book has been accepted for the past hundred years by white audiences who may not understand the layers of contradiction, how patronizing it is.

EZ: There's a lot of talking in the new piece. Why use all that text in a dance work?

BTJ: I don't have any other way of dealing with such a polemical novel. I've always been interested in words, in the very specific. I continue to be interested in what Arnie and I used to call "the collision of media." There's a power in the language and something about polemic that I'm very attracted to: the way language changes in the context of abstraction.

Do we need more good dances? Sometimes I just want to walk away from these *issues* to do Mendelssohn's Trio in A. Those Beethoven late quartets are calling to me. But I have to do this. I'm not a fatalist. I do believe we're responsible for our own actions, but there's something in me that has to come out through this piece, the polemic. This is how I hope to earn the final image of its last section, *The Promised Land.*

Using political language in modern dance is subversive. It links dance to the large world. Dance has seemed to me like a little esoteric corner of the cultural world. I love it, but it doesn't resonate nearly as much as it could, or should.

EZ: How come you don't appear in most of the piece?

BTJ: It's really difficult. I'm not such a great choreographic genius as to be able to be in and out. I need to see it, see that the movement is not solely generated from my body, my ability. I haven't given up dancing, but because this piece is so demanding of me, it's good to relax the performing side of myself. *Faith* [a section of the work in which he appears with several gospel singers, including two of his sisters] was sort of a study for this piece. *Faith* is myself.

EZ: What is your relation to Scripture?

BTJ: Harriet Beecher Stowe quotes Scripture a lot. I was supposed to have been a preacher; I have this introspective, otherworldly side. There's a tendency on my part to preach, a kind of catharsis that black ministers understand. I was being groomed emotionally for that. I would sit with my father after Sunday school and read the Bible. But I got derailed when I was fourteen by the big questions: where did we come from? Here I am, left with the desire to express, as my mother would have expressed, this belief, this catharsis, but I'm not equipped.

When I use "the good book," it's with a kind of nostalgia for what was, and what might have been. My lifestyle, my company, represents a kind of hyper-contemporary aesthetic. We're a marginal group of people. So when I use the antiquated, authoritative voice of the Scriptures, it has a particular ring to the context of this group.

EZ: The context of the group or the context of the choreography?

BTJ: I confuse the two a lot. Am I making an organization or am I making a piece? Sometimes I get confused about it.

EZ: Should people prepare themselves to see this work by reading *Uncle Tom's Cabin* and LeRoi Jones' *Dutchman*, which is also used in the piece?

BTJ: I think it's a very good idea. Guy Darmet of the Maison de la Danse in Lyons [where the work was presented in September 1990] said *Uncle Tom's Cabin* is very popular in France. I would hope everyone would read it. I asked a couple of historians why it's so important. They said it was such a uniquely American document. All of the questions are there: issues of race and class, of government responsibility at the federal and state level, of the individual's rights and responsibilities, of women's rights and of religion.

I read the book the way I collect black memorabilia: it's a testament to where we've been. The real question is, were we ever really there, or is that where a well-meaning, white liberal Christian woman said we were? In a way, isn't that what makes the black memorabilia so painfully intriguing? When you look at it as a contemporary person, white or black, it shouts "This is a lie." So then the question is "What is the truth?"

I've never talked about a piece so much while it was being made. It's going to address things that people are interested in. One sponsor only wanted to show three sections, because the last section has nudity in it. Another sponsor has been waving a banner—he thinks that on principle, because the artist is being threatened, the sponsor should go out on a limb. The piece operates from a point of view that asks some hard questions. It isn't meant to be a cudgel—or is it? Ultimately, it longs to be a purging and a healing. I'm interested in presenting historical, thematic material with moral force.

EZ: How do you use video in the construction of the work?

BTJ: It's been a notebook for me this year. It's the record. I've been making these elaborate studies to be honed into a work. I began in November 1989 in New York, then had a long residency in Minneapolis, then a period in England, then the Catskills and now Los Angeles. Jacob's Pillow is next, and then a rehearsal period at the Brooklyn Academy of Music before we open in November 1990. I'm more relaxed, and the group is more focused. We can really concentrate on the work, give it a kind of respect, when we're in another city.

EZ: How and where do you find your dancers?

BTJ: There are so many people who would like to work with us. They see that it's an "everyman" company. The "523 Handsome Nudes" section [for which Jones has attempted to recruit a multiracial group of dancers, including college students, in each city sharing the development of the work] is a sort of catch-all for those people. In Minneapolis, I requested that Northrop Auditorium and the Walker Arts Center recruit a diverse group of dancers. Nearly everyone who showed up was white. They tried to tell me there were no blacks, or that the blacks were interested in commercial work. I'm interested in diversity: race, class, age, body type, sexual preference. You name them, I

Bill T. Jones/Arnie Zane & Co. performing *The Last Supper at Uncle Tom's Cabin/The Promised Land.* (1990). Photo: © 1991 Martha Swope, courtesy Martha Swope Associates/Carol Rosegg.

want them. I would like to work with handicapped people, but the piece must be tailored for them in some way.

What I'm proud about is that the piece puts a demand on a community and on a sponsor's ability to rally around a work of art. Sometimes, just the effort to bring together a diverse group reveals so much about the community. It's very important right now to make a community look at itself. Every community is responsible for this. What does it take to extend a special invitation to blacks and Asians, to minority communities?

The "dominant culture" mentality has worked its magic: it will be a long time before the United States has a sense of itself as anything but WASP. The question the piece asks is "What is our commonalty?" The body is what we focused on. That's highlighted only too well by mortality. Many of my generation have run into a brick wall on this issue, and you know the other topic that I'm talking about.

The issue of faith is connected to this issue. Why does one care to live in a world where there are so many problems? What is the nature of belief?

EZ: What about the music for the piece?

BTJ: I commissioned a score by Julius Hemphill, formerly of the World Saxophone Quartet, who now has the Long Tongue Saxophone Sextet. We're in a crisis right now, because some of the members of the presenting consortium and the other presenters involved can't really pay what it costs to have live music all the time. We're going to be traveling more and more with tape. That saddens me. Dancers are used to working for less, but the musicians are not so willing to do that. □

Projects

In conjuring a conceivable media arts companion to the thirteen installations documented through interviews and images in the preceding pages, it seemed a reasonable idea to ask five film or video artists to contribute pages for this book: "projects" based on or catalyzed by their own ongoing production history. What these five artists—Shu Lea Cheang, Steve Fagin, Tom Kalin, Leslie Thornton and Julie Zando—have produced are not precisely script extracts nor precisely page-bound static renditions of their time-based work. What they have produced is, overall, an irony: artists who create moving images being asked to deliver words and pictures (scripts, scriptograms, commentaries or markings in advance/arrears of those) frozen and spread across a book's pages.

It's a mild irony, still, as such phenomena go, thanks to the circumstance of these particular artists being casual opponents of film or video "purity" as previous decades might have avowed it. Working in what seems to be a transitional moment in the wake of the last two decades' preferred tendencies within independent media—which roughly might be characterized as "structural cinema," "new narrative" and "new documentary"—these artists are located within what Fredric Jameson has termed the "cultural logic" of postmodernism.

In the context of alternative film and video production, that logic is placed in relief by the pleasures of "cinephilia" being questioned by "cinephobia" (a struggle echoing Gaston Bachelard's prescription to doubt one's "philia" as instinctively as one's "phobia"). What the five artists share (they share little else) is an aesthetic affinity for mongrel thought and deed: for mixing high-end with low-end; for estranging image from referent and acoustic effect from its origin; for sensing that they stand in a rhetorically terminal relation to a landfill of always expanding image-making; and hence for acting on the faith that the only way left is up.

Asian-American video artist and film producer Shu Lea Cheang offers visual notes toward a collaborative work-in-progress with scriptwriter Jessica Hagedorn and researcher Kelly Anderson, tentatively titled *For Whom the Air Waves*. Based in New York, Cheang coordinated *...Will Be Televised: Video Documents From Asia*, a five-part video series focusing on political activism and unrest, which was shown as part of the Wexner Center's first anniversary programming. "Notes for the Airwaves" continues Cheang's interest in alternative media, here addressing environmental issues. A visiting artist during the Wexner Center's inaugural year and a faculty member at the University of California at San Diego, video producer Steve Fagin offers an illustrated internal rumination on a suite of film stills. His "Casanova's Homecoming" in this way sheds light on the evolution of his current project based on Casanova's life.

Swoon, which writer/director Tom Kalin recently completed filming, dwells on the notorious duo of Nathan Leopold and Robert Loeb. Kalin's "Notes on Swoon" offers a counterpart to the film's critical reinterpretation of desire. A member of Gran Fury (a group of artists affiliated with New York's ACT UP), Kalin is one of the participants in *Video Against AIDS*, a six-hour compilation of independent media exhibited by the Wexner Center as part of its ongoing commitment to provide informed and engaged knowledge on the epidemic. Brooklyn-based Leslie Thornton is best known for her remarkable series of hybrid film/video productions centered around her ongoing and "endless" serial *Peggy and Fred in Hell*. Her "Character in Unconventional People" refers to the legendary Saharan adventuress Isabelle Eberhardt, as does her earlier work, *There Was An Unseen Cloud Moving*. Videotapes by Buffalo-based Julie Zando have been featured in a Wexner Center program of lesbian and gay independent media. Zando's "Symptoms and Stories: The Narrative Cure" provides a conceptual background, in terms borrowed from a therapeutic intervention, to the challenges posed by her tapes.

William Horrigan

Some 25 years ago, the U.S.
Navy accidentally dropped an
H-bomb into the ocean, 200
miles from Japan's densely
populated island, Okinawa.

24 years later, the Pentagon
admitted that the bomb
exploded in the deep ocean.

ABC News, May 15, 1989

Peter Jennings concludes his
report on the "Lost H-Bomb"

".........the Pentagon says, yes,
the bomb was crushed as it sank
to the sea bed, but the Pentagon
ran tests which it says shows
that nuclear material would
have dissolved harmlessly on
the ocean floor."

TOXIC TERRORISM

Remember the endlessly traveling vagabond garbage barge?

Rejected from one port to the next, it got on the Johnny Carson show.

Johnny expresses the sentiment shared by some Americans about the barge. Pointing at a map of the Mid-East, he says, "Take the barge up to the gulf of Persia, and there's Iran. Dump it right there."

(all around applause from the audience)

The newly appointed anchorwoman for the recently merged ACC News–American Communications Corporation, WE BRING INTELLIGENT NEWS TO YOU, announces in the Global News Tonight,

"ACC Network is experiencing severe interference from satellite break-ins these days. Tele-aggression of unauthorized news has severely interrupted our Sky Rider's Dishing Out Service to millions of home satellite disk owners. Unable to ascertain the source of this video terrorism, chairman Roger Bailey has issued a warning to the intruders........."

VIDEO TERRORISM

A few examples of the unauthorized news:

item 1:

item 2:

Shot of an African boy, skinny, healthy, no sorrowful eyes but determined closed-shut lips, looking straight into the invisible camera lens. Body turning sideways, he is squatting under the tropical sun taking a shit.

Words crawl across the bottom screen,

BROTHERS AND SISTERS, HAVE YOU BEEN RECEIVING OUR MESSAGES? AFRICAN UNITY NETWORK NEEDS YOU!

JOIN OUR CALL FOR A MASSIVE ANTI-TOILET PAPER RALLY FOR ALL AFRICAN NATIONS.

BOYCOTT THE TOILET PAPER MADE FROM LEAD-TAINTED ENGRAVING PAPER SOLD BY THE U.S. TREASURY DEPARTMENT.

WE WOULD RATHER WIPE OUR ASSES CLEAN WITH LEAVES!

Evening rush hour at Fresh Kill Road, Staten island. Traffic is backed up, bumper to bumper, for miles. Drivers get out of their cars; some of them gather in small groups to chitchat. The cars are not moving, but people seem patient and resigned to the situation. Burning debris and overturned automobiles can be seen in the background.

A home-video camera operated by a commuter catches this traffic jam tableau, moving past car after car until it reaches the head of the motionless procession. Thousands of seagulls swoop low across the road that cuts through the world's largest dump, the 3000-acre, 150-foot-high Fresh Kill landfill. The flocks of diving birds blacken the sky. Traffic is stalled until the seagulls finish their evening stroll.

Words flashing on the screen read,

LATEST BIRD COUNT 87,000

CASANOVA'S

The most imaginable film in the world.

In fact the only film I couldn't make

JOURNEY INTO FEAR

it's magic. she appears in a puff of smoke, she's been hijacked from some amateur allegory, yes Milton, she's playing the character Lust. the lights go dark and there is a shooting. Lust is love's excitement. its proximity to death.

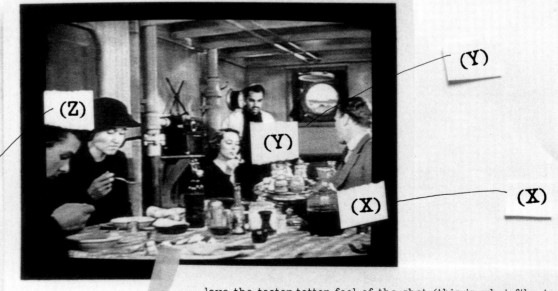

love the teeter-totter feel of the shot (this is what film is good for), he looking over his shoulder

background l u s t (Y) w i t h chaperone

mid-ground he, the American, the confused one, the moral one   (X)   just like Custer, surrounded

foreground (music)   harpies (Z) chirping away

HOMECOMING

would be THE SON OF SHOAH.

as he slurps and slurps and slurps and.................
I want this sound and banality to put a wedge between the
lovers

"he knows he has the look of fear all over him"
what does fear look like? perhaps ask the question about
fear and also love, then have a sort of Kuleshov effect
sequence, i.e. the
same look on the person's face intercut with different things
and/or people. all of the things/people shown will have
already appeared, in a different context, at an earlier/later
moment of the film

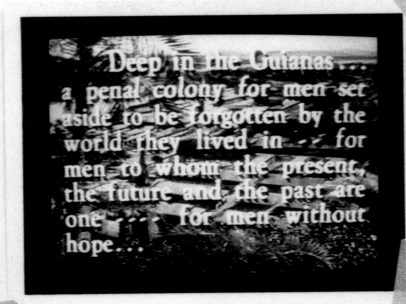

I want language to be used diaphanously

what I like the most about the movie is some of the prisoners' names. Gable is Verne, another Flaubert, etc., very difficult to get these names to work. THE IMAGE. the way the look on her face is controlled by what's going on under her waist (unbeknownst to the passersby), twisting an ankle must be the tactile version of bending an ear. Hollywood is like a kosher butcher. only those cuts above the waist are suitable for public consumption (the lower half of the anatomy is unceremoniously devoured)

I want the piece to start a bit like SIGNORA DI TUTTI, close-up of records playing, different ones: tango, country and western chanteuse, etc., hand with gloves, elegant with holes, going on frame changing records. cut to overhead (same room) swanky (a la italiano) flowers, vases, encore encore, then woman/maid with gloves straightens things up walks out of room cut to camera slowly do(a)llying alongside her. man walks in camera dollies reversing through the space it just passed (a la Ophuls), he goes to a door other side of room from where he entered. camera stops. says a name, he looks, we don't see. he screams then camera tries to keep up same tracking as he runs back through the elegant room knocking over the flowers, vases, glasses that the maid had just been straightening. he hits the record player and it starts sticking on a phrase. camera holds still on the room in shambles sound of record sticking after he has left the room

(truth)

(truth)
the moment suspended between fantasy and
psychodrama. is it death or only a drug? truth, that is.

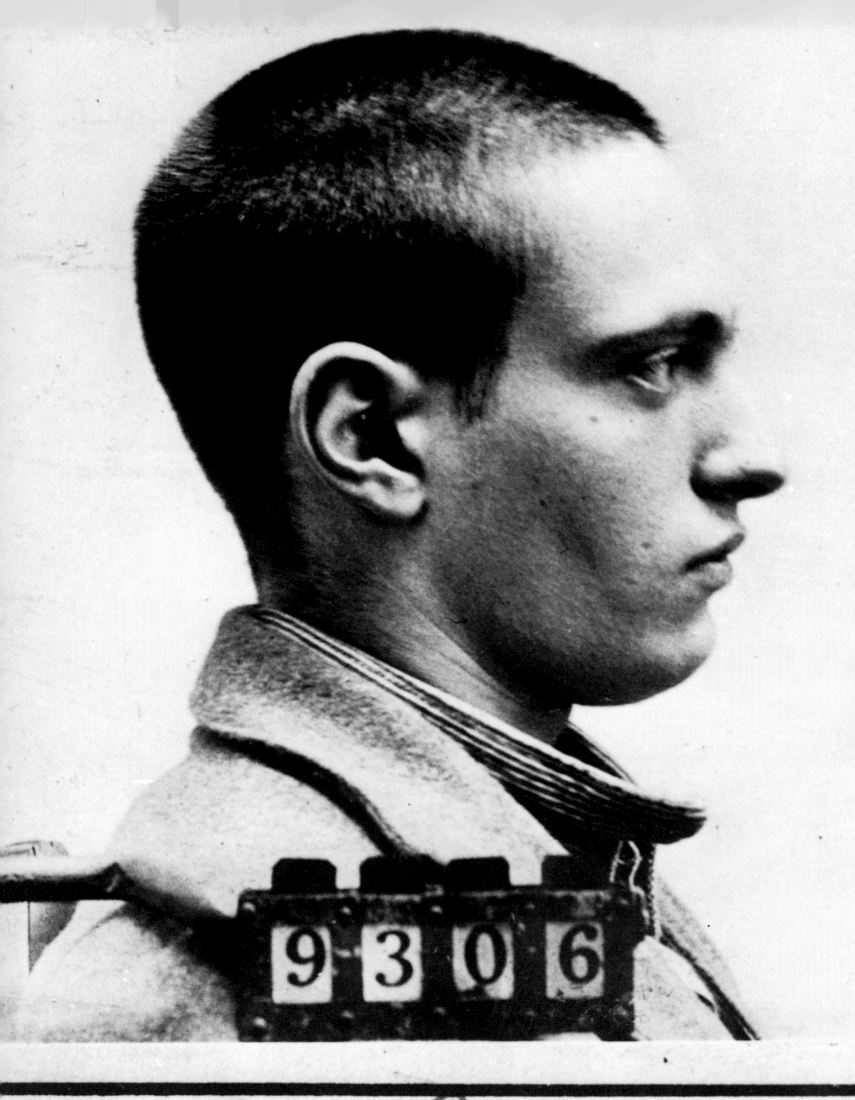

His first actual sex experience, namely, the use or misuse of his organ, was when a boy, Henry, two years older than himself, masturbated by rubbing his genitals with a towel, producing an erection and ejaculation.

This quite interested the patient.

The two boys saved the discharge and put it in a jar. Later they lost interest in it.

The boy acts as if he were a law unto himself alone.

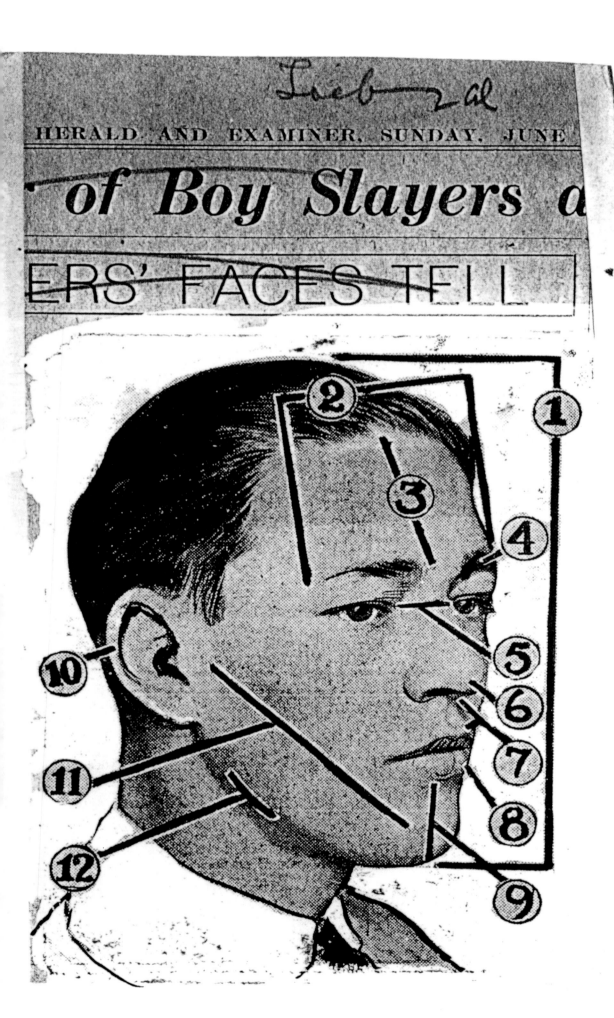

The patient spoke about his compulsive fantasies. He thought of himself as being confined behind bars. The men and women that surrounded him were naked. He himself was often abused or beaten. He would see people peering at him through the bars commenting upon the fact that he was a great criminal, looking upon him with curiosity.

I was abused, but it was a very pleasant thought. The punishment inflicted upon me in jail gave me pleasure. I enjoyed being looked at through the bars, because I was a famous criminal.

PHRENOLOGICAL CHARACTER

Isabelle Eberhardt

CHARACTER IN UNCONVENTIONAL PEOPLE

Isabelle Eberhardt
Writer, Traveler, Journalist, Adventurer

From personal examination by A. Monito, Phrenologist

Only by carefully studying all of the elements of human nature, both agreeable and disagreeable, can we hope to gain accurate and comprehensive knowledge. To this end, we propose here to make a little excursion into the realm of unconventional mentality. Our purpose is to show the relation between peculiar ideas of life and certain types of physical organization. Of course, we shall enter into no discussion as to the merit of the views held by today's subject, although it is only justice to say that she repudiates the commonly accepted idea that she breeds subversion and sedition on her travels in North Africa. Having recently interviewed and examined this young woman, we hope to be able to point out certain facts about her which will be of interest.

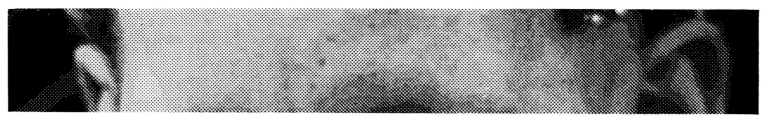

Isabelle Eberhardt professes to be of Turkish descent although it is known that she is the fille naturelle of Mme de Moerder, wife of Senator-General Pavel Carlovitch de Moerder, and the family tutor Alexander Nikolaevitch Trophimovsky, a Russian Orthodox priest who was excommunicated for his anarchist activities. It is surprising, given her notoriety, that Isabelle is still a young woman, not over twenty-two or twenty-four. She is five feet six and only ninety-five pounds, with a jutting chin, a wide mouth, and a domed forehead. She has rather thick dark hair, which has been clipped short, and green-grey eyes of which the expression is very peculiar. Her head measures twenty-one and a half inches in basilar circumference, and the principle developments are above this line. The back head is rather long, showing friendship, domestic attachment, and love of the opposite sex. There is considerable width over the ears at destructiveness, and acquisitiveness, which the portrait does not adequately show. But with the further exception of the upper forehead, which in this picture is not included, the likeness is remarkably accurate. This is especially true as to the expression of the eyes and the mouth. The facial signs of destructiveness and acquisitiveness are very pronounced in the form of the mouth, and it is chiefly in the mouth and eyes that we may detect the signs of quality and temperament which account for the woman's disposition to attack the present social fabric.

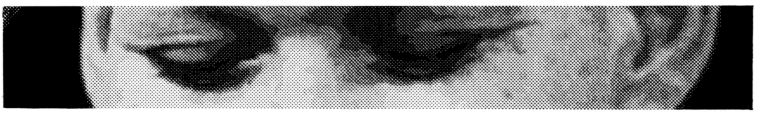

There is very considerable development in the rear of the crown. Appropriateness and firmness are especially strong. Conscientiousness is difficult to define. These is a latent sense of justice, but everything in the organization points to a lack of discipline, and there are evidences of what might be called a habit of willfulness, an abandon to the dominant impulses. In that form of chin and mouth, with the large firmness in the brain, we have the phase of persistence that may be called tenacity, and which is often referred to in the popular parlance by a comparison with the wild boar. It is a vehement clutch which is seldom relaxed and it differs from a more rational obstinacy or perseverance in being independent of opposing forces or other external conditions. Like an animal, she nurses her joys or griefs whether anyone is present to contradict or not. Her stubbornness is always active and stamps her character with an indelible dye.

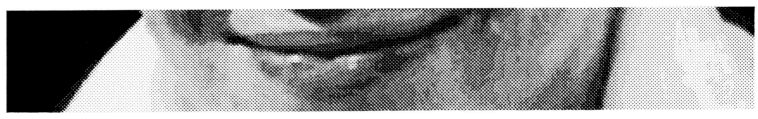

The incorrigibility of such a nature is also greatly augmented, as in the present instance, by the almost utter lack of reverence and faith. Hope is also weak. This combination leaves the intellect without incentive to search for evidences of optimism, and as such a nature readily finds itself at war with the conventionalities, ill adapted to compete in the struggle for existence with those more harmoniously constituted, a pessimistic view of life with a consequent desire to either alter or "escape" from existing conditions. Of course there are thousands of people who have many of these peculiarities of feeling, but who are endowed with ordinary intellect, so that they make no outcry, no protest, and indeed have few opinions beyond the consciousness that are uncomfortable. But Isabelle Eberhardt, obviously of a lineage aristocratic and learned in tone, is endowed with the philosophical cast of mind which is very rare. Her upper forehead is beautifully developed and our portrait utterly fails to do her justice in this respect.

The development of causality and comparison, stimulated by her melancholy emotion, renders her a person of radical action. In her conversation she manifests that familiarity with the vocabulary of philosophy which is ordinarily expected only among cultivated professional men. However, her lower forehead is almost as defective as the upper portion is fine. The eyebrows barely exist, and the space between them (the glabella) is depressed much more than appears in the portrait. This shows a want of precision and accuracy in her observations. In other words, she will reason profoundly, but often upon insufficient evidence. As may be seen by the flattened outer angle of the brow, she has scarcely a trace of order.

There are, doubtless, certain biases or tendencies in this woman which she owes to some marked peculiarities or habits of her ancestors. She says that her father was a man of almost tyrannical disposition, and that her mother was very weak-willed. Thus, there is quite a difference between the indications in her head and in her hand as regards firmness. Her hand is quite long, very flexible, but with a poorly developed thumb, the first and second phalanx being very short. It is in the first joint that cheirognomists locate will-power, while the second phalanx is, according to its length, a sign of logic. This imperfect first joint, and shortened second joint are often found in people who are undeveloped or askew in some particular. This peculiarity in Mademoiselle Eberhardt shows how important it is to study the brain and not to rely upon one isolated or remote sign.

Prepared by A. Monito, Paris, 1901

Natalie Eberhardt

Alexander Trophimovsky

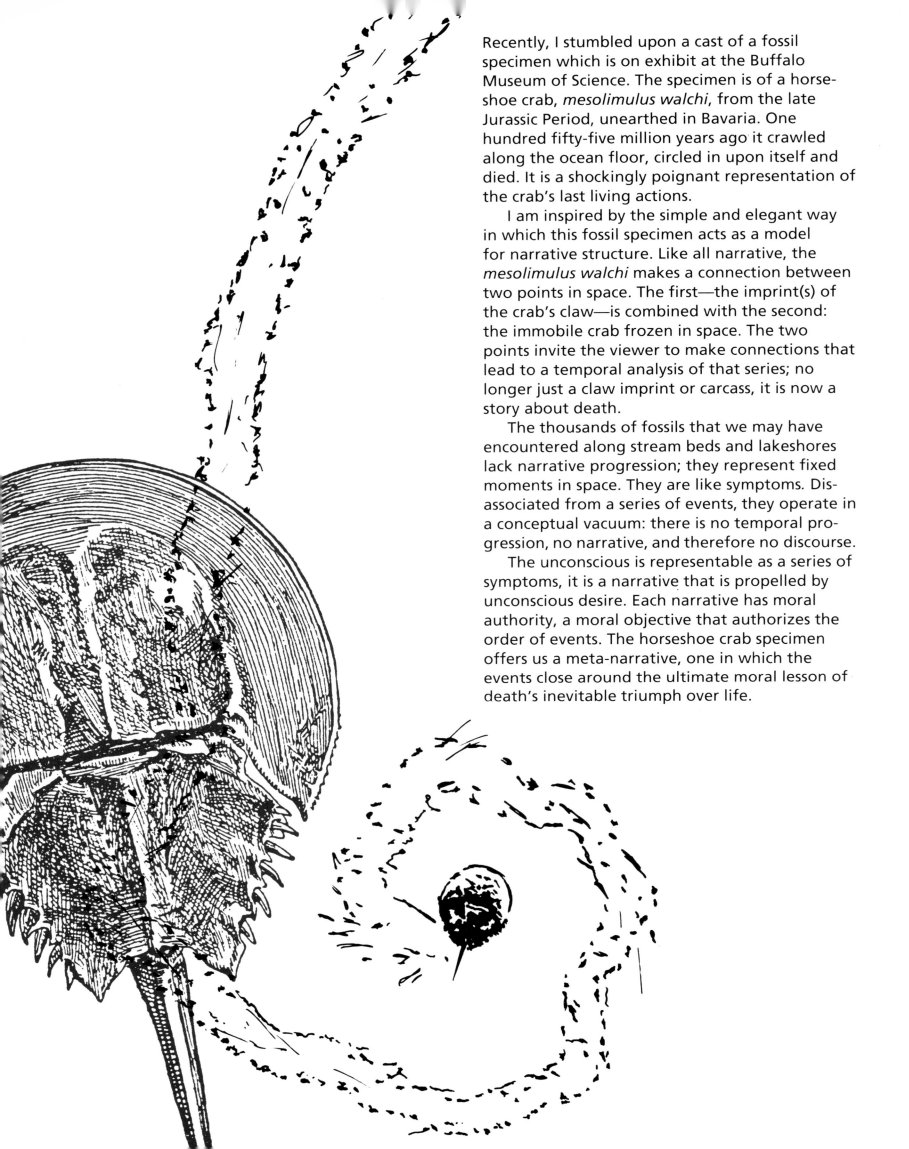

Recently, I stumbled upon a cast of a fossil specimen which is on exhibit at the Buffalo Museum of Science. The specimen is of a horseshoe crab, *mesolimulus walchi*, from the late Jurassic Period, unearthed in Bavaria. One hundred fifty-five million years ago it crawled along the ocean floor, circled in upon itself and died. It is a shockingly poignant representation of the crab's last living actions.

I am inspired by the simple and elegant way in which this fossil specimen acts as a model for narrative structure. Like all narrative, the *mesolimulus walchi* makes a connection between two points in space. The first—the imprint(s) of the crab's claw—is combined with the second: the immobile crab frozen in space. The two points invite the viewer to make connections that lead to a temporal analysis of that series; no longer just a claw imprint or carcass, it is now a story about death.

The thousands of fossils that we may have encountered along stream beds and lakeshores lack narrative progression; they represent fixed moments in space. They are like symptoms. Disassociated from a series of events, they operate in a conceptual vacuum: there is no temporal progression, no narrative, and therefore no discourse.

The unconscious is representable as a series of symptoms, it is a narrative that is propelled by unconscious desire. Each narrative has moral authority, a moral objective that authorizes the order of events. The horseshoe crab specimen offers us a meta-narrative, one in which the events close around the ultimate moral lesson of death's inevitable triumph over life.

So I am inspired by the fossil because it acts as a metaphor for the structure of both narrative and the unconscious. I am drawn to this method of analysis: taking a symptom or series of symptoms, each a displaced signifier in need of interpretation, and ordering them into a conscious narrative. This is hardly a novel idea, for it is the work of psychoanalysis, but it is also a guiding principle for me. When you work in film or video you become an analyst, you see something that might look shocking, disorienting or disassociated from reality and you read it as symptomatic of something else—economics, politics, desire, whatever. You get to order the scenes in such a way as to provide a larger interpretation, and I am constantly aware of this privilege. In my work I want to remind my audiences of my privilege and also to point out their own, because after I tell my story, they go home to their friends and tell them what the tape is about, they make their own connections and create their own version of the story. (I suppose that therapeutic success is for my story to jive with yours, regardless of the accuracy or truthfulness of either.) In much of my work I've examined power relations, and this is often one person's story or psychological space dominating another's. My latest tape, *The Bus Stops Here* (1990), is precisely about this problem, particularly how it affects women, who are

The Bus Stops Here 1990. Photos: © Fred Ciminelli.

always struggling to have their voices heard. In another work, *Let's Play Prisoners* (1988), the narrative describes the childhood experience of peer pressure and examines the dynamic behind domination and submission. The tape is divided into two sections, "Remembrance" and "Recognition." The first sets up a series of painful childhood memories. In the second, the seemingly random events are understood to originate from an unconscious pattern. It is only after the tape reconstructs, reorders and nar- rativizes the pain that the analysis can surface.

The A Ha! Experience (1988) is another tape that explores the value of "recognition" to analysis. The "aha-erlebnis" (a ha experience) is the moment when a child first recognizes his own image in a mirror. It is an experience that is critical to the development of intelligence and identity. It is also a moment when the self is surrendered to the control of an external influence. In the tape the narration describes a scene in which a young woman, on the brink of adolescent sexual awakening, is shocked by the presence of her mother in her bed. The image haunts her, and the imagined presence of the mother's body provides the backdrop for all further sexual encounters. All desire is sub- sequently understood to be derived from that experience. It is the mother's desire (her presence in the bed) that directs and controls the scene of passion; she is the ultimate subject whose love confers sexual and psychical identity.

Let's Play Prisoners 1988. Photos: © Ellen R. Spiro.

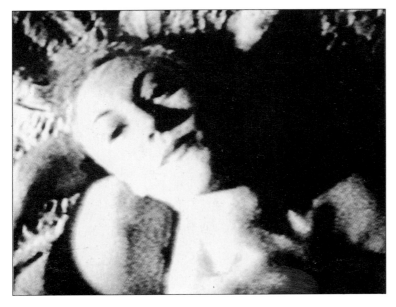

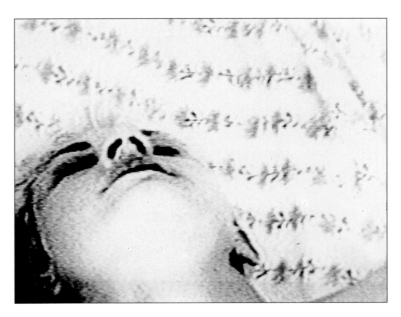

The A Ha! Experience 1988. Photos: © Ellen R. Spiro.

Just as an analyst directs the therapeutic session, the camera directs perception and experience. In psychoanalytic terms the camera "normalizes" experience in a deliberate, self-conscious way; my tapes often remind the audience of the camera's analytic privilege (its power to interpret and mediate experience). Like Bertolt Brecht, I am interested in self-conscious direction, except that I interpret the process as a kind of "counter-transference."

The camera as analyst is most evident in *Hey Bud* (1987), which revolves around the suicide of Bud Dwyer, a government official who killed himself before a live television audience. The suicide was choreographed like an analytic session, in which its "success" depended on a reaction from the audience that could be counter-transferred. The role of analyst was forced upon the viewer, much the way an exhibitionist throws himself into the gaze of an unsuspecting audience.

I also like to play with the gaze and to point out the role of the audience in the work of the narrative. Occasionally I'll put viewers on the spot by having the characters speak or look at the camera directly. By making viewers feel slightly uncomfortable I can emphasize their roles as voyeurs.

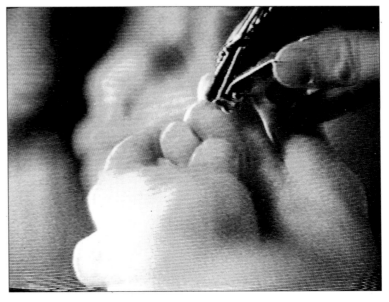

Hey Bud 1987. Photos: © Ellen R. Spiro.

Notes

Art in Europe and America: The 1950s and 1960s

Dore Ashton
The Long and Short of It

1. "The American Action Painters," *The Tradition of the New* (New York: Horizon Press, 1959), p. 25.

2. Dubuffet's lecture *Anticultural Positions* was delivered at The Arts Club of Chicago on 20 December 1951. Its original English language text has been published in *Dubuffet and the Anticulture* (New York: Richard L. Feigen & Co., 1969) in a facsimile edition and in *Arts Magazine* 53 (April 1979), pp. 156–157.

3. "What Abstract Art Means to Me: Statements by Six American Artists," *The Museum of Modern Art Bulletin* 17 (Spring 1951), p. 7.

4. "Content is a Glimpse…," excepts from an interview with David Sylvester of the BBC, reprinted from *Location* 1 (Spring 1963) in Thomas B. Hess, *Willem de Kooning* (New York: The Museum of Modern Art, 1968), p. 148.

5. From an interview with David Sylvester of the BBC, recorded at Edisto Beach, South Carolina, in the spring of 1965 and first broadcast on 10 October 1965; excerpts published in *Jasper Johns: Drawings* (London: Arts Council of Great Britain, 1974), p. 7.

Roy Close
The Future of Music: The Fifties and Sixties in Retrospect

1. Letter to Rita LaPlante Raffman, dated 11 February 1977.

2. "Composition as Process," *Silence: Lectures and Writings by John Cage* (Middletown, Connecticut: Wesleyan University Press, 1961), p. 18.

3. Calvin Tomkins, *The Bride and the Bachelors* (New York: Viking Press, 1965), p. 120.

4. *4'33"* (New York: C. F. Peters Corporation, 1960). This was not the complete score but a single page listing three movements, all *tacet*.

5. Michael Nyman, *Experimental Music: Cage and Beyond* (New York: Schirmer Books, 1974), p. 70.

Paul Arthur
The Redemption of the City in Postwar Avant-Garde Film

1. Leo Marx, *The Machine in the Garden: Technology and the Pastoral Ideal in America* (New York: Oxford University Press, 1964), passim.

2. The notion of illegibility as the loss of fixed and rational spatial relations in the modern city is already present in Lewis Mumford's characterization of the "non-plan of a non-place," but it receives its most influential elaboration in Kevin Lynch, *The Image of the City* (Cambridge, Massachusetts: MIT Press, 1960). See also: William Sharpe and Leonard Wallock, "From 'Great Town' to 'Nonplace Urban Realm': Reading the Modern City," in *Visions of the Modern City*, Sharpe and Wallock, editors (Baltimore: Johns Hopkins University Press, 1987), pp. 1–50.

3. These tropes are derived from a venerable literary tradition that is briefly sketched by Sharpe and Wallock, pp. 36–38. A more extensive review is found in Burton Pike, *The Image of the City in Modern Literature* (Princeton: Princeton University Press, 1981).

4. Perhaps the best recent overview of Chicago social theory is in Michael P. Smith, *The City and Social Theory* (New York: St. Martins Press, 1979), pp. 2–35.

5. "The Idea of the City in European Thought: Voltaire to Spengler," in *The Historian and the City*, Oscar Handlin and John Burchard, editors (Cambridge, Massachusetts: Harvard University Press, 1963), p.112.

6. David James examines avant-garde film's documentation of Beat culture in *Allegories of Cinema: American Film in the Sixties* (Princeton: Princeton University Press, 1989), pp. 87–94, 96–101.

7. Thomas Bender, "New York as a Center of 'Difference': How America's Metropolis Counters American Myth," *Dissent* 34 (Fall 1987), pp. 429–436.

8. The attribution of the aesthetic tenets of modernist art to ecological conditions of the modern city is quite widespread. Even otherwise astute urban commentators such as Marshall Berman fall at times into the reflectionist trap of equating speed or fragmentation in social relations with, say, the rhythmic components of Cubism or bebop. See Berman, *All That is Solid Melts into Air* (London: Verso, 1982), p. 18. Music critic John Rockwell tries, somewhat naïvely, to locate a range of musical styles in the mythology of New York City in "Why New York Has a Sound All its Own," *The New York Times*, 3 April 1988, Section 2, pp. 1, 22–23.

9. P. Adams Sitney, *Visionary Film* (New York: Oxford University Press, 1974), passim.

10. *Film-makers' Cooperative Catalogue No. 7* (New York: The New American Cinema Group, Inc., 1989), p. 272.

11. Quoted in Annette Michelson, "Toward Snow," *Artforum* 9 (June 1971), p. 38. Michelson extrapolates from Farber's remark a well-known and extremely elegant argument around the phenomenological implications of the "action film," yet nowhere does she pick up on Farber's documentary clue.

12. Here I am in solid disagreement with the standard line on Structural film (including some of my own earlier pronouncements) as epitomized by Sitney and also with its materialist reworking by David James, who concludes that the reductionist ethos erases all textual hints of social context: "The formal concerns, the absence of content, and the insistent reflexivity all corresponded to an absence of any positive social function, the denial of any audience but the specialist. Its symbolic utopia of uncompromised film was achieved not merely by negating all previous uses and situations of film, but by negating cinema." *Allegories of Cinema*, p. 275.

13. Scott Macdonald, "Interview with Jonas Mekas," *October* 29 (Summer 1984), p.88.

14. Michel de Certeau, "Practices of Space," in *On Signs*, Marshall Blonsky, editor (Baltimore: Johns Hopkins University Press, 1985), pp. 78–96.

15. Walter Benjamin, *Charles Baudelaire: A Lyric Poet in the Era of High Capitalism* (London: Verso, 1973), p. 36.

16. Sharpe and Wallock assert that the decentered nature of the "urban field" provokes a crisis in language in sociology's efforts to describe current spatial configurations. They relate the ambivalence of naming to tendencies in the urban novels of Thomas Pynchon and others; Sharpe and Wallock, "From 'Great Town' to 'Nonplace Urban Realm': Reading the Modern City," pp. 25–34.

17. See Fredric Jameson, "Postmodernism or the Cultural Logic of Late Capitalism," *New Left Review* 146 (July–August 1984), p. 62. Jameson ties the belief in a unique style with the concept of the centered subject as terms on which the efficacy of modernism has foundered. I have avoided locating a break in avant-garde film between modernism and its "post-" condition because, except in relation to television, there is little to distinguish older and more recent manifestations of filmic subjectivity.

Art in Europe and America:
The 1960s and 1970s

Lucy Lippard
Intruders: Lynda Benglis
and Adrian Piper

1. Piper, *Talking to Myself: The Ongoing Autobiography of an Art Object* (Bari, Italy: Marilena Bonomo, 1975), p. 17.

2. Benglis too, by coincidence, has been involved in philosophy. As a college student she was attracted to logic in particular: "I excelled in logic but found that I didn't want to go into logic at that time because it seemed to go nowhere; it seemed to be an argument about arguments, although I loved the theory, making propositions, arguments, the thinking process, the whole idea of inductive and deductive reasoning…The philosophy experience would keep me awake all night; the art experience didn't at that point, and I think it was largely because I didn't know what it was to *look* at something." Benglis in Ned Rifkin, "Lynda Benglis: Interview by Ned Rifkin," *Early Work* (New York: The New Museum, 1982), p.6.

3. Benglis, "Interview" (interviewer anonymous), *Ocular* 4 (Summer 1979), p. 36.

4. Benglis, *Ocular* interview, p. 40.

5. Benglis, Rifkin interview, *Early Work*, p. 11.

6. Benglis, *Ocular* interview, p. 40.

7. Ned Rifkin, *Early Work*, p. 12.

8. Benglis, Rifkin interview, *Early Work*, p. 8.

9. "Eccentric Abstraction" was the title of an exhibition I organized at the Fischbach Gallery in 1966; it included Louise Bourgeois, Eva Hesse, Alice Adams, Bruce Nauman, Frank Lincoln Viner, Gary Kuehn, Keith Sonnier and Don Potts.

10. Benglis, Rifkin interview, *Early Work*, p. 9.

11. Piper, in Lucy R. Lippard, "Catalysis: An Interview with Adrian Piper," *The Drama Review* 16 (March 1972); reprinted in Lippard, *From the Center* (New York: E. P. Dutton, 1976), p. 169

12. Benglis originally offered the image as an artist's project, but the editors insisted that it appear as an advertisement.

13. Benglis, Rifkin interview, *Early Work*, p. 14.

14. Benglis, Rifkin interview, *Early Work*, p. 15.

15. Angela Carter, *The Sadeian Woman and the Ideology of Pornography* (New York: Pantheon Books, 1978), p. 3.

16. Benglis, *Ocular* interview, p. 32.

17. Dick Hebdige, "Posing…Threats, Striking…Poses: Youth, Surveillance, and Display," *SubStance,* 37/38 (1983), p. 86.

18. Benglis, Rifkin interview, *Early Work*, pp. 13–14.

19. Piper, Lippard interview, *From the Center*, p. 171.

20. Benglis, Rifkin interview, *Early Work*, p. 13.

21. Benglis, *Ocular* interview, p. 35.

22. Piper, in "Flying," *Adrian Piper, Reflections 1967–1987* (New York: Alternative Museum, 1987), p. 22.

Lucy Lippard
Intruders: Lynda Benglis
and Adrian Piper
(continued)

23. Piper, "Flying," p. 23.

24. Piper, "Flying," pp. 23-24.

25. Piper, 1986 lecture at Antioch College, Yellow Springs, Ohio.

26. Craig Owens, "Posing," *Difference* (New York: The New Museum of Contemporary Art, 1985), p. 7.

27. James Baldwin, "A Talk to Teachers" (1963), *The Graywolf Annual Five: Multicultural Literacy* (St. Paul: Graywolf Press, 1988), p. 8.

Walter Grasskamp
"Give Up Painting" or the Politics
of Art: A West German Abstract

1. Günter Grass, "Geschenkte Freiheit" (Speech on 8 May 1985, West Berlin) *Anmerkungen zur Zeit der Akademie der Künste*, no. 24.

2. See the catalogue *Grauzonen Farbwelten. Kunst und Zeitbilder 1945–1955* (Gray zones color worlds: Art and pictures of the era 1945–1955), Bernhard Schulz, editor (West Berlin and Vienna: Neue Gesellschaft für Bildende Kunst, Medusa, 1983); also Walter Grasskamp, "Images of Space," in Christos M. Joachimides et al, editors, *German Art in the Twentieth Century: Painting and Sculpture 1905–1985* (Munich: Prestel, 1985), pp. 137–147.

3. Such were the arguments of, say, the painter Bernard Schultze (*Die Zeit,* 31 May 1985) or the art historian Eberhard Roters in an open letter to Grass.

4. Eduard Beaucamp, *Frankfurter Allgemeine Zeitung*, 29 June 1985.

5. The action was minutely reconstructed and described in Peter Moritz Pickshaus, *Kunstzerstörer. Fallstudien. Tatmotive und Psychogramme* (Art destroyers: Case studies: Motives and psychograms), (Reinbek: 1988), pp. 341–374.

6. Jörg Immendorff, *Hier und Jetzt: Das tun, was zu tun ist* (Here and now: To do what has to be done), (Cologne and New York: Gebrüder König, 1973).

7. Rolf-Gunter Dienst, *Deutsche Kunst: eine neue Generation* (German art: A new generation), (Cologne: M. DuMont Schauberg, 1970), unpaged.

Sally Banes
American Dance and Performance Art:
The Sixties and Seventies

1. See Noël Carrol, *The Philosophy of Horror; or, Paradoxes of the Heart* (New York: Routledge, 1989), for an analysis of the horror genre as the representative genre of our present time, incorporating anxieties about the body and its vulnerability suitable for a postmodern, post–Pax Americana age—a mood exactly opposite to what I am describing in the sixties.

2. Ann Halprin and her improvisational approach to kinesiology was an important early influence on Forti as well as on other postmodern dancers of the sixties.

3. See Simone Forti, *Handbook in Motion* (Halifax, Nova Scotia: The Press of the Nova Scotia College of Art and Design; New York: New York University Press, 1974) for documentation of her early work and its inspirations.

4. Yvonne Rainer, Program, *The Mind is a Muscle*, Anderson Theater, 11, 14, 15 April 1968; reprinted in *Rainer, Work 1961–1973* (Halifax, Nova Scotia: The Press of the Nova Scotia College of Art and Design; New York: New York University Press, 1974), p. 71.

5. See Rainer, *Work 1961–1973* for a full description of these and other dances, her choreographic process, and her trajectory into performance and filmmaking.

6. Normal O. Brown, in *Life Against Death: the Psychoanalytical Meaning of History* (Middletown, Connecticut: Wesleyan University Press, 1959; paperback edition, New York: Random House, 1961), titled the last chapter "The Resurrection of the Body" after Tertullian. Brown's influential book reworked Freudian notions of repression and sublimation and applied them on a cultural (rather than individual) and eschatological level. In the final chapter, Brown calls for a lifting of repression—which can only take place when humankind accepts death as part of life and forsakes genital fixation for the polymorphously perverse sexuality of children—in order to reawaken bodily consciousness and heal the mind-body dualism of Western culture.

For a description of the works by Judson Dance Theater, see Sally Banes, *Democracy's Body: Judson Dance Theater 1962–1964* (Ann Arbor, Michigan: UMI Research Press, 1983).

7. See Michael Kirby, *Happenings: An Illustrated Anthology* (New York: E. P. Dutton, 1966).

8. The most comprehensive work to date on Fluxus is Jon Hendricks, editor, *Fluxus Codex* (Detroit: The Gilbert and Lila Silverman Fluxus Collection; and New York: Harry Abrams, 1989).

9. The description is Jill Johnston's, from her review column "Paxton's People," *Village Voice*, 4 April 1968; reprinted in Jill Johnston, *Marmalade Me* (New York: E. P. Dutton, 1971), pp. 135–137. All of Johnston's dance, performance and art reviews in the *Voice*, *ARTnews* and other publications shed valuable light on this extraordinary period.

10. See Moira Roth, editor, *The Amazing Decade: Women and Performance Art in America, 1970–1980* (Los Angeles: Astro Artz, 1983).

11. See my chapter on the Grand Union in *Terpsichore in Sneakers: Post-Modern Dance* (Boston: Houghton Mifflin, 1980; reprint edition, Middletown, Connecticut: Wesleyan University Press, 1987); and Margaret Ramsay, *The Grand Union: An Improvisational Performance Group* (Ann Arbor, Michigan: UMI Research Press, 1990).

12. See Babette Mangolte's film of *Calico Mingling*.

13. Michael Kirby, Introduction, *The Drama Review* 19 (March 1975) p. 3.

14. For a discussion of the use of the terms postmodern and postmodernist in dance, see the Introduction to the Wesleyan edition of *Terpischore in Sneakers*.

15. See Charles Jencks, *What Is Post-Modernism?* (London: Academy Editions; New York: St. Martin's Press, 1986).

B. Ruby Rich
Don't Look Back: Film and Video from Then to Now

1. By this comment, I do not mean to discount the very rich history of independent, particularly avant-garde, film that developed in the forties, fifties and early sixties. Paul Arthur discusses this epoch in an essay in part one of this volume. I am dealing here only with the currents that led most directly to the concerns of the seventies and eighties that motivate this piece.

2. For more on this perspective, see the article "Avant-Garde and Political Film in the United States," which I coauthored with Chuck Kleinhans. Originally presented as a paper at the Society for Cinema Studies conference in Syracuse, New York, spring 1980, it was published in French in *Cinemaction* 12 (1980).

B. Ruby Rich
Don't Look Back: Film and Video
from Then to Now
(continued)

3. Here, I refer to the Anthology of that time and its symbolic enterprise then, recognizing that the programs taking place at Anthology today are markedly different.

4. See Lillian Jimenez, "From The Margin To The Center: Puerto Rican Cinema in New York" in *Centro* II, no. 8 (New York: Centro de Estudios Puertorriqueños, Hunter College), pp. 28–43, for a discussion of the *Realidades* history in context. Information on *Black Journal* came from discussions at the Whitney Museum's symposium on African-American cinema, 1990.

5. For more details on this epoch, see Clyde Taylor's "The L.A. Rebellion: A Turning Point in Black Cinema" published by the Whitney Museum of American Art (New York, January 1986) and Renee Tajima's "Lights, Camera...Affirmative Action" in *The Independent* 7 (March 1984), pp. 16–18.

6. The New York State Council on the Arts, the agency where I direct the Electronic Media and Film Program, is one of the few funding entities that actually saw its budget increase in the eighties. This is a result of a unique set of circumstances: founded by a Republican governor (Nelson Rockefeller) and today administered by a Democratic governor (Mario Cuomo), the Council benefits from having its own charismatic leader (chairman Kitty Carlisle Hart) as well as from the centralization of arts in New York City that makes economic-support arguments viable. Yet despite these distinct advantages, it has never outstripped the real-dollar budget it had in the economically kinder era of the mid-seventies.

7. This point is acknowledged by the Sundance U.S. Film Festival program staff; see Alberto Garcia and Tony Safford's essay on reviving the raw edge of low-budget independent cinema, "Optimistically toward a 'Cinema of the Rejected'," in the festival's 1990 catalogue.

8. For informed and informative perspectives on two different traditions of relevance here, see: Martha Gever, "Video Politics: Early Feminist Projects" in *Cultures in Contention,* Douglas Kahn and Diane Neumaier, editors (Seattle: Real Comet Press, 1985) and "Seduction Hot And Cold," in *Screen* 28 (Autumn 1987); also, see Deirdre Boyle, "American Documentary Video: Subject To Change," catalogue essay accompanying her exhibition of the same name at the Museum of Modern Art in November 1988 (currently distributed by the American Federation of Arts).

9. At the level of exhibition, see the first curated appearance of AIDS videotapes as a part of *Only Human: Sex, Gender, and Other Misrepresentations,* which I organized together with Bill Horrigan for the American Film Institute's 1987 video festival. Since then, Horrigan has co-organized (with John Greyson) the Video Data Bank's home-video anthology *Video Against AIDS* and curated a number of programs based on that initial AFI presentation. I organized a series of seminars with Douglas Crimp at the New York Institute for the Humanities at New York University in 1988, and Crimp edited a special issue of *October* (Winter 1987) dedicated entirely to AIDS and the media, which was published as *AIDS: Cultural Analysis, Cultural Activism,* Douglas Crimp, editor (Cambridge, Massachusetts: MIT Press, 1988).

10. This is no utopian caveat. The formation of the ITVS, the independent television service created by a national consortium bent on providing funding outside of the CPB umbrella, means that $6 million a year will now be available for film and video makers, hopefully free of the inherited-wisdom that chained the public television money to endless repetition of the same formulae.

New Works for New Spaces:
Into the Nineties

Patricia C. Phillips
Collecting Culture: Paradoxes
and Curiosities

1. Susan Stewart, *On Longing: Narratives of the Miniature, the Gigantic, the Souvenir, the Collection* (Baltimore: Johns Hopkins University Press, 1984), p. 151.

2. Kenneth Hudson, *Museums of Influence* (London: Cambridge University Press, 1987), p. 21.

3. Stewart, *On Longing*, p. 151.

4. Jean-Francois Lyotard, "A Response to Kenneth Frampton," in Lisa Appignanesi, editor, *Postmodernism* (London: Free Association Books, 1989), p. 91.

5. Rene d'Harnoncourt, "Challenge and Promise of Modern Art and Society," *Art News* 48 (November 1949), p. 252.

6. Quotation from a May 1986 interview with Daniel Buren by Suzanne Page in *Daniel Buren*, catalogue conceived and produced by Daniel Buren and Ph. Robert (with l'Association Francaise d'Action Artistique).

A P P E N D I X

The Wexner Center's
Inaugural-Year Progams

The Ohio State University and the Wexner Center for the Arts are deeply grateful to the
following organizations and agencies for their generous support of the Wexner Center's
inaugural-year programs:

The Battelle Memorial Endowment for Technology and Human Affairs; the Wexner Art
Fund of the Columbus Foundation; the New Works Program of the Ohio Arts Council; the
National Endowment for the Arts; Arts Midwest members and friends in partnership with
the National Endowment for the Arts; The Ohio State University; the Ohio Arts Council;
the Ethel Manley Long Fund established by Dr. Frank Clarke Long, Jr.; the Carl E. Haas
Trust; the Fiftieth Anniversary Class Gift contributions of The Ohio State University Class
of 1934; the Class Gift contributions of The Ohio State University Class of 1988; and the
contributions from members of The Ohio State University faculty and staff through the
University Campaign Campaign.

The Wexner Center's series of inaugural exhibitions is dedicated to the architectural vision
and accomplishments of the late Richard W. Trott, FAIA.

Exhibition Checklists

Art in Europe and America: The 1950s and 1960s

Dimensions are for unframed works and are given in inches; unless otherwise noted, height precedes width precedes depth.

Willem de Kooning

Woman 1949–50
oil on canvas
64 ¼ x 46 ¼
Weatherspoon Art Gallery, University of North Carolina at Greensboro; Lena Kernodle McDuffie Memorial Gift, 1954.

Woman 1965
oil on wood
80 x 36
Hirshhorn Museum and Sculpture Garden, Smithsonian Institution, Washington, D.C.; gift of Joseph H. Hirshhorn, 1966.

Woman Accabonic 1966
oil on paper, mounted on canvas
79 x 35
Whitney Museum of American Art, New York; purchase, with funds from the artist and Mrs. Bernard F. Gimbel, 67.75.

Lucio Fontana

Concetto spaziale, "Attese" 1959
aniline on canvas
38 ¾ x 52
Fondazione Lucio Fontana, Milan.

Concetto spaziale, "Attese" 1959
aniline on canvas
40 ⅜ x 50
Collection of Teresita Fontana.

Concetto spaziale, "Attesa" 1960
waterbase paint on canvas
46 ⅜ x 35 ⅝
Collection of Teresita Fontana.

Concetto spaziale, "Venice Moon" 1961
oil on canvas
60 x 60
Collection of Teresita Fontana.

Concetto spaziale 1968
oil on canvas
40 x 32 ⅛
Fondazione Lucio Fontana, Milan.

Eva Hesse

Area 1968
latex on wire mesh and metal wire
240 x 36
Wexner Center for the Arts, The Ohio State University, Columbus; purchased in part with designated funds from Helen Hesse Charash, 1977.001.

Jasper Johns

White Target 1957
wax and oil on canvas
30 x 30
Whitney Museum of American Art, New York; purchase, 71.211.

0 Through 9 1961
oil and charcoal on canvas
54 ⅛ x 41 ⅜
Hirshhorn Museum and Sculpture Garden, Smithsonian Institution, Washington, D.C.; gift of Joseph H. Hirshhorn, 1966.

Subway 1965
sculpmetal over plaster and wood
7 ⅝ x 9 ⅞ x 3
Collection of the artist.

Yves Klein

Anthropometry: Princess Hélena 1960
oil on wood
78 x 50 ½
The Museum of Modern Art, New York; gift of Mr. and Mrs. Arthur Wiesenberger.

ANT 85 1960
blue pigment on paper, mounted on linen
61 ½ x 138 ¾
Private collection.

Piero Manzoni

Merda d'artista 1961
Nos. 003, 006, 010
mixed media
1 ⅞ (height) x 2 ⅜ (diameter)
Courtesy Galleria BLU, Milan.

Linea m. 6 1959
ink on paper
10 ¼ (height) x 2 ⅜ (diameter)
Courtesy Galleria BLU, Milan.

Corpo d'aria No. 11 1959–60
wood box containing a balloon and a metallic base
4 ¹³⁄₁₆ x 19 ³⁄₁₆ x 4 ¹³⁄₁₆
Courtesy Galleria BLU, Milan.

Achrome 1960
polystyrene soaked in cobalt chloride
13 ¾ x 10 ¼
Private collection; courtesy Sperone Westwater, New York.

Achrome 1960
polystyrene soaked in cobalt chloride
25 x 19 ¼
Private collection; courtesy Sperone Westwater, New York.

Linea di lunghezza infinita 1960
wood cylinder
5 ¹⁵⁄₁₆ (height) x 1 ¹⁵⁄₁₆ (diameter)
Courtesy Galleria BLU, Milan.

Linea lunga, 7200 meters 1960
zinc and paper
26 ⅜ (height) x 38 ⅜ (diameter)
Herning Kunstmuseum, Denmark.

Laine de Verre 1961
fiberglass and felt on board
15 ¼ x 17 ¼ x 1 ⅜
Albright-Knox Art Gallery, Buffalo; The Martha Jackson Collection at the Albright-Knox Art Gallery, 1974.

Socle du Monde 1961
iron
32 ¹³⁄₁₆ x 40 x 40
Herning Kunstmuseum, Denmark.

Louise Nevelson

Sky Cathedral Presence 1951–64
painted wood
117 x 174 x 29
Walker Art Center, Minneapolis; gift of Judy and
Kenneth Dayton, 1969.

Young Shadows 1959–60
painted wood
115 x 126 x 7 ¾
Whitney Museum of American Art, New York;
purchase, with funds from the Friends of the Whitney
Museum and Charles Simon, 62.34.

Sky Cathedral: Night Wall 1963–70
painted wood
114 x 171
Columbus Museum of Art, Ohio; gift of Eva Glimcher
and Derby Fund Purchase.

Claes Oldenburg

Soft Pay-Telephone 1963
vinyl filled with kapok, mounted on painted wood
panel
46 ½ x 19 x 9
Solomon R. Guggenheim Museum, New York; gift,
Ruth and Philip Zierler in memory of their dear
departed son, William S. Zierler, 1980.

Giant Pool Balls 1967
sixteen fiberglass balls, each 24" diameter, on
wood rack
24 x 120 x 108
Los Angeles County Museum of Art; anonymous gift
through the Contemporary Art Council, M.69.88.

Three-Way Plug—Scale A, Soft, Brown 1975
naugahyde
144 x 77 x 59
Walker Art Center, Minneapolis; gift of the artist,
1979.

Robert Rauschenberg

Minutiae 1954 (replica)
freestanding construction: oil, fabric, paper, metal,
plastic, wood with mirror on string
84 ¾ x 81 x 30 ½
Cunningham Dance Foundation Inc., New York.

Memorandum of Bids 1957
combine painting
59 x 44 ½
Sonnabend Collection, New York.

Gift for Apollo 1959
freestanding combine
43 ¾ x 29 ½
The Museum of Contemporary Art, Los Angeles;
The Panza Collection.

Niki de Saint Phalle

Nana c. 1965
mixed media
50 x 36 x 31
Albright-Knox Art Gallery, Buffalo; gift of Seymour H.
Knox, 1978.

Black Venus 1967
painted polyester
110 x 35 x 24
Whitney Museum of American Art, New York; gift of
the Howard and Jean Lipman Foundation, Inc., 68.73.

Frank Stella

Untitled 1959
cardboard and enamel paint on wood
33 x 61 ¼
Wexner Center for the Arts, The Ohio State University,
Columbus; purchased in part with funds from the
National Endowment for the Arts.

Union Pacific 1960
aluminum paint on canvas
77 ¼ x 148 ½
Nathan Emory Coffin Collection of the Des Moines Art
Center; Coffin Fine Arts Trust Fund, 1976.

Jean Tinguely

Relief métamécanique 1956
mixed media
18 ¹³⁄₁₆ x 49 ³⁄₁₆ x 6 ¹³⁄₁₆
Louisiana Museum of Modern Art, Humlebaek,
Denmark.

Balouba vert 1962
mixed media
54 x 20 ¹³⁄₁₆ x 16 ¹³⁄₁₆
Louisiana Museum of Modern Art, Humlebaek,
Denmark.

Jean Tinguely with Niki de Saint Phalle

M.O.N.S.T.R.E. 1964
freestanding motorized assemblage: cast iron and
welded steel, rubber, painted papier-mâché with
newsprint and gauze over wire; with plastic flowers,
plastic panther and soldiers, metal wheel, plaster skull,
rubber knife, cord, lace and cloth fibers.
88 ⅝ x 60 ¾ x 38, without base
Menil Collection, Houston.

Andy Warhol
Daisy 1970
mixed-media installation with photographs, pipes,
tanks, water
132 x 248 x 96
Private collection; courtesy Ronald Feldman Fine Arts,
Inc., New York.

Art in Europe and America:
The 1960s and 1970s

John Baldessari

Examining Pictures 1967
acrylic on canvas
67 ⅞ x 56 ½
Courtesy Sonnabend Gallery, New York.

Space 1967
acrylic on canvas
67 ¾ x 56 ⅜
Courtesy Sonnabend Gallery, New York.

Subject Matter 1967
acrylic on canvas
67 ¾ x 56 ½
Courtesy Sonnabend Gallery, New York.

Lynda Benglis

Untitled 1968
encaustic-damar resin on masonite
36 x 4 ½
Collection of Nancy and George Rosenfeld.

Contraband 1969
poured pigmented latex
1 x 108 x 405
Courtesy Paula Cooper Gallery, New York.

For Carl Andre 1970
pigmented polyurethane foam
56 ¼ x 53 ½ x 46 ³⁄₁₆
Modern Art Museum of Fort Worth; museum
purchase, The Benjamin J. Tillar Memorial Trust.

Plum 1971
purified pigmented beeswax and damar resin on
masonite and wood
35 x 5 ⅛ x 2 ¾
Collection of Mr. and Mrs. Harry W. Anderson.

Joseph Beuys

Untitled 1963
child's red wool glove holding candy in a wooden box
12 ³⁄₁₆ x 4 ⅝ x 2 ⅝
Collection of Lucio Amelio, Naples, Italy.

JaJaJaJaNeeNeeNeeNee 1969
felt sculpture containing a recorded tape
6 x 10 x 10
Collection of Lucio Amelio, Naples, Italy.

Sled 1969
sled of wood, felt, belt, torch, lard
14 x 36 x 14
Collection of Lucio Amelio, Naples, Italy.

Sulphur Box 1970
zinc box covered with sulphur and containing gauze
25 ³⁄₁₆ x 12 ³⁄₁₆ x 7 ³⁄₁₆
Collection of Lucio Amelio, Naples, Italy.

*Backrest for a Fine-Limbed Person (Hare-Type) of the
20th Century A.D.* 1973
iron corset
38 ⅜ x 18 x 6 ⅜
Collection of Lucio Amelio, Naples, Italy.

Joseph Beuys (continued)

Enterprise 1973
zinc box, black-and-white photo, camera, felt
16 x 12 x 6 ⅜
Collection of Lucio Amelio, Naples, Italy.

Record: Scottish Symphony/Requiem of Art 1973
2 long-playing records in double jacket
12 ⅜ x 12 ⅜
Collection of Lucio Amelio, Naples, Italy.

The Silence 1973
five reels of the movie by Ingmar Bergman "The
Silence" covered with zinc and contained in a
cardboard box
10 x 17 ³/₁₆ x 17 ³/₁₆
Collection of Lucio Amelio, Naples, Italy.

Sun Disc 1973
metal disc with felt in a cardboard box
15 ³/₁₆ x 15 ³/₁₆ x 1 ⅝
Collection of Lucio Amelio, Naples, Italy.

Green Violin 1974
green violin
24 x 8 ¹³/₁₆ X 4
Collection of Lucio Amelio, Naples, Italy.

Telephon S_____ ꟻ 1974
two tin cans connected with a string of jute
81 ⅝ x 40
Collection of Lucio Amelio, Naples, Italy.

Bruno Corà-Tee 1975
box with bottle containing an herbal tea
11 ⅝ x 4 ⅜ x 4 ³/₁₆
Collection of Lucio Amelio, Naples, Italy.

Fish Bone 1985
wooden box with fishbone
11 ⅝ x 4 ⅝ x 4 ³/₁₆
Collection of Lucio Amelio, Naples, Italy.

Scala Napoletana 1985
wooden ladder and two spheres of lead
176 x 10; diameter of spheres, 20
Estate of Joseph Beuys; courtesy of Lucio Amelio,
Naples, Italy.

Louise Bourgeois

Labyrinthine Tower c. 1962
plaster
height: 18
Courtesy Robert Miller Gallery, New York.

Rondeau for L 1963
bronze
11 x 11 x l0 ½
Courtesy Robert Miller Gallery, New York.

Torso, Self Portrait 1963–64
bronze, white patina
24 ¾ x l6 x 7 ⅛
Courtesy Robert Miller Gallery, New York.

Janus in Leather Jacket 1968
bronze
12 x 22 x 6 ½
Courtesy Robert Miller Gallery, New York.

Noir Veine l968
black marble
23 x 24 x 27
Collection of Jerry Gorovoy; courtesy Robert Miller
Gallery, New York.

Gilbert & George

Lick 1977
95 x 79
Collection of Martin Sklar.

The Queue 1978
95 x 79
Collection of Robert J. Dodds III.

Taxi 1978
95 ¼ x 74 ⅜
The Arthur and Carol Goldberg Collection.

Donald Judd

Untitled 1965
lacquer paint on aluminum
8 ¼ X 161 X 8 ¼
Wexner Center for the Arts, The Ohio State University,
Columbus; purchased in part with funds from the
National Endowment for the Arts, 77.24.

Untitled 1966
amber plexiglass and stainless steel
20 x 48 x 34
Froehlich Collection, Stuttgart, West Germany.

Untitled 1969
anodized aluminium
114 x 27 x 24, ten units, each unit 6 x 27 x 24
Walker Art Center, Minneapolis; gift of Mr. and Mrs.
Edmond R. Ruben, 1981.

Jannis Kounellis

Untitled 1980
propane gas torches attached to a cello, mandolin,
flute, trumpet, drum, violin and trombone
dimensions variable
Collection of Marielle and Paul Mailhot.

Agnes Martin

White Flower l960
oil on canvas
7l ⅞ x 72
Solomon R. Guggenheim Museum, New York;
anonymous gift, 1963.

Falling Blue 1963
oil and pencil on canvas
71 ⅞ x 72
San Francisco Museum of Modern Art;
gift of Mr. and Mrs. Moses Lasky.

Nam June Paik

Magnet TV 1965
black-and-white, 17-inch television set with magnet
28 ⅜ x 19 ¼ x 24 ½
Whitney Museum of American Art, New York;
purchase, with funds from Dieter Rosenkranz, 86.60a-b.

TV Chair 1968
standard metal-frame chair, lucite seat, plastic
backing, suspended TV set
30 x 20 x 20
Collection of Allan Kaprow.

18th Century TV late 1960s
vintage wood TV cabinet with antique oriental scroll,
aerial, electric light and stand, masking tape
17 ¾ x 15 ¾ x 7; aerial height: 18
Collection of Peter and Barbara Moore.

TV Glasses 1971
Reconstruction by the artist
mixed media
12 x 12 (estimated)
Collection of the artist.

TV Buddha 1974
2-part video-installation with wooden, 18th-century
Buddha, camera, monitor
dimensions variable: 64 x 86 x 32
Stedelijk Museum, Amsterdam, The Netherlands.

Adrian Piper

Four Intruders Plus Alarm Systems 1980
installation: bounded environment, four silkscreened
light boxes, four audio monologues, audio music
soundtrack
72 (height) x 60 (diameter)
Wexner Center for the Arts, The Ohio State University,
Columbus; purchased in part with funds from The
National Endowment for the Arts, 83.15.

Sigmar Polke

Untitled 1971
acrylic and chalk on cloth
51 ¾ x 61
Collection of Bette Ziegler.

Menschkin 1972
oil on fabric
39 ½ x 31 ½
Collection of Elaine and Werner Dannheiser.

Susan Rothenberg

Siena Dos Equis 1974
acrylic and tempera on canvas
144 x 274
Private collection; courtesy Sperone Westwater,
New York.

Blue Frontal 1978
acrylic, flashe and tempera on canvas
77 x 88 ½
Private collection; courtesy Sperone Westwater, New York.

Robert Smithson

Gravel Mirror with Cracks and Dust 1968
mirrors and gravel: six leaning wall mirrors and six floor mirrors, each 36" x 36"
36 x 216 x 36
Estate of Robert Smithson; courtesy John Weber Gallery, New York.

New Works For New Spaces: Into the Nineties

Magdalena Abakanowicz

Winged Trunk 1989
wood and iron
Courtesy, Marlborough Gallery, New York.

Gretchen Bender

Aggressive Witness–Active Participant 1990
multi-monitor installation with videotape, live television and sound
Commissioned by the Wexner Center for the Arts; collection of the artist. The artist wishes to thank Mitsubishi International.

Chris Burden

The Wexner Castle 1990
lumber, foam and paint
Commissioned by the Wexner Center for the Arts; collection of the artist.

Malcolm Cochran

Western Movie 1990
16mm film, coin-operated horses, lead, wood, theater seats; transparency of Frederic Edwin Church's *Niagara* (Corcoran Gallery of Art)
Commissioned by the Wexner Center for the Arts; collection of the artist. The artist wishes to thank Skip Stander, Clayton Wolf, Bruce Thompson, Juan Granados, Henry Zinck, David Driscoll and Diane Craft.

Fortuyn/O'Brien

Marble Public 1990
marble
Commissioned by the Wexner Center for the Arts; collection of the artist. The artist wishes to thank Claudio Giannini, Studio Balderi.

Ann Hamilton

dominion 1990
corn cobs, corn husks, corn meal, paper, bassinet, fabric, wood and moths
Commissioned by the Wexner Center for the Arts; collection of the artist. The artist wishes to thank George Keeney, Debbie Griffins, Dareth Gerlach, Monny Postle; Beth, Dean, and Diane Henry; Dana Wrensch, Herb and Nancy Postle, Jo and Bill Ketcham, Ann Jackson, Beth and Bob Hamilton, Carol Clark and the Columbus School for Girls art students, Jane and Dick Paul, Gay Hadley, Sue and Norval Goss, Clara Owens, Teen Harter, Liz Galbreath, Emalene Hoover, Sally Meier, Sally McDonald, Marty and Gale Johnson, Wendy Johnson, Kate Haller, Leah Reis, Lydia Hadley, Todd DeVreise, Jeff Freppon, Nole Giulini, Britta Kathmeyer, Carolyn Eicher, Marguerite Kahn, Randy Moore, Ann Lewis, Miriam Ferrari, Marjorie Snouffer, Elaine Smith, Susie Taylor, Jo Duran, Lili-Beth Hamilton, Rachel Timmons, The Ohio State University College of Agriculture and Department of Entomology and all the crew at the Wexner Center.

Tadashi Kawamata

Sidewalk in Columbus, Ohio 1990
lumber
Commissioned by the Wexner Center for the Arts; collection of the artist. The artist wishes to thank Pug Heller, Stephen Montague, Edward Myers and The Ohio State University community.

Joseph Kosuth

'Ex Libris, Columbus (for W.B.)' 1990
neon
Commissioned by the Wexner Center for the Arts; collection of the artist.

Barbara Kruger

Untitled (Why Are You Here?) 1990
silkscreen on paper
Commissioned by the Wexner Center for the Arts; collection of the artist.

Untitled (What Makes History While It Does Business?) 1990
silkscreen on paper
Commissioned by the Wexner Center for the Arts; collection of the artist.

Untitled (Whose Body Is a Battleground?) 1990
silkscreen on paper
Commissioned by the Wexner Center for the Arts; collection of the artist.

Untitled (Your Body Is a Battleground) 1990
outdoor billboard project, Columbus, 7 locations
Commissioned by the Wexner Center for the Arts; collection of the artist.

Sol LeWitt

The Tower 1990
concrete block and mortar
Commissioned by the Wexner Center for the Arts; collection of the artist.

Christian Marclay

The Clock 1990
aluminum clamps, mechanical strikers and timer
Commissioned by the Wexner Center for the Arts; collection of the artist.

MICA-TV
Carole Ann Klonarides, Michael Owen

The Inbetween 1990
color, stereo, 12-minute videotape
Commissioned by the Wexner Center for the Arts; collection of the artist.

Gilberto Zorio

La Sedia di Marzio (Marzio's chair) 1988
metal, compressor, plastic, rubber, copper and water
Courtesy, Sonnabend Gallery, New York.

La Canoa di Columbus (The Columbus canoe) 1990
fiberglass, canoe, motor, one timer, one lamp, two copper tubes, six metal bars and one transformer
Commissioned by the Wexner Center for the Arts; collection of the artist.

Performing Arts

The privilege of developing a performing arts program at the Wexner Center lies in the breadth of the territory we are able to explore in dance, music, theater and performance art. We have an unusual and welcome mandate to present classical works alongside recent experiments and so to provide a forum in which to investigate connections between the two.

A vital contemporary art center should be an environment responsive to the multiplicity of creative ideas that reflect and confront contemporary society. The ideas we express through music, light, movement and dialogue are like artifacts that document our aspirations. Too often we forget that the cultural contributions that will best represent those aspirations to future audiences are ones that offer critical observations, challenge assumptions and contribute to the exchange of ideas.

The dangers potentially facing the arts in a democratic system were outlined as early as 1835, when de Tocqueville's *Democracy in America* was published. De Tocqueville predicted that, in a democracy without aristocratic patronage, the demand for increased artistic productivity would diminish the time available for artists to make great strides in their disciplines, to create great works. He suggested that art produced in this democracy would adorn or entertain rather than illuminate social or political conditions.

Living in a culture that often regards art as entertainment or commodity, we tend to measure quality by success in the marketplace. We fail to separate the values of capitalism and democracy. Patronage in the arts has spread itself thin in this century. The easy course has been to fall back on time-tested, time-honored artistic products, to trust the market's values. A more difficult approach is to invest in artists, to give them significant creative time in which to work. This is still the greatest gesture a patron can make. As the performing arts programs at the Wexner Center evolve, we plan to focus on the creative artist, the originator or conceiver of a work, as well as on the performers; we hope to be a patron as well as a presenter. Through commissions and residencies, we will endeavor to give artists time to work with themes that recognize the complexity of our society.

This nation's experiment in democracy is a remarkable contribution to humankind. But it's an experiment that needs to be reinforced with constant dialogue. Art, the humanities and education are perhaps the most useful tools in maintaining that dialogue. The United States is no longer a society dominated by a single Western European tradition. The rapid changes that have created this situation have been disconcerting and alienating for many. Art has the ability to draw people back together, to open new lines of communication. But if we only present and support art from past cultures and time periods, we will leave a legacy of silence about the complex present.

This country must focus its mind and resources on creating and supporting art that breaks that silence and, in doing so, strikes an intellectual or emotional common chord. Striking that common chord has become increasingly difficult in a time of intolerance, strident opinions and radically opposing views. Many of us seek respite from controversy by refusing to confront upsetting ideas, and, as a result, we become ever more isolated and frozen in our own convictions. Unless we can engage in the kind of dialogue that rigorous art engenders, we will remain trapped. But if we can help provide rigorous and inclusive art, we each can make significant contributions to a dialogue about our world as it is today. The work we accomplish will provide a window through which future creators and audiences will be able to view our ideas and our struggles. If music is, as Plato described it, "the medium of the soul in its most ecstatic condition of wonder and terror," and other art forms continually juggle the balance between passion and reason, we have very powerful tools with which to build a common language out of our diversity.

The eventual strength of a performing arts program such as that at the Wexner Center will derive from a curious blend of anticipating the tastes of the community and developing a point of view in the programming that is put forward. Through the presentations of our inaugural year, we have begun to develop and enunciate our point of view.

William B. Cook, Director of Performing Arts

Performing Arts Checklist

Martha Graham Dance Company
17–18 November 1989

The Best of Serious Fun: Charles Moulton, Guy Klucevsek, Scott Johnson, Frank Maya, Dan Kotlowitz
6 December 1989

And More . . .: Shrimps, Jawole Willa Jo Zollar, Joe Goode, Golden Sea with David Murray and Kahil El'Zabar, Olu Dara and his Natchezsippi Dance Band
8–9 December 1989

John Cage
16 January 1990

Rhythm in Shoes and the Horseflies
19–20 January 1990

David Parsons Company*
26 January 1990

Paul Dresher Ensemble with Rinde Eckert
27 January 1990

Herbie Hancock Trio
2 February 1990

Pinchas Zucherman
8 February 1990

John Jesurun*
8–11 February 1990

Merce Cunningham Dance Company
16–17 February 1990

Spalding Gray
21–25 February 1990

David Cale
1-3 March 1990

Laurie Anderson
7 March 1990

Stephen Petronio and Company*
9 March 1990

Reggie Workman Ensemble
31 March 1990

Mabou Mines
4–8 April 1990

Academy of St. Martin in the Fields
5 April 1990

Dana Reitz
27–28 April 1990

Edwina Lee Tyler
10–12 May 1990

Los Angeles Philharmonic
16 May 1990

Molissa Fenley
17–19 May 1990

Steve Reich and Musicians
2 June 1990

Grand Kabuki Theater
4–5 June 1990

Columbus Dance Works
21–23 June 1990

Spalding Gray
25–26 September 1990

Jay Bolotin with Bebe Miller
4–6 October 1990

Bebe Miller and Company
11–14 October 1990

Moscow Virtuosi
12 October 1990

Edward Adelson & Thomas Wells
(in cooperation with the School of Music, The Ohio State University)
21 October 1990

John Kelly
25–27 October 1990

Japan Philharmonic Symphony
28 October 1990

Trisha Brown, The Early Years
31 October 1990

Trisha Brown Company*
2 November 1990

Sankai Juku
10 November 1990

Stephan Möller
(in cooperation with the School of Music, The Ohio State University)
11 November 1990

Women of the Calabash
(cosponsored with the Frank W. Hale, Jr. Black Cultural Center, The Ohio State University)
17 November 1990

The White Oak Dance Project with Mikhail Baryshnikov, choreography by Mark Morris
17 November 1990

Karen Finley
14–17 November 1990

Alwin Bar
(in cooperation with the School of Music, The Ohio State University)
25 November 1990

Dianne McIntyre
29 November–1 December 1990

Kronos Quartet
30 November-1 December 1990

The Paul Taylor Dance Company
17 January 1991

Emerson String Quartet
20 January 1991

Eiko & Komo
23-26 January 1991

Juilliard String Quartet/Billy Taylor Trio
25 January 1991

Joe Goode Performance Group
7–9 February 1991

Bill T. Jones/Arnie Zane & Co.
15 February 1991

Da Capo Chamber Players
21–22 February 1991

Art Ensemble of Chicago
23 February 1991

Susan Marshall & Company
28 February-3 March 1991

Meredith Monk/Houston Grand Opera
9 March 1991

Schoenberg Quartet
15 March 1991

Ivo Pogorelich
21 March 1991

New World Symphony/Michael Tilson Thomas
2 April 1991

Guillermo Gómez-Peña
5–6 April 1991

The Wooster Group*
10–14 April 1991

Arditti String Quartet
11 April 1991

John Zorn's Naked City
19 April 1991

Henry Threadgill
20 April 1991

Metropolitan Opera Orchestra/James Levine
1 May 1991

Susan Hadley/Bradley Sowash*
1–4 May 1991

Programming by William B. Cook, Director of Performing Arts, and Carla Peterson, Assistant Director of Performing Arts.

* Presentations featuring works commissioned or cocommissioned by the Wexner Center for the Arts.

Media Arts

As in thinking about the history of an industrially based cinema, it would be possible to imagine a history of the traditions of independent (or "avant-garde") film and video from the viewpoint of "breaking" texts—works that break ground, break through or break away. It's one description of history. A different description would involve positing a structural or lyrical or critical essence, then tracking its persistence across time and adversity to a final yielding of tradition. The former idea is based on a mechanical empiricism unembarrassed by the concomitant thirst for aesthetic "masterpieces" (and never has to wonder why there are so few). It is also, like the latter idea, serenely able and willing to divine history before it's realized in word and deed, since history is construed as a fulfillment of a system of values, signs, urgencies and occasions—a transcendent system falling to some people as birthright, to some as a legacy and to some as a curse.

Of the available chronicles of this country's independent film and video traditions, as many have been illuminated by ardent reason as have plodded with none. In imagining a series of film and video events unevenly paralleled but nonetheless suggested by the first two components of the Wexner Center's inaugural trilogy of painting and sculpture exhibitions—that is, in admitting a selective version of the historical record—the goal was neither just to interpret that history nor from tendentiousness to assault it, but to propose a modest, admiring configuration staying mostly, though not wholly, within the idea of this avant-garde, this independence, as many observers would recognize it. It's a further figure in the carpet.

Hence, these two series (*An American Avant-Garde: 1935–1970; Independents: 1970–1990*) were as little interested in protecting a canon as in overturning one, two activities better left to those for whom the will to power is a hedge against chaos. And yet it's clear that for this country's alternative cinema and video accomplishments, something close enough to a chain of canons has been forged, emerging, as canons will, from the collusion of factors including partisan interpretive commentary, curatorial taste and alliance, professional and personal patronage, the fashion and spirit of the moment and the fluctuating opportunities and demands of the market. That's a given, a point of departure.

Of the ten film artists featured in *An American Avant-Garde*, the earliest, Joseph Cornell, produced intermittently (aided by such stellar assistants as Stan Brakhage, Rudy Burckhardt and Larry Jordan, among others) a series of short films sharing with his coveted boxes a fondness for pastiche and gentle reverie but having, some of them, a *plein-air* vivacity rarely associated with the boxes, which speak precisely as interiors. Predating his short works, Cornell's *Rose Hobart* (1936) remains astonishing in the way it anticipates with such rigor the pursuit of visual obsession, artifice and star-gazing that will come to move throughout the personal film practices of subsequent decades. *Rose Hobart* is, among other miracles, a record or admittance of failure: the desire to possess the fantasized object, the pretext for the delirium, is ruthlessly (not a word commonly credited to Cornell) acknowledged and enacted, but only in the shadowy terms the fantasy extends.

The nine filmmakers subsequent to Cornell included in the series are not overly beholden, so far as one knows, to his example (though Ken Jacobs recalls the shock of influence). That acknowledgment counters the inclination to regard this group as having, or as having imposed on it, a linear coherence—as forming a tradition or an atelier of filmmaking. That denial persists despite what they do share: eight of them—Cornell, Jacobs, Marie Menken, Peter Emanuel Goldman, Carolee Schneemann, Barbara Rubin, Alfred Leslie and Jonas Mekas (who wrote about them all)—worked or work primarily in and around, and hence visualize, New York City, often having drifted amid overlapping turfs. Paul Arthur remarks upon that coincidence elsewhere in this volume, asking, "In what ways can the American avant-garde be construed as a branch of documentary practice whose primary, though not exclusive, focus is the visual patterning of New York?"

But what these artists share as a more binding feature comes from the figurative location they all inherit and cultivate—the speaking position they own. As film artists, their medium has been (prior to television) the century's global medium, which in its industrial/Hollywood incarnation—the studio-made fiction film—has in this epoch determined how a culture proclaims and denies all that it would be. The film artists here have taken up the same basic tools, but their relation to the medium has by and large been artisanal rather than industrial. That has a bearing certainly on everything else: on the internal and external constraints and contours of their work, on where it might be expected to be seen and by whom, on a radically different relation between the maker and the audience, on the relativity of production values and of values related to acting standards, emotional engagement and so on.

By triumphing worldwide, the studio-made fiction film has been confirmed as the standard of cinematic measure; and in producing work for a public, for any "public," these film artists inevitably are seen to be maneuvering in relation to that standard. Sometimes it's a relation of authentic disregard: Marie Menken, a miniaturist who *assumed* film with the same joy as one assumes painting. Sometimes it's a relation of authentic malregard: Jonas Mekas, the diarist, tilting at protocol; or Barbara Rubin, a libertarian theologian of the physical and universally wounded body; or Carolee Schneemann, demanding full control of *her* image.

Sometimes the regard is quizzical, then piercing: Ken Jacobs, the fixer of appearances; or Alfred Leslie, sensitive to beatific manner and structure; or Bruce Conner, whose invention of *trouvaille* is virtually scientific. Sometimes there's a regard of honest, hence lonely, longing: the Cornell of *Rose Hobart*, a masterpiece of really judicious desire; and sometimes of ambivalent aspiration, as with Peter Emanuel Goldman's *Echoes of Silence*, his downbeat portrait of the artist as a young *flâneur*. And sometimes when the regard is in some respects the closest, it's at heart the most deeply distanced. Spencer Williams produced narrative feature films, more or less on the studio system model, yet the visitations he was able to make within these stories (*The Blood of Jesus, Go Down Death*) of a profoundly held religious sensibility shaped by the structures and sentiments of African-American musical and folk idioms free his work from the inhibiting secularity of the narrative feature films of his time: here is visionary cinema.

•

As B. Ruby Rich argues elsewhere in this volume, the practice and direction of independent film over the past several decades was radically altered by, among other factors, the emerging availability of video as a flexible, affordable medium. More fundamental differences between the "heroic" period of the American avant-garde (a moment given lapidary finality by P. Adams Sitney in his book *Visionary Film*) and the eventual trajectory of independent work in the subsequent decades of the seventies and eighties, as Rich elaborates them, include the gravitation of avant-garde film towards the mainstream (taking the form of dozens of artists all of a sudden "working on my feature"), the efflorescence of engaged documentaries alert to new tendencies in anthropology, ethnography and historiography and, most crucially, the entry of new practitioners—women, people of color, lesbians and gay men—into film and video institutions.

The representation of artists in *Independents* was intended to keep faith with those developments—again, not to propose an orthodoxy but to recognize the field's contours and to pay admiration to artists whose ongoing work enriches their already salutary contributions. Continuing to alternate among several artistic fronts, Nancy Holt and Vito Acconci engaged video early on, subjecting it to inquiries compatible with the conceptual interrogations each was making elsewhere of the art object as both experience and commodity. Another video pioneer, the late Lyn Blumenthal, is recognized as much for her own production as an artist as for her cofounding, with Kate Horsefield, of the Video Data Bank, which grew from a virtually unfunded labor of love into one of this country's most estimable distributors and defenders of video art. General Idea, a Canadian trio working in video, film, gallery exhibitions and publications, produce interventions targeted at an art world too often pleased by its own devices and besotted by "glamour."

In some respects extending the achievements of the tradition of "personal" film-making, Marjorie Keller and James Herbert both produce works of astonishing visual resonance, with Keller producing meticulous variations on the diaristic mode and Herbert, with his signature strategy of rephotography, elaborating upon the painterly preoccupation with the nude. Equally celebrated as a photographer, Danny Lyon brings to his films the range of his interests, particularly with reference to subcultures and family relationships. Ohio-based Richard Myers has been producing remarkable feature-length films for over three decades, works each different from the last but all evincing his capacity for speaking of personal preoccupations within continually inventive formal terms. Also working with, and thereby reinventing, the feature-film format are Mark Rappaport and Charles Burnett, the New York–based Rappaport producing witty and idiosyncratic commentaries on overly cultured urban lives and the Los Angeles–based Burnett opening a view onto the dreams and frustrations of African-Americans in a frequently stultifying culture.

Starting out as a dancer and choreographer, Yvonne Rainer, by remaining attuned to the misgivings and perceived contradictions triggered by sexual difference and political inequality, continues to produce feature films noted for their provocations; too seldom acknowledged is their evocation of compassion. Vietnamese-born Trinh T. Minh-ha, making common cause with "the new ethnography," has decisively challenged the complacencies and the obscuring of those documentary practices that allege to reveal "alien" cultures.

Filmmaker Curt McDowell, who died prematurely from AIDS, had, judging from the record of his work, a happy life, happiest perhaps when deploying film as an agent in the fulfillment of sexual desire. As one of the growing number of artists consumed by the AIDS epidemic and as such, like everyone else touched by this blight, "innocent," McDowell and the example of his work serve as a bracing caution against the looming wave of legislative and demagogically organized reprisals that intend to turn back the victories scored in recent decades for freedom of expression and fundamental civil rights.

●

When told of the filmmakers to be included in the first series, *An American Avant-Garde*, a friend pondered a bit before remarking, by way of conditional endorsement, "fragments of a failed enterprise." Let it stand for both projects. In the understanding this epithet discloses of these artists' aspirations to discover ways of making mechanical vision bear the gift and burden of inner vision (enterprises majestically destined to "fail" except in epiphanic fragment: hence the origin of grace), it might remain to authorize the decisions whereby this work and these people have been brought together here.

William Horrigan, Curator of Media Arts

Media Arts Checklist

An American Avant-Garde: 1935–1970

Joseph Cornell

Rose Hobart (1936/39)
Aviary (1955; photographed by Rudy Burckhardt)
Joanne, Union Square (1955; photographed by Rudy Burckhardt)
Centuries of June (1955; photographed by Stan Brakhage)
GniR RednoW (1955; Cornell's "mirrored" version of *The Wonder Ring*, photographed by Stan Brakhage)
Mulberry Street (1957; photographed by Rudy Burckhardt; edited by Larry Jordan)
Nymphlight (1957; photographed by Rudy Burckhardt)
A Legend for Fountains (1957/70; photographed by Rudy Burckhardt, edited by Larry Jordan)
Bookstalls (date unknown; restored 1978)
Vaudeville De-Luxe (date unknown; restored 1978)
New York–Rome-Barcelona-Brussels (date unknown; restored 1979)
By Night with Torch and Spear (date unknown; restored 1979)
2 March 1990

Marie Menken

Visual Variations on Noguchi (1945)
Hurry! Hurry! (1957)
Dwightiana (1957)
Glimpse of the Garden (1957)
Eye Music in Red Major (1961)
Arabesque for Kenneth Anger (1961)
Bagatelle for Willard Mass (1961)
Go! Go! Go! (1963)
Wrestling (1964)
Andy Warhol (1965)
9 March 1990

Spencer Williams

The Blood of Jesus (1941)
Go Down Death (1944)
16 March 1990

Ken Jacobs

Blonde Cobra (1958–69; images gathered by Bob Fleischner, sound-film composed by Jacobs)
Little Stabs at Happiness (1958/63)
Little Stabs at Happiness addenda: Orchard Street (1956, unfinished); *Sat. Afternoon Blood Sacrifice: TV Plug: Little Cobra Dance* and *Reveling in the Dumps* (1957–64); *The Death of P'town* (1961); *Naomi Is A Vision of Loveliness* (1965)
Globe (1969)
Grandma's House (Bob Fleischner; 1965)
Two Wrenching Departures (1989; A Nervous System Film Performance)
30–31 March 1990

Alfred Leslie

Pull My Daisy (1959; directed, adapted and photographed by Alfred Leslie and Robert Frank; written and narrated by Jack Kerouac)
11 April 1990

Bruce Conner

A Movie (1958)
Cosmic Ray (1961–62)
Report (1963–67)
Marilyn Times Five (1969–73)
Crossroads (1976)
Mongoloid (1977)
America Is Waiting (1981)
11 April 1990

Jonas Mekas

Film Magazine of the Arts (1963)
Award Presentation to Andy Warhol (1964)
Walden (filmed 1964–68; edited 1968–69)
Lost, Lost, Lost (filmed 1949–63; edited 1976)
18 April 1990

Carolee Schneemann

Fuses (1964–67)
Plumb Line (1968–72)
25 April 1990

Barbara Rubin

Christmas on Earth (1963)
Emunah (aka *Emouna*) (1972–73; made in collaboration with Pamela Badyk Mayo and City College of New York film students)
25 April 1990

Peter Emanuel Goldman

Echoes of Silence (1965)
4 May 1990

Independents: 1970–1990

Trinh T. Minh-ha

Surname Viet Given Name Nam (1989)
26 May 1990

Curt McDowell

A Visit to Indiana (1970)
Ronnie (1972)
True Blue and Dreamy (1974)
Confessions (1971)
Nudes: A Sketchbook (1975)
Loads (1980)
7 June 1990

Nancy Holt

East Coast, West Coast (1969; Nancy Holt and Robert Smithson)
Locating No. 2 (1972)
Underscan (1974)
Art in the Public Eye: The Making of Dark Star Park (1988)
14 June 1990

Lyn Blumenthal

Lyn Blumenthal Memorial Tape (1988; produced by Kate Horsefield and Branda Miller)
Joseph Beuys (1975; produced by Lyn Blumenthal and Kate Horsefield)
Louise Bourgeois (1975; produced by Lyn Blumenthal and Kate Horsefield)
14 June 1990

Richard Myers

Moving Pictures (1989)
13 July 1990

Vito Acconci

Home Movies (1973)
10 October 1990

Danny Lyon

Social Sciences 127 (1969)
Little Boy (1977)
10 October 1990

Marjorie Keller

Misconception (1977)
Daughters of Chaos (1980)
17 October 1990

James Herbert

Apalachee (1974)
Two Figures (1980)
Automan (1989)
Piano (1989)
17 October 1990

General Idea

Loco (1985)
Cornucopia (1982)
Shut the Fuck Up (1985)
24 October 1990

Mark Rappaport

Imposters (1979)
24 October 1990

Yvonne Rainer

The Man Who Envied Women (1985)
Privelege (1990)
1, 3 November 1990

Charles Burnett

Killer of Sheep (1978)
6 December 1990

Lenders to the Exhibitions

Lucio Amelio
Mr. and Mrs. Harry W. Anderson
Gretchen Bender
Estate of Joseph Beuys
Chris Burden
Malcolm Cochran
Elaine and Werner Dannheiser
Robert J. Dodds III
Teresita Fontana
Fortuyn/O'Brien
J. W. Froehlich Collection
The Arthur and Carol Goldberg Collection
Jerry Gorovoy
Ann Hamilton
Jasper Johns
Tadashi Kawamata
Allan Kaprow
Joseph Kosuth
Barbara Kruger
Sol LeWitt
Christian Marclay
Marielle and Paul Mailhot
MICA-TV (Carole Ann Klonarides,
    Michael Owen)
Peter and Barbara Moore
Nam June Paik
Nancy and George Rosenfeld
Martin Sklar
Estate of Robert Smithson
Sonnabend Collection
Bette Ziegler
Gilberto Zorio
Private Collectors

Albright-Knox Art Gallery, Buffalo
Columbus Museum of Art, Ohio
Paula Cooper Gallery, New York
Cunningham Dance Foundation Inc.,
    New York
Des Moines Art Center
Ronald Feldman Fine Arts, Inc., New York
Fondazione Lucio Fontana, Milan, Italy
Galleria BLU, Milan, Italy
Solomon R. Guggenheim Museum,
    New York
Herning Kunstmuseum, Denmark
Hirshhorn Museum and Sculpture Garden,
    Smithsonian Institution,
    Washington, D.C.
Los Angeles County Museum of Art
Louisiana Museum of Modern Art,
    Humlebaek, Denmark
Marlborough Gallery, New York
Menil Collection, Houston
Robert Miller Gallery, New York
Modern Art Museum of Fort Worth
The Museum of Contemporary Art,
    Los Angeles
The Museum of Modern Art, New York
San Francisco Museum of Modern Art
Sonnabend Gallery, New York
Sperone Westwater, New York
Stedelijk Museum, Amsterdam,
    The Netherlands
Walker Art Center, Minneapolis
Weatherspoon Art Gallery,
    University of North Carolina at
    Greensboro
John Weber Gallery, New York
Whitney Museum of American Art,
    New York

Acknowledgments

The undertaking of preparing this publication and simultaneously presenting a trilogy of inaugural exhibitions and related programs at the Wexner Center for the Arts has been dependent on the committed efforts of so many people that it would be impossible to name everyone involved. But I would first offer my sincerest thanks to the writers and other contributors, whose observations have provided critical perspectives on the complex topics explored in this volume.

The visual arts exhibitions that served as a basis for this book were organized as a collaborative effort of the Curators of Exhibitions, Claudia Gould and Sarah Rogers-Lafferty. Antonella Soldaini, former Assistant Curator of Exhibitions, provided continuous support in research. William B. Cook, Associate Director and Director of Performing Arts, and Carla Peterson, Assistant Director of Performing Arts, developed the programming in the performing arts and advised on that component of this volume. William Horrigan, Curator of Media Arts, and Jason Simon, Assistant Curator of Media Arts, provided similar insight regarding the areas of film and video.

The inaugural exhibitions were completely dependent on the artists who created the assembled works and on the museums, collectors and artists themselves who agreed to lend us these objects. On behalf of the Wexner Center and The Ohio State University, I express to all of them our deepest appreciation and gratitude. Special thanks are also due to all those who cooperated in facilitating the loan arrangements and to those whose generous advice led us to objects, collections and other resources.

The commitment to build a major visual arts center at The Ohio State University was made in 1982 by former University President Edward H. Jennings; its realization was made possible by a historic financial contribution from Leslie H. Wexner, in honor of his father, Harry Wexner. Their first commitment was to constructing an extraordinary facility for the arts. I thank them both for their encouragement to construct, as well, an extraordinary program for that facility. I also want to thank E. Gordon Gee, University President, for his continuing support and enthusiasm for this project; Frederick Hutchinson, Provost, for the administrative assistance of the Office of Academic Affairs; and Donald Harris, Dean, for the cooperative artistic environment provided by the College of the Arts.

Assistance in research, information about artists and cooperation in locating and obtaining illustration materials have come from the staffs of the numerous lending institutions and of other museums, galleries, archives, publicity firms and organizations, as well as from individual collectors and artists. At the university, research assistance has come from the university library faculty and staff, especially from Susan Wyngaard of the Fine Arts Library, and from the Wexner Center's talented graduate student associates.

Further acknowledgments are due to many individuals specifically involved in the production of this publication. Maureen Alvim, Annetta Massie, Elizabeth Ann Krouse, Darnell Lautt and M. Christopher Jones of the Wexner Center staff, along with Wendy Ernst, Kathleen Kopp and Norma Roberts deserve special mention for their contributions. Charles Miers, Associate Editorial Director, Rizzoli International Publications, Inc., and guest editor John Howell offered supportive advice and guidance. Ann Bremner attended to every detail as Associate Editor. In addition, we are indebted to the Wexner Center design department, guided by Oscar Fernandez; Alan Jazak was responsible for the design, layout and production of this book.

Numerous other staff members at the Wexner Center also have contributed to this project, assisting with everything from contracts to photography sessions. Finally, I would like to offer my sincere thanks to all of them. It would be any director's greatest pleasure to lead such a dedicated and talented team.

Robert Stearns

Index of Names

Abakanowicz, Magdalena, 184, 186–87
Acconci, Vito, 162, 196
Adams, John, 79
Agee, James, 83–84
Ailey, Alvin, 259
Albers, Josef, 24
Allendy, Colette, 36
Alloway, Lawrence, 44
Alpert, Richard (see Ram Dass)
Anders, Günter, 27
Andersen, Eric, 135
Anderson, Laurie, 157, 162–63, 247
Andre, Carl, 104, 125–26, 142–43
Anger, Kenneth, 84
Anselmo, Giovanni, 122, 244
Archambault, John, 43
Argabright, Stuart, 190
Arman (Armand Fernandez), 33, 36, 43–44
Armitage, Karole, 162
Arp, Jean, 38, 93
Artaud, Antonin, 72
Ashbery, John, 39
Ashley, Robert, 78
Ashton, Frederick, 72

Babbitt, Milton, 75–78
Baillie, Bruce, 81
Baj, Enrico, 43–44
Balanchine, George, 11, 69–70
Baldessari, John, 96, 98, 115–17
Baldwin, James, 131
Ballacca, Mario, 24
Bambara, Toni Cade, 172
Banham, Reyner, 44
Barry, Robert, 115
Baruchello, Gianfranco, 44
Baselitz, Georg, 133, 138–39
Baudelaire, Charles, 14, 18, 21, 81, 86
Beaucamp, Eduard, 133
Beckmann, Max, 133
Behrman, David, 78
Béjart, Maurice, 11, 69, 72–73
Bellamy, Richard, 40
Bender, Gretchen, 184, 188–91, 259
Benglis, Lynda, 90–93, 96, 124–29, 131, 141
Bengt at Klintberg, 134
Benjamin, Walter, 86, 184, 221–22
Bérard, Christian, 69
Berio, Luciano, 75
Berlioz, Hector, 158
Berman, Eugene, 69
Beuys, Joseph, 91–93, 96, 100–01, 113, 120–22, 133–39, 141, 148–49
Bickerton, Ashley, 57
Birnbaum, Dara, 169
Birtwistle, Harrison, 78
Bladen, Ronald, 196
Blair, Dike, 237–38
Blake, Peter, 44
Blum, Andrea, 238
Boccioni, Umberto, 49
Bochner, Mel, 64, 162
Boetti, Alighiero, 244
Bogosian, Eric, 162
Bontecou, Lee, 43
Borde, Percival, 259
Boulez, Pierre, 11, 75–77
Bourgeois, Louise, 92–93, 99, 102–3, 106–9, 126–27, 129
Boyce, Johanna, 162, 259
Braderman, Joan, 169
Brakhage, Stan, 81, 84
Braque, Georges, 49
Brecht, Bertolt, 253
Brecht, George, 39–40, 42–43, 79, 159
Breer, Robert, 38
Breton, André, 107

Broomfield, Nick, 171
Brouwn, Stanley, 115, 135
Brown, Earle, 13, 77
Brown, Trisha, 158, 162, 246–51
Buba, Tony, 171
Buchloh, Benjamin H.D., 137, 223
Burckhardt, Rudy, 84
Burden, Chris, 162, 184, 192–97
Burnett, Charles, 167, 171
Burri, Alberto, 24–26, 244

Cage, John, 4, 11, 40, 42, 50, 71, 74–79, 134, 156–57, 162, 255
Calder, Alexander, 38
Calzolari, Pier Paolo, 244
Canaday, John, 60, 62
Capogrossi, Giuseppe, 24
Carlomusto, Jean, 170
Carrà, Carlo, 49
Carter, Angela, 127
Castellani, Enrico, 27–28, 244
Castelli, Leo, 6–7, 40, 43, 44
Cavalcanti, Alberto, 83
Celant, Germano, 244
César (Baldaccini), 36, 43
Cézanne, Paul, 13
Chamberlain, John, 38, 43–44
Chapman, George, 59, 66
Charlip, Remy, 70
Cheang, Shu Lea, 169, 265, 266–69
Chia, Sandro, 23
Chicago, Judy, 126, 128
Childs, Lucinda, 158, 161–62
de Chirico, Giorgio, 121
Choy, Christine, 171
Christiansen, Henning, 135
Christo (Javachef), 33, 36, 44, 120
Chryssa, 43
Church, Frederic Edwin, 198–202
Citron, Michelle, 168
Clark, Larry, 167
Clarke, Shirley, 84
Clemente, Francesco, 23
Clert, Iris, 36, 38
Cochran, Malcolm, 184, 198–203
Cocteau, Jean, 83
Cole, Thomas, 199
Colla, Ettore, 24
Condit, Cecilia, 169
Conner, Bruce, 38, 43
Consagra, Pietro, 24
Corbusier, Le (Charles Eduoard Jeanneret), 24, 148
Cordier, Daniel, 36
Cornell, Joseph, 39, 80–81
Corner, Philip, 158
Croce, Benedetto, 23
Cucchi, Enzo, 24
Cunningham, Merce, 4, 11, 42, 47, 50, 68–72, 79, 157, 247, 251

Darboven, Hanne, 115–116
Davies, Peter Maxwell, 78
DeAk, Edit, 128
Dean, Laura, 162
de Antonio, Emile, 82, 171
Debussy, Claude, 76
de Certeau, Michel, 86
de Gaulle, Charles, 154
de Groat, Andy, 162
de Kooning, Willem, 4, 12–14, 16–18, 49–53, 77, 91, 103
De Maria, Walter, 116–19
Demme, Jonathan, 253, 256
Deschamps, Gérard, 36
Dewey, Kenneth, 152
Diaghilev, Serge, 69–73
Dibbets, Jan, 115, 244

Dine, Jim, 36, 40, 44, 158
Ding, Loni, 171
Dilley, Barbara, 162
Dix, Otto, 133
Dobujinsky, Mstislav, 69
van Doesburg, Theo, 149
Dorazio, Piero, 24
Dove, Arthur, 50
Downey, Juan, 169
Drew, John, 49
Drexler, Rosalyn, 40
Dubuffet, Jean, 14–15, 24
Duchamp, Marcel, 3, 5, 18, 28–29, 38–39, 44, 56, 70, 96, 107, 121, 181, 222
Dufrêne, François, 36
Dunn, Douglas, 162, 248
Dunn, Robert, 247

Eisenman, Peter, 180–85, 187, 193, 196–97, 199, 202, 205, 210, 221–22, 231, 233, 238–40
Eluard, Paul, 141
Erdman, Jean, 152

Fabro, Luciano, 120, 122
Fagin, Steve, 169, 265, 270–73
Fahlströhm, Oyvind, 44
Farber, Manny, 85
Fassbender, Joseph, 133
Fautrier, Jean, 16, 24
Feldman, Morton, 11, 13, 65–66, 77–78
Fenley, Molissa, 162
Filliou, Robert, 135
Flavin, Dan, 43, 63, 65, 114, 116
Fontana, Lucio, 4, 8, 18, 20, 22, 25–27, 91, 244
Forti, Simone, 157–58, 247
Fortuyn, Irene (see Fortuyn/O'Brien)
Fortuyn/O'Brien (Irene Fortuyn and Robert O'Brien), 184, 204–07
Frampton, Hollis, 85–86
Frank, Robert, 83–84
Frankenthaler, Helen, 103, 125–26
Franklin, Aretha, 127
Freud, Sigmund, 14, 23, 222
Friedrich, Su, 171
Fulton, Hamish, 115

Gass, William, 239
Gehr, Ernie, 85
Gerima, Haile, 167
Gerson, Barry, 85
Gilardi, Pietro, 244
Gilbert and George, 96–97, 121, 140–41, 145–49
Glass, Philip, 79, 162
Godard, Jean Luc, 173
Godmilow, Jill, 171
Goetry, K.O., 133–34, 137–38
Goldman, Peter Emanuel, 81–82
Goldstein, Malcolm, 158
Goldwater, Robert, 107
Gordon, David, 162, 248
Gordon, Peter, 259
Gorewitz, Shalom, 169
Gorky, Arshile, 13
Gosewitz, Ludwig, 135
Gottlieb, Adolph, 15
Graham, Dan, 237–38
Graham, Martha, 11, 69–72, 242
Grass, Günter, 133
Graubner, Gotthard, 138
Graves, Nancy, 126
Gray, Spalding, 162, 252–57
Green, Vanalyne, 169
Greenberg, Clement, 91, 106
Griffith, D.W. (David Wark), 49
Gris, Juan, 49, 70
Grooms, Red, 40, 158
Gropius, Walter, 24

Grosz, George, 133, 135
Guston, Philip, 13

Haacke, Hans, 134, 223
Hains, Raymond, 33, 36, 43–44
Halprin, Ann, 247
Hamilton, Ann, 185, 208–13
Hamilton, Richard, 44
Hansen, Al, 42
Haring, Keith, 259
Harnett, William M, 50
Harrison, Amy, 172
Harten, Jürgen, 138
Hawkins, Erick, 152
Hay, Alex, 158, 251
Hay, Deborah, 158–59, 162
Haynes, Todd, 171
Heartfield, John, 135
Heizer, Michael, 116–19
Heldt, Werner, 133
Helms, Jesse, 168
Hemphill, Julius, 263
Henson, Robby, 172
Henze, Hans Werner, 78
Herko, Fred, 158
Hesse, Eva, 3, 10, 18, 59, 64–67, 126–27
Heubach, Friedrich W., 137
Higgins, Dick, 42, 134, 159
Hill, Gary, 169
Hiller, Lejaren, 78
Hockney, David, 44
Hödicke, Karl Horst, 138
Hoehme, Gerhard, 133–34, 137
Holzer, Jenny, 57
Horn, Rebecca, 121
Horst, Louis, 247
Huebler, Douglas, 115, 126
Humphrey, Ralph, 103
Hunter, Sam, 38
Huntington, David C., 200
Husserl, Edmund, 23

Immendorf, Jörg, 133–34, 136–37
Indiana, Robert, 40, 44
Inglesby, Mona, 72
Ivens, Joris, 83

Jacobs, Ken, 81, 84–85, 87
Jacquet, Alain, 33
Janis, Sydney, 43–44
Janowitz, Tama, 87
Jencks, Charles, 162
Jersey, Bill, 171
Joffe, Roland, 253
Johns, Jasper, 4, 8–10, 18, 20, 33, 36, 40, 43–45, 49–50, 53–56, 70, 96, 126, 142
Johnson, Ray, 43
Jones, Allen, 44
Jones, Bill T., 162, 258–63
Jones, LeRoi, 262
Jouffroy, Alain, 40
Judd, Donald, 63, 65, 93–96, 103–8, 111–14, 116, 141–43, 149, 196

Kalin, Tom, 170, 265, 274–77
Kandinsky, Vasily, 24
Kaprow, Allan, 2, 33, 36, 40, 42–43, 92, 150–55, 158
Karp, Ivan, 40
Kawamata, Tadashi, 185, 214–19
Kawara, On, 115
Keats, John, 13, 21, 59, 66
Kelly, Ellsworth, 111
Kelly, Mary, 166
Kerouac, Jack, 83–84
Khlebnikov, Velimir, 13
Kiefer, Anselm, 120, 133, 139

Kienholz, Ed, 43
King, Kenneth, 162
Kirby, Michael, 162
Kirchner, Ernst Ludwig, 133
Kirstein, Lincoln, 69
Klee, Paul, 24
Klein, Yves, 4–6, 28–29, 33–36, 38, 43–44, 121
Kline, Franz, 87
Klonarides, Carole Ann (see MICA-TV)
Klüver, Billy, 33, 38
Knoebel, Imi, 134
Knowles, Alison, 134, 159
Koberling, Bernd, 136, 138
Koch, Kenneth, 6, 47
Kochno, Boris, 69
Köpcke, Arthur, 134–35
Kopple, Barbara, 171–72
Kosuth, Joseph, 115–16, 184, 220–23
Kounellis, Jannis, 91–93, 96, 120–23, 244
Kozloff, Max, 44
Kruger, Barbara, 57, 184, 224–29
Kuchar, George, 85
Kuchar, Mike, 85
Kybartas, Stashu, 170

Lane, Charles, 171
Larcade, Jean, 36, 43
Larsen, Ernie, 169
Latham, John, 43–44
Lebel, Jean–Jacques, 40, 155
LeComte, Elizabeth, 253
Lee, Spike, 168
Léger, Fernand, 83, 107
Lehmbruck, Wilhelm, 133
Leslie, Alfred, 39, 83–84
Levine, Neil, 43
Levitt, Helen, 83–84
LeWitt, Sol, 64–65, 114–16, 141–43, 162, 184, 230–31
Leyda, Jay, 84
Lhote, André, 107
Lichtenstein, Harvey, 260
Lichtenstein, Roy, 43–44, 49, 54–56, 104, 244
Lifar, Serge, 72
Lincoln, Abraham, 152
Lippard, Lucy, 64–65, 93, 115
Loeb, Janice, 83–84
Logue, Joan, 169
Long, Richard, 116, 126, 244
Longo, Robert, 259
Louis, Morris, 103, 125
Lowell, Robert, 254
Lucier, Alvin, 78
Lucier, Mary, 169
Luening, Otto, 76
Lumiere, Auguste, 81
Lumiere, Louis, 81
Lüpertz, Markus, 138

McDowell, John Herbert, 158
McLuhan, Marshall, 141
Maciunas, George, 134–35, 159
Mack, Heinz, 134
Maderna, Bruno, 75
Malraux, André, 38, 154
Man Ray, 38, 49
Manet, Éduoard, 62
Manzoni, Piero, 3–6, 23, 26–31, 91, 121
Marclay, Christian, 184, 232–34, 237–38
Marcuse, Herbert, 91–93
Marden, Brice, 103
Marioni, Tom, 196
Martin, Agnes, 93–96, 109–11, 143
Marx, Karl, 23, 115
Marx, Leo, 81
Mason, Jackie, 254
Massiah, Louis, 172
Masson, André, 107

Matthews, Harry, 39
Matisse, Henri, 69
Meidner, Ludwig, 133
Meistermann, Georg, 133
Mekas, Jonas, 81–83, 85–86
Melotti, Fausto, 244
Menken, Marie, 84
Merleau–Ponty, Maurice, 13
Merz, Mario, 120, 122–23, 244
Merz, Marisa, 123
Messiaen, Olivier, 75–76
MICA-TV (Carole Ann Klonarides and Michael Owen), 235–241
Miës van der Rohe, Ludwig, 24
Milner, Sherry, 169
Minh-ha, Trinh T., 172
Miró, Joan, 93
Mock, Ed, 260
Moholy–Nagy, László, 24, 29
Mondrian, Piet, 27, 148–49
Monk, Meredith, 159–62
Monroe, Marilyn, 49, 56
Moog, Robert, 78
Moore, George Edward, 115
Moore, Michael, 171
Moorman, Charlotte, 156
Morris, Erroll, 171
Morris, Robert, 70, 127, 141–42, 158
Mosher, Gregory, 253
Moskowitz, Robert, 43
Mumma, Gordon, 78
Murphy, Gerald, 49
Myers, Rita, 169

Nagrin, Daniel, 259
Namuth, Hans, 5
Nay, Ernst Wilhelm, 133
Nevelson, Louise, 2–5, 244
Newman, Barnett, 13, 15–16, 143
Nietzsche, Friedrich Wilhelm, 15, 73
Nijinsky, Vaslav, 72
Nizzoli, Marcello, 26
Noguchi, Isamu, 70
Noland, Kenneth, 103, 125
Nono, Luigi, 75, 78
Noren, Andrew, 85
Noriega, Manuel, 171
Norman, Jessye, 260

O'Brien, Robert (see Fortuyn/O'Brien)
O'Hara, Frank, 39
Oldenburg, Claes, 3–4, 8–10, 15, 18–19, 21, 33, 36, 40, 43–44, 157–58
Olitski, Jules, 103, 125
Olmstead, Frederick Law, 183
Ono, Yoko, 159
Oppenheim, Dennis, 126
Owen, Michael, (see MICA-TV)
Owens, Craig, 131
Ozenfant, Amédée, 107

Paik, Nam June, 92–95, 134, 141–43, 149, 156, 159, 169
Palermo, Blinky, 134, 138
Paolini, Giulio, 120, 123
Park, Robert, 82
Pascalli, Pino, 244
Patterson, Benjamin, 134
Paulhan, Jean, 14
Paxton, Steve, 158–59, 161
Penck, A. R., 138
Penone, Giuseppe, 123, 244
Perilli, Achille, 24
Perron, Wendy, 162
Petipa, Marius, 72
Peto, John Frederick, 50, 53–54
Petronio, Stephen, 157
Phillips, Peter, 44

Piano, Renzo, 182
Picasso, Pablo, 49–50, 70–71
Piene, Otto, 134
Piper, Adrian, 92, 97, 125–131
Pirandello, Luigi, 72
Pistoletto, Michelangelo, 244
Polke, Sigmar, 96, 132–34, 137–38
Pollock, Jackson, 5, 13, 39, 77, 103, 141–42
Portillo, Lourdes, 168, 171
Pousseur, Henri, 75
Presley, Elvis, 56, 151
Primus, Pearl, 259
Prini, Emilio, 244
Proust, Marcel, 72

Rainer, Yvonne, 158–59, 164–65, 167, 171, 247, 259
Ram Dass, 255
Rappaport, Mark, 167
Rauschenberg, Robert, 3–4, 6–8, 16, 18, 33–36, 38–40, 42–44, 47–53, 56, 68, 70–72, 158, 244, 247, 250–51, 256
Raysse, Martial, 33, 36, 44, 47
Reeves, Dan, 169
Reich, Steve, 79, 162
Reinecke, Chris, 136
Restany, Pierre, 4, 8, 29
Richter, Gerhard, 133, 137–38
Riggs, Marlon, 169
Riley, Terry, 79
Rimmer, David, 85
Rivers, Clarice, 6
Rivers, Larry, 6, 39
Roach, Max, 259
Robbins, Jerome, 72
Rochlin, Sheldon, 82
Rogers, Richard, 182
Rosenberg, Harold, 14, 20
Rosenquist, James, 43–44
Rosler, Martha, 169
Ross, Bertram, 71
Rotella, Mimmo, 36, 44
Rothenberg, Susan, 96, 141, 143–45, 148–49
Rothko, Mark, 15–16, 103, 143
Rubin, William, 62
Russolo, Luigi, 78
Ruthenbeck, Reiner, 134
Ruttman, Walter, 83
Ryman, Robert, 103–04
Rzewski, Frederic, 78

de Saint Phalle, Niki, 4–6, 29, 32, 36, 38–40, 42–43, 47
Samaras, Lucas, 40, 43
Sartre, Jean–Paul, 23–24
Schaeffer, Pierre, 78
Shaffer, Deborah, 171
Shearer, Jacqueline, 171
Schechner, Richard, 253
Shepard, Sam, 253
Schifano, Mario, 44
Schlemmer, Oskar, 24
Schlichter, Rudolf, 133
Schmit, Tomas, 134–35
Schnabel, Julian, 222
Schneemann, Carolee, 81, 158, 165–66
Schönberg, Arnold, 75–76
Schönebeck, Eugen, 138
Schorske, Carl, 83
Schultze, Bernard, 133
Schumacher, Emil, 133
Schwitters, Kurt, 39, 44, 50
Scorsese, Martin, 173
Segal, George, 43–44
Seitz, William C., 42–43, 62
Self, Jim, 162
Seligmann, Kurt, 69
Selz, Peter, 38
Sheeler, Charles, 84
Sherman, Cindy, 237

Sherman, Stuart, 162
Siegelaub, Seth, 115, 223
Sironi, Mario, 49
Sitney, P. Adams, 83
Smith, Jack, 84
Smith, Willi, 259
Smithson, Robert, 64, 91, 93, 96, 113, 116–19, 126, 141–43, 149
Snow, Michael, 84–85
Sonderborg, K. H. R., 133
Sperone, Gian Enzo, 244
Spiro, Ellen, 170
Spoerri, Daniel, 36, 44, 134
Stankiewicz, Richard, 36, 38, 40–41, 43–44
Stauffacher, Frank, 84
Stein, Gertrude, 13
Steiner, Ralph, 84
Stella, Frank, 4, 10, 20, 58–63, 65–66, 70, 104, 111
Stockhausen, Karlheinz, 11, 75–76, 78, 134
Stowe, Harriet Beecher, 261–62
Strand, Paul, 84
Stravinsky, Igor, 78
Stuart, Michelle, 126
Summers, Elaine, 158
Sweeney, James Johnson, 47

Tadeusz, Norbert, 134
Tajima, Renee, 171
Tanning, Dorothea, 69
Tchelitchev, Pavel, 69
Tenney, James, 158
Tharp, Twyla, 162
Thieler, Fred, 133
Thompson, Francis, 84
Thoreau, Henry David, 81
Thornton, Leslie, 278–81
Tilson, Joe, 44
Tinguely, Jean, 3–7, 18, 32–39, 42–44, 47, 120
Tomlin, Lily, 254
Tremlett, David, 115
Trier, Hann, 133, 138
Trini, Tomaso, 244
Trökes, Heinz, 133
Trott, Richard, 180–85, 187, 193, 231
Trowbridge, Frank, 134
Tudor, David, 75–76, 134
Turcato, Giulio, 24
Turner, Ted, 169
Tzara, Tristan, 38

Uecker, Günther, 134, 138
Ultvedt, Per Olof, 44, 47

Van Dyke, Willard, 84
Vedova, Emilio, 23
Vermeer, Jan, 59
Vertov, Dziga, 83
Vico, Giovanni Battista, 13–14
Villeglé, Jacques de la, 33, 36
Viola, Bill, 169
Vogel, Amos, 172
Vostell, Wolf, 18, 40, 134–35, 155

Wagner, Richard, 70
Warfield, David, 49
Warhol, Andy, 4, 8–10, 33, 40, 43–44, 49, 54–57, 70, 85, 104, 142
Watts, Robert, 43, 159
Webern, Anton, 75–76
Wegman, William, 196
Weiner, Lawrence, 115
Welk, Lois, 259
Werner, Michael, 139
Werner, Theodor, 133
Wesselmann, Tom, 43
Whitman, Robert, 40, 158–59
Whitman, Walt, 254, 256

Wilder, Thornton, 253
Williams, Emmett, 134–35
Wilson, Ian, 115–16
Wilson, Robert, 162
Winsor, Jackie, 143
Winter, Fritz, 133–34
Wittgenstein, Ludwig, 96, 115
Wolfe, Thomas, 255
Wolff, Christian, 77
Wright, Frank Lloyd, 24–26, 243

Young, LaMonte, 79, 159
Youngerman, Jack, 111

Zaloom, Paul, 162
Zando, Julie, 282–85
Zane, Arnie, 162, 259–60
Zevi, Bruno, 24
Zimmerman, Bernd, 28
Zola, Emile, 6
Zorio, Gilberto, 123, 184, 242–45
Zucker, Joe, 143